The United States Space Force and the Future of American Space Policy

Studies in Space Law

VOLUME 18

The titles published in this series are listed at *brill.com/slaw*

The United States Space Force and the Future of American Space Policy

Legal and Policy Implications

By

Jeremy Grunert

BRILL
NIJHOFF

LEIDEN | BOSTON

US Air Force PA#: USAFA-DF-2022-2

The Library of Congress Cataloging-in-Publication Data is available online at https://catalog.loc.gov
LC record available at https://lccn.loc.gov/2022035084

Typeface for the Latin, Greek, and Cyrillic scripts: "Brill". See and download: brill.com/brill-typeface.

ISSN 1871-7659
ISBN 978-90-04-52312-8 (hardback)
ISBN 978-90-04-52406-4 (e-book)

This book is printed on acid-free paper and produced in a sustainable manner.

Rules and responsibilities: these are the ties that bind us. We do what we do because of who we are. If we did otherwise, we would not be ourselves.

NEIL GAIMAN
The Sandman: The Kindly Ones

I am putting myself to the fullest possible use, which is all I think that any conscious entity can ever hope to do.

HAL 9000
2001: A Space Odyssey

Contents

Appendices

Acknowledgements

This book[1] is a revised and updated publication of my master's thesis, originally written to satisfy the thesis requirement of my Masters of Law program in "Air and Space Law" at the University of Mississippi School of Law. My family's time in Oxford, Mississippi, was an extremely pleasant time of our lives—despite the onset of the COVID-19 pandemic slightly over halfway through our year there. Though the lockdown accompanying the pandemic was unfortunate and, at times, extremely difficult, being forced to lockdown and stay at home did prove beneficial to focused work on this thesis! The success of this work, however, is by no means mine alone: there are a great many people to whom I owe a debt of gratitude and thanks and who have contributed immeasurably to this work.

First, I am extremely grateful to Professor Michelle Hanlon and Professor Charles Stotler, the Directors of the Center of Air and Space Law at the University of Mississippi School of Law. Professor Hanlon and Professor Stotler were my advisors during my time at the Masters of Law program. Professor Stotler and Professor Hanlon assisted me with multiple draft versions of chapters and the completed thesis, and I owe much to their advice, source recommendations, and editing. This work could not have been as thoroughly researched without their help.

Second, gratitude and thanks are owed to my military superiors in the United States Air Force Judge Advocate Generals (JAG) Corps. It was the JAG Corps that both stimulated my interest in the field of outer space law and sent me, as a preparatory assignment for my teaching position at the United States Air Force Academy, to the LL.M. program at Ole Miss to study the topic. The encouragement I have received from the larger JAG Corps, as well as my immediate superiors at the Air Force Academy, including Colonel Tara Villena, Department Head of the Department of Law, have been critical to my ability to research and write about the field of space law and to complete the revision of this book. While the Air Force has encouraged and assisted me in my research endeavors, however, it is imperative that I provide the following disclaimer: this work is a product of my own research, and the views reflected in this work are my own. Nothing in this work is, or ought to be construed as, the official

---

1 The views expressed are those of the author and do not necessarily reflect the official policy or position of the United States Air Force Academy, the Air Force, the Department of Defense, or the U.S. Government.

US Air Force PA#: USAFA-DF-2022-2.

position of the United States Government, the United States Department of Defense, or the United States Department of the Air Force.

Finally, and most importantly of all, my wife, Miriam, and my children, Tzipora, Asher, and Naomi, have tirelessly supported me during the over two years I have written and developed this project. This book is dedicated to them, and I am extremely grateful for their love and support.

Major Jeremy Grunert
Colorado Springs, April 2022

Abbreviations

ABM	Anti-Ballistic Missile
ADIZ	Air Defense Identification Zone
AFDD	Air Force Doctrine Document (United States Military)
AFM	Air Force Manual (United States Military)
ARDC	Air Research and Development Command (United States Military)
ASAT	Anti-satellite (i.e. "ASAT missile," "ASAT weapon")
C4ISR	Command, Control, Communications, Computers, Intelligence, Surveillance, and Reconnaissance
CIA	Central Intelligence Agency
COPUOS	United Nations Committee on the Peaceful Uses of Outer Space
COVID-19	Coronavirus Pandemic of 2019 (ongoing as of December 2021)
DoD	United States Department of Defense
GPS	Global Positioning System
ICBM	Intercontinental Ballistic Missile
IGY	International Geophysical Year
JP	Joint Publication (United States Military)
NASA	National Aeronautics and Space Administration
NDAA	National Defense Authorization Act
NOAA	National Oceanic and Atmospheric Administration
NRO	National Reconnaissance Office
NSC	National Security Council
NSCA	National Security Council Action
NSDD	National Security Decision Directive
NSDM	National Security Decision Memorandum
NSP	National Space Policy
NSSS	National Security Space Strategy
PAROS	Prevention of an Arms Race in Outer Space
PD	Presidential Directive
PRM	Presidential Review Memorandum
SAC	Strategic Air Command (United States Military)
SDI	Strategic Defense Initiative
SPD	Space Policy Directive
SPoC	Space Operations Command (United States Space Force)
SSC	Space Systems Command (United States Space Force)
STARCOM	Space Training and Readiness Command (United States Space Force)
UNOOSA	United Nations Office of Outer Space Affairs
USAF	United States Air Force

USNORTHCOM	United States Northern Command (United States Military)
USSF	United States Space Force
USSPACECOM	United States Space Command (United States Military)
USSR	Union of Soviet Socialist Republics
USSTRATCOM	United States Strategic Command (United States Military)

CHAPTER 1

Introduction

On June 18, 2018, during the signing of a Presidential Space Policy Directive (SPD) on the issue of outer space traffic management, President Donald J. Trump surprised the audience that had gathered for his remarks by announcing his intent to create a new branch of the armed forces: the United States Space Force. "[America's] destiny, beyond the Earth," President Trump stated, "is not only a matter of national identity, but a matter of national security …. I'm here by [sic] directing the Department of Defense and Pentagon to immediately begin the process necessary to establish a space force as the sixth branch of the armed forces."[1] President Trump's surprise announcement was followed, eight months later, by the issuance of SPD-4, which reiterated the importance of a Space Force to US national security and directed the Secretary of Defense to develop and submit "a legislative proposal … that would establish the United States Space Force as a new armed service within the Department of the Air Force."[2] A legislative proposal for the creation of the Space Force was duly introduced, passed by Congress as part of the National Defense Authorization Act for Fiscal Year 2020 and signed into law by President Trump on 20 December 2019.[3] The United States Space Force became a reality.

President Trump's initial Space Force announcement was met with a range of reactions. Some (mainly on the late-night talk show and comedy circuits) greeted the proposal with mockery and even derision.[4] Others applauded the

1 "Remarks by President Trump at a Meeting with the National Space Council and Signing of Space Policy Directive-3," Trump White House Archives, June 18, 2018, https://trumpwhitehouse.archives.gov/briefings-statements/remarks-president-trump-meeting-national-space-council-signing-space-policy-directive-3/.

2 Donald J. Trump, "Space Policy Directive—4," White House, Office of the Press Secretary, February 19, 2019, https://media.defense.gov/2019/Mar/01/2002095015/-1/-1/1/SPACE-POLICY-DIRECTIVE-4-FINAL.PDF.

3 Sandra Erwin, "Trump signs defense bill establishing US Space Force: What comes next," *Space News*, December 20, 2019, https://spacenews.com/trump-signs-defense-bill-establishing-u-s-space-force-what-comes-next/.

4 For instance, comedian and *Late Show* host Stephen Colbert, in an opening monologue eventually posted to YouTube with the subtitle "To Infinity and Beyond Stupid," described the Space Force as President Trump's "boldest idea that he got from a Buzz Lightyear Happy Meal toy." Stephen Colbert, "Mike Pence Tries to Make Space Force Sound Less Dumb," *The Late Show with Stephen Colbert*, YouTube.com, Aug. 9, 2018, https://www.youtube.com/watch?v=7ipwho-kxkI. Similarly, Steve Carrell, who played Michael Scott, the bumbling boss of NBC's *The Office*, produced *Space Force*—a "workplace comedy 'centered around the people tasked

 | DOI:10.1163/9789004524064_002

move toward a space-centered military branch, which some military members and researchers had been proposing for decades. Still others saw the creation of the Space Force as dangerous—a grim reflection of the United States' intent to "militarize" outer space and a destabilizing policy decision that would ultimately encourage other nations to pursue outer space military capabilities. Lost, to some degree, in the political scrum surrounding the proposal (and in the unceasing news-cycle involving various aspects of the Trump Administration, including personnel changes, presidential Tweets, and, of course, the President's impeachment and Senate trial) were a number of important questions: why should the United States have a Space Force? How will the Space Force work? What will the Space Force do? What *should* it do?

Initial answers to these questions have begun to emerge, as General John W. Raymond, who was appointed the first Chief of Space Operations for the Space Force on December 20, 2019, and the Department of the Air Force, the military department under which the Space Force is organized, trained, and equipped, developed the Space Force during the waning years of the Trump Administration and the early years of the Biden Administration. The Space Force now has unique uniform accoutrements for its servicemembers (and is working on even more distinctive Space Force uniforms); a number of operating bases, shifted to the control of the Space Force from the United States Air Force; mottos and symbols; and a service-specific name for its servicemembers, who are now referred to as 'Guardians.' Significant questions concerning the Space Force's operational scope, specific missions, and, particularly, future direction and development remain. The current development of the Space Force and what is currently known about its organization, mission set, and doctrine will be further discussed in Chapter 4.

What *is* clear, given other space-related Trump Administration policy initiatives,[5] and, especially, the Biden Administration's continued support for these

---

with creating a sixth branch of the armed services'"—for streaming giant Netflix. Sandra Gonzalez, *Sorry, Trump. Netflix is creating its own 'Space Force,'* CNN.com, Jan. 17, 2019, https://www.cnn.com/2019/01/16/entertainment/space-force-netflix/index.html.

5 Such initiatives include the reconstitution of the National Space Council—an Executive Branch council, chaired by the Vice President, meant to advise the President on outer space policy and strategy—and the resurrection of United States Space Command as a Geographic Combatant Command of the US military. *See* President Donald J. Trump, "Executive Orders: Presidential Executive Order on Reviving the National Space Council," June 30, 2017, https://trumpwhitehouse.archives.gov/presidential-actions/presidential-executive-order-reviving-national-space-council/; Jim Garamone, "Pentagon Rolls Out Space Command," US Dept. of Defense, Aug. 29, 2019, https://www.defense.gov/Explore/News/Article/Article/1948420/pentagon-rolls-out-space-command/.

policy initiatives,[6] is that the United States' recent expansion of national and military space organizations constitutes a continuation of national policies that have been growing more space-focused for at least the past 40 years. The early 1980s saw the initial creation of uniquely space-focused military organizations: the US Air Force's Space Command and the larger, multiservice US Space Command—the space-focused Combatant Command that was decommissioned after the September 11, 2001, terrorist attacks and resurrected by President Trump in 2019.[7] The work of these organizations and the US military's development and enhancement of space technologies more generally would result in a watershed moment for military space operations in the Gulf War of 1991. Less than a year after Iraqi dictator Saddam Hussein's fateful decision to invade the neighboring country of Kuwait, the United States military's pervasive use of satellite communications, GPS navigation signals, multispectral remote sensing imagery, and satellite-based meteorological monitoring—as well as the denial of satellite and remote-sensing information to the Iraqis—was instrumental to the American-led coalition's rapid, low-casualty victory over the Iraqi Army and the successful liberation of Kuwait.[8] The Gulf War was, in the words of General Merrill A. McPeak, then Chief of Staff of the United States Air Force, "the first space war"[9]—and it demonstrated, both to the United States and its adversaries, that space-based support systems had profound force-multiplying effects in a terrestrial war.

Since the 1950s, space had mainly been the purview of the Air Force.[10] The successful application of space-based technology to the Desert Storm

---

6 Christian Davenport, "The Biden administration has set out to dismantle Trump's legacy, except in one area: Space," *Washington Post*, Mar. 2, 2021, https://www.washingtonpost.com/technology/2021/03/02/biden-space-artemis-moon-trump/.

7 For more information on these organizations, *see infra* Chapter 3, sec. 3.5.

8 *See* Steven Lambakis, "Space Control in Desert Storm and Beyond," *Orbis*, vol. 39, no. 3 (Summer 1995), 421–22.

9 Steven J. Bruger, "Not Ready for the First Space War: What About the Second?," *Naval War College Review*, vol. 48, no. 1 (Winter 1995), 73 (citing Craig Covault, "Desert Storm Reinforces Military Space Direction," *Aviation Week & Space Technology*, no. 4 (Apr. 8, 1991)). Other notable descriptions of the importance of outer space in Operation Desert Storm came from science fiction writer Arthur C. Clarke, who described Desert Storm as "[t]he first satellite war," John Burgess, "Satellites' Gaze Provides New Look at War," *Washington Post*, Feb. 19, 1991, https://www.washingtonpost.com/archive/politics/1991/02/19/satellites-gaze-provides-new-look-at-war/768b19e4-a1da-4f40-8267-28a5dda48726/, and, later, from Everett C. Dolman—professor of military strategy at the Air Force's Air Command and Staff College and a prominent space strategy theorist—who described the Gulf War as "the coming-out party for space support," Everett C. Dolman, *Astropolitik* (London: Frank Cass, 202), 150.

10 *See infra* Chapter 3, secs. 1 and 2.

battlefield, however, represented the beginning of the now-successful push for an independent space service. In a May 2000 paper on the topic of creating a separate Space Force, for instance, one Air Force Colonel noted: "Since the end of the [Persian Gulf] war on 28 February 1991, the debate over whether space should become a separate service, equal with the Air Force, Army, and Navy, has grown in proportion to its indispensable value to our nation's defense."[11] Indeed, as American reliance on space-based systems has increased in both the civilian and military realms, as space technology has advanced, and as reduced costs and increased technological expertise allowed a wider array of civilian actors to participate in space operations, gaps and disparities between the Air Force's traditional operations and doctrine and the potential uses and doctrine of outer space assets only increased. As the differences between the Air Force's aerial and space-based operations grew starker, some began to compare the arguments for a Space Force with those made decades earlier in favor of an independent Air Force.[12] Even before President Trump's June 18, 2018, announcement concerning his desire to create a new Space Force or Space Corps,[13] a significant number of military academics and even senior officers had examined the issue and also advocated for an independent, space-oriented

11 Michael C. Whittington, *A Separate Space Force: An 80-Year-Old Argument*, Air War College, Maxwell Paper No. 20 (2000), 1, https://apps.dtic.mil/dtic/tr/fulltext/u2/a378853.pdf, last visited Aug. 19, 2021.

12 *See generally id.* Whittington describes the concerns of early air power activists like Billy Mitchell and their push for an independent air service separate and distinct from the US Army Air Corps as "strikingly similar to the concerns of the space community in today's Air Force. With leadership skills equal, space operators argue that space, as the fourth dimension of warfare, will never reach its full potential until freed from the fetters of the 'air' commander." *Id.* at 15. *See also* John D. Cinnamon, *US Department of the Space Force: A Necessary Evolution*, Joint Forces Staff College, National Defense University, May 15, 2012 ("The most obvious parallel to creating a new military Department of the Space Force from the NSS structure is the genesis of the USAF from the Army. The rationale used in those debates in 1947 mirror the same arguments made today about space forces and their possible future organization.").

13 The difference between a 'force' and a 'corps' is organizational in nature. Generally, within the US military's organization structure, a 'corps' is a subdivision of a larger organization—rather than being an independent military branch with its own separate military Department (i.e. the US Army, organized under the Department of the Army). For example, the US Marine Corps is a military *service* that is a subdivision of the Department of the Navy. Generally speaking, a 'force' would be an independent service with its own military department—for example, the US Air Force, organized under the Department of the Air Force. With the creation of the Space Force in 2019, however, this distinction seems largely pedantic, as the Space Force is, as we will see in Chapter 4, largely operating as a 'corps.'

service.[14] The US House of Representatives itself had entertained the possibility of creating a "Space Corps" in mid-2017, during the passage of its version of the 2018 National Defense Authorization Act (the proposal was later removed from the final bill).[15] Contrary to popular opinion, then, the creation of the Space Force was not a grandiose, spur-of-the-moment scheme by a frenetic and ignorant President; it was the culmination of a debate concerning the nature of military space power that had been raging for nearly three decades.

The establishment of the Space Force as an independent service may have settled the issue of who, or, rather, what organization, would be responsible for space security and defense within the American military system, but questions concerning the full breadth of the Space Force's responsibilities—what the Space Force will and, just as significantly, *should* do—remain in flux. While answers may be inferred from the space-oriented actions of the Air Force, such questions are not insignificant. Outer space is a vast area of operation, but a State's actions in space have dramatic consequences in both the terrestrial and extraterrestrial realms. In Earth's orbits, ever-increasing use of near-Earth space by both national governments and commercial entities, along with significantly increasing amounts of potentially harmful space debris, have created an environment that, in the Department of Defense's own words, is "increasingly congested, contested, and competitive."[16] The increased focus on space-based capabilities and, indeed, the creation of the Space Force itself, are reflections of the United States' desire to remain competitive in this environment (or, in

14 *See generally* Franz J. Gayl, "Time for a Military Space Service," *Proceedings* 130:7 (July 2004); Peter C. Norsky, *The United States Space Force: Not If, But When*, A Thesis Presented to the Faculty of the School of Advanced Air & Space Studies, Air University, June 2016, available at https://apps.dtic.mil/dtic/tr/fulltext/u2/1030447.pdf, last visited Aug. 19, 2021); Cinnamon, *supra* note 12; Whittington, *supra* note 11. Perhaps the highest-ranking military member to advocate for the creation of space-specific service during the early 2000s was Major General James Armor, then the Director of the National Security Space Office, who urged the creation of a Space Corps several times during the 2007/2008 timeframe. *See* James B. Armor, Jr., "The Air Force's Other Blind Spot," *The Space Review*, Sept. 15, 2008, https://www.thespacereview.com/article/1213/1; Jeremy Singer, "Armor Urges Creation of Space Corps Within the US Air Force," *Space News*, Nov. 16, 2007, https://spacenews.com/armor-urges-creation-space-corps-within-us-air-force/.

15 *See* H.R. 2810, 115th Cong., 1st Sess., §1601, July 6, 2017, available at https://www.congress.gov/115/bills/hr2810/BILLS-115hr2810rh.pdf.

16 US Dept. of Defense & Office of the Director of National Intelligence, "National Security Space Strategy—Unclassified Summary," January 2011, 1 (hereinafter, "2011 National Security Space Strategy").

the somewhat more internationally tone-deaf words of some senior American officials, to "ensur[e] American dominance in space"[17]).

Of particular importance to the questions concerning the Space Force's operations and scope are questions related to American space policy and American perceptions of the rule of law in outer space more generally. The United States, as one of the two original preeminent space powers, played a significant role in the development of international outer space law, both the binding treaty regimes and non-binding 'principles,' 'guidelines,' and other systems established to regulate State behavior in outer space. The United States has long maintained its compliance with international space law, as well as to a policy commitment from the Eisenhower Administration in the earliest days of the Space Age to using outer space for peaceful purposes—though, the US has broadly defined this to include national security and intelligence-related uses of outer space. But, with a greater emphasis on military uses of outer space by the United States over the past four decades—and, now, with the creation of the Space Force, an entire military service devoted to space-oriented operations—the question of how past, current, and future activities in space will contribute to militarization and instability in outer space has once again come to the fore.

There are those who argue that the United States' actions, possibly even from the early days of the Space Age, have been self-defeating. According to this view, the United States' fears of technological inferiority after the *Sputnik* launch, and its continuous attempts to maintain "superiority" in outer space to avert potential space-oriented threats from its international rivals, actually encourage the very competition in outer space the United States' claims to want to avert. To use a literary analogy, the United States is akin to the protagonists in Umberto Eco's novel *Foucault's Pendulum*. These men, bored editors at a vanity publishing house for books of the occult, decide to amuse themselves by making up, and drafting a manuscript about, a vast conspiracy. Their "Plan" is all good fun, a way to subtly mock their self-important and largely delusional clients … until key personalities related to their imaginary conspiracy, as well as the editors themselves, are threatened by a mysterious occult cabal, which has taken the fictitious "Plan" as true. As Casaubon, the novel's narrator, laments:

17 C. Todd Lopez, "Shanahan: Space Force to Preserve Margin of Dominance, $19 Trillion Economy," US Dept. of Defense, Mar. 20, 2019, https://www.defense.gov/Explore/News/Article/Article/1790830/shanahan-space-force-to-preserve-margin-of-dominance-19-trillion-economy/.

> We invented a nonexistent Plan, and They not only believed it was real but convinced themselves that They had been part of it for ages, or rather They identified the fragments of their muddled mythology as moments of our Plan, moments joined in a logical, irrefutable web of analogy, semblance, suspicion.
>
> But if you invent a plan and others carry it out, it's as if the Plan exists. At that point it does exist.
>
> …
>
> The same applies to everyday life. Take stock-market crashes. They happen because each individual makes a wrong move, and all the wrong moves put together create panic. Then whoever lacks steady nerves asks himself: Who's behind this plot, who's benefitting? He has to find an enemy, a plotter, or it will be, God forbid, his fault.[18]

Eco, through Casaubon and the fictional "Plan," recognizes three points. The first is the power of belief in the creation of reality. To some extent, the perceptions and beliefs of individuals or nations do not simply reflect reality; instead, they shape and create it—often bringing a new, previously non-existent objective reality into being simply through their subjective belief that that reality does, in fact, exist. The second point is that of action and reaction, the *acting on* of beliefs that, ultimately, can bring about the creation of a new objective reality and even result in unforeseen catastrophe. Finally, if, or when, catastrophe does strike, the participants will seek to place blame … and will very rarely find it to lie with themselves.

Students of international relations theory will be familiar with the situation outlined by Eco/Casaubon: it describes, at its heart, the concept of the 'security dilemma.' The security dilemma theory is used to illustrate the way in which perceptions of external threats[19] lead a State, which we will refer to here as 'State 1,' to take steps to protect its perceived national security interests. These steps—weapons developments and arms build-ups, increased military spending, mandatory conscription, or other military-oriented activities—do not occur in a vacuum; as they are observed by State 1's neighbors and international

---

18 UMBERTO ECO, FOUCAULT'S PENDULUM 603 (1988).

19 While these external threats can be either real *or* imagined, the security dilemma often posits (at least at the triggering point of the 'dilemma') a largely imaginary 'threat'—similar to the fictional "Plan" concocted by Casaubon and his friends.

rivals, one or more of *those* States, in turn, feel threatened by State 1's activities. These other States undertake their own methods of (again, perceived) national security preservation, which are observed by the original State, State 1. These actions appear to corroborate State 1's original perceptions of external threats, which then leads to a cycle of measures and counter-measures by State 1 and the other State (or States) that may ultimately lead to war. The cruel irony of the security dilemma, however, is that the 'threats' that trigger the cycle of measure and counter-measure were never inexorable: they were, largely, imaginary perceptions by the participants that are ultimately actualized by State behavior.

Is the security dilemma theory applicable to State activity in outer space—and, as certain academics and space policy researchers we will meet in these pages suggest, are the United States' activities in space, both past and present, contributing to this dilemma? Or are the accusations that the United States is contributing to outer space instability themselves naïve and misguided? After all, there has not yet been a physical domain—on land, in the air, or on or under the sea—that has been free from the blight of human conflict. Would it not, then, be foolish and, indeed, dangerous, for the United States (or any country) to *not* take steps to prepare for conflict in outer space or to find ways to better protect its outer space assets?

This book seeks to use the establishment of the Space Force to examine these questions. It will begin, in Chapter 2, by examining the current international legal regime for outer space, particularly the Treaty on Principles Governing the Activities of States in the Exploration and Use of Outer Space, including the Moon and Other Celestial Bodies, more commonly known as the "Outer Space Treaty." The Outer Space Treaty, the first widely-accepted treaty to deal with outer space law, created the framework for all subsequent international law related to outer space and activities that take place there. It has also served as the primary source document for American interpretations of what is and is not 'legal' behavior in outer space. Chapter 2 will also examine one of the key concepts of the outer space legal regime: the idea that international law constrains States solely to "peaceful" uses of outer space. While, as is to be expected, legal scholars disagree on this point, Chapter 2 ultimately concludes, with respected outer space legal expert Bin Cheng, that this pillar of the outer space regime is based on a misinterpretation of the text of the Outer Space Treaty—which, for the vast majority of outer space, has no such requirement. The United States, however, appears to have largely accepted the concept of "peaceful use" and, thus, attempts to justify most of its actions in outer space through references to "peaceful purposes." Chapter 2 will examine the United States' space policies and interpretations of the concept of "peaceful purposes" from the beginning of the Space Age to the present, demonstrating the way in which—even accepting the possibility that the United States itself may be misinterpreting the Outer Space Treaty—the American interpretation preserves a broad range of action for the United States' military operations in space.

Moving from an international to a national perspective, Chapter 3 will delve into the history of American space security policy from the 1940s to the present. This chapter will start with the theoretical beginnings of the US satellite program in the immediate aftermath of World War II, describing the development of early American ballistic missile technology and the shock of the Soviet Union's *Sputnik 1* launch in 1957. While the United States had already been working toward the development of its own Earth-orbiting satellites, and the Eisenhower Administration had already promulgated national policies concerning satellite development, *Sputnik's* inauguration of the "Space Age" pressed President Eisenhower to more explicitly develop American national space policy. Chapter 3 will examine Eisenhower's creation of American space policy, as well as the space security policy developments and national space policies of every subsequent US President, ending with the Trump Administration's creation of the US Space Force and the Biden Administration's early space policies. This chapter will describe how different Presidential Administrations address key aspects of international space law, and, particularly, the United States' claimed policy of 'peaceful use' of outer space. It will also, when appropriate, examine the domestic laws and regulations passed during the various Presidential Administrations to examine how they intersect with the United States' space security policies and international space law.

Chapter 4 will serve as a more in-depth examination of the US Space Force itself. Moving beyond the overarching, big-picture policies described in Chapter 3, Chapter 4 will provide a detailed discussion of the Space Force's development so far, including its organizational structure, its new basing locations, the role it currently anticipates playing in the United States' national security and military framework, and the way in which its operations will implicate international space law and the United States' stated policy positions.

Chapters 2 and 3 touch on the security-related issues that contributed to certain developments in American space security and military space policies, and Chapter 4 examines the US Space Force in greater detail. Chapter 5 will examine a danger that has dogged the United States' space security policies for decades, but may be becoming far more significant in a multipolar, post-Cold War world in which an increasing number of States (not all of which are friendly to the United States) develop ever more advanced outer space launch and operational capabilities. This is the danger of the 'security dilemma,' briefly discussed above—the international relations theory in which one State's attempts to ensure its own security are misinterpreted by others as threatening, or, worse, potentially aggressive, actions. This triggers a cycle of mutual misunderstanding, recrimination, and mistrust between the original State and its imagined (and now, potentially, *actual*) adversaries that can ultimately result in conflict. The prospect of an arms race in outer space has been a worrisome threat since the days of the Cold War, and there is simply no question that action-and-reaction triggering events have previously played a significant role in the development of outer space policy. Indeed, the "Space Race" itself, triggered by the Soviet Union's launch of *Sputnik I* and the rapid development of the American outer space program that resulted from that launch, demonstrates the significance of State perception and reaction—particularly when it comes to perceived threats. The United States' current dominance in the outer space realm is a direct consequence of its response to the Soviet space program. But, with the *Sputnik* example in mind, is the United States' current course in outer space, particularly its focus on military uses and applications of space, likely to bring about a similar situation with its current peer or near-peer competitors? With the creation of the US Space Force, following a significant period of renewed focus on military and security-related applications of outer space, the United States has signaled its intended direction. As other States, particularly powerful and technologically advanced States like the People's Republic of China, react to American actions, is there a risk that the United States will have created the very threats and instabilities the development of the Space Force and extensive space security capabilities were meant to protect against?

Finally, this book will conclude, in Chapter 6, with a brief discussion of the likely future of American space policy and American interpretations of international outer space law. Particularly given recent Biden Administration and Department of Defense support for the development of international 'norms' for responsible behavior in outer space, the United States may be entering a period when increased military use of space is coupled with an increased willingness to reorient national policy toward the development of new, more specific legal regimes for outer space. Chapter 6 will examine these efforts and conclude with several recommendations for how the United States and, particularly, the US Space Force, can maintain a robust military, intelligence, and security-related space program, while complying with international outer space law and minimizing potential 'security dilemma'-related threats.

CHAPTER 2

Outer Space Law and the Concept of "Peaceful Purposes"

1 Introduction

In order to understand the legal context in which the US Space Force, or USSF, will be operating, it is imperative to understand the regime of treaties, United Nations resolutions, international regulations, and "soft law" that forms the basis of law in outer space. Of primary significance are the four international outer space-related treaties to which the United States is a party: the Treaty on Principles Governing the Activities of States in the Exploration and Use of Outer Space, including the Moon and Other Celestial Bodies ("Outer Space Treaty");[1] the Agreement on the Rescue of Astronauts, the Return of Astronauts and the Return of Objects Launched into Outer Space ("Rescue and Return Agreement");[2] the Convention on International Liability for Damage Caused by Space Objects ("Liability Convention");[3] and the Convention on Registration of Objects Launched into Outer Space ("Registration Convention").[4] The development of outer space law, and the key provisions of these treaties that are—or may be—applicable to the Space Force and the United States' military operations in space will be discussed in the first section of this chapter. Of primary significance to military operations in space are the prohibitions contained in the Outer Space Treaty related to certain weapons systems and uses of celestial bodies, and, most importantly of all, the principle, which has been recognized almost since the beginning of human spaceflight, that outer space be used for "peaceful purposes." An examination of the interpretations of the "peaceful purposes" and peaceful "use" language in the outer space treaties, as well as

1 Treaty on Principles Governing the Activities of States in the Exploration and Use of Outer Space, Including the Moon and Other Celestial Bodies, Jan. 27, 1967, 18 U.S.T. 2410, 610 U.N.T.S. 205 [hereinafter "Outer Space Treaty"].

2 Agreement on the Rescue of Astronauts, the Return of Astronauts and the Return of Objects Launched into Outer Space, Apr. 22, 1968, 19 U.S.T. 7570, 672 U.N.T.S. 119 [hereinafter Rescue and Return Agreement].

3 Convention on International Liability for Damage Caused by Space Objects, Mar. 29, 1972, 24 U.S.T. 2389, 961 U.N.T.S. 187 [hereinafter Liability Convention].

4 Convention on Registration of Objects Launched into Outer Space, Jan. 14, 1975, 28 U.S.T. 695, 1023 U.N.T.S. 15 [hereinafter Registration Convention].

 | DOI:10.1163/9789004524064_003

conclusions regarding the most likely meaning of this language, will be discussed in the third section of this chapter.

2 Outer Space Law: The Legal and Treaty Regime

2.1 *The Committee on the Peaceful Uses of Outer Space and Declaration of Legal Principles*

While theoretical discussions concerning the application of law beyond Earth's atmosphere predate the invention of rocket technology capable of reaching orbit, such ideas were largely academic until October 1957, when the Soviet Union successfully launched the first man-made satellite, *Sputnik I*, into orbit. In addition to jolting the United States into a 'Space Race' with the Soviets[5] (a 'race' that ultimately contributed to significant national defense and military outer space capabilities, and to which the development of organizations like USSPACECOM and the USSF can be traced), the launch of *Sputnik* triggered an international effort to create a legal regime for outer space.[6] Less than a year after the *Sputnik* launch, Henry Cabot Lodge, the United States' Representative to the United Nations, proposed the creation of a "programme for international co-operation in the field of outer space," which would involve the formation of an ad hoc committee

> to make ... studies and recommendations as to what specific steps the [UN General] Assembly might take to further man's progress in this field [i.e. the peaceful use of outer space] and to assure that outer space will be used solely for the benefit of all mankind.[7]

The United States' proposal for the creation of the Ad Hoc Committee on the Peaceful Uses of Outer Space was approved in December 1958,[8] and, despite initial Soviet Bloc objections to the forum, was formalized into the permanent Committee on the Peaceful Uses of Outer Space (COPUOS) the following year.[9]

---

5 *See* James Clay Moltz, *The Politics of Space Security: Strategic Restraint and the Pursuit of National Interests*, 3rd ed., (Stanford, CA: Stanford University Press, 2019), 91–92.

6 *See* Moltz, *Politics of Space Security*, 92–93, 98.

7 Henry Cabot Lodge, "Letter dated 2 Sept. 1958 from the Permanent Representative of the United States of America to the United Nations, addressed to the Secretary-General," U.N. General Assembly, 13th Sess., U.N. Doc A/3902, Sept. 2, 1958.

8 G.A. Res. 1348(XIII), ¶ 1, U.N. Doc. A/RES/1348(XIII), Dec. 13, 1958.

9 G.A. Res. 1472(XIV), ¶ A.1.a, U.N. Doc. A/RES/1472(XIV) A-B, Dec. 12, 1959.

As directed by the General Assembly, one of COPUOS's primary purposes is "study[ing] the nature of legal problems which may arise from the exploration of outer space."[10]

In 1963, COPUOS produced what would become one of the foundations of outer space law: the Declaration of Legal Principles Governing the Activities of States in the Exploration and Use of Outer Space (the "Declaration of Legal Principles" or, more simply, the "Declaration").[11] Approved unanimously, first within COPUOS itself and then, on 13 December 1963, by the General Assembly, the Declaration of Legal Principles elaborates nine legal principles that should "guide" the "exploration and use of outer space."[12] These include the principles that "[t]he exploration and use of outer space shall be carried on for the benefit and in the interests of all mankind," that outer space be "free for exploration and use by all States on a basis of equality," that "[o]uter space and celestial bodies are not subject to national appropriation," and that international law, including the UN Charter, applies to States' activities in, and uses of, outer space.[13] Additionally, the Declaration of Legal Principles recognized that concepts such as international responsibility and liability would apply in outer space, and formulated the potentially multi-State liability scheme (which considers the State(s) that launched or procured the launch of a space object *and* the State from whose territory the space object was launched to be potentially liable parties in the event that space object causes damage or harm) that would later be formally recognized in both the Outer Space Treaty and the Liability Convention.[14] Finally, the Declaration elaborates principles related to the "due regard" States must show one another in carrying out their respective space activities, the "jurisdiction and control" that States retain over their space objects, the recognition of astronauts as "envoys of mankind" (rather than spies or military combatants), and the return of both astronauts and space objects to their country of origin in the event they land in some other State or territory.[15] As we will see, all of these principles would later be formalized and expanded upon in later international treaties.

---

10 G.A. Res. 1472(XIV).

11 G.A. Res. 1962 (XVIII), Declaration of Legal Principles Governing the Activities of States in the Exploration and Use of Outer Space, 18th Sess., U.N. Doc A/RES/1962(XVIII), Dec. 13, 1963 [hereinafter Declaration of Legal Principles].

12 Declaration of Legal Principles, Preamble.

13 Declaration of Legal Principles, ¶¶ 1–4.

14 Declaration of Legal Principles, ¶ 5, ¶ 8.

15 Declaration of Legal Principles, ¶ 6, ¶ 7, and ¶ 9.

2.2 *The Outer Space Treaty: "Hard" Law for a New Domain*

As the United States and the Soviet Union advanced their outer space programs and capabilities during the 1960s, each sought to build on the framework outlined in the Declaration of Legal Principles to establish binding international law that would prevent the other from "exploiting any territorial or other advantages" it might gain from landing on the Moon or another celestial body.[16] To this end, the two nations worked with their allies in COPUOS to develop the text of an international treaty concerning the exploration and use of outer space. The draft treaty text was approved by the General Assembly in a unanimous vote on 19 December 1966,[17] and the Outer Space Treaty was officially open for signature beginning 27 January 1967. Less than ten months later, in October 1967, the Treaty went into effect.[18] The Outer Space Treaty has proven to be among the most successful international instruments: as of the end of 2021, 111 States—including all of the major space-faring powers—had signed and ratified the Treaty, while another 23 had signed, but not ratified.[19] The provisions of the Outer Space Treaty constitute the first binding treaty law established to govern outer space, and, as such, all post-1967 outer space law—on both the national and international levels—flows from the legal framework established in the Outer Space Treaty. For this reason, the Outer Space Treaty is the primary document to examine when considering the international legal framework within which the US Space Force will be obliged to act.

The Outer Space Treaty "recogniz[es] the common interest of all mankind in the progress of the exploration and use of outer space for peaceful purposes" and aims "to contribute to broad international cooperation in the scientific as well as the legal aspects of the exploration and use of outer space for peaceful purposes."[20] Taking the Declaration of Legal Principles (which is also referenced in the Treaty's Preamble) as its basis, the Outer Space Treaty is composed of thirteen substantive Articles that reframe—and, in several instances, expand upon—the Declaration's nine principles.

---

16 Moltz, *Politics of Space Security*, 98.

17 G.A. Res. 2222 (XXI), Treaty on Principles Governing the Activities of States in the Exploration and Use of Outer Space, including the Moon and Other Celestial Bodies, 21st Sess., Dec. 19, 1966.

18 COPUOS Legal Subcommittee, "Status of International Agreements relating to activities in outer space as at 1 January 2021," 60th Sess., U.N. Doc. A/AC.105/C.2/2021/CRP.10, May 31, 2021 [hereinafter "International Space Agreements"]. Pursuant to Article XIV of the Outer Space Treaty, the Treaty would enter into force upon the deposit of ratification instruments by five States. *See* Outer Space Treaty, art. XIV.

19 *See* COPUOS International Space Agreements, 10.

20 Outer Space Treaty, Preamble.

Article I of the Outer Space Treaty expands upon the first and second principles of the Declaration to, first, reiterate that exploration of outer space should be "for the benefit and in the interests of all"—although the Treaty establishes a State-focused regime by replacing "mankind" (the term used in the first principle of the Declaration)[21] with "countries."[22] Article I also recognizes the right of all States to access, explore, and scientifically investigate outer space:

> The exploration and use of outer space, including the Moon and other celestial bodies, shall be carried out for the benefit and in the interests of all countries, irrespective of their degree of economic or scientific development, and shall be the province of all mankind.
>
> Outer space, including the Moon and other celestial bodies, shall be free for exploration and use by all States without discrimination of any kind, on a basis of equality and in accordance with international law, and there shall be free access to all areas of celestial bodies.
>
> There shall be freedom of scientific investigation in outer space, including the Moon and other celestial bodies, and States shall facilitate and encourage international cooperation in such investigation.

The principles codified in Article I are among the foundational principles of outer space law. Indeed, a number of commentators even assert that the freedoms of access, use, and exploration had entered into *customary* international law by 1967—meaning that even the Outer Space Treaty itself was simply "enunciate[ing] preexisting legal principles based on the practice of States dating back to the launching of the first satellite."[23]

Articles II and III of the Outer Space Treaty codify principles 3 and 4 of the Declaration. Article II prohibits "national appropriation [of outer space or celestial bodies] by claim of sovereignty, by means of use or occupation, or by any other means."[24] Article III reiterates that the corpus of international law is fully applicable to the actions of States as they use and explore outer space: States must undertake their outer space activities "in accordance with international law, including the Charter of the United Nations, in the interest

21 Declaration of Legal Principles, ¶ 1.

22 Outer Space Treaty, art. I.

23 Christopher M. Petras, "'Space Force Alpha': Military Use of the International Space Station and the Concept of 'Peaceful Purposes,'" *Air Force Law Review*, vol. 53 (2002): 135–181, 153.

24 Outer Space Treaty, art. II.

of maintaining international peace and security and promoting international cooperation and understanding."[25] The UN Charter, including its security-oriented provisions (Articles 2(3), 2(4), and 51), and "the full breadth of codified and customary international law" is applicable in outer space—and, thus, will govern and, to some degree, restrict the possible actions of the Space Force.[26]

Article IV presents the first significant deviation of the Outer Space Treaty from the Declaration of Legal Principles. Article IV addresses *military* uses of outer space—a subject that the Declaration entirely avoids. With Cold War tensions still high, and the proxy war between the Communist Bloc and the West in Vietnam expanding, Article IV reflected the superpowers' desire that the Cold War arms race not extend into outer space. With this goal in mind, limits were placed on the types of weapons that could legally be stationed in outer space and the types of military actions that could be undertaken in outer space and on celestial bodies:

> States Parties to the Treaty undertake not to place in orbit around the Earth any objects carrying nuclear weapons or any other kinds of weapons of mass destruction, install such weapons on celestial bodies, or station such weapons in outer space in any other manner.
>
> The Moon and other celestial bodies shall be used by all States Parties to the Treaty exclusively for peaceful purposes. The establishment of military bases, installations and fortifications, the testing of any type of weapons and the conduct of military manoeuvres on celestial bodies shall be forbidden. The use of military personnel for scientific research or for any other peaceful purposes shall not be prohibited. The use of any equipment or facility necessary for peaceful exploration of the Moon and other celestial bodies shall also not be prohibited.[27]

Notably, Article IV's prohibition on the stationing of "nuclear weapons" and "any other kinds of weapons of mass destruction" does not prohibit the stationing of conventional weapons *not* rising to the level of "weapons of mass destruction."[28] Additionally, the Treaty text indicates a clear distinction in the

---

25 Outer Space Treaty, art. III.

26 Jeremy Grunert, "Grounding the Humā: Space Denial and (Potential) American Interference in the Iranian Space Program," *Air Force Law Review*, vol. 81 (2020): 75–132, 98.

27 Outer Space Treaty, art. IV.

28 It should be noted that the term "weapons of mass destruction" is not defined in the Outer Space Treaty. While some disagreement exists as to the full extent of the term, generally speaking, and applying understandings of the term from other areas of international law, "weapons of mass destruction" in the context of international space law is thought to

nature of legal military activities taking place in outer space versus those taking place on the surface of the Moon or other celestial bodies: while the use and exploration of outer space is, at least aspirationally per the language of the Treaty's Preamble, supposed to be for "peaceful purposes," the use of the Moon and other celestial bodies may be used only for "*exclusively* peaceful purposes" (emphasis added).[29] The potential significance of Article IV to the activities of the Space Force is obvious and will be discussed further in Chapter 4.

While the operations of the Space Force are unlikely to involve manned outer space missions at any point in the near future, Article V of the Outer Space Treaty (and its treaty-length expansion, the Rescue and Return Agreement, discussed below) is significant as increasing numbers of States either establish, or consider establishing, military space forces. Article V governs the status of astronauts under international space law, as well as astronauts' and States' responsibilities to render assistance to the astronauts of other nations and inform other States and astronauts of potentially dangerous phenomena. In full, Article V states:

> States Parties to the Treaty shall regard astronauts as envoys of mankind in outer space and shall render to them all possible assistance in the event of accident, distress, or emergency landing on the territory of another State Party or on the high seas. When astronauts make such a

mean "nuclear, chemical, biological, or radiological weapons capable of causing indiscriminate death to masses of people, or devastation to large areas of property." John E. Parkerson, Jr., "International Legal Implications of the Strategic Defense Initiative," *Military Law Review*, vol. 116 (1987), p. 87 (internal citations omitted).

29 Outer Space Treaty, art. IV. The distinction between permissible activities in space, as opposed to on the Moon or on the surface of celestial bodies, was not lost on the delegates of COPUOS during the debates concerning the draft Treaty text. During discussions on July 22, 1966, the Indian delegate, Mr. Krishna Rao, stated he "regretted that both texts [the proposed American and Soviet drafts of the Treaty text] omitted the concept of the use of outer space as well as the celestial bodies for peaceful purposes only." COPUOS Legal Sub-Committee, "Summary Record of the Sixty-Fifth Meeting—Held at the Palais des Nations, Geneva, on Friday, 22 July 1966, at 10:30 a.m.," 5th Sess., UN Doc. A/AC.105/C.2/SR.65, Oct. 24, 1966, 11. An identical sentiment was voiced by the Argentine delegate, Mr. Ruda, on July 25, 1966, who stated he would support the text of Article IV as eventually approved in the Outer Space Treaty in order not to delay the Treaty's development, but still "regrett[ed] that it [the text of Article IV] did not expressly stipulate that *outer space as a whole* was to be used *solely* for peaceful purposes" (emphasis added). COPUOS Legal Sub-Committee, "Summary Record of the Sixty-Fifth Meeting—Held at the Palais des Nations, Geneva, on Monday, 25 July 1966, at 10:30 a.m.," 5th Sess., UN Doc. A/AC.105/C.2/SR.66, Oct. 21, 1966, 3.

> landing, they shall be safely and promptly returned to the State of registry of their space vehicle.
>
> In carrying on activities in outer space and on celestial bodies, the astronauts of one State Party shall render all possible assistance to the astronauts of other States Parties.
>
> States Parties to the Treaty shall immediately inform the other States Parties to the Treaty or the Secretary-General of the United Nations of any phenomena they discover in outer space, including the Moon and other celestial bodies, which could constitute a danger to the life or health of astronauts.[30]

In the context of military operations in outer space, this Article raises significant questions. If manned military outer space missions become a reality, would Active Duty members of the Space Force (or, potentially, other military branches) conducting operations in space retain the protections astronauts enjoy under Article V? Would military astronauts have an obligation to render assistance to another State's astronauts, even if those astronauts were, themselves, Active Duty members of the other State's military space forces? Does the requirement to "immediately inform" other States Parties to the Outer Space Treaty apply to threats or dangers that, if revealed, would also reveal secret or sensitive outer space capabilities to the United States' adversaries? These and similar questions will likely grow in significance as military operations—and, particularly, manned military operations—in outer space increase.

Articles VI, VII, and VIII of the Outer Space Treaty deal with issues related to international responsibility, liability, and jurisdiction and control of space objects respectively.[31] Article VI stipulates that States Parties "shall bear international responsibility" for their national activities in outer space (with "national activities" comprised of activities of both "governmental and non-governmental agencies") and for "assuring that national activities are carried out in conformity with the provisions set forth in the [Outer Space] Treaty."[32] While Article VI governs State responsibility for activities, Article VII establishes a liability scheme for damage caused by outer space objects or their "component parts."[33] Any State Party that "launches or procures the launching" of a space object *and* any State Party "from whose territory or facility an object

30 Outer Space Treaty, art. V.
31 *See* Outer Space Treaty, arts. VI–VIII.
32 Outer Space Treaty, art. VI.
33 Outer Space Treaty, art. VII.

is launched" are internationally liable for such damage.[34] (These provisions are echoed and expanded in the Liability Convention). Finally, Article VIII stipulates that a State Party that registers a space object "shall retain jurisdiction and control over such object"[35]—essentially, this is recognized as meaning that a State retains an ownership or jurisdiction over a space object that is comparable to its jurisdiction/ownership of national territory.

The implications of Articles VI–VIII on national military activities in space are profound. Articles VI and VII ensure that, at least to some degree, a space power like the United States would be subject to international responsibility even for its national military activities and, potentially, subject to liability for damage caused by its military space objects. The jurisdiction and control provisions of Article VIII, particularly if interpreted as establishing quasi-territorial ownership of space objects, is extremely significant in the context of self-defense and national security: if a State's space object is attacked, this may constitute an attack on the State itself under a 'quasi-territorial' understanding of Article VIII. This would be similar, at least in principle, to the treatment of ships, other ocean-going vessels, and aircraft, all of which are generally 'flagged,' or registered, in specific States. Their quasi-territorial status allows the State in question to exert certain types of legal jurisdiction over these vessels, and, in some circumstances, to interpret an attack on such a vessel as an act of war.[36]

---

34 Outer Space Treaty, art. VII.

35 Outer Space Treaty, art. VIII.

36 It should be noted that space objects' quasi-territorial status, and, especially, the proposition that an attack on a space object could constitute an act of war are by no means self-evident, and significant controversy exists with respect to how Article VIII's characterization of jurisdiction and control over space objects applies, in a practical sense, to military and self-defense scenarios. For example, "Armed Conflicts in Outer Space: Which Law Applies?," a 2021 article published by international space law expert Frans von der Dunk in *International Law Studies*, examines this issue extensively. Drawing on the requirements of the UN Charter and the Outer Space Treaty's structural principle concerning prohibitions on territorial sovereignty in outer space (i.e. Article II), von der Dunk posits that "unless an armed attack against a space object would in itself threaten the political independence of a State, it would not violate Article 2(4) of the U.N. Charter[,]" which prohibits the use of force against "the territorial integrity or political independence" of another state. Frans G. von der Dunk, "Armed Conflicts in Outer Space: Which Law Applies?," *International Law Studies*, vol. 97, 2021, p. 209. An attack on a space object, however, could potentially trigger a State's internationally-recognized right to self-defense, though this right to self-defense would be based on the specific principles associated with Article 51 of the UN Charter, principles of customary self-defense under international law that preexisted the UN Charter, and the nature of the attack itself, rather than the quasi-territorial status of the attacked space object. *See* von der Dunk, "Armed Conflicts in Outer Space," pp. 210–11, 218, 220, 225, 230–31. A third possibility is that a State attack on,

Out of all the Articles in the Outer Space Treaty, none may be open to wider interpretation than Article IX. This is partially due to the length and complexity of the Article. Essentially, there are six primary responsibilities delineated in Article IX. With respect to the outer space activities of States Parties to the Treaty, such activities must be (1) "guided by the principle of cooperation and mutual assistance" and (2) "conduct[ed] ... with due regard to the corresponding interests of all other States Parties to the Treaty."[37] Further, States must avoid both (3) "harmful contamination" to the Moon and other celestial objects and (4) "adverse changes in the environment of the Earth resulting from the introduction of extraterrestrial matter" during the course of their outer space activities.[38] Finally, Article IX establishes dual responsibilities for States that believe either that their own activities may "cause potentially harmful interference" with the activities of another State Party *or* that believe another State's activities would "cause potentially harmful interference" with their own activities.[39] In the first case, Article IX stipulates (5) the State seeking to conduct the activity "*shall* undertake appropriate international consultations before proceeding with any such activity or experiment" (emphasis added).[40] In the second case, (6) the State fearing harm "*may* request consultation concerning the activity or experiment" (emphasis added).[41] As with almost all the significant terminology in the Outer Space Treaty, no specific definitions are provided for the relevant treaty terms—"principle[s] of cooperation and mutual assistance," "due regard," "harmful contamination," or "harmful interference"—contained in Article IX. Similarly, no explanation is provided for what might constitute "appropriate international consultations" between States in the event of expected harmful interference, or, indeed, what remedy might be available for a State that "request[s] consultation" about a space activity, but is denied by the State Party to whom the request was made.

---

or other State interference with, an on-orbit space object could trigger a right by the State party owning/operating that space object to engage in *counter-measures* (potentially of a military nature) against the attacking/interfering State. von Der Dunk, "Armed Conflict in Outer Space," *International Law Studies*, pp. 210–11. Counter-measures "are State actions, or omissions, directed at another State that would otherwise violate an obligation owed to that State and that are conducted by the former in order to compel or convince the latter to desist in its own internationally wrongful acts or omissions." Michael N. Schmitt, "'Below the Threshold' Cyber Operations: The Countermeasures Response Option and International Law," *Virginia Journal of International Law*, vol. 54:3, 700 (2014).

37 Outer Space Treaty, art. IX.

38 Outer Space Treaty, art. IX.

39 Outer Space Treaty, art. IX.

40 Outer Space Treaty, art. IX.

41 Outer Space Treaty, art. IX.

The last three substantive Articles of the Outer Space Treaty, Articles X–XII, involve provisions to "promote international cooperation" and foster transparency between States engaged in outer space activities.[42] Article X stipulates that, "in order to promote international cooperation," a State Party "shall consider on a basis of equality any requests by other States Parties to the Treaty to be afforded an opportunity to observe the flight of space objects launched by [that State]."[43] Article XI requires that State Parties conducting outer space activities "agree to inform the Secretary-General of the United Nations as well as the public and the international scientific community, to the greatest extent feasible and practicable, of the nature, conduct, locations and results of such activities."[44] Finally, Article XII provides a curious dual right/responsibility for State Parties: that "[a]ll stations, installations, equipment and space vehicles on the Moon and other celestial bodies shall be open to representatives of other States Parties to the Treaty on a basis of reciprocity."[45] As Article XII indicates, this "right of visit" or "right of inspection" is only applicable to space objects and facilities "on the Moon and other celestial bodies," and, thus, is not applicable to space objects, space stations, or space vehicles in orbit around

42 Outer Space Treaty, arts. X, XI. While the explicit language "[i]n order to promote international cooperation" is not found in Art. XII, as it is in Arts. X and XI, the text of Art. XII and its inclusion among the similar Arts. X and XI indicate its natural similarity with the two previous articles.

43 Outer Space Treaty, art. X. It should be noted, however, that this already somewhat equivocal stipulation ("shall consider" is hardly language easily interpreted as mandating particular action) is further tempered by the requirement that "[t]he nature of such an opportunity for observation and the conditions under which it could be afforded shall be determined by agreement between the States concerned." Outer Space Treaty, art. X.

44 Outer Space Treaty, art. XI.

45 Outer Space Treaty, art. XII. This article traces its history to the Antarctic Treaty, which contains a similar provision regarding designated observers appointed by the Contracting Parties to that Treaty. Pursuant to Article VII, "[a]ll areas of Antarctica, including all stations, installations and equipment within those areas ... shall be open at all times to inspection" by these observers "[i]n order to promote the objectives and ensure the observance of the provisions" of the Treaty. The Antarctic Treaty, Dec. 1, 1959, 12 U.S.T. 794, 402 U.N.T.S. 71, art. VII [hereafter Antarctic Treaty]. Because of the similar nature of other provisions of the Antarctic Treaty with provisions of the Outer Space Treaty (see, for example, the extended discussion of the 'peaceful purposes' provisions of the Treaties later in this chapter), the extent to which Article VII of the Antarctic Treaty and Article XII of the Outer Space Treaty relate to one another is a subject of much debate. That said, even when granting the limitations of Article XII's more equivocal language (the caveat that facilities be open "on the basis of reciprocity," indicating the rights of visit and inspection are limited by whether similarly-situated States agree to allow mutual inspection rights), the Article's potential implications for military-run or military-sponsored activities on celestial bodies are clear.

the Earth or otherwise located in the vacuum of outer space. Thus, despite the imperative "shall" language of the Article,[46] the type and nature of the facilities to which Article XII would apply are, at least at the present time, fairly limited. Still, when considering potential Space Force operations, Articles X–XII provide several significant factors to consider—particularly in the event that American military space operations progress to the point of involving facilities or equipment constructed on celestial objects (which would also, of course, have to comply with the limitations and requirements of Article IV).

3 "Peaceful Purposes" under the Outer Space Treaty

As noted above in the discussion of the Outer Space Treaty, the idea that outer space ought to be used "for peaceful purposes" is deeply ingrained in the outer space legal regime—although, as we shall see below, there is disagreement concerning the extent to which utilizing outer space and celestial bodies for "peaceful" or "exclusively peaceful" purposes is a legal obligation. Nowhere in the Outer Space Treaty, however, is the term "peaceful" defined, nor is any clear guidance provided with respect to differentiating uses of outer space for "peaceful" versus "non-peaceful" purposes. As innumerable scholars have noted, this lack of definition has resulted in the development of at least two schools of thought with respect to the proper interpretation of "peaceful purposes" in the context of the outer space law: the "non-aggressive" interpretation, which holds that military—and even weaponized—uses of outer space are permissible so long as they comply with both (1) the specific prohibitions of certain weapons/actions outlined in Article IV of the Outer Space Treaty, and (2) other international law, including UN prohibitions on aggressive behavior; and the "non-military" interpretation, which holds that *all* military uses of space are prohibited under the "peaceful purposes" language.[47]

---

46 In the *Cologne Commentary on Space Law*, Dr. Lesley Jane Smith notes that "[t]he use of the imperative form—'shall'—in the language of Article XII suggests that proposed visits should not be subject to the discretionary decision of the State receiving the request. It was stated that the provision 'does not confer, or imply the existence of any right or power to veto proposed visits to other countries' facilities on a celestial body'." Lesley Jane Smith, "Article XII," in Stephan Hobe, Bernhard Schmidt-Tedd, & Kai-Uwe Schrogl, eds., *Cologne Commentary on Space Law: Volume I Outer Space Treaty* (Cologne: Carl Heymanns Verlag, 2009), 210.

47 *See* Manfred Lachs, *The Law of Outer Space: An Experience in Contemporary Lawmaking* (Leiden: Brill Nijhoff, 2010) 105–106. *See also* Stephan Hobe and Niklas Hedman, "Preamble," in *Cologne Commentary on Space Law*, 22. In the *Cologne Commentary* on the Outer Space Treaty, Hobe and Hedman actually posit *three* potential interpretations of the

The "non-aggressive" interpretation, advocated by the United States and every significant space power, is the more widely accepted of the two; indeed, given the growing ubiquity of the "non-aggressive" interpretation, advocacy of the "non-military" interpretation is of less and less practical significance. Although the "non-military" interpretation has largely "been overtaken by [S]tate practice,"[48] this section will examine both the "non-aggressive" and the "non-military" interpretations of the "peaceful purposes" language.

3.1 *"Peaceful Purposes" as "Non-military" Use: A Fading, or Inapplicable, Interpretation?*

The "non-military" interpretation of the Outer Space Treaty's "peaceful purposes" language is significant for two primary reasons. First, it has been a preferred interpretation for many States that lack the technological capability to conduct launches into outer space; this was particularly true at the beginning of the Space Age, as international outer space law was first being contemplated and developed.[49] (It should be noted that, as we will see below in the case of

"peaceful purposes" language: "One opinion holds that if the mention of "peaceful purposes" would make any sense, it should include a complete demilitarisation.. Therefore, "peaceful" would mean "non-military" because any aggressive use was already prohibited by Article III of the Outer Space Treaty. On the other hand, space powers like the United States refer to the legitimate right of self-defence, which should also be exercised in outer space. Only an aggressive use, in the sense of UNGA Resolution 3314, will be a prohibited non-peaceful use of outer space. Finally, there is a third opinion that holds that "peaceful" means "non-weaponized". [sic] This opinion stresses that any military use of outer space must not be contrary to a promotion of peace and concludes that any use that threatened peace in outer space would be prohibited." Hobe and Hedman, "Preamble," in *Cologne Commentary on Space Law*, 22. The "non-weaponized" interpretation described by Hobe and Hedman seems to be a hybrid position of sorts—an idea that some military uses of outer space that are non-aggressive but also non-weapon (perhaps remote sensing and satellite surveillance?) would constitute uses for "peaceful purposes," while any space weapon (even one not explicitly excluded by Article IV of the Outer Space Treaty) would be inherently non-peaceful. Because the so-called "non-weapon" interpretation, depending on its gradations, seems to shift into either the non-military or non-aggressive interpretations, it will not be considered in this paper as a separate and distinct interpretation of the meaning of the "peaceful purposes" language.

48 Patrick K. Gleeson, "Legal Aspects of the Use of Force in Outer Space" (A Thesis Submitted to McGill University in partial fulfillment of the requirements for the degree of Master of Laws (LL.M.)) (Montreal: Institute of Air & Space Law, McGill University, 2005), 110.

49 *See* Bin Cheng, *Properly Speaking, Only Celestial Bodies Have Been Reserved for Use Exclusively for Peaceful (Non-Military) Purposes, but not Outer Space Void*, in Michael N. Schmidtt, ed., *International Law Across the Spectrum of Conflict: Essays in Honor of L.C. Green on the Occasion of His Eightieth Birthday* (Newport, RI: Naval War College, 2000), 81 (Cheng notes that, after the launch of *Sputnik*, "[t]here was an overwhelming yearning that the whole of outer space, including all the celestial bodies, should be reserved

the United States, and as has been repeated by other States, protestations that outer space be used for exclusively peaceful purposes generally only last until the State in question has *developed* an outer space capability). Second, the "non-military" interpretation reflects the legal analyses of several of the most prominent legal scholars of space law, including Manfred Lachs, the diplomat, legal scholar, and former judge on the International Court of Justice who wrote one of the earliest treatises on outer space law, and—at least in the context of Article IV of the Outer Space Treaty—Professor Bin Cheng, the former Dean of the Faculty of Laws at University College London and an internationally-recognized expert in the fields of air and space law.

Lachs takes up the issue of "peaceful use" of outer space in Chapter IX of his ground-breaking space law treatise, *The Law of Outer Space: An Experience in Contemporary Lawmaking*. Citing UN General Assembly Resolutions, the Outer Space Treaty, and "documents emanating from non-governmental organizations and ... legal scholars," Lachs notes that "ever since man-made instruments [of law] moved into outer space, the claim has been asserted that, in view of the dangers involved, outer space should be used solely for peaceful purposes, and endeavours have been pursued to ensure that this be so."[50] Recognizing the already-established conflict between the "non-aggressive" and "non-military" interpretations of the "peaceful purposes" language, Lachs is dismissive of any attempt to minimize the scope of the term "peaceful." "[T]here seems to be little doubt," Lachs writes, "as to the real meaning of ['peaceful use']."[51] He goes on:

> If [the "peaceful use" language] was intended to forbid aggressive use only, mere reference to international law and the Charter of the United Nations would have sufficed. Is it not evident that such actions are prohibited in terrestrial environments? .... For the Charter, reflecting as it does contemporary international law, imposes upon States the obligation to "refrain in their international relations from the threat or use of force". A restrictive interpretation of this obligation ... has no legal foundation .... Thus an attack or any other constraint against a ship, aircraft or any

---

for exploration and use for peaceful purposes only" and that "[p]opular opinion and a number of governments were clamouring for the whole of outer space, including all the celestial bodies, to be preserved for exclusively peaceful, i.e., non-military, exploration and use.").

50 Lachs, *Law of Outer Space*, 105.

51 Lachs, *Law of Outer Space*, 106.

other vehicle moving in other dimensions, such as outer space, constitutes a violation of the law.

> Had only this prohibition [i.e. prohibiting "aggressive use"] been contemplated, the additional words "for peaceful purposes" would have been redundant. And yet they were expressly written into the basic international instruments governing the question. They can therefore hardly be considered as meaningless, the expression of a pious desire devoid of legal effects. Moreover, the same term "peaceful purposes" has been employed in other contemporary instruments and at the same time given an authentic interpretation which is unequivocal. Suffice it to mention the provision concerning "the contribution of atomic energy to peace, health and prosperity throughout the world", which is linked with the goal that it be "not used in such a way as to further any military purposes". Or another provision, where the term "peaceful purposes" is linked with the prohibition of "any measures of a military nature".[52]

In addition to his assertions that the "peaceful purposes" language must be understood in the context of similar language in other international instruments and would be redundant if it did not connote anything more than what would otherwise be unlawful under international law, Lachs further argues that "the whole trend of the development of the law of outer space from its general principles to specific and detailed rules" cuts against the "non-aggressive" interpretation of "peaceful."[53] He cites Article IV's stipulation that celestial bodies "shall be used … exclusively for peaceful purposes" as the culmination of this trend and further evidence of the definition of "peaceful" as meaning "non-military." It should be noted that Lachs makes no distinction in *The Law of Outer Space* between the Moon/celestial bodies and the rest of outer space with respect to the nature and context of use for "peaceful purposes."

Cheng, a contemporary of Lachs who wrote dozens of articles and books about outer space law both before and after the publication of *The Law of Outer Space*, largely agreed with Lachs' interpretation of the "peaceful purposes" language—at least in the context of Article IV of the Outer Space Treaty. Citing the early history of the Space Age, Cheng notes that both the United

52 Lachs, *Law of Outer Space*, 106 (internal citations omitted). The quotations Lachs uses in the final two sentences of this selection are drawn from the Statute of the International Atomic Energy Agency (Statute of the International Atomic Energy Agency, July 29, 1957, 8 U.S.T. 1093, 276 U.N.T.S. 3 (amended Oct. 4, 1961, 14 U.S.T. 135, 471 U.N.T.S. 333)) and the Antarctic Treaty respectively.

53 Lachs, *Law of Outer Space*, 107.

States and the Soviet Union advanced proposals in the late 1950s "that outer space and celestial bodies should be used only for genuinely peaceful purposes and the common benefit of mankind."[54] He also argues that such an interpretation of "peaceful" appears to be reflected in the United States' domestic space legislation from that time period[55]—specifically, in the 1958 National Aeronautics and Space Act, which declares in its introductory "Declaration of Policy and Purpose" that "[t]he Congress declares that it is the policy of the United States that activities in space should be devoted to peaceful purposes for the benefit of mankind."[56] Moving from historical State declarations to the text of the Outer Space Treaty itself, Cheng echoes Lachs in his application of legal comparative analysis between the language of the Antarctic Treaty and the language of Article IV of the Outer Space Treaty. Noting that the language regarding "peaceful purposes" is nearly identical in both treaties,[57] Cheng reaches three conclusions concerning how "peaceful" ought to be interpreted.

---

54 Bin Cheng, *Studies in International Space Law* (Oxford: Oxford University Press, 2004), 514.

55 Cheng, *Studies in International Space Law*, 514.

56 Act of July 29, 1958 (National Aeronautics and Space Act of 1958), Pub. L. No. 85–568, §102(a), 72 Stat. 426 (1958). It should be noted, however, that in the Act's very same "Declaration of Policy and Purpose" section, Congress also explicitly declares "that the general welfare and security of the United States require that adequate provision be made for aeronautical and space activities" and, even more significantly "that activities peculiar to or primarily associated with the *development of weapons systems, military operations, or the defense of the United States* (including the research and development necessary to make effective provision for the defense of the United States) shall be the responsibility of, and shall be directed by, the Department of Defense[.]" (emphasis added). National Aeronautics and Space Act, sec. 102(b). Thus, in almost the same breath as its recognition of the 'peaceful purposes' principle, Congress also explicitly recognized the legality (in its view) of military uses of outer space—and even the development of space-related weapons!

57 Article I of the Antarctic Treaty reads:

1. Antarctica shall be used for peaceful purposes only. There shall be prohibited, inter alia, any measures of a military nature, such as the establishment of military bases and fortifications, the carrying out of military maneuvers, as well as the testing of any type of weapons.

2. The present treaty shall not prevent the use of military personnel or equipment for scientific research or for any other peaceful purposes.

Antarctic Treaty, art. I. The stipulation that "Antarctica shall be used for peaceful purposes only" language is quite similar to the Outer Space Treaty's mandate that "[t]he Moon and other celestial bodies shall be used by all States Parties to the Treaty exclusively for peaceful purposes," and the references to prohibited activities (establishment of military bases and fortifications, military maneuvers, weapons testing) and permitted use of military personnel and equipment for "scientific research or for any other peaceful purposes" are largely identical.

First, "peaceful" means non-military.[58] Second, "references to military installations, military manoeuvres and so forth in the provision are *exemplificative and not exhaustive*" (emphasis added).[59] Third, and finally, "the possibility of using military personnel and equipment for scientific research or other peaceful purposes in no way invalidates" the interpretation of "peaceful" as meaning "non-military."[60] Based on these conclusions, Cheng is adamant that Article IV's reference to "exclusively peaceful purposes" means precisely what it says: that only "non-military" activities are permitted on the Moon and other celestial bodies.

In contrast to Lachs, however, Cheng argues, based on his analysis of the text of the Outer Space Treaty, that a State's legal obligation to use outer space for "peaceful purposes" only applies to the use of "the Moon and other celestial bodies" as mandated in Article IV. Unlike Lachs, who steadfastly sought to apply "the whole trend" of outer space law development toward an interpretation of the Outer Space Treaty mandating the exclusively peaceful use of all of outer space,[61] Cheng notes that "[n]owhere ... in the 1967 Space Treaty, is outer space in the narrow sense of the term, i.e., the void between all the celestial bodies ... confined to 'peaceful uses' only."[62] Indeed, recognizing that the Preamble is the only other place in the Outer Space Treaty in which the term "peaceful purposes" is used in a context pertaining to potential military uses of space, Cheng points out that the language utilized in the Preamble ("Recognizing," "Desiring," "Recalling") is hardly imperative or obligation-imposing.[63] More importantly, "[i]n law," Cheng writes, "it is well established that preambles to treaties do not normally contain provisions with binding obligations. They may at best serve as an aid in interpreting the substantive provisions of the Treaty."[64] Other references to "peaceful" uses of outer space in the Outer Space Treaty, specifically to "peaceful exploration" in Articles IX and XI, likewise do not indicate that outer space void, as Cheng describes it, may only be used for non-military purposes.[65] Thus, while the Outer Space

58 Cheng, *Studies in International Space Law*, 519.
59 Cheng, *Studies in International Space Law*, 519.
60 Cheng, *Studies in International Space Law*, 519.
61 Lachs, *Law of Outer Space*, 107.
62 Cheng, *Studies in International Space Law*, 517.
63 *See* Cheng, "Properly Speaking ...," in Schmidtt, ed., *International Law Across the Spectrum of Conflict*, 89.
64 Cheng, "Properly Speaking ...," in Schmidtt, ed., *International Law Across the Spectrum of Conflict*, 90.
65 *See* Cheng, "Properly Speaking ...," in Schmidtt, ed., *International Law Across the Spectrum of Conflict*, 91.

Treaty may reflect a high-minded desire that outer space as a whole, including the celestial bodies floating in space and the void between them, ought to be used for peaceful purposes, Cheng posits that, other than the normal limits of other international law and the provisions of the UN Charter (as applied to outer space pursuant to Article III) and the prohibitions on certain weapons described in Article IV, the Outer Space Treaty provides no legal prohibition on non-peaceful, military uses of outer space void. Only the Moon and other celestial bodies are off-limits for military use.

Cheng's interpretation of the different legal requirements for outer space void versus the Moon and other celestial bodies has profound implications for any State seeking to use or exploit outer space for military advantage, as we shall see in later chapters. It also explains why Cheng is highly critical of the United States' "non-aggressive" interpretation of the Outer Space Treaty's "peaceful purposes" language (see Section B, below). If the only legally binding reference to using outer space for "peaceful purposes" can be found in Article IV's requirement that the Moon and celestial bodies be used for "exclusively peaceful purposes," then the United States' "non-aggressive" interpretation is legally relevant and applicable *only to the activities described in Article IV*. In other words, if "peaceful" means "non-aggressive," then couldn't the United States find militarily significant, though purportedly "non-aggressive," uses for the Moon and other celestial bodies despite Article IV's apparent prohibition of using those bodies for such purposes?

For Cheng, this is an affront to the plain language of the Treaty. Describing the United States' interpretation of "peaceful" as "needless," "wrong," and "potentially noxious," Cheng devotes a multi-page analysis in *Studies in International Space Law* to attacking the United States' concept of "peaceful-as-non-aggressive."[66] The US interpretation is "needless," according to Cheng, first, because "the United States does not seek to apply it to Article IV(2)"—as Cheng notes, "there is [currently] no evidence to suggest that the United States intends to conduct military activities on the moon and other celestial bodies."[67] Second, the United States' interpretation and announcements of this interpretation at international bodies, carry no legal significance: without

66 Cheng, *Studies in International Space Law*, 520–522. This portion of Cheng's book is adapted from a previously published article, "The Legal Status of Outer Space Issues: Delimitation of Outer Space and Definition of Peaceful Use," which was originally published in the University of Mississippi School of Law's *Journal of Space Law* in 1983. *See* Bin Cheng, "The Legal Status of Outer Space Issues: Delimitation of Outer Space and the Definition of Peaceful Use," *Journal of Space Law*, vol. 11 (1983): 103–105.

67 Cheng, *Studies in International Space Law*, 520.

accompanying State practice—that is, in the context of Article IV—the United States' simple announcement that it interprets a provision of the Outer Space Treaty in a certain way has no bearing on the creation of customary norms or law related to that provision.[68] Further, Cheng argues, the United States' interpretation is simply "wrong" for all the reasons (plain language of Article IV, comparative analysis of Article IV with Article I of the Antarctic Treaty, redundancy of "non-aggressive" interpretation in light of Article III's application of international law to outer space and international law's existing prohibition on aggressive acts, etcetera) previously elaborated by both Lachs and Cheng himself.[69]

Most significantly of all, however, Cheng derides the United States' interpretation as "potentially noxious" because it threatens the foundations of *any other international treaty or agreement* that uses language identical or similar to the "peaceful purposes" language contained in the Outer Space Treaty. As Cheng acidly observes:

> For as long as the United States restricts its idiosyncratic interpretation of the word "peaceful" to some non-existent limitation on the military use of the outer void space, perhaps no more harm is done than the emperor preening himself in his non-existent clothes. But this rather whimsical interpretation carries with it seeds of serious consequences.
>
> The United States is a party to the Antarctic Treaty. It is also a party to many multilateral and bilateral agreements for international cooperation in nuclear matters, under which nuclear materials, equipment, and facilities which have been transferred from one contracting party to another contracting party may be used by the latter only for "peaceful purposes." Is the United States prepared to allow the word "peaceful" in these treaties to be interpreted by the other parties as meaning also "non-aggressive" and not "non-military"? Is that the reply that the United States is getting from some of the States which have already misused the nuclear assistance they have received in order to make bombs, non-aggressive bombs no doubt? If not, it should not take them long to learn what is the interpretation of the word "peaceful" favoured by the United States, unless the United States itself takes immediate steps to revise its attitude in the matter.[70]

---

68 *See* Cheng, *Studies in International Space Law*, 520.
69 Cheng, *Studies in International Space Law*, 521.
70 Cheng, *Studies in International Space Law*, 521–522.

It is a fair point. Without the benefit of a definition of "peaceful" in the treaty texts of the Outer Space Treaty, the Antarctic Treaty, and other international agreements utilizing the term "peaceful purposes," or similar language, can the United States really purport to have differing interpretations of the same term in the context of different treaties—by, for example, defining "peaceful" as "non-military" in the context of the Antarctic Treaty, and "peaceful" as "non-aggressive" in the context of the Outer Space Treaty? And, as Cheng ponders, would the United States accept such an interpretation of "peaceful purposes" from another State—particularly one the United States considered to be dangerous? Iran and North Korea, for instance, serve as excellent examples of Cheng's prediction that other States will eventually seek to justify (or shield) their nefarious actions under the auspices that such actions are being undertaken "peaceably." Both State have argued that their space programs are being undertaken for purely "peaceful" purposes—and, in keeping with Cheng's prediction, these protestations have failed to persuade the United States that the Iranian and North Korean space programs are not merely covers for the development of intercontinental ballistic missiles.

As noted at the beginning of this section, the belief that outer space ought to be used exclusively for peaceful, non-military purposes, was by no means confined to international legal scholars like Lachs and Cheng. Especially during the early years of the Space Age, the exclusively peaceful interpretation was the officially stated goal for State behavior in outer space by a range of State governments. At the conclusion of the 1961 Conference of Non-Aligned States (sometimes referred to as the 'Belgrade Conference' or the 'Conference of Heads of State or Government of Non-Aligned Countries') in Belgrade, Serbia, for example, the participating States issued a declaration that, among many other topics, "call[ed] upon all States in general, and States exploring outer space at present in particular, to undertake to use outer space exclusively for peaceful purposes."[71] Many of these same States (including Brazil, Lebanon, India, and Morocco) would further advocate the exclusively peaceful use of outer space during the COPUOS Legal Subcommittee's drafting and development of the non-binding Declaration of Legal Principles—and would

71 "Text of the Final Declaration of the Belgrade Conference of Nonaligned Nations," *New York Times*, Sept. 7, 1961, 8, available at https://timesmachine.nytimes.com/timesmachine/1961/09/07/118518779.html?pageNumber=8. The States participating in the Belgrade Conference were, in alphabetical order: Afghanistan, Algeria, Burma, Cambodia, Ceylon, Congo, Cuba, Cyprus, Ethiopia, Ghana, Guinea, India, Indonesia, Iraq, Lebanon, Mali, Morocco, Nepal, Saudi Arabia, Somalia, Sudan, Tunisia, the United Arab Republic, Yemen, and Yugoslavia, with Bolivia, Brazil, and Ecuador represented by observers.

be joined by other States (such as Argentina, Japan, Mongolia, and Hungary) that had not been part of the previous Belgrade Conference.[72] Given the final language of the Declaration, these concerns largely carried over into the later discussions of the Outer Space Treaty itself. Despite their preferred, non-military interpretation, however, at least some of these States would wind up agreeing with what would later be Cheng's interpretation: the language of the Declaration and the Outer Space Treaty did not contain mandates that outer space be used for exclusively peaceful purposes.[73] As noted above, the views of States on the "peaceful purposes" issue tend to change in direct relation to their technological ability to use outer space for wider purposes. India is a good example of this phenomenon: though it advocated strongly for the "exclusively peaceful" interpretation of the "peaceful purposes" language during the 1960s, it has since come to accept the use of space technology for military purposes, has tested an anti-satellite (ASAT) missile,[74] and has established a joint military organization, the Defense Space Agency, devoted to space warfare and satellite intelligence.[75]

There are several critical counterpoints to Lachs', Cheng's, and the "exclusively peaceful" camp of States' argument regarding the "peaceful purposes" language. The first is the radical limitations such an interpretation places on

72 *See* Bhupendra Jasani and Maria A. Lunderius, "Peaceful Uses of Outer Space—Legal Fiction and Military Reality," *Bulletin of Peace Proposals*, vol. 11, no. 1 (1980), p. 62. These States' opinions with respect to the "peaceful purposes" question were conveyed during the COPUOS Legal Subcommittee's meetings between April 23, 1963, and May 1, 1963, which can be found in UN Documents A/AC.105/C.2/SR.21, A/AC.105/C.2/SR.22, A/AC.105/C.2/SR.23, A/AC.105/C.2/SR.24, and A/AC.105/C.2/SR.26, which are available at https://www.unoosa.org/oosa/en/ourwork/spacelaw/treaties/travaux-preparatoires/declaration-of-legal-principles.html.

73 In April 1963, Mr. Birendra Chakravarty, India's representative during the negotiations leading to the drafting of the Declaration of Legal Principles, lamented that "[t]he possibility of the use of outer space for military purposes presented a serious threat to mankind" and that India and its delegation "regretted … that neither the United States nor the Soviet Union drafts [of the Declaration of Legal Principles] included a provision limiting the use of outer space to peaceful purposes." COPUOS Legal Subcommittee, "Provisional Summary Record of the Twenty-Second Meeting, Held at Headquarters, New York, on Wednesday, 24 April 1963, at 10:55 a.m.," UN Doc. A/AC.105/C.2/SR.22, Apr. 26, 1963, p. 7.

74 *See generally* Shounak Set, "India's Space Power: Revisiting the Anti-Satellite Test," Carnegie India, Carnegie Endowment for International Peace, September 2019, available at https://carnegieendowment.org/files/7-30-19_Set_India_ASAT_Test.pdf.

75 Asian News International, "Defence Space Research Agency: Modi govt approves new body to develop space warfare weapon systems," *India Today*, June 11, 2019, https://www.indiatoday.in/india/story/defence-space-research-agency-modi-govt-approves-new-body-to-develop-space-warfare-weapon-systems-1546951-2019-06-11.

State uses of outer space. Indeed, if Lachs' perception that use of *all* areas of outer space is legally limited to exclusively non-military "peaceful purposes" is correct, any space activity having dual military and civilian application (the problem of so-called "dual use" objects, recognized by the United States' representatives early in the Space Age, see below) would be prohibited. So, too, would any use of outer space or outer space objects for the purposes of self-defense or for passive, non-kinetic national security purposes. The implications of this blanket prohibition would be significant: telecommunications, geonavigational, and remote sensing technology—all of which have critical civilian as well as military applications—might run afoul of such a legal requirement. It might not be an exaggeration to say that, due to the wide applicability of space technology to military activities (not just in a kinetic sense, but in administration, communication, navigation, and other areas as well), Lachs' interpretation of the "peaceful purposes" language would effectively prohibit many critical outer space technologies.

Additionally, there is a wider international law conflict at play that may largely nullify the arguments of the "exclusively peaceful" use of outer space camp. This is the tension between different areas and instruments of international law: questions of *lex generalis* (laws governing general subject matters or legal areas), *lex specialis* (law governing a specialized subject matter or legal area), and *lex superior* (law having greater legitimacy than another law or body of law). As Frans von der Dunk has persuasively argued, the United Nations Charter's self-imposed status as *lex superior* over other international agreements[76] has significant implications for military activity in the space domain.[77] Particularly because the term "peaceful purposes" is not explicitly defined in either the binding space law treaties or other, non-binding space law instruments, there is no space law-based *lex specialis* on the issue of exclusively peaceful use, nor any obvious conflict between international space law and the Charter of the United Nations on the "peaceful purposes"/"peaceful use" issue. As such (and, it is likely, even if there *was* some degree of contradiction between understandings of the concept in international space law versus the UN Charter), the "right to use force in self-defense against an armed attack or if sanctioned or mandated by the Security Council," as described in

76 United Nations, Charter of the United Nations, 24 October 1945, 1 UNTS XVI, art. 103 ("In the event of a conflict between the obligations of the Members of the United Nations under the present Charter and their obligations under any other international agreement, their obligations under the present Charter shall prevail").

77 Frans G. von der Dunk, "Armed Conflicts in Outer Space: Which Law Applies?," *International Law Studies*, vol. 97, 2021, pp. 217–20, 225.

the text of the UN Charter, "applies in outer space."[78] That these rights exist in outer space naturally implies that a State is legally authorized to have (or develop) the physical or technological methods of exercising those rights in the space domain. Because the "exclusively peaceful" interpretation advocated by Lachs and others would prevent States from developing methods of exercising their self-defense rights or rights to lawful force in outer space, it follows that "exclusively peaceful" interpretation does not comport with international law as elaborated in the UN Charter. It should be noted that Cheng's interpretation of the Outer Space Treaty's "peaceful purposes" language (specifically, his argument that no legal requirement to use outer space void, or interplanetary space, for "peaceful purposes" actually exists) largely avoids the problematic, wide-ranging prohibition that seems to characterize Lachs' interpretation.

3.2 *"Peaceful Purposes" as "Non-aggressive" Use: The US (and Modern) Approach*

With the exception of a brief period in the immediate aftermath of the *Sputnik I* launch, during which the United States sought to limit the influence of the Soviets' perceived advantage in outer space,[79] the United States has consistently

---

78 Frans G. von der Dunk, "Armed Conflicts in Outer Space," *International Law Studies*, p. 225. The United Nations Charter mandates, in Article 2, that "[a]ll Members shall settle their international disputes by peaceful means in such a manner that international peace and security, and justice, are not endangered" and that "[a]ll Members shall refrain in their international relations from the threat or use of force against the territorial integrity or political independence of any state, or in any other manner inconsistent with the Purposes of the United Nations." UN Charter, art. 2. However, one of the ways in which armed force *can* be used consistently with the Purposes of the United Nations is through the recognition by the UN Security Council of "the existence of any threat to the peace, breach of the peace, or act of aggression" and a decision by the Security Council to "take such action by air, sea, or land forces as may be necessary to maintain or restore international peace and security." UN Charter, arts. 39, 42.

79 *See* Moltz, *Politics of Space Security*, 92–94. *See also* Paul B. Stares, *The Militarization of Space: U.S. Policy, 1945–1984* (Ithaca, NY: Cornell University Press, 1985), 54–57. Less than a week after the *Sputnik I* launch, Henry Cabot Lodge, the United States' Representative to the United Nations, proposed not only that the United States was willing to agree that outer space be used *exclusively* for peaceful purposes, but that it was supporting the creation of a technical verification committee to conduct "prelaunch inspections of all space rockets to ensure their peaceful intentions." Moltz, *Politics of Space Security*, 92. Comparing outer space technology to nuclear weapons, and the United States' previous efforts to control nuclear proliferation, Lodge made an impassioned speech to the UN's Political and Security Committee on October 10, 1957, stating: "Mr. Chairman, in 1946 when the United States alone had nuclear weapons, it proposed to the United Nations a plan to ensure the peaceful use of the new and tremendous force of atomic energy by putting it under international control. The world knows now that a decade of anxiety and

advocated the "non-aggressive" interpretation of the "peaceful purposes" language. Despite the United States' initial shock at the Soviets' satellite launch, the US military had been undertaking satellite research and development for almost a decade (see Chapter 4, below). With additional support from

---

trouble could have been avoided if that plan had been accepted. We now have a similar opportunity to harness for peace man's new pioneering efforts in outer space. We must not miss this chance. We have therefore proposed that a technical committee be set up to work out an inspection system which will *assure the use of outer space for exclusively peaceful and scientific purposes*. If there is general agreement to proceed with this study on a multilateral basis, the United States is prepared to join in this initiative *without awaiting the conclusion of negotiations on the other substantive proposals*" [emphasis added].

Department of State, U.S. Participation in the UN—Report by the President to the Congress for the Year 1957 (DoS Publication 6654, June 1958), 25 [hereinafter Lodge Speech]. Lodge's speech was not simply US posturing at an international forum. Approximately ten months later, on August 26, 1958, State Department Legal Advisor Loftus E. Becker echoed Lodge'os sentiments—and repeated claims of America's commitment to exclusively peaceful uses of outer space—in an address at the American Bar Association's 81st annual meeting in Los Angeles, California. "The most immediate problem in the field of space foreign policy," Becker stated, "is how to ensure that space is *used for peaceful purposes only*" (emphasis added). Loftus E. Becker, "The Control of Space," Address made before the 81st annual meeting of the American Bar Association, Aug. 26, 1958, in *Department of State, The Department of State Bulletin Vol. XXXIX, No. 1003* (DoS Publication 6701, Sept. 15, 1958), 417. Lauding the United States' efforts at the United Nations to encourage the development of an inspection framework for ensuring peaceful uses of outer space, Becker eventually concluded his speech by noting the State Department's desire for the development of additional outer space legal frameworks, with an emphasis on demilitarization in outer space: "From the viewpoint of the United States proposed solutions [to the development of law applicable in outer space] must reflect our policy aims to develop systems of institutional adjustment conducive to long-range objectives. These objectives include *the demilitarization of space and its devotion to peaceful purposes*, the encouragement of scientific research and the rapid achievement of practical benefits from such science to increase human welfare, and the encouragement of international cooperation and institutions of world community" [emphasis added]. Becker, "The Control of Space," in *Department of State Bulletin Vol. XXXIX, No. 1003*, 420. The language of "peaceful purposes" made its way into the legislative realm as well: in the United States' first space-related legislation, the National Aeronautics and Space Act of 1958 (which created the National Aeronautics and Space Administration, or NASA), Congress, in its "Declaration of Policy and Purpose," stated "that it is the policy of the United States that activities in space should be devoted to peaceful purposes for the benefit of all mankind." 72 Stat. 426, Pub. L. No. 85–568, 85th Congress (1958). Despite the United States' public willingness to advocate for exclusively peaceful uses of outer space, however, the official space policy of the Eisenhower Administration, NSC 5918, *U.S. Policy in Outer Space, see infra* Chapter 3, recommended that "a study of the implications for the [sic] national security of the expression 'peaceful uses of outer space' [be conducted] with a view to *defining this expression in a manner that would best serve the interests of the U.S.*" (emphasis added). NSC 5918, *U.S. Policy in Outer Space*, Dec. 17, 1959, at ¶ 44.

President Eisenhower, American spy satellites launched under the auspices of the Central Intelligence Agency's (CIA's) and USAF's joint "Project Corona," were orbiting earth by August 1960.[80] The success of the Corona satellites—in terms of the quality of the imagery and intelligence they were able to provide—effectively ended American calls for "exclusively peaceful" uses of outer space. Instead, "peaceful" use of outer space would, henceforward, be interpreted as including "non-aggressive" activities, such as the operation of non-weaponized military reconnaissance satellites.

While US policy under first the Eisenhower Administration and then the Kennedy Administration proceeded under this interpretation, it would be several years before the United States' "non-aggressive" interpretation of "peaceful" use would be presented at an international body. This occurred in December 1962, in an address given by Senator Albert Gore, Sr. (father of former Vice President and presidential candidate Albert "Al" Gore, Jr.) to the United Nations' First Committee. "It is the view of the United States," Senator Gore declared,

> that outer space should be used only for peaceful-that is, non-aggressive and beneficial-purposes. The question of military activities in space cannot be divorced from the question of military activities on earth. To banish these activities in both environments we must continue our efforts for general and complete disarmament with adequate safeguards. Until this is achieved, the test of any space activities must not be whether it is military or non-military, but whether or not it is consistent with the United Nations Charter and other obligations of law.
>
> There is, in any event, no workable dividing-line between military and non-military uses of space. For instance, both American and Russian astronauts are members of the armed forces of their respective countries; but this is not reason to challenge their activities or to deprecate their accomplishments. A navigation satellite in outer space can guide a submarine as well as a merchant ship. The instruments which guide a space vehicle on a scientific mission can also guide a space vehicle on a military mission.

---

80 *See* Sean N. Kalic, *US Presidents and the Militarization of Space, 1946–1967* (College Station, TX: Texas A&M University Press, 2012), 49–50.

> One of the consequences of these facts is that any nation may use space satellites for such purposes as observation and information-gathering. Observation from space is consistent with international law, just as is observation from the high seas. Moreover, it serves many useful purposes .... Observation satellites obviously have military as well as scientific and commercial applications. But this can provide no basis for objection to observation satellites.
>
> With malice toward none, science has decreed that we are to live in an increasingly open world, like it or not, and openness, in the view of Government, can only serve the cause of peace. The United States, like every other nation represented here in this Committee, is determined to pursue every non-aggressive step which it considers necessary to protect its national security and the security of its friends and allies, until that day arrives when such precautions are no longer necessary.[81]

Senator Gore's emphasis on man-made satellites demonstrated the United States' primary goal with the speech: carving out a place for military reconnaissance satellites under the canopy of "peaceful" uses of outer space. Particularly after the Soviet Union itself developed photoreconnaissance technology and began fielding its own spy satellites in mid-1962,[82] the Soviets, too, concluded that the use of satellites for military reconnaissance ought to be permissible—at least in their own practice and use of outer space, if not always in their public pronouncements.

The definition of "peaceful purposes" came to the fore again during the Senate Foreign Relations Committee ratification hearings for the Outer Space Treaty after President Johnson signed the treaty in January 1967. While a number of the advocates for the Treaty testifying before the Senate largely glossed over issues related to the definition of "peaceful" (Secretary of State Dean Rusk, for instance simply reiterated the military-related provisions of the Treaty and their significance for international arms control, before adding, "[t]here is, of course, no prohibition on the use of military personnel and equipment for peaceful purposes [in outer space]"[83]), definitional issues were addressed

81 United Nations, First Committee, "Verbatim Record of the Twelve Hundred and Eighty-Ninth Meeting," 17th Session, U.N. Doc. A/C.1/PV.1289, Dec 3., 1962, at 13–14.

82 *See* Moltz, *Politics of Space Security*, 128–29.

83 "Statement of Hon. Dean Rusk, Secretary of State" in *Treaty on Outer Space. Hearings before the Committee on Foreign Relations*, United States Senate, Ninetieth Congress, first session, on Executive D. March 7, 13, and April 12, 1967, at 4 [hereinafter *Senate Outer Space Treaty Hearings*].

directly during the testimony of Arthur J. Goldberg, the Ambassador to the United Nations. In an exchange with Goldberg, Senator Gore expressed his concerns with the treaty text in relation to the issue of satellite use—the same subject on which he had spoken at the United Nations approximately four years earlier—specifically with respect to the interaction between "peaceful" uses of outer space and the Outer Space Treaty's requirement that the exploration and use of space "shall be carried out for the benefit and in the interests of all countries."[84] Describing such a requirement as "indefinite" and "fuzzy," Senator Gore worried that, as satellite reconnaissance was a "peaceful" use, the Treaty would require sharing sensitive satellite data with other nations.[85] In the course of his remarks, he reminded the Committee of the debate concerning the definition of "peaceful purposes":

> There has been a long argument between the United States and Russia about the definition of a peaceful purpose. I engaged in that argument for some weeks.
>
> ...
>
> ... We interpret peaceful purposes as being non-aggressive and beneficial. The Soviet Union insists that it must mean nonmilitary. This involves communications satellites, and it is that particular issue that concerns me very much here.[86]

Neither Goldberg, nor any other testifying witness or Senator, contradicted Senator Gore's definition of "peaceful purpose." By this time, it appears that the "non-aggressive" interpretation was sufficiently well-established within the United States' space policy that Gore's statement was considered an uncontroversial description of American perceptions of the phrase.

While there were no further explicit discussions of the underlying meaning of the Outer Space Treaty's "peaceful purposes" language, or any further attempts to offer a clear definition of the phrase, later witnesses from the

84 Outer Space Treaty, art. 1.

85 "Statement of Hon. Arthur J. Goldberg, Ambassador to the United Nations in Senate," *Outer Space Treaty Hearings*, 30. As an aside, it should be noted that Senator Gore's concerns regarding reconnaissance data-sharing were ultimately unfounded. The United States has never interpreted the Outer Space Treaty to require sharing sensitive satellite imagery with other States.

86 "Statement of Hon. Arthur J. Goldberg, Ambassador to the United Nations; Accompanied by Leonard C. Meeker, Legal Advisor, Department of State," in *Senate Outer Space Treaty Hearings*, 59.

Department of Defense made it clear that they shared Senator Gore's perception of how "peaceful purposes" should be interpreted. In testimony before the Committee on April 12, 1967, the Deputy Secretary of Defense, Cyrus R. Vance, described the Outer Space Treaty's importance to national security, while emphasizing that it did not completely prohibit military activity in space:

> The treaty does not mean that military personnel or equipment will be excluded from space. Only weapons of mass destruction are barred from space. Military space programs concerned with communications, navigation, or observation are permitted. These programs, too, are peaceful uses of space. Our Vela satellite program, to take but one example of a military space program, is designed to observe to watch for nuclear tests in space or in the upper atmosphere, and thereby to safeguard the Nuclear Test Ban Treaty. We plan two additional Vela satellite launches in April to maintain and to enhance this peaceful military capability ....
>
> ...
>
> In short, the Department of Defense plans to continue its activities in space and to complement the work of NASA in those space endeavors in which the Defense Department has achieved a high degree of technical competence.[87]

General Earle G. Wheeler, the Chairman of the Joint Chiefs of Staff, testified immediately after Deputy Secretary Vance, reiterating Vance's position that the military ultimately supported the ratification of the Outer Space Treaty. General Wheeler cautioned, however, that national security threats involving space would not disappear upon approval of the Treaty, and that the military intended to continue its work on military-oriented (though not necessarily weaponized) space technology, at least partially for the purpose of ensuring compliance with the Outer Space Treaty:

> [This Treaty] should not mislead us into believing that we can ignore the feasibility and reality of future security threats from space or *into retarding our military space efforts*. Of crucial significance to the Joint Chiefs of Staff is the proposition that the United States *will not permit the authority of this treaty to become meaningless by diminishing U.S. military efforts in*

87 "Statement of Cyrus R. Vance, Deputy Secretary of Defense" in *Senate Outer Space Treaty Hearings*, 81.

> *space technology*. Confident that our Government is strongly resolved toward this end, the Joint Chiefs of Staff have no military objection to the United States becoming a party to this treaty, and the articulated goals of this treaty are fully acceptable to them. [Emphasis added][88]

Again, though neither Vance nor Wheeler offered a definition of "peaceful purposes," their comments indicate that both agreed with Senator Gore that there were legally permissible "military space efforts"—certainly in the field of satellite remote sensing, but also potentially in other areas—that constituted "peaceful" uses of outer space.

Even after the acceptance of the Outer Space Treaty, and despite the widely accepted American understanding of "peaceful purposes," official US space policy documents largely lacked a clear description of the term. It took until 1978, with the publication of Presidential Directive/NSC-37, President Jimmy Carter's National Space Policy—the first comprehensive space policy since the Eisenhower Administration[89]—for the United States' interpretation of "peaceful purposes" to be formally recognized in a national policy document. NSC-37 addressed the issue almost immediately. In the document's description of the principles in accordance with which "[t]he United States space program shall be conducted," the first is "[c]ommitment to the principle of the exploration and use of outer space for peaceful purposes and for the benefit of all mankind."[90] "Peaceful purposes," however, "*allow for military and intelligence-related activities in pursuit of national security and other goals*" (emphasis added).[91] Additionally, "[t]he United States will pursue activities in space in support of its right of self-defense" and will "maintain a national intelligence space program"—a clear reference to the satellite reconnaissance capabilities the United States had maintained since 1960.[92] Here, for the first time, was a clear articulation by the Executive Branch of the United States' interpretation of the "peaceful purposes" language, and, surprisingly, it seemed to be even more expansive than the merely "non-aggressive" uses described previously

88 "Statement of Gen. Earle G. Wheeler, U.S. Army, Chairman of the Joint Chiefs of Staff" in *Senate Outer Space Treaty Hearings*, 85.

89 *See* R. Cargill Hall, "The Evolution of U.S. National Security Space Policy and Its Legal Foundations in the 20th Century," 22 J. SPACE L. 1, 33 (2007). *See also, infra* notes 209–228 and accompanying text.

90 President Jimmy Carter, PD/NSC-37, *National Space Policy*, May 11, 1978, at 1–2, available at https://www.jimmycarterlibrary.gov/assets/documents/directives/pd37.pdf (last visited Apr. 2, 2020) [hereinafter PD/NSC-37].

91 PD/NSC-37, *National Space Policy*, 2.

92 PD/NSC-37, *National Space Policy*, 2.

by Senator Gore and others. While the reference to the right of self-defense in paragraph 1.f indicated a tacit recognition of international legal principles, the description of "peaceful purposes" as encompassing apparently *any* "military or intelligence-related" activity in pursuit of "national security" and, ominously, undescribed "other goals"[93] seemed to go well beyond prior interpretations of the term.

After the publication of NSC-37, whatever reticence may or may not have previously existed concerning the articulation of the United States' interpretation of "peaceful purposes" in even classified documents evaporated. With the exception of the new Biden Administration, every President since President Carter has issued his own National Space Policy (NSP). All have echoed the Carter Administration's formulation of "peaceful purposes" as "allow[ing] for military and intelligence-related activities in pursuit of national security or other goals."[94] Only two, the National Space Policies of the George W. Bush Administration and the Obama Administration, have altered that language, and the alterations were so slight as to entail no meaningful substantive difference: President Bush's NSP characterized "peaceful purposes" as "allow[ing] U.S. defense and intelligence-related activities in pursuit of *national interests*," (emphasis added)[95] while President Obama's states that "'peaceful purposes' allows for space to be used for *national and homeland security activities*" (emphasis added).[96]

Similarly, shortly after the publication of NSC-37, in the early years of the Reagan Administration, definitions and interpretations of "peaceful purposes" began to appear in military documents as well. In conjunction with standing up the United States' first official space-oriented military organization, the Air Force Space Command, the USAF also drafted the military's first "space doctrine." Published in October 1982, Air Force Manual (AFM) 1–6,

93 Clues about the extent of national security-related space activities and those in pursuit of "other goals" can be found in paragraph 2 of PD/NSC-37, which reads in part: "The United States will conduct those activities in space which are necessary to national defense. The military space program shall support such functions as command and control, communications, navigation, environmental monitoring, warning, tactical intelligence, targeting, ocean and battlefield surveillance, and space defense." PD/NSC-37, *National Space Policy*, 3.

94 *See infra* Chapter 3.

95 United States, *U.S. National Space Policy*, NSPD-49, Aug. 31, 2006, available at https://fas.org/irp/offdocs/nspd/space.pdf [hereinafter *2006 NSP*].

96 United States, *National Space Policy of the United States of America* (June 28, 2010), at 3 [hereinafter *2010 NSP*].

Military Space Doctrine,[97] utilized an interpretation of "peaceful purposes" that seemed to combine the Carter Administration's interpretive language with the earlier, "non-aggressive" description used by Senator Gore. In section 1–5, "Executive Guidance—National," AFM 1–6 mirrors the language of President Reagan's NSDD-42 (which had superseded NSC-37 in July 1982, but, as noted above, used identical "peaceful purposes" language), stating that "'[p]eaceful purposes' allows activities in pursuit of national security goals."[98] Section 1–9, "International Law," however, reflects Senator Gore's perspective, sweepingly declaring that "[i]nternational law allows non-aggressive military activities in space (that is, activities which do not constitute an attack upon, or threat against the territorial integrity or political independence of another country)."[99]

The Air Force's use of both formulations in AFM 1–6 reemphasizes the question that was originally raised by President Carter's NSC-37: is there a difference between "non-aggressive" activities and activities "in pursuit of national security or other goals?" Do references to "non-aggressive" behavior impose limits on the "military and intelligence-related activities" that can be used to support national security, or is the NSC-37 formulation a more expansive interpretation of the "peaceful purposes" language? The answer to this question is unclear, and little clarity has been provided in the military's doctrinal documents since the publication of AFM 1–6. In both Air Force and Joint Force doctrine publications related to outer space operations, references to "peaceful purposes" seesaw between the two formulations—if the Outer Space Treaty, international law, or "peaceful purpose" requirements are mentioned at all. Within the Air Force, for instance, a late 1990s doctrine document, Air Force Doctrine Document (AFDD) 2–2, *Space Operations*, mentions neither the concept of "peaceful purposes" nor the Outer Space Treaty's restrictions on certain space-based weapons.[100] By 2006, AFDD 2–2 had been updated to include a "Legal Issues" section, in which the "non-aggressive" formulation of peaceful purposes is on full display:

> The majority of nations have traditionally held that the "peaceful purposes" language does not prohibit military activities in outer space;

97 Department of the Air Force, Air Force Manual 1–6, *Military Space Doctrine*, Aerospace Basic Doctrine (Oct. 15, 1982).

98 AFM 1–6, *Military Space Doctrine*, 2.

99 AFM 1–6, *Military Space Doctrine*, 3.

100 *See generally* Department of the Air Force, Air Force Doctrine Document 2–2, *Space Operations*, Aug. 23, 1998.

> such activities have taken place throughout the space age without significant international protest. The phrase, rather, has been interpreted to require that activities in space be non-aggressive, or in other words, in compliance with the requirements under the United Nations Charter and international law to refrain from the threat or use of force except in accordance with the law, such as in self-defense or pursuant to United Nations Security Council authorization.[101]

Nearly six years later, in mid-2012, AFDD 2–2 had become defunct—replaced in Air Force doctrine by a new doctrinal annex: Annex 3-14, *Space Operations*. Annex 3-14 scrapped reference to the "non-aggressive" interpretation, opting for a formulation of "peaceful purposes" similar to the one typically used in the Presidential NSPs. While recognizing the United States' commitment to the use of outer space for "peaceful purposes," the Annex stipulates, first, that "US use of space systems in support of its defense activities is consistent with the use of space for peaceful purposes,"[102] and, second, that "peaceful purposes" allows "US defense and intelligence- related activities in pursuit of national interests."[103] The current version of Annex 3-14, now titled *Counterspace Operations*, contains no reference to "peaceful purposes" or any sections discussing legal considerations related to space operations at all.[104]

Similar inconsistencies exist when comparing the development of Joint Doctrine related to the outer space domain. First published in 2002, the earliest version of Joint Publication (JP) 3-14, *Joint Doctrine for Space Operations*, details the provisions of the Outer Space Treaty in a "Legal Considerations" section, including the statement that "[outer space] is to be used for peaceful purposes with due regard for all."[105] No additional information concerning "peaceful purposes" is mentioned. The 2009 update to JP 3-14 adopts the language of the Presidential NSPs, particularly the then-current Bush Administration NSP of 2006: "peaceful purposes" allows "US defense and intelligence-related

101 Department of the Air Force, Air Force Doctrine Document 2-2, *Space Operations*, Nov. 27, 2006, 27.

102 United States Air Force, Curtis E. LeMay Center for Doctrine Development and Education, Annex 3-14, *Space Operations*, June 19, 2012, at 10, available at https://fas.org/irp/doddir/usaf/3-14-annex.pdf [hereinafter 2012 Annex 3-14, *Space Operations*].

103 2012 Annex 3-14, *Space Operations*, 72.

104 *See generally* United States Air Force, Curtis E. LeMay Center for Doctrine Development and Education, Annex 3–14, *Counterspace Operations*, Aug. 27, 2018, https://www.doctrine.af.mil/Portals/61/documents/AFDP_3-14/AFDP-3-14-Counterspace-Ops.pdf [hereinafter 2018 Annex 3–14, *Counterspace Operations*].

105 Joint Publication 3–14, *Joint Doctrine for Space Operations*, Aug. 9, 2002, at I-4.

activities in pursuit of national interests."[106] The next update, in 2013, did not alter this formulation of "peaceful purposes," although an additional sentence was added to the document's discussion of the Outer Space Treaty's prohibition of military activities on the Moon or other celestial bodies noting that "the use of military personnel for scientific research and for any other peaceful purpose [on celestial bodies] is permitted."[107] The current version contains no explicit discussion of the Outer Space Treaty, its provisions, or interpretations of "peaceful purposes," instead simply stating in a brief "Legal Considerations" section that "[s]pace activities and operations must comply with the law of war and any other applicable treaties or international agreements to which the US is a party, with all applicable domestic law and policy, and with any applicable host nation laws."[108]

Regardless of whether the United States' and the US military's interpretation of "peaceful purposes" has subtly shifted over the years from allowing only "non-aggressive" activities and uses of outer space to something (at least somewhat) more expansive, the United States believes, and has believed since at least the early 1960s, that "peaceful purposes" encompass more than merely non-military uses of space. While there may have been a time when significant numbers of States would have opposed this position,[109] the continued use and dramatic expansion of military and national defense activities in outer space indicate that the United States' "non-aggressive" interpretation has come to be widely viewed as correct. In their actions, if not always their public pronouncements, other prominent spacefaring States, such as China and the Russian Federation, are emulating the United States—particularly in the realm of space-based C4ISR (the military acronym for "command, control, communications, computers, intelligence, surveillance, and reconnaissance") and similar space-based support capabilities for terrestrial military forces.[110] China and Russia have also indicated their acceptance of the American position through their own efforts to mold international space law—most notably through their draft "Treaty on the Prevention of the Placement of Weapons in Outer Space, the Threat or Use of Force Against Outer Space Objects"—in ways that would constrain the United States from fielding space weapons, which they

106 Joint Publication 3–14, *Joint Doctrine for Space Operations*, Jan. 6, 2009, at V–8.

107 Joint Publication 3–14, *Joint Doctrine for Space Operations*, May 29, 2013, at V–8, V–9.

108 Joint Publication 3–14, *Joint Doctrine for Space Operations*, Apr. 10, 2018, at IV-5.

109 See, for instance, the views of Argentina and India during the drafting of the Outer Space Treaty, previously discussed, *supra* note 43.

110 *See* Defense Intelligence Agency, *Challenges to Security in Space*, Jan. 2019, at iii, 18–21, 26–29.

believe are not prohibited under the current outer space legal regime. While a firm definition of "peaceful purposes" remains lacking in both international law and in States'—including even the United States'—domestic policies, it is clear that the United States' "non-aggressive" interpretation of "peaceful purposes" is sufficiently well-accepted that even its potential adversaries operate under the US interpretation.

4 Conclusions for United States' Military Space Policy

The foregoing examination of the international legal regime for outer space, and, particularly, the definition of the term "peaceful purposes" in relation to a State's lawful use of outer space, leads to a number of conclusions. First, the most interesting and most significant: the "non-military" versus "non-aggressive" approach to the Outer Space Treaty's "peaceful purposes" language has been flawed since at least the Treaty's ratification. Questions concerning what uses of outer space were or were not "peaceful" were, to a degree, meaningful prior to the drafting and ratification of the Outer Space Treaty—when binding international law on the subject did not exist and when the two States primarily engaged in space activities both insisted they intended to use outer space for peaceful purposes. With the Treaty's placement of the "peaceful purposes" principle in the non-binding Preamble, however, and its implicit, if not explicit, indication in Article IV that a difference exists between the "exclusively peaceful purposes" for which celestial bodies may be used and the largely unbounded uses (with the exception of the placement of certain weapons) that can be made of the vast expanse of "outer space void," any true limitation imposed by States' previous references to using outer space for "peaceful purposes" were largely voided. It seems that we can only conclude, with Bin Cheng, that "[w]hether 'peaceful' means 'non-military' or 'non-aggressive' consequently has no effect whatsoever on the contracting States' freedom to use the outer void space for military purposes in accordance with international law."[111] While outer space activities on celestial bodies are, to some degree, limited by the treaty obligations imposed by the Outer Space Treaty, no limits (again, save for the prohibition on nuclear weapons and "weapons of mass destruction") on military activity exist in the rest of space, the void between planets, and, perhaps most significantly, within Earth's orbits.

111 Cheng, "Properly Speaking ...," in Schmidtt, ed., *International Law Across the Spectrum of Conflict*, 109.

Second, the United States has never subscribed to the proposition that uses of space ought to be entirely non-military. Even during the brief period at the very beginning of the Space Age, when its disadvantage in space relative to the Soviet Union triggered diplomatic proposals for using space "exclusively for peaceful and scientific purposes," the United States was pressing forward with its development of photoreconnaissance spy satellites and other military space projects. The subsequent history of the United States' advocacy for the "non-aggressive" interpretation of "peaceful purposes," its input into the development of the Outer Space Treaty, the interpretations related to "peaceful" use of space espoused during the Treaty's ratification debates in the US Senate, and the evolution of official interpretations of the term in military and policy documents since President Carter's NSC-37 have consistently demonstrated that the United States believes—correctly, as we have seen in the previous paragraph and prior discussion—that there are a wide range of military activities that can be conducted in or through outer space for the purpose of protecting national security, or, even more broadly, of furthering national interests. This point has significant implications for the operations of the Space Force: with uses of the whole of outer space void constrained only by the Outer Space Treaty's Article IV prohibition on certain weapons systems, the ability of the USSF to operate in, conduct military flights or maneuvers through, or even station conventional weapons system in outer space is, at least from a *legal* standpoint, largely unconstrained.

From an international law standpoint, then, the United States has a wide range of options available for space-based military and even warfighting activities. With the exception of clear prohibitions on militarized uses of celestial bodies (or, perhaps, not so clear, if Bin Cheng's criticism of the United States' "peaceful purposes" interpretation is accurate—could an argument be made for "non-aggressive" fortifications, for instance?) and the stationing of nuclear weapons and weapons of mass destruction in orbit, any other military or security-related action in space would be lawful under the existing international law framework. The United States' "non-aggressive" interpretation of "peaceful purposes" and the relatively permissive military environment for interplanetary space under Article IV seem to track with broader international law principles—including States' inherent right to self-defense, recognized under Article 51 of the United Nations Charter, and, with Article III of the Outer Space Treaty's application of international law (including the UN Charter) to outer space, the right of States to engage in UN-mandated uses of force pursuant to Articles 2, 39, and 42 of the Charter. Given these fairly wide-ranging permissions with respect to lawful State action in outer space, the extent to which military uses of space, or as critics more darkly describe it, "space militarization," can and should go on, is a *policy*, rather than legal, question. The next chapter will discuss the basic history of United States space policy, particularly in the space security realm, in order to frame where we currently stand with the formation of the USSF.

CHAPTER 3

American Space Security Policy: US Space Policies and Military Involvement from President Eisenhower to President Biden

1 Introduction

On 2 May 1946, just under a year after Nazi Germany's surrender to the Allied Powers, the newly-formed Project RAND (which would go on to become the RAND Corporation, but was then a subsidiary organization within the Douglas Aircraft Company's Engineering Division) published a ground-breaking study. The nearly 350-page work, commissioned by US Army Air Force Major General Curtis LeMay, was entitled *Preliminary Design of a World-Circling Spaceship*.[1] The RAND study addressed not only the scientific and engineering requirements that would be necessary for the successful launch of a satellite vehicle into orbit—the fuels, weights, propulsion velocities, and other factors—but also the political and military implications such a satellite would have on the world at large. In the political realm, the Introduction of *Preliminary Design* makes two predictions that have proven to be incredibly prophetic:

> 1. A satellite vehicle with appropriate instrumentation can be expected to be one of the most potent scientific tools of the Twentieth Century.
> 2. The achievement of a satellite craft by the United States would inflame the imagination of mankind, and would probably produce repercussions in the world comparable to the explosion of the atomic bomb.[2]

With respect to military applications, RAND theorized that orbital satellites would have revolutionary effects on targeting and precision strike ("precise observations of the position of [a] missile can be made from [a] satellite, and a final control impulse applied to bring the missile down on its intended target"[3]), Earth observation and reconnaissance, weather forecasting, and even

1 *See* RAND Corporation, *Preliminary Design of a World-Circling Spaceship*, 1946, https://www.rand.org/pubs/special_memoranda/SM11827.html (last visited May 25, 2020).
2 RAND Corporation, *Preliminary Design*, 1–2.
3 RAND Corporation, *Preliminary Design*, 10.

 | DOI:10.1163/9789004524064_004

kinetic strike using the satellite vehicle itself.[4] In both its political and its military predictions, the RAND study proved to be decades ahead of its time.

Despite RAND's forward-thinking technical research and revolutionary predictions, it would be over ten years before a man-made satellite was launched into orbit. To the chagrin of the United States' national security establishment, politicians, and public, the honor of that historical achievement would belong to the Soviet Union. Still, RAND's *Preliminary Design* demonstrates that there was considerable US interest in the possible uses of outer space, and practical study in the mechanics necessary to place a man-made satellite vehicle in Earth orbit, as early as the mid-1940s. That it was the United States military that sponsored the study is indicative of another important point: the potential national security and military applications of outer space-based technology have been a primary concern of planners, policy-makers, and the national defense establishment since before the advent of the Space Age.

Outer space, in early post-war American policy, then, was viewed as an area of military interest: a prospective realm of military operation, a source of potential danger from terrestrial adversaries, and, in the words of many, the "ultimate high ground." Particularly after the launch of *Sputnik* in 1957, the eerie prospect of the United States' adversaries exploiting outer space to the detriment of American security and prestige reiterated this view. Indeed, as with many space-related matters, the United States military's focus on "space control" and even "space dominance" can be traced to the *Sputnik* launch. No less a military luminary than Lieutenant General James M. Gavin, the Commanding General of the 82nd Airborne Division during World War II, articulated the foundations of military "space control" theory in the immediate aftermath of *Sputnik*. Rattled by the Soviets' outer space success, and writing less than a year after the launch, Gavin argued:

> In order to win [a military and ideological race with the Soviet Union], the strategic initiative must be ours. We appear to be losing it, but we can regain it by proper study and the selection and training of imaginative and farsighted scientists and officers. We can develop a strategy of technology that will regain the technological initiative for the West .... Of one thing we may be sure, *the nation that first achieves the control of outer space will control the destiny of the human race.* [Emphasis added][5]

4 RAND Corporation, *Preliminary Design*, 10–11.

5 James M. Gavin, *War and Peace in the Space Age* (New York: Harper, 1958), 247–48.

Gavin's proposed strategy, and, as articulated in the last sentence of the passage quoted above, his opinion concerning the importance of outer space, would not sound out of place in a modern military document or policy book concerning space-based threats from China, Russia, or other potential American competitors. As we will see, over 75 years since RAND's *Preliminary Design*, the perception of outer space as a militarily significant domain in which the United States must excel has persisted, with its ultimate expression being the recent formation of the USSF. This chapter will outline the general history of the American military's interest in outer space-related capabilities, as well as examine the United States' "official" outer space policies as articulated by Presidents Eisenhower through Biden.

2 The Early Years: Military Missile Development and *Sputnik 1*

RAND's 1946 *Preliminary Design* study laid the groundwork for the military's and, more broadly, the United States Government's interest in outer space capabilities. It certainly convinced LeMay and others in the Army Air Force that the military possibilities of satellite technology were worth pursuing. As Cold War tensions rose in the late 1940s, however, more immediate concerns—the reconstruction of war-ravaged Europe and the protection of Western European nations from Soviet domination—prevailed over seemingly fantastic outer space escapades. Especially after the Soviet Union's test of its own atomic bomb in August 1949, the United States' interest in outer space became largely a subsidiary part of the nuclear arms race between the United States and the Soviet Union. Nazi Germany had proven with its V-2 rocket that a missile tipped with an explosive payload could be launched into the upper reaches of the atmosphere and brought down on a terrestrial target. What if such a missile could carry a nuclear warhead? For the better part of the decade after RAND's satellite study was published, the United States Government would focus not on satellite research, but on ballistic missile development.[6] The goal was to create a long-range weapon that could, if necessary, evade the

6 Although, as history proved and as noted by historians of the United States' (and the Soviet Union's) outer space program, without ballistic missile development, the United States would not have had a sufficiently powerful launch vehicle for placing satellites in orbit. Indeed, as noted by Everett C. Dolman, "every successful national space launch program to date has its lineage based in a direct path to a ballistic missile development program." Dolman, *Astropolitik*, 91–92.

anti-aircraft defenses that threatened traditional manned bomber aircraft and deliver a nuclear payload to targets in the Soviet Union.

The United States Air Force (USAF), established as an independent branch of the United States military in 1947, took the lead in this effort, albeit with certain internal divisions that threatened to delay missile development.[7] General LeMay, the progenitor of the RAND study, had, in 1948, become the commander of Strategic Air Command (SAC)—the USAF's strategic airpower bombing force, which, until the development of Atlas and other inter-continental ballistic missiles (ICBMs), served as the United States' sole method of long-range bombing. As SAC Commander, LeMay turned away from a focus on space. In the cutthroat bureaucratic battles for funding, development, and prime-of-place within the USAF and, more broadly, within Cold War military strategy, LeMay fully embraced his role as the Don of the so-called "Bomber Mafia." Ballistic missiles, which threatened to replaced LeMay's well-loved bombers, were at best a nuisance and at worst a dangerous and "extravagant boondoggle that wouldn't perform as anticipated," sapping money and resources that could have been better spent on SAC's fleet of manned nuclear bombers.[8] With SAC refusing to sufficiently fund ballistic missile development, General Thomas White, the USAF's Vice Chief of Staff, ordered the creation of a new organization, the Western Development Division (WDD), to take charge of the United States' ballistic missile program.[9] Semi-autonomous from its ostensible parent-organization, the USAF's Air Research and Development Command (the ARDC, which, at the time, was controlled by General Thomas Power—a LeMay ally

7 The United States Army and Navy, it should be noted, played significant roles in ballistic missile—and, ultimately, US space launch vehicle—development as well. Indeed, the Army and Navy, working with captured Nazi V-2 technology, undertook the initial post-World War II rocketry research and development programs. The Naval Research Laboratory developed the Viking sounding rocket in the late 1940s, which was later used as the basis for the Vanguard rockets selected by the Eisenhower Administration (at least initially) as the primary launch vehicles for the first American satellite launches. *See* John P. Hagen, "The Viking and the Vanguard," *Technology and Culture*, vol. 4, no. 4 (Autumn 1963), 435–51. The Army, working with the famed German rocket scientist Werner von Braun, developed the Redstone missile from the late 1940s into the early 1950s. Despite Eisenhower's initial selection of the Vanguard program as the United States' satellite programs launch vehicle, the Redstone (in its modified Jupiter derivative) would ultimately be used to launch both the first American satellite, *Explorer 1*, and, with Commander Alan Shepherd's May 1961 suborbital flight, the first crewed American space mission. US Army, "Redstone Rocket," US Army Aviation and Missile Life Cycle Management Command, https://history.redstone.army.mil/space-redstone.html (last visited Mar. 19, 2022).

8 Lawrence J. Spinetta, "White vs. LeMay: The Battle Over Ballistic Missiles," *Air Force Magazine*, vol. 96, no. 1 (January 2013), 56.

9 Spinetta, "White vs. LeMay," *Air Force Magazine*, 56, 59.

who would succeed LeMay as Commander of SAC),[10] the WDD would be run by Brigadier General Bernard A. Schriever, a former Pentagon development planner and chief of scientific liaison familiar with the theoretical benefits of missile technology.[11] Schriever and his team at the WDD accomplished the goal set by ballistic missile proponents: with the successful testing of the Atlas ICBM in December 1957, the United States had an unmanned missile, capable of striking targets in the Soviet Union, that could be launched from the continental United States.

General Schriever's work with the ballistic missile program convinced him not only that ICBMs provided an excellent weapons system, but that similar rocket technology could be used to place satellites in orbit and, perhaps, even reach other celestial bodies. Eight months before the Soviets' *Sputnik* launch and ten months before the first successful launch of the Atlas missile, Schriever gave a speech in San Diego at the Astronautics Symposium entitled "ICBM: A Step Toward Space Conquest." As its title suggests, Schriever's speech focused on the WDD's work on ICBMs as only the beginning of the possibilities outer space presented for the United States. Far beyond the mere military benefits that could be derived from the successful development of ballistic missiles, Schriever predicted that the research his team had conducted on "airframe, propulsion, [the] guidance and control subsystems," and other aspects of ICBMs would lead to revolutionary "follow-on projects" in space:

> It is reasonable to expect that it will not be too difficult to extend these present developments to surface-to-surface transport of personnel

10 Spinetta, "White vs. LeMay," *Air Force Magazine*, 58–59. It should be noted, however, that despite the level of autonomy provided to the WDD, as a subsidiary organization to ARDC, Schriever was a subordinate of General Power. As USAF Major and author Brent Ziarnick describes in a lengthy paper on General Power's role in the development of the USAF's space operations, the initial tension between Schriever and Power would give way to a close working relationship that ultimately propelled the development of both the ICBM and, later, successful satellite launch vehicles. *See* Brent D. Ziarnick, *Tough Tommy's Space Force: General Thomas S. Power and the Air Force Space Program* (Maxwell AFB, AL: Air University Press, Drew Paper No. 34, 2019), 31–35.

11 *See* Bernard A. Schriever, "Military Space Activities Recollections and Observations," in R. Cargill Hall & Jacob Neufeld, eds., *The US Air Force in Space: 1945 to the Twenty-First Century* (Washington, D.C.: USAF History & Museums Program, 1998), 14–15. Schriever described his pre-WDD job in the Air Staff's Development Planning Office at the Pentagon as "try[ing] to relate long-range technology [i.e. missile technology] to operational requirements and enhance the overall capability of the Air Force"—experience that likely contributed significantly to his selection as the commander of the WDD. Schriever, "Military Space Activities Recollections and Observations," *The US Air Force in Space*, 14.

> by rocket propulsion, or space travel of personnel at some time in the future ....
>
> ...
>
> Now, where does all this [ballistic missile and outer space research] lead? My thought is that the evolution of space vehicles will be a gradual step-by-step process, with the first step beyond ballistic missiles being unmanned, artificial earth satellites and then perhaps unmanned exploratory flights to the Moon or Mars. These first flights would no doubt be research vehicles to gather scientific data and to accumulate information on space environmental conditions for future design use. The information gathered from these flights will supplement the information gathered from ballistic missile test flights.
>
> Many of the things that [w]e can learn from satellites will lead not only to a better understanding of conditions to be encountered in space, but will lead to a better understanding of our own planet. Weather reconnaissance can be accomplished in a more effective manner. This will lead to a better understanding of the movements of polar air masses and the course of jet streams and will permit improved long range weather forecasts and improved aircraft and missile operations. A better understanding of the earth's magnetic field will lead to better radio communications, more reliable navigation instruments, and perhaps new ideas for propulsive devices. Refined data on the earth's gravitational effects will lead to improved guidance. Much remains to be known about cosmic rays. Unmanned satellites will be the means for obtaining this information.[12]

Schriever's description of the developmental steps from ballistic missile development, to the launch of unmanned satellites, to the ever-more-ambitious, unmanned research missions to other celestial bodies would prove to be incredibly accurate.

At the same time, as a military man concerned with the national security of the United States and the ongoing ideological battle against Soviet Communism, Schriever harbored no illusions that outer space would be a realm of cooperation and peace. While recognizing the myriad scientific benefits of space technology, Schriever insisted there was a "military need" for such

12 Bernard A. Schriever, *ICBM: A Step Toward Space Conquest*, Speech to the Astronautics Symposium, Feb. 19, 1957, at 2, 3, 4–5, available at https://www.airforcemag.com/PDF/MagazineArchive/Documents/2007/February%202007/0207keeperfull.pdf.

technology, prophesying (as many high-ranking military officers would, and have continued to, ever since) that warfare in outer space was likely inevitable:

> In the long haul our safety as a nation may depend upon our achieving 'space superiority'. Several decades from now the important battles may not be sea battles or air battles, but space battles, and we should be spending a certain fraction of our national resources to insure that we do not lag in obtaining space supremacy. Besides the direct military importance of space, our prestige as world leaders might well dictate that we undertake lunar expeditions and even interplanetary flight when the appropriate technological advances have been made and the time is ripe. Thus it is indeed fortunate that the technological advances required in support of military objectives can, in large part, directly support these more speculative space ventures ....[13]

This portion of the speech caught the attention of Schriever's superiors. As we shall see below, at the time, the Eisenhower Administration's official policy—despite ongoing military research into both ballistic missiles and satellite surveillance systems—was the encouragement of weapons-free, peaceful uses of outer space. The Department of Defense duly chastised their renegade general. Reflecting nearly four decades later on his speech, and on the Department of Defense's negative reaction to it, Schriever makes it clear that, in his opinion, he had the last laugh:

> In February 1957, in San Diego, I made a speech concerning military space and indicated that space would play an important role for national security in the future. The next day I received a wire from the Secretary of Defense's office: "Do not use the word 'space' in any of your speeches in the future." The launch of Sputnik I a few months later, in October of that year, changed everything. Suddenly, everyone got space-minded.[14]

The Soviet Union's launch of *Sputnik 1* just eight months after Schriever's February 1957 speech certainly convinced the American public and significant numbers of America's government officials that the threat presented by a foreign nation's operations in outer space was real—and that the United States ought to do something about it.

---

13 Schriever, *ICBM: A Step Toward Space Conquest*, 4.

14 Schriever, "Military Space Activities Recollections and Observations," *The US Air Force in Space*, 15.

3 Official United States Outer Space Policy and Law

The launch of *Sputnik* was hardly the beginning of official US policy toward outer space. The early, post-WWII research into both the technological underpinnings and political/societal implications of orbital man-made satellites conducted by RAND has been previously described, and, despite the somewhat ambivalent attitude towards satellites and outer space expressed by the Truman Administration,[15] President Eisenhower recognized the importance of outer space early in his Presidency. The Eisenhower Administration became the first presidential administration to establish official outer space-oriented policies, including policies related to the development of military reconnaissance satellites—a number of which had been instituted even prior to the *Sputnik* launch. Indeed, given the Eisenhower Administration's plans concerning space and its intent to pursue a "freedom of space" policy—in other words, a free over-flight policy for space objects (in contrast to terrestrial airspace, which was viewed as national territory and, thus, could not be flown into without permission)—the Soviets' "victory" in the Space Race proved to be surprisingly providential. As Assistant Secretary of Defense for Research and Development Donald Quarles would comment at a meeting of the National Security Council convened in response to the *Sputnik* launch: "the Soviets have now proved very helpful. Their Earth satellite has overflown practically every nation on Earth, and there have thus far been no protests."[16] Regardless

15 Sean Kalic describes President Truman as "reluctan[t] to support the development of satellites," stating, "[t]he Truman administration did not share the [Air Force's and RAND's] vision [that satellites had profound scientific and military applications], and his assistant secretary of war for air … Stuart Symington did not see any reasonable prospect for space as a military environment." Kalic, *US Presidents and the Militarization of Space*, 17.

16 Document 348, "Memorandum of Discussion at the 339th Meeting of the National Security Council, Washington, October 10, 1957," in *U.S. Department of State, Foreign Relations of the United States, 1955–1957, Vol. XI*, "United Nations and General International Matters" (1988), available at https://history.state.gov/historicaldocuments/frus1955-57v11/d348. A description of Quarles' comments at the National Security Council can also be found in Mike Moore's *Twilight War: The Folly of U.S. Space Dominance*. *See* Mike Moore, *Twilight War: The Folly of U.S. Space Dominance* (Oakland, CA: Independent Institute, 2008), 198. Eisenhower himself seems to have expressed similar sentiments: during Cabinet meetings the day after the *Sputnik* launch "… Eisenhower reaffirmed the deliberate separation of the military and scientific space effort and emphasized the "peaceful character" of the US programme. He also insisted that, as there had never been a "race" with the Russians to get a satellite into orbit, the United States had not 'lost.' Moreover the Soviet Union had *probably done the United States a favour* as Sputnik had set the precedent of freedom of passage in outer space. This was viewed with some significance given the possible international repercussions to US satellite reconnaissance." Stares, *The Militarization of Space*, 40.

of whether *Sputnik* was an expected, or even beneficial, event for the United States, it forced the Eisenhower Administration—and every subsequent Presidential Administration—to develop official space-related policies that, with varying degrees of classification, could be articulated to the American people.

This section will briefly examine the "official" outer space policies of the United States, covering every presidential administration from President Eisenhower to President Biden. It should be noted at the outset that the purpose of this section is not to provide a comprehensive account of every space-related law, act, policy, or presidential statement made or enacted during a given presidency. Instead, it is to provide an overview of American policy, particularly in the military and space security realms, one that will assist the reader in understanding the general evolution of official outer space policy since its origins in the 1950s.

3.1 *President Dwight D. Eisenhower (1953–1961)*

As the first US President to directly formulate American space policy, and because he was the sitting president at the time of the paradigm-shifting *Sputnik* launch, President Eisenhower looms large in any discussion of US outer space policy. R. Cargill Hall, a leading historian of astronautics and Emeritus Chief Historian for the National Reconnaissance Office, describes Eisenhower's importance:

> Of all the Presidents who have taken an active role in formulating national space policy ... Eisenhower remains the most significant because he framed the U.S. space policy edifice. His successors either embraced the Eisenhower design or, at most, refined it by adding a window here and a door there.[17]

President Eisenhower's early recognition of the possible benefits of orbital satellites in the fields of reconnaissance, intelligence gathering, and communication led to the drafting and promulgation of NSC 5520, "U.S. Scientific Satellite Program," in May 1955—arguably the United States' first "official" policy related to activities in outer space.[18] In addition to Eisenhower's approval

17 R. Cargill Hall, "The Evolution of U.S. National Security Space Policy and Its Legal Foundations in the 20th Century," *Journal of Space Law*, vol. 22, no. 1 (2007), 6.

18 *See* Hall, "The Evolution of U.S. National Security Space Policy," *Journal of Space Law*, 10; Kalic, *US Presidents and the Militarization of Space*, 31.

of both military and civilian satellite programs, his Administration also contributed to the overarching idea that space ought not to be weaponized, but should be used for peaceful (though not entirely non-military) purposes, the recognition of an international right of free overflight of space objects, and the development of international bodies, such as the United Nations Committee on the Peaceful Uses of Outer Space (COPUOS), to contribute to international cooperation in outer space. These policy contributions can be found in NSC 5814/1 and NSC 5918, respectively the "Preliminary U.S. Policy on Outer Space" (published in August 1958) and the "U.S. Policy on Outer Space" (published in December 1959), as well as in the Eisenhower Administration's actions at the United Nations. In addition to all this, President Eisenhower also signed into law the National Aeronautics and Space Act of 1958, Congress's first foray into outer space legislating, which created the National Aeronautics and Space Administration (NASA)—the organization which would, just over a decade later, go on to achieve glory by successfully landing American astronauts on the Moon.[19]

NSC 5520, which was largely based on the recommendations and research of the Technological Capabilities Panel of the Eisenhower Administration's Science Advisory Committee, may bear little resemblance to the outer space policies of the 21st Century, but it ultimately laid the groundwork for the development of the United States' outer space-based intelligence infrastructure. Focusing specifically on the development of small, scientific satellites, NSC 5520 details the possible scientific and military benefits that could be derived from such satellites[20] (a discussion of benefits not remarkably different from those elaborated in RAND's *Preliminary Design of a World-Circling Spaceship* from nearly a decade prior), and notes that these benefits "warrant an immediate program leading to a very small satellite in orbit around the earth ...."[21] It recognized that military leaders "have stated their belief that intelligence applications strongly warrant the construction of a large surveillance satellite," and posits that a small scientific satellite program will prove technologically

19 72 Stat. 426, Pub. L. No. 85–568, 85th Congress (1958) (hereafter the National Aeronautics & Space Act of 1958).

20 *See* National Security Council Planning Board, NSC 5520, "Draft Statement of Policy on U.S. Scientific Satellite Program General Considerations," *Dwight D. Eisenhower Presidential Library and Museum* 2–3, ¶¶ 4–5 (May 20, 1955), available at https://aerospace.csis.org/wp-content/uploads/2019/02/NSC-5520-Statement-of-Policy-on-U.S.-Scientific-Satellite-Program-20-May-1955.pdf (last visited May 25, 2020) [hereinafter NSC 5520].

21 NSC 5520, 1, ¶ 2.

helpful to this goal "so long as [it] ... does not impede development of the large surveillance satellite."[22]

Correctly noting that "[c]onsiderable prestige and psychological benefits will accrue to the nation which first is successful in launching a satellite," NSC 5520 predicted that a successful satellite launch "might have important repercussions on the political determination of the free world countries to resist Communist threats, especially if the USSR were to be the first to establish a satellite."[23] To develop the United States' satellite launch capabilities, to counter the possibility that the Soviet Union would beat the United States into space, and to advance the Eisenhower Administration's proposed policies with respect to "freedom of space" (see above), NSC 5520 directed the following course of action:

> 11. Initiate a program in the Department of Defense to develop the capability of launching a small scientific satellite by 1958, with the understanding that this program *will not prejudice continued research directed toward large instrumented satellites for additional research and intelligence purposes*, or materially delay other major Defense programs.
> 12. Endeavor to launch a small scientific satellite under international auspices, such as the International Geo-physical Year, in order to emphasize its peaceful purposes, provided such international auspices are arranged in a manner which:
>   a. *Preserves U.S. freedom of action in the field of satellites and related programs.*
>   b. *Does not delay or otherwise impede the U.S. satellite program and related research and development programs.*
>   c. Protects the security of U.S. classified information regarding such matters as the means of launching a scientific satellite.
>   d. Does not involve actions which imply a requirement for prior consent by any nation over which the satellite might pass in its orbit, and thereby does not jeopardize the concept of "Freedom of Space." [Emphasis added][24]

As the italicized text in the selection above indicates, NSC 5520 sought to balance the public pursuit of a "peaceful," scientific satellite, which could be launched to public fanfare during the International Geophysical Year (IGY) or

22 NSC 5520, 3, ¶ 5.
23 NSC 5520, 3, ¶ 6.
24 NSC 5520, 6, ¶¶ 11–12.

another occasion, with the more secretive "large surveillance satellite" mentioned in paragraph 5. This was likely a reference to the WS-117L satellite program then being developed by the USAF's ARDC. The WS-117L program was split in early 1958, when the Central Intelligence Agency (CIA), working jointly with the Air Force, was put in charge of fast-tracking a surveillance satellite. Ultimately, the goals of NSC 5520—the launch of a small scientific satellite and the successful development of larger surveillance satellites—would be realized with the launch of the *Explorer I* satellite in January 1958[25] (a partial realization of American goals, of course, since the US had failed to "beat" the Soviets into space) and the development and successful deployment of the CIA's "Project Corona" photoreconnaissance satellites beginning in 1960.

In the aftermath of *Sputnik*, the Eisenhower Administration developed more comprehensive policies toward outer space, using a dual track of, first, pursuing international cooperation and mechanisms to limit the perceived Soviet advantage in rocketry and satellite technology, and, second, creating more robust domestic space policies to guide American efforts in outer space. With respect to the Eisenhower Administration's efforts on the international stage, we have already seen, in Chapter 2, the proposal by Henry Cabot Lodge, the United States' representative at the United Nations, for the creation of an international, United Nations-run technical committee to assure the use of outer space for exclusively peaceful and scientific purposes.[26] When this idea was rejected by the Soviet Union, the United States and its allies then proposed the creation of an Ad Hoc Committee on the Peaceful Use of Outer Space, which would examine "areas of international co-operation and programmes in the peaceful uses of outer space which could be appropriately undertaken under United Nations auspices," "future organizational arrangements to facilitate international co-operation" in outer space, and "the nature of legal problems which may arise in … [the exploration of] outer space."[27] The UN General

25 *See* Moltz, *Politics of Space Security*, 96.

26 *See* Lodge Speech, 25.

27 G.A. Res. 1348(XIII), ¶ 1 (Dec. 13, 1958). In pursuit of its goal of creating an international body to help oversee the peaceful use of outer space, the Eisenhower Administration reached across the aisle to Democratic Senator, and future President, Lyndon Johnson, who addressed the United Nations General Assembly on November 17, 1958, to urge the adoption of Resolution 1348. Emphasizing the American political parties' bipartisan support for the Resolution, Johnson declared, "On the goal of dedicating outer space to peaceful purposes for the benefit of all mankind there are no differences within our Government, between our parties, or among our people. The executive and legislative branches of our Government are together. United we stand." "Address by Senator Lyndon B. Johnson to the First Committee of the General Assembly, November 17, 1958," in *United States Senate, Document No. 18, Documents on International Aspects of the Exploration and*

Assembly approved the creation of this Ad Hoc Committee on December 13, 1958, in General Assembly Resolution 1348,[28] and the Ad Hoc Committee was formalized into the permanent Committee on the Peaceful Uses of Outer Space (COPUOS) the following year.[29] As we saw in our discussion of the Outer Space Treaty in Chapter 2, COPUOS, with the participation of the United States, the Soviet Union, and its other constituent UN member States, would go on to play a starring role in the early development of international outer space law.

In the realm of national policy, the Eisenhower Administration blazed a trail for later Presidential Administrations by publishing not one, but two national space policies. The first, released in the second half of 1958, was NSC 5814/1, "Preliminary U.S. Policy on Outer Space,"[30] followed, slightly over a year later, by NSC 5918, "U.S. Policy on Outer Space."[31] These policies, unlike NSCC 5520, did not focus on merely a single aspect of the United States' outer space endeavors; instead, setting the tone for future space policies, they were comprehensive—encompassing discussions of the various uses of outer space, comparisons of US and Soviet space capabilities, the implications of space activities in the context of the Cold War and in international affairs, as well as providing policy guidance and objectives for the United States' space activities. NSC 5814/1 (dubbed "preliminary" because "man's understanding of the full implications of outer space is only in its preliminary stages"[32]), begins with an ominous introductory note:

> The USSR has surpassed the United States and the free World in scientific and technological accomplishments in outer space, which have captured the imagination and admiration of the world. The USSR, if it maintains its present superiority in the exploitation of outer space, will be able to use that superiority as a means of undermining the prestige and leadership of the United States and of threatening U.S. security.[33]

Use of Outer Space, 1954–1962 85 (Staff Report Prepared for the Committee on Aeronautical and Space Sciences, May 9, 1963).

28 G.A. Res. 1348(XIII), ¶ 1 (Dec. 13, 1958).

29 G.A. Res. 1472(XIV), ¶ A.1.a (Dec. 12, 1959).

30 NSC 5814/1, *Preliminary U.S. Policy on Outer Space*, National Security Council (Aug. 18, 1958).

31 NSC 5918, *U.S. Policy on Outer Space*, National Security Council (Dec. 17, 1959).

32 NSC 5814/1, 1.

33 NSC 5814/1, 1.

The ominous tone reflected the gravity of the moment: whether strictly true or not, the widespread perception that the Soviet Union had technologically outpaced the United States required action and urgency.

Ultimately, the aim of NSC 5814/1 was to reverse the United States' fortunes in outer space, encouraging continued space-related research and development, with the goal of equaling or, preferably, surpassing the Soviets. The policy listed four primary goals, or "Objectives," for the US space program:

(1) The "[d]evelopment and exploitation of U.S. outer space capabilities as needed to achieve U.S. scientific, military, and political purposes, and to establish the U.S. as a recognized leader in this field."[34]
(2) "As consistent with U.S. security, [the] achievement of international cooperation in the uses of and activities related to outer space; [sic] for peaceful purposes, and with selected allies for military purposes."[35]
(3) "As consistent with U.S. security, the achievement of suitable international agreements relating to the uses of outer space for peaceful purposes that will assure orderly development and regulation of national and international outer space programs."[36]
(4) The "[u]tilization of the potentials of outer space to assist in opening up the Soviet Bloc through improved intelligence and programs of scientific cooperation."[37]

These four objectives, as we shall see below, were altered significantly in Eisenhower's second Space Policy. While they may not have been restated in either NSC 5918 or subsequent policies, these objectives guided the United States' outer space actions for decades to come. Perhaps even more radically (especially now, in an age when the gap between policy goals and reality is often glaringly stark), they were largely achieved over the course of the following several decades.[38]

---

34 NSC 5814/1, 18, ¶ 44.
35 NSC 5814/1, 18, ¶ 45.
36 NSC 5814/1, 18, ¶ 46.
37 NSC 5814/1, 18, ¶ 47.
38 The first, though ongoing, could largely be considered accomplished with the successful manned Moon Landing of 1969, which ended the Space Race and definitively established the United States as the preeminent space power. The second, another continuous, ongoing objective, continues to be pursued with significant outer space-related partnerships between the United States, its allies, and, in the case of the International Space Station, even its old Soviet adversary, Russia. The third utilized COPUOS, created via the United States' successful proposal for such an organization at the United Nations, to develop outer space law at the international level, successfully resulting in the Outer Space Treaty,

Finally, it should be noted that, from a military perspective, NSC 5814/1's discussions of military uses of outer space were almost solely devoted to the use of satellites. "Military reconnaissance" satellites were the only military use of outer space labeled as "Now Planned or In Immediate Prospect," with satellite use for "weather observation," "communications," "electronic counter-measures," and "navigation" considered "Feasible in the Near Future."[39] Reconnaissance satellites (which, as noted above in the discussion concerning NSC 5520, were of primary concern to the Eisenhower Administration) were described as being "of critical importance to U.S. national security."[40] They were also proposed as a key method "of implementing [Eisenhower's] 'open skies' proposal or policing a system of international armaments control."[41] While several more ambitious military uses of space were described—including "manned defensive outer space vehicles" and manned or unmanned "bombardment satellites"[42]—the emphasis on reconnaissance and sensing satellites reflected the Eisenhower Administration's interest in practical and arguably peaceful uses of outer space, even when those uses had military significance, and its desire to prevent the weaponization of space.

NSC 5814/1 was superseded, at the end of 1959, by NSC 5918. While very similar to its predecessor, NSC 5918 contained several key changes. First, as noted above, the four US objectives described in NSC 5814/1 were replaced with a single, "bureaucratized" objective: to

> [c]arry out energetically a program for the exploration and use of outer space by the U.S., based upon sound scientific and technological progress, designed: (a) to achieve that enhancement of scientific knowledge, military strength, economic capabilities, and political position which may be derived through the advantageous application of space technology and through appropriate international cooperation in related matters, and

and its follow-on treaties: the Rescue and Return Agreement, the Liability Convention, and the Registration Convention. Finally, while "scientific cooperation" with the Soviet Union was always touch-and-go even at the best of times during the Cold War, the fourth goal was realized with the advent of largescale satellite surveillance of the Soviet Union and its allies beginning with the first Corona satellite launched in 1960. It is a testament to the Eisenhower Administration and its successors that the objectives set for the United States in NSC 5814/1 were well on their way to accomplishment only a decade after its initial publication.

39 NSC 5814/1, 7.

40 NSC 5814/1, 8.

41 NSC 5814/1, 8.

42 NSC 5814/1, 8.

> (b) to achieve and demonstrate an over-all U.S. superiority in outer space without necessarily requiring United States supremacy in every phase of space activities.[43]

While the practical, substantive differences between this monolithic, single objective and the four objectives described in NSC 5814/1 is open to debate, the differences in clarity are obvious.

Luckily, NSC 5918 cannot be overly criticized for its lack of specificity. While the "Objectives" may have succumbed to the language of bureaucratic obfuscation, the "Policy Guidance" section of the policy provides a number of concrete instructions that would have significant implications for US space policy. First, in order to catch up with the Soviet Union, NSC 5918 called on the United States to, "[a]t the earliest practical time, proceed with manned space flight and exploration, starting with the recovery from orbit of a manned satellite."[44] As previously discussed in Chapter 2, NSC 5918 called for an examination "of the implications for the [sic] national security of the expression 'peaceful uses of outer space' with a view to defining this expression in a manner that would best serve the interests of the U.S."[45] Noting that "peaceful uses" "does not necessarily exclude military applications," NSC 5918 sought to establish a clear US interpretation of the "peaceful uses" language in order to "ensure that no international agreements might be reached which would result in net disadvantage to the United States by sustaining or enhancing over-all Soviet military capabilities while restricting those of the United States."[46] The "Policy Guidance" section of NSC 5918 also addressed specific actions the United States ought to take with respect to working toward the establishment of international regulations related to "the identification and registration of space vehicles," "liability for injury or damage" caused by space objects, the "reservation of radio frequencies" for space communications, avoiding "interference between space vehicles and aircraft," and the "re-entry and landing of space vehicles … in the territory of other nations"[47]—all questions of immense importance to space exploration, which, over the coming decades, would be addressed via international conventions and agreements.

A discussion of the United States' outer space policies during the Eisenhower Administration would be incomplete without mention of the National

43 NSC 5918, 10.
44 NSC 5918, 12.
45 NSC 5918, 12.
46 NSC 5918, 13.
47 NSC 5918, 14.

Aeronautics and Space Act of 1958—the primary *legislative* activity related to the American outer space program that took place during Eisenhower's presidency. Though the National Aeronautics and Space Act was primarily focused on the United States' national civil space program, the Congressional policies contained in the Act are still significant from the perspective of overall development of American space policy, particularly with respect to the underlying concept of whether—and how—outer space ought to be used for "peaceful purposes." As noted above in Chapter 2, the Act's opening Declaration of Policy and Purpose explicitly declares "that it is the policy of the United States that activities in space should be devoted to peaceful purposes for the benefit of all mankind."[48] This language of "peaceful" use and purposes is repeated several more times in the Act's listed objectives. Among those Congressional objectives are

> [t]he preservation of the role of the United States as a leader in aeronautical and space science and technology and in the application thereof to the conduct of *peaceful* activities within and outside the atmosphere[,] (emphasis added)

and "[c]ooperation by the United States with other nations and groups of nations in work done pursuant to this Act and in the *peaceful* application of the results thereof" (emphasis added).[49]

The meaning of the word "peaceful" and the term "peaceful purposes" is not defined in the National Aeronautics and Space Act; however, the drafting and passage of the Act took place in between Henry Cabot Lodge's October 1957 speech to the United Nations' Political and Security Committee advocating for "exclusively peaceful" uses of outer space (see Chapter 2) and the publication of President Eisenhower's "Preliminary U.S. Policy on Outer Space," which at least to some degree contemplated broader military uses of the space domain. While this likely means that Congress's intentions with respect to the meaning of "peaceful purposes" was closer to Lodge's "exclusively peaceful" formulation of the term—a theory that seems to be borne out by public statements by then-Senate Majority Leader Lyndon Johnson (whose views would evolve by the time he became President half a decade later)[50]—it is not clear, given the

48 National Aeronautics & Space Act of 1958, § 102(a).

49 National Aeronautics & Space Act of 1958, § 102(c).

50 *See* "Conversation with Eilene Galloway," in *Legislative Origins of the National Aeronautics and Space Act of 1958*, Proceedings of an Oral History Workshop Conducted April 3, 1992, John M. Logsdon (Moderator), Monographs in Aerospace History No. 8 (Washington,

largely civilian nature of the National Aeronautics and Space Act, that the Act's "peaceful purposes" languages necessarily imposed constraints on American military activity related to space. Whether it was intended as such a constraint or not, the Act's Declaration of Policy and use of the "peaceful purposes" language throughout its text did not deter the Eisenhower Administration from amending its interpretation of the "peaceful purposes" language in its two space policies (NSC 5814/1 and NSC 5918) to reflect the United States' evolving "non-aggressive" formulation, nor, as we will see, has the Act provided any meaningful constraint on subsequent Presidential Administrations with respect to the "peaceful purposes" issue.

President Eisenhower had the unenviable task of serving as Commander-in-Chief during a time of immense technological change, all taking place in an international system increasing characterized by mutual animosity and distrust between the United States and the Soviet Union. Eisenhower, however, was up to the challenge: he "seized the initiative to take advantage of space for military purposes, worked to keep space free of weapons, and championed the establishment of NASA."[51] Eisenhower steadfastly maintained the United States' official stance of seeking to utilize space for solely peaceful purposes, cultivating a military space program that would develop and improve upon satellite reconnaissance and other force-enhancing uses of satellite technology, rather than space-based weapons. As noted by R. Cargill Hall at the beginning of this section, it is no exaggeration to say that Eisenhower and his Administration created the US outer space policy framework that has governed American actions in outer space ever since. This framework ultimately "emphasize[s] the use of the military and civilian space programs working in concert to reestablish [or, in the present, to maintain] the technological superiority of the United States."[52]

3.2 *President John F. Kennedy (1961–1963) and President Lyndon B. Johnson (1963–1969)*

President Eisenhower's framework for the United States' outer space policy was inherited by his young successor, President John F. Kennedy, who, during his tragically brief presidency, would not publish his own national outer space policy. While no "official" Kennedy Administration space policy exists in the form of a single policy document, this does not mean that Kennedy was not

D.C.: NASA Headquarters, 1998), p. 42, available at https://history.nasa.gov/40thann/legislat.pdf.

51 Kalic, *US Presidents and the Militarization of Space*, 57.

52 Kalic, *US Presidents and the Militarization of Space*, 59.

interested in, or did not, as President, have a significant effect on, American outer space policy. Indeed, Kennedy would, in some ways, receive much of the glory for American space achievements that President Eisenhower set in motion but which he could not, due to classification considerations, make public. One early example of such an achievement was the United States' first successful manned suborbital flight, by American astronaut Alan Shepard, on May 5, 1961—though this flight, and, indeed, much of Kennedy's civil space policy, was also a response to another *Sputnik*-like shock: the Soviet Union's groundbreaking manned space mission on April 12, 1961, when Major Yuri Gagarin became the first human being to travel into orbit.[53]

Perhaps no clearer articulation of President Kennedy's space policy can be found than that contained in one of his most famous speeches: his address at Rice University in Houston, Texas, on September 12, 1962. The now-famous "We Choose to Go to the Moon," speech, which he delivered during a cross-country tour of NASA facilities,[54] would cement Kennedy's reputation as the "Space President."[55] As we read the following excerpt of the speech, it is easy to understand why:

> … [F]or the eyes of the world now look into space, to the moon and to the planets beyond, and we have vowed that we shall not see it governed by a hostile flag of conquest, but by a banner of freedom and peace. We have vowed that we shall not see space filled with weapons of mass destruction, but with instruments of knowledge and understanding.
>
> Yet the vows of this Nation can only be fulfilled if we in this Nation are first, and, therefore, we intend to be first. In short, our leadership in science and in industry, our hopes for peace and security, our obligations to ourselves as well as others, all require us to make this effort, to solve these mysteries, to solve them for the good of all men, and to become the world's leading space-faring nation.

53 Moltz, *The Politics of Space Security*, 107.

54 *See* Abigail Malangone, "We Choose to Go to the Moon: The 55th Anniversary of the Rice University Speech," *John F. Kennedy Presidential Library Archives Blog* (Sept. 12, 2017), https://jfk.blogs.archives.gov/2017/09/12/we-choose-to-go-to-the-moon-the-55th-anniversary-of-the-rice-university-speech/.

55 Brittany Britto, "JFK's 1962 moon speech—though deliberate, political—is still inspiring after all these years," *Houston Chronicle* (June 11, 2019), https://www.houstonchronicle.com/local/space/mission-moon/article/JFK-s-1962-moon-speech-though-deliberate-13960428.php.

> We set sail on this new sea because there is new knowledge to be gained, and new rights to be won, and they must be won and used for the progress of all people. For space science, like nuclear science and all technology, has no conscience of its own. Whether it will become a force for good or ill depends on man, and only if the United States occupies a position of pre-eminence can we help decide whether this new ocean will be a sea of peace or a new terrifying theater of war. I do not say that we should or will go unprotected against the hostile misuse of space any more than we go unprotected against the hostile use of land or sea, but I do say that space can be explored and mastered without feeding the fires of war, without repeating the mistakes that man has made in extending his writ around this globe of ours.
>
> There is no strife, no prejudice, no national conflict in outer space as yet. Its hazards are hostile to us all. Its conquest deserves the best of all mankind, and its opportunity for peaceful cooperation may never come again. But why, some say, the moon? Why choose this as our goal? And they may well ask why climb the highest mountain? Why, 35 years ago, fly the Atlantic? Why does Rice play Texas?
>
> We choose to go to the moon. We choose to go to the moon in this decade and do the other things, not because they are easy, but because they are hard, because that goal will serve to organize and measure the best of our energies and skills, because that challenge is one that we are willing to accept, one we are unwilling to postpone, and one which we intend to win, and the others, too.[56]

President Kennedy's stirring words not did not simply throw down a gauntlet in the Cold War space race (albeit one that Kennedy had already, less dramatically, thrown during a speech before a joint session of Congress the previous year[57]). Whether his audience knew it at the time, President Kennedy was also

56 President John F. Kennedy, "Address at Rice University, Houston, Texas," Sept. 12, 1962 (the paragraph breaks follow those in the official version of President Kennedy's remarks released by the Office of the White House Press Secretary, Address at Rice University, Houston, Texas, Sept. 12, 1962, *John F. Kennedy Presidential Library and Museum*, https://www.jfklibrary.org/asset-viewer/archives/JFKPOF/040/JFKPOF-040-001).

57 This occurred on May 25, 1961, when President Kennedy addressed a special joint session of Congress to address "urgent national needs in the areas of foreign aid, international and civil defense, and outer space." During the speech, President Kennedy first announced his goal of putting a man on the Moon by the end of the 1960s: "I therefore ask the Congress, above and beyond the increases I have earlier requested for space activities, to provide

succinctly describing key aspects of the United States' overarching space policy. The vows Kennedy describes—that the United States "shall not see [outer space] governed by a hostile flag of conquest" and "shall not see space filled with weapons of mass destruction"—were two key part of the United States' outer space policy. Even then, American representatives at the United Nations were working to advocate the proposition that outer space was not an arena of "conquest," but, instead, an area that would be "free from national appropriation."[58] Kennedy's speech also referenced the universal (no pun intended) nature of space exploration: outer space's mysteries must be solved "for the good of all men," the new rights related to outer space "must be won and used for the progress of all people," the conquest of space "deserves the best of all mankind," and space activities present an "opportunity for peaceful cooperation [that] may never come again." Kennedy's internationalist language, along with his call for non-appropriation and prohibition on weapons of mass destruction in outer space, would be reflected in the language of the Outer Space Treaty.

Despite Kennedy's internationalist rhetoric, the duality of the American approach to outer space—a recognition of international rights and rule of

---

the funds which are needed to meet the following national goals: First, I believe that this nation should commit itself to achieving the goal, before this decade is out, of landing a man on the moon and returning him safely to earth. No single space project in this period will be more exciting, or more impressive, or more important for the long-range exploration of space; and none will be so difficult or expensive to accomplish. … . We propose additional funds for other engine development and for unmanned explorations—explorations which are particularly important for one purpose which this nation will never overlook: the survival of the man who first makes this daring flight. But in a very real sense, it will not be one man going to the moon—it will be an entire nation. For all of us must work to put him there." President John F. Kennedy, "Address to Joint Session of Congress," May 25, 1961, *John F. Kennedy Library & Museum*, https://www.jfklibrary.org/learn/about-jfk/historic-speeches/address-to-joint-session-of-congress-may-25-1961 (last visited Apr. 11, 2020). Though less stirring than his Rice Speech, President Kennedy, with his characteristic rhetorical skill, still succeeded in communicating the excitement and significance of the quest to land a man on the Moon. Kennedy's Congressional address was also the first articulation of his plans to find some way to "*beat* the Soviets" in outer space, after the Soviet Union's dramatic space "firsts." Moltz, *The Politics of Space Security*, 108.

58 This American position—which was not opposed by the Soviet Union and, as we have seen, would become a key provision of both the Declaration of Legal Principles and the Outer Space Treaty—would be described in a letter and draft Declaration of Principles Relating to the Exploration and Use of Outer Space from Senator Albert Gore to the Chairman of the U.N.'s First Committee on December 8, 1962. Albert Gore, "Letter dated 8 December 1962 from the representative of the United States of America to the Chairman of the First Committee," U.N. Doc. A/C.1/881 (Dec. 8, 1962).

law, coupled with an emphasis on, and preference for, American superiority—is evident in his Rice address. Key among Kennedy's points, after all, are the ideas that America's goals "can only be fulfilled if [the United States is] first" and that "only if the United States occupies a position of pre-eminence can we help decide whether this new ocean [of outer space] will be a sea of peace or a new terrifying theater of war." Such rhetoric would not be out of place in the modern era—indeed, not only has Kennedy's argument been echoed by space-minded members of the military establishment since the earliest days of the Space Age, but "America First Among the Stars" is, as we shall see, a key principle of President Trump's National Space Strategy.[59] The idea has evolved into the military concept of "space control," which we will examine further in a later chapter. Further, though couched in rhetorical turn-of-phrase, Kennedy's speech recognized the necessity of militarizing, perhaps even weaponizing, the United States' spacefaring capabilities: how else to interpret Kennedy's comment that the United States neither "should [n]or will go unprotected against the hostile misuse of space any more than we go unprotected against the hostile use of land or sea"?

Without a written Kennedy Administration national space policy, Kennedy's Rice speech is about the closest single speech or document to articulate an overarching American policy during the Kennedy years. It is clear, however, that, despite Kennedy's willingness to "race" the Soviets to the Moon ("racing" the Soviet Union was something President Eisenhower had steadfastly believed to be counter-productive[60]), the Kennedy Administration's official policy was not significantly different than that of Kennedy's predecessor. Indeed, among President Kennedy's other significant outer space-related activities was the promulgation of another National Security Council directive, National Security Council Action (NSCA) 2454, that, in an echo of the Eisenhower Administration's focus on satellite technology, "focused exclusively on securing international acceptance of overhead reconnaissance conducted from outer space."[61] NSCA 2454 emphasized the necessity of molding international law on this topic, advising that the United States (1) "should maintain the legal position that the principles of international law and the UN Charter apply to activities in outer space and, specifically, that outer space is free, as are the high seas;" (2) "should ... continue to avoid any position implying that reconnaissance activities in outer space are not legitimate;" (3) "should avoid any

---

59 *See infra* pages 112-13.

60 *See* Moltz, *Politics of Space Security*, 94, 106; Kalic, *US Presidents and the Militarization of Space*, 48.

61 Hall, "The Evolution of U.S. National Security Space Policy," *Journal of Space Law*, 19.

position declaring or implying that [reconnaissance activities] are not 'peaceful uses;'" and (4) "should avoid any indication that physical countermeasures to reconnaissance vehicles would be justified ... [and] make a positive effort to propagate the idea that interference with or attacks on any space vehicle of another country in peacetime are inadmissible and illegal."[62]

As the Outer Space Treaty and other binding principles of outer space law had not yet been established, questions related to the legality of satellite photoreconnaissance were still extant. Kennedy's NSCA, therefore, contributed not merely to the United States' position regarding satellite reconnaissance, but also, more overarchingly, to the continued development of the United States' position regarding the definition of "peaceful," and, specifically, peaceful *military*, uses of outer space. The Kennedy Administration continued the Eisenhower Administration's international space law-making efforts at the United Nations, with renewed success. The Soviet Union largely ended its early non-participation in COPUOS, allowing the Committee to meet in 1961 and begin discussions concerning the development of outer space law in the Committee's Legal Subcommittee. The efforts of the Kennedy Administration's representatives at COPUOS would help lead to the development of the Declaration of Legal Principles—although, tragically, Kennedy himself would not live to see the Declaration passed by the UN General Assembly.

Though not solely an outer space-related endeavor, President Kennedy's successful shepherding of the Treaty Banning Nuclear Weapon Tests in the Atmosphere, in Outer Space and Under Water (more commonly known as the "Partial Nuclear Test Ban Treaty" or "Limited Test Ban Treaty")[63] constituted another important development in international space law. The United States' signing and ratification of the Limited Test Ban Treaty was a significant step in preventing the use of outer space for weapons testing and maintaining a safe space environment for manmade satellites. Though by no means the sole motivating factor underlying the Limited Test Ban Treaty, the United States' Starfish Prime nuclear test—an exo-atmospheric detonation of a 1.4 megaton nuclear device approximately 400 kilometers above the Pacific Ocean, which took place July 9, 1962—provided a dramatic demonstration of the dangers of

---

62 Hall, "The Evolution of U.S. National Security Space Policy," *Journal of Space Law*, 20, 21 (citing NSCA 2454, "Space Policy and Intelligence Requirements," National Security Council (July 10, 1962)).

63 Treaty Banning Nuclear Weapon Tests in the Atmosphere, in Outer Space and Under Water, Aug. 5, 1963, 14 U.S.T. 1313, 480 U.N.T.S. 43 [hereinafter Partial Nuclear Test Ban Treaty].

orbital nuclear explosions.[64] Starfish Prime ultimately resulted in the complete incapacitation of seven orbital satellites from exposure to ionizing radiation.[65] This would be a significant number of satellites even now, but, according to one source, at the time it constituted the effective destruction of "*all* publicly acknowledged space assets" (emphasis added).[66] The Limited Test Ban Treaty ensured that, so long as the States Parties to the treaty (including the United States and Soviet Union) complied with its terms, the grave consequences of orbital nuclear testing would be prevented.

As his Administration advocated further development of international space law and as he himself pressed the US space program to "put a man on the Moon," President Kennedy also allowed the United States military, primarily the Air Force, to pursue a number of more militaristic space projects. Kennedy, who, as we have seen, was elected partially due to national security concerns related to the non-existent "missile gap," continued to worry about Soviet ICBMs and space weapons after his election. As a result, he was the first President to actively encourage the military to develop anti-satellite (ASAT) weapons, supposedly ordering Secretary of Defense Robert McNamara "to develop an ASAT system at the 'earliest practicable time.'"[67] With Kennedy's support, the Army began adapting its Nike-Zeus anti-ballistic missiles to the purpose of satellite (rather than missile) interception. The new project, code-named Program 505, conducted its first successful test in May 1963.[68] Meanwhile, the Air Force had also entered the ASAT-development arena, undertaking a project called Program 437, which sought to modify the Air Force's Thor intermediate-range ballistic missiles into viable ASAT weapons. These efforts were successful, with Program 437 Thors successfully intercepting orbital targets in a series of tests conducted between February and May 1964.[69] While Kennedy's

---

64 E.G. Stassinopoulos, "The STARFISH Exo-atmospheric, High-altitude Nuclear Weapons Test," Hardened Electronics and Radiation Technology (HEART) 2015 Conference, Chantilly, VA, April 22, 2015, available at https://nepp.nasa.gov/files/26652/2015-561-Stassinopoulos-Final-Paper-Web-HEART2015-STARFISH-supplemental-TN26292.pdf.

65 Stassinopoulos, "The STARFISH Exo-atmospheric, High-altitude Nuclear Weapons Test."

66 Michael J. Frankel, James Scouras, & George W. Ullrich, *The Uncertain Consequences of Nuclear Weapons Use*, National Security Report, Johns Hopkins University Applied Physics Laboratory (2015), 5.

67 Clayton K. S. Chun, "Shooting Down a 'Star': Program 437, the US Nuclear ASAT System and Present-Day Copycat Killers," The Cadre Papers, Cadre Paper #6 (Maxwell AFB, AL: Air University Press, 2000), 6 (citing Wayne R. Austerman, *Program 437: The Air Force's First Antisatellite System* (Peterson AFB, Colo.: Air Force Space Command, 1991), 13).

68 Brian Weeden, "U.S. Direct Ascent Anti-Satellite Testing," Secure World Foundation, May 2022, available at https://swfound.org/media/207368/swf-us-da-asat-may-2022.pdf.

69 Chun, "Shooting Down a 'Star,'" 17–18.

support of military ASAT development implies that he may have had fewer scruples than Eisenhower with respect to space weaponization, Kennedy also reduced or canceled a number of space-related defense programs, including de-weaponizing the Air Force's Dynamic Soaring Vehicle (or 'Dyna-Soar')[70]—a proposed spaceplane the Air Force hoped to use as an orbital bomber, and the design for which would go on to influence the creation of both NASA's Space Shuttle and the Air Force's unmanned X-37B spaceplane.[71]

President Kennedy's assassination in November 1963 brought Lyndon B. Johnson to the presidency. Johnson was no stranger to outer space policy, having, during his time as Senate Majority Leader, chaired the Preparedness Subcommittee set up by the Senate Armed Services Committee to investigate Soviet success in outer space technology and recommend an American response. The recommendations ultimately proposed by Johnson's subcommittee in 1958—though "focus[ed] primarily on strengthening and modernizing America's traditional, terrestrial military forces"[72]—would set the stage for the future outer space activities in both the civilian and military sectors.[73] After being sworn in as President, Johnson, like Kennedy before him, would not publish his own national space policy. However, he continued pursuing President Kennedy's goal of putting American astronauts on the Moon by the end of the decade—a goal that, thanks to President Johnson's continued support of NASA and its groundbreaking Apollo program, would be achieved six months after the inauguration of Johnson's successor, President Richard Nixon. But while the United States' civilian space endeavors were momentous, President Johnson and his Administration would leave behind a legacy in the international outer space law arena likely no less significant than NASA's dramatic achievements.

70 Nicholas Michael Sambaluk, *The Other Space Race: Eisenhower and the Quest for Aerospace Security* 212–17 (Annapolis, MD: Naval Institute Press, 2015).

71 Robert F. Dorr, "X-20 Dyna-Soar Spaceplane Was Decades Ahead of Its Time," *Defense Media Network*, Sept. 19, 2018, https://www.defensemedianetwork.com/stories/what-might-have-been-x-20-dyna-soar/.

72 Grunert, "Grounding the Humā," *Air Force Law Review*, 98.

73 *See Preparedness Subcommittee Recommendations for America's Defenses*, Senate Armed Services Committee, 104 Cong. Rec., Pt. 15, 18, 887–89 (1958). Among the Subcommittee recommendations applicable to the United States' efforts in outer space are Recommendation #8, "Set Up Production Schedules of Atlas, Thor, Jupiter, and Accelerate Development of Titan;" Recommendation # 11, "Start Work at Once on the Development of a Rocket Motor with a Million-Pound Thrust;" and Recommendation #16, "Put More Effort Into Development of Manned Missiles." *Preparedness Subcommittee Recommendations for America's Defenses*, 887–89.

Shortly after President Kennedy's assassination, efforts by the United States and its allies at COPUOS achieved a breakthrough success in creating a legal framework for outer space with the passage of the Declaration of Legal Principles Governing the Activities of States in the Exploration and Use of Outer Space by the U.N. General Assembly.[74] While the Declaration of Legal Principles was nonbinding, its unanimous adoption indicated widespread international acceptance of its principles. But in the aftermath of the adoption of the Declaration of Legal Principles, progress on international outer space law stalled.[75] The Johnson Administration would break the deadlock:

> [b]eginning in mid-1966, the United States began an international effort to codify in a formal treaty the legal issues previously contained in the 1963 U.N. resolution by ... submit[ting] a new U.S. draft treaty to COPUOS and by opening negotiations in Vienna with the Soviet Union.[76]

The Soviets, like the Americans, were concerned with preventing their geopolitical rival from "exploiting any territorial or other advantages" it might accrue by winning the Space Race, and, thus, negotiations on the treaty progressed remarkably quickly.[77] There is no need to rehash the contents of the Outer Space Treaty here, since these were discussed at length in Chapter 2, but suffice to say that President Johnson was successful, both in the efforts of American diplomats at the United Nations to prepare a draft treaty conducive to the United States' perceived interests and in the ultimate ratification of that treaty by the US Senate on April 25, 1967.[78]

The success of the Johnson Administration's efforts codified, in a binding treaty, the key principles of international outer space law that remain the basis of the outer space legal framework to this day: the principles of free access, use, and non-appropriation; the prohibition on nuclear weapons and weapons of mass destruction; the basic rules relating to liability, the rescue and return of astronauts, and the jurisdiction and control over space objects. In addition to the Outer Space Treaty, the Johnson Administration and its representatives at COPUOS successfully negotiated the Rescue and Return Agreement—an

---

74 *See supra* notes 26–30.

75 *See* Moltz, *Politics of Space Security*, 149. As Moltz notes, for several years after the adoption of the Declaration of Legal Principles, "there had been no progress of any sort in the legal subcommittee of COPUOS."

76 Moltz, *Politics of Space Security*, 149.

77 Moltz, *Politics of Space Security*, 149.

78 Moltz, *Politics of Space Security*, 149–51.

international convention reaffirming the Outer Space Treaty's characterization of astronauts as "envoys of mankind"[79] and establishing an international framework for their safe return to their country of origin in the event they landed in a foreign State.[80] Johnson himself considered the Outer Space Treaty and the Rescue and Return Agreement to be tremendous successes, later reflecting in his memoir that "history may record that one of the greatest triumphs of the space program of the 1960s was the basis it provided for reaching accommodation with old adversaries"[81] and listing both treaties among his key achievements in American-Soviet relations during his presidency.[82]

Thus, despite the fact that neither President Kennedy nor President Johnson published explicit national space policies, it is fairly easy to trace the policies and principles guiding American outer space policy during their presidencies. One need only look to the Declaration of Legal Principles and the Outer Space Treaty, both of which were advanced and at least partially drafted by the United States' representatives at the United Nations, to see what was important to the United States. The Kennedy and Johnson Administration not only assumed the mantle of President Eisenhower's original conception of American space policy—involving joint civilian and military operations, a focus on satellite technology (and, particularly, reconnaissance satellite technology) and the legality of satellite overflight and observation, and, as we have seen, definitions of "peaceful" use of outer space that encompassed certain military activities—but, through their efforts at the United Nations, molded the development of then-nascent international space law to reflect (or, at worst, to not actively hinder) American aims. By the end of the Johnson Administration, the goals the Eisenhower Administration had set for the American space programs, both military and civilian, were well on their way to completion: international recognition of the legality of satellite overflight had largely been accomplished, an international legal framework governing space activities was in place, and the United States was on the cusp of winning the race to the Moon thanks to massive expenditures on NASA's revolutionary Apollo program. Additionally, while neither Kennedy nor Johnson had released official space policies during their presidencies, each had contributed—primarily through the United States'

79 Outer Space Treaty, art. V.

80 Rescue and Return Agreement, arts. 1–4. The Rescue and Return Agreement also provided for the return of space objects and pieces of space objects that landed in foreign territory. Rescue and Return Agreement, art. 5.

81 Lyndon B. Johnson, *The Vantage Point: Perspectives on the Presidency, 1963–1969* (New York: Holt, Rinehart and Winston, 1971), 284.

82 Johnson, *The Vantage Point*, 476.

efforts at COPUOS and the United Nations, but also through their continuation and expansion of President Eisenhower's satellite reconnaissance programs and other military and intelligence-related space activities—to the development of the overarching concept of what it meant to use outer space for "peaceful purposes."[83] The first decade of American space policy-making had been a resounding success, and reflected significant political achievements in goal-setting, bipartisan cooperation, and execution of American policy at the international level. It would also set the stage for the further military development of the American space program, and, more widely, military space activities by other States as well.

3.3 *President Richard Nixon (1969–1973) and President Gerald Ford (1973–1977)*

On July 20, 1969, six months after President Richard Nixon's inauguration, American astronauts Neil Armstrong and Edwin "Buzz" Aldrin, Jr., made history by landing on the surface of the Moon. The United States' successful Moon landing more than made up for its shock at being bested by the Soviet Union with the launch of *Sputnik* over a decade earlier. But with the Space Race won, and the massive expenditures the had allowed NASA to win it viewed as no longer necessary, what was to be the future of the United States' space endeavor?

President Nixon and his successor, President Gerald Ford, presided over a period during which the international legal framework of outer space law would be further fleshed out, but American space policy would, with certain exceptions, largely remain static. The newly-formed international outer space legal regime, which, at the time of Nixon's inauguration, consisted of the Outer Space Treaty and the Rescue and Return Agreement, required additional specificity with respect to issues of liability, responsibility, international registration, and jurisdiction. Indeed, many nations felt that an additional agreement regarding the Moon, other celestial bodies, and, particularly, the ownership and use of the resources that might be found on those celestial bodies was

83 As we previously saw in Chapter 2, and above during the discussion of President Eisenhower's space policies, the United States' original push for exclusively peaceful uses of outer space quickly became more nuanced. The evolution of the United States' policy position toward defining "peaceful use"/"peaceful purposes" as meaning "non-aggressive" may have begun with the Eisenhower Administration's recognition that the "peaceful use" terminology "[did] not necessarily exclude military applications" (NSC 5918), this interpretation solidified as US representatives and policy-makers during the Kennedy and Johnson Administrations negotiated the terms of the Declaration of Legal Principles and the Outer Space Treaty.

necessary.[84] While this push for binding international law governing the Moon and its potential resources proved controversial, the issue of liability was not nearly as contentious. The basic framework for State liability for space objects was already laid out in the Outer Space Treaty.[85] In the aftermath of the Outer Space Treaty's passage, proposals, working papers, and draft agreements on the issue of liability proliferated at COPUOS.[86] Over the next four years, the United States would work with its allies and adversaries at COPUOS to hammer out the final text of the Liability Convention, which was adopted by the General Assembly in November 1971[87] and ratified by the United States in October 1973.[88]

The Liability Convention was not the only binding international treaty impacting outer space-related matters pursued by the Nixon Administration.

---

84 This was the basis of negotiations at COPUOS for what would become the Agreement Governing the Activities of States on the Moon and Other Celestial Bodies (more commonly known as the "Moon Agreement"). The first draft of an agreement regulating activities on the Moon and other celestial bodies was proposed by Argentina in 1970. *See* COPUOS Legal Subcomm., "Activities being carried out or to be carried out on the Moon and other celestial bodies, international and national rules governing those activities and information received from States parties to the Agreement Governing the Activities of States on the Moon and Other Celestial Bodies about the benefits of adherence to that Agreement," 47th Sess., U.N. Doc. A/AC.105/C.2/L.271 (Jan. 25, 2008), 2 [hereinafter Moon Agreement Information]. Interestingly, the Nixon Administration "was generally supportive of the negotiations to develop a CHM [common heritage of mankind] regime in [sic] the moon" and "supported the Argentine Draft Moon Treaty." J.M. Spectar, "Elephants, Donkeys, or Other Creatures? Presidential Election Cycles & International Law of the Global Commons," *American University International Law Review*, vol. 15, no. 5 (2000), 1011. The United States' support for the Moon Agreement, however, would not last. Ultimately, while the Moon Agreement would be finalized and adopted by the United Nations General Assembly in 1979, it would fail to achieve widespread international support. *See* COPUOS Legal Subcomm., "Moon Agreement Information," 2. As of mid-2021, only 18 States (none of which were significant spacefaring States) had ratified the Moon Agreement, with only 4 other States having signed, but not ratified, the Agreement. *See* COPUOS Legal Subcomm., "Status of International Agreements relating to activities in outer space as at 1 January 2021," 60th Sess., U.N. Doc. A/AC.105/C.2/2021/CRP.10 (May 31, 2021), 10.

85 *See* Outer Space Treaty, art. VII.

86 *See* United Nations Office for Outer Space Affairs, "Convention on International Liability for Damage Caused by Space Objects—Travaux Préparatoires," *UNOOSA.org*, https://www.unoosa.org/oosa/en/ourwork/spacelaw/treaties/travaux-preparatoires/liability-convention.html (last visited Sept. 6, 2021).

87 G.A. Res. 2777(XXVI) (Nov. 29, 1971).

88 *See* United Nations Treaty Collection, *Convention on the international liability for damage caused by space objects*, treaties.un.org, https://treaties.un.org/pages/showDetails.aspx?objid=08000002801098c7 (last visited Mar. 31, 2020).

Shortly after assuming office, President Nixon embarked on a multi-year series of negotiations with the Soviet Union that had been prepared (and, indeed, had been scheduled to begin) during the Johnson Administration: the Strategic Arms Limitation Talks (SALT). The first round of these negotiations, starting in Helsinki in November 1969 and continuing in Helsinki and Vienna over the next two and half years, would result in two significant agreements. The first, the Limitation of Anti-Ballistic Missile Systems Treaty (more commonly referred to as the Anti-Ballistic Missile Treaty or ABM Treaty), provided specific limitations on the number and type of anti-ballistic missile systems the United States and the Soviet Union could deploy.[89] While, at the time, the types of systems contemplated by the ABM Treaty were terrestrial, a mere ten years later the ABM Treaty would lead to significant outer space-related controversy when President Ronald Reagan proposed his Strategic Defense Initiative of space-based missile interceptors (as we will see below).

The second agreement, the Interim Agreement Between the United States and the Union of Soviet Socialist Republics on Certain Measures with Respect to the Limitation of Strategic Offensive Arms (more commonly known as the SALT I Agreement), was designed to limit both sides' nuclear weapons inventories—including both land-based and submarine-launched ballistic missiles.[90] The SALT I Agreement contained an extremely important space-related provision in its Article V, which dealt with the United States' and the Soviet Union's "national technical means of verification," a diplomatic euphemism for photoreconnaissance satellites.[91] Article V states that the two States "shall use [the] national technical means of verification at [their] disposal in a manner consistent with generally recognized principles of international law," that neither would "interfere with the national technical means of verification of the other," and that neither would seek to subvert the arms limitation provisions of the agreement by using "deliberate concealment measures which impede verification by national technical means of compliance."[92] This recognition by both of the major Cold War Space Powers (1) that space-based photoreconnaissance and remote sensing (in the Agreement's parlance, "national technical means of verification") were critical, lawful methods of treaty

89 Treaty on the Limitation of Anti-Ballistic Missile Systems, May 26, 1972, U.S.-U.S.S.R., 23 U.S.T. 3435, T.I.A.S. No. 7503.

90 Interim Agreement Between the United States and the Union of Soviet Socialist Republics on Certain Measures with Respect to the Limitation of Strategic Offensive Arms, May 26, 1972, U.S.-U.S.S.R., 23 U.S.T. 3462, T.I.A.S. No. 7504 [hereafter SALT I Agreement].

91 SALT I Agreement, art. V.

92 SALT I Agreement, art. V.

verification, and (2) that these previously extremely controversial reconnaissance methods should, in fact, be *explicitly protected* due to the role they play in increasing trust and reducing international tensions was wholly unique in the history of arms control agreements up to that time, and would provide the basis for continuing recognition of the freedom of space principle for these systems into the present day.

In addition to the signing and ratification of the Liability Convention, the ABM Treaty, and the SALT I Agreement, President Nixon's other major outer space policies consisted of policy actions designed to reduce the costs of outer space exploration without sacrificing American supremacy, and, with the Space Race won, pursuing President Eisenhower's previous goal of utilizing space as a method of "opening up" the Soviet Bloc via scientific cooperation. Indeed, as the Nixon Administration's National Security Decision Memorandum (NSDM) 70, *International Space Cooperation: US–USSR Activities*, alludes, these goals could potentially be pursued simultaneously:

> Cooperation with the Soviet Union in space matters is desirable. Such cooperation, if it involves substantive scientific and technical content, could be useful intrinsically as well as from the viewpoint of raising the level of political confidence between ourselves and the Soviets and of easing international tensions. It could yield greater economic and social benefits from applications of space technology on a worldwide basis. *It could possibly lead to some cost sharing and to budgetary savings through the synergistic effect of applying both programs to common tasks*. Many of these benefits could be realized without impinging on U.S. national security requirements or export control policies [emphasis added].[93]

NSDM 70's proposal for cooperative ventures with the Soviet Union was not merely aspirational. In May 1972, during a bilateral summit in Moscow, President Nixon and Soviet Premier Alexei Kosygin signed the "Agreement Concerning Cooperation in the Exploration and Use of Outer Space for Peaceful

93 Hall, "The Evolution of U.S. National Security Space Policy," *Journal of Space Law*, 27 (citing Henry Kissinger, NSDM 70, "International Space Cooperation: US–USSR Activities," National Security Council, July 10, 1970). The cited text does not specifically appear in the one-page memorandum from Henry Kissinger, then Nixon's National Security Advisor, that constitutes the main body of NSDM 70, but, rather, from a report by the ad hoc National Security Study Memorandum (NSSM) 72 committee, entitled *Cooperation Between the US and USSR in Space Activities, Prospects and Opportunities*. Hall writes that "[o]n the President's approval," this report "became NSDM 70." Hall, "The Evolution of U.S. National Security Space Policy," *Journal of Space Law*, 27.

Purposes"—the agreement that would result, after three years of planning and cooperation, in the successful joint Apollo-Soyuz mission in July 1975.[94]

In addition to policies improving cooperation with the Soviet Union, the Nixon Administration also sought to strengthen international ties between the United States and its allies in the outer space field. Nixon's two other major space-related security policies—NSDM 72, *Exchange of Technical Data Between the United States and the International Space Community*, and NSDM 187, *International Space Cooperation—Technology and Launch Assistance*—both emphasized international cooperation via (as their names suggest) the sharing of technical data, potential transfer of satellite technology, and the extension of launch assistance to allied countries seeking cooperative ventures with the United States.[95] Finally, to return to the Nixon Administration's focus on cutting costs within the space program, President Nixon approved the development of NASA's iconic Space Shuttle—which he described as a vehicle that would "revolutionize transportation into near space[] by routinizing it" and, thanks to its reusability, "take the astronomical costs out of astronautics."[96]

Gerald Ford, unexpectedly thrust into the Presidency in 1974 due to the resignations of Vice President Spiro Agnew, and, in the wake of the Watergate Scandal, President Nixon himself, had only a brief time in which to leave a mark on outer space policy. Despite his abbreviated presidency, however, President Ford presided over several significant outer space policy actions. First, the Ford Administration and its representatives at the United Nations successfully concluded negotiations for the Registration Convention, the last of the major outer space treaties to receive widespread support from the

---

94 *See* Moltz, *Politics of Space Security*, 169. *See also* Jennifer Ross-Nazzal, "Détente on Earth and in Space: The Apollo-Soyuz Test Project," *OAH Magazine of History* (July 2010), 30–31. The 1972 summit between the United States and the Soviet Union would also result in the successful negotiation, via the SALT I talks, of the Anti-Ballistic Missile Treaty. *See* Moltz, *Politics of Space Security*, 169–70.

95 *See* Hall, "The Evolution of U.S. National Security Space Policy," *Journal of Space Law*, 28–29. *See generally* NSDM 187, "International Space Cooperation—Technology and Launch Assistance," National Security Council, Aug. 30, 1972, https://aerospace.csis.org/wp-content/uploads/2019/02/NSDM-187-International-Space-Cooperation-30-Aug-1972-.pdf; NSDM 72, "Exchange of Technical Data Between the United States and the International Space Community," National Security Council, July 17, 1970, https://aerospace.csis.org/wp-content/uploads/2019/02/NSDM-72-Exchange-of-Technical-Data-between-the-United-States-and-the-International-Space-Community-17-Jul-1970-.pdf.

96 National Aeronautics & Space Administration, "President Nixon's 1972 Announcement on the Space Shuttle," history.nasa.gov, https://history.nasa.gov/stsnixon.htm (last visited Apr. 1, 2020).

international community, which was ratified by the United States in the fall of 1975.[97] In addition to the ratification of the Registration Convention, the Ford Administration also would publish the first Executive Branch policies related to a more kinetic and bellicose aspect of outer space security: anti-satellite systems, or "ASATs."

While the United States military and the Soviet Union had both explored the possibility of developing kamikaze, kinetic-kill ASAT systems in the early 1960s and later 1960s, respectively,[98] and the United States had also explored the possibility of utilizing anti-ballistic missile systems like the Nike Zeus and Thor missiles as ASAT systems,[99] ASAT testing and development in both countries had been radically reduced during the détente of the Nixon years. By the mid-1970s, however, relations between the United States and the Soviet Union were deteriorating, and both countries renewed ASAT weapon-testing.[100]

As Soviet ASAT testing ramped up in 1976, and as a report on satellite security requested by President Ford revealed that "the DoD's satellite survivability efforts had been negligible," President Ford became increasingly concerned about the threat ASAT weapons posed to the United States' satellites.[101] In response, Ford issued NSDM 333, *Enhanced Survivability of Critical U.S. Military and Intelligence Space Systems*, which directed the Department of Defense and the Central Intelligence Agency to "prepare an aggressive time-phased, prioritized action plan" to develop "short-term," "intermediate-term," and "long-term" measures to "enhance the survivability of critical military and intelligence satellites" against kinetic and non-kinetic threats.[102] But the defensive "hardening" of satellite systems would not be enough for President Ford. In late December 1976, upset by what he viewed as the "relaxed approach of the Defense Department" to ASAT threats and spurred by yet another Soviet test of a satellite interceptor, Ford decided that another written policy

97 *See* United Nations Treaty Collection, *Depositary—Convention on registration of objects launched into outer space*, treaties.un.org, Mar. 31, 2020, https://treaties.un.org/Pages/ViewDetailsIII.aspx?src=TREATY&mtdsg_no=XXIV-1&chapter=24&Temp=mtdsg3&clang=_en.

98 *See* Moltz, *Politics of Space Security*, 100–101, 156–57; Stares, *The Militarization of Space*, 112–17.

99 *See* Stares, *The Militarization of Space*, 117–28.

100 *See* Moltz, *Politics of Space Security*, 178–79.

101 Stares, *The Militarization of Space*, 169.

102 NSDM 333, "Enhanced Survivability of Critical U.S. Military and Intelligence Space Systems," National Security Council, July 3, 1976, available at https://aerospace.csis.org/wp-content/uploads/2019/02/NSDM-333-Enhanced-Survivability-of-Critical-Space-Systems.pdf (last visited May 27, 2020).

was necessary.[103] This new policy, NSDM 345, would explicitly state that "the President has decided that the United States should acquire a non-nuclear anti-satellite capability which could selectively nullify certain militarily important Soviet space systems, should that become necessary."[104] It went on to direct the Secretary of Defense to "take immediate steps" for such a system, which should "includ[e] means for electronic nullification as well as physical destruction."[105] NDSM 345, issued just two days prior to the end of his presidency, would be President Ford's final presidential action related to outer space. While NSDM 345 represented a dual-track strategy that recognized the need for both defensive and offensive measures, the fact that Ford would issue such a significant policy even as a new, Democratic presidential administration was about to enter office is surely a reflection of the profound significance he attached to the operational security of the United States' satellites.

3.4 *President James Earl "Jimmy" Carter (1977–1981)*

President Jimmy Carter's one-term presidency, bedeviled by domestic economic malaise (partially the result of a Ford-era economic downturn, but exacerbated by rising inflation and the 1979 oil crisis) and international instability (including the Iranian Revolution of 1979, which deposed a key American ally and resulted in the seizure of American hostages, and the Soviet invasion of Afghanistan), is not remembered for significant outer space-related achievements. Indeed, a cursory search of President Carter's Wikipedia page (the ultimate, crowdsourced font of knowledge!) reveals no mention of outer space at all.[106] But appearances can be deceiving, for, as we saw in Chapter 2 during our discussion of American interpretations of "peaceful" uses of outer space, the Carter Administration would do what no American President since Eisenhower had done: produce a self-contained, single-document national space policy.

Just over two months after taking office, President Carter (apparently spurred on by Major General Robert Rosenberg, a National Security Council staff member who had been held over from the Ford Administration[107]) issued

103 Stares, *The Militarization of Space*, 171 (citing *Author Interview with a Former Senior Official of the National Security Council Staff (Alpha)*, Washington, D.C., June 4, 1981).

104 NSDM 345, "U.S. Anti-Satellite Capabilities," National Security Council, Jan. 18, 1977, available at https://aerospace.csis.org/wp-content/uploads/2019/02/NSDM-345-US-Anti-Satellite-Capabilities.pdf (last visited May 27, 2020).

105 NSDM 345, "U.S. Anti-Satellite Capabilities."

106 *See* Wikipedia, *Jimmy Carter*, Wikipedia.org, Mar. 30, 2020, https://en.wikipedia.org/wiki/Jimmy_Carter#Presidency_(1977–1981) (lasted visited Apr. 1, 2020).

107 *See* Stares, *The Militarization of Space*, 182.

Presidential Review Memorandum/NSC 23, *A Coherent U.S. Space Policy*. This memorandum expressed President Carter's concern "that the United States does not have a coherent national space policy guiding our civil, military, and national intelligence programs" and directed a "thorough[] review [of] existing space policy and prior efforts."[108] But this was to be much more than a review. PRM/NSC 23 mandated the development of "a coherent, inclusive Statement of National Policy" and the establishment of "the necessary framework for its implementation;" the determination of "the relative importance ... of the use of space for the different yet interrelated goals of [the] civil, military, and national intelligence programs;" the establishment of "rules for the balance and control of the interaction among the [various space] sectors;" and, finally, the making of

> specific, mutually supportive recommendations in each of the areas of: modifications to existing policies, agreements, and practices; appropriate extent of overlapping technology, performance, application, and product dissemination by the three sectors; degree of application of civil and intelligence assets to military needs; maintenance of the principle of free use of space and a favorable international legal environment; appropriate degree of system survivability, defensive, and offensive capabilities in space, and arms control initiatives; guidelines for security and public disclosure; goals for international cooperative agreements; and guidance for military, civil and national intelligence use of the space shuttle.[109]

In short, President Carter was asking for nothing less than a complete, comprehensive review of all aspects of US space policy—to be followed by the development of single, coherent national policy explaining and setting the direction for American outer space endeavors during his Presidency.

The report and recommendations from the comprehensive review mandated by PRM/NSC 23 resulted in the development and publication of Presidential Directive/NSC-37 (PD/NSC-37, or, alternatively the Carter NSP)—the first National Space Policy since the Eisenhower Administration.[110] PD/NSC-37 opened with an explanation of its purpose: to establish "national policies" to "guide the conduct of United States activities in and related to" outer

108 President Jimmy Carter, PRM/NSC 23, "A Coherent U.S. Space Policy," Mar. 28, 1977, available at https://www.jimmycarterlibrary.gov/assets/documents/memorandums/prm23.pdf (last visited Apr. 1, 2020).

109 PRM/NSC 23, "A Coherent U.S. Space Policy."

110 *See generally* PD/NSC-37.

space and the US space program, with the goals of (1) "advanc[ing] the interests of the United States through the exploration and use of space," and (2) "cooperat[ing] with other nations in maintaining the freedom of space for all activities which enhance the security and welfare of mankind."[111] As we have seen with previous Administrations, particularly in the words of President Kennedy's "We Choose to Go to the Moon" speech and in President Eisenhower's development of early US space policy, there is an inherent tension in the Carter Administration's approach. Based on the goals described in Carter's NSP, the United States seeks, on the one hand, to encourage international cooperation with respect to outer space and to continue to protect key aspects of the international legal regime for space. On the other hand, it recognizes its own interests as paramount; indeed, the vast majority of PD/NSC-37 (perhaps unsurprisingly, considering that it is a *National* Space Policy) details the policies the United States is pursuing, and will pursue, to advance its interests on the global stage.

With respect to international law, PD/NSC-37 acknowledges several principles originating from within the international legal regime for outer space in accordance with which the United States' space programs must operate. First among these, as we noted in Chapter 2, is the American "[c]ommitment to the principles of the exploration and use of outer space by all nations for peaceful purposes and for the benefit of all mankind."[112] (As the potential differences between international and American interpretations of "peaceful purposes" has been previously discussed, it will not be rehashed here). In keeping with Article II of the Outer Space Treaty, the second significant international legal principle cited by the PD/NSC-37 is the United States' "[r]ejection of any claims to sovereignty over outer space or over celestial bodies, or any portion thereof."[113] The United States, per PD/NSC-37, also rejects "any limitations on the fundamental right to acquire data from space"—a reflection of the "free use" principle of international space law (though also, as we shall see, likely a reference to the United States' policies regarding satellite remote sensing and photoreconnaissance). Finally, PD/NSC-37, recognized that "[t]he space systems of any nation are national property" and, again echoing the "free access" and "free use" principles, that these systems "have the right of passage through and operation in space without interference."[114] Despite these references to key principles of international law related to outer space, neither the Outer

111 PD/NSC-37, 1.
112 PD/NSC-37, 2.
113 PD/NSC-37, 2.
114 PD/NSC-37, 2.

Space Treaty, nor any of the other three space treaties/conventions to which the United States is a party, is ever explicitly mentioned or referenced as a basis for the United States' positions or policies.[115]

After these largely cursory references to international legal principles, PD/NSC-37 turned to the specific policies the United States was either already pursuing, or intended to pursue, to preserve its interests in and related to outer space. During our discussion of "peaceful purposes" in Chapter 2, we saw that PD/NSC-37's interpretation of that term left a broad range of military-related uses available to the United States. Because "peaceful purposes" purportedly allowed for "military and intelligence-related activities in pursuit of national security and other goals,"[116] the United States would continue to "pursue activities in space in support of its right of self-defense," "maintain a national intelligence space program," and "conduct those activities in space which are necessary to national defense."[117] Continuing the policies of every President since Eisenhower, President Carter made the United States' reliance on satellite technology an explicit part of PD/NSC-37: the United States would continue to

> develop and operate on a global basis *active and passive remote sensing operations* in support of *civil, military, and national intelligence objectives*. Such operations [would] occur under conditions which protect classified technology, deny sensitive data, and promote acceptance and legitimacy of such activities [emphasis added].[118]

In addition to continuing the United States' unbroken insistence that satellite remote sensing operations constituted legitimate, peaceful uses of outer space (and its dedication to arguing this point on the international stage), this was the clearest description of United States policy with respect to satellite use since President Eisenhower's NSC 5814/1.

After elucidating its primary policy principles, President Carter's NSP divided space activities into three types: military, national intelligence, and civilian.[119] In the military realm, PD/NSC-37 recognized what would become a

115 *See generally* PD/NSC-37.

116 PD/NSC-37, 2.

117 PD/NSC-37, 2–3.

118 PD/NSC-37, 2.

119 This differentiation between military and national intelligence space activities was an official recognition of the continuing, separate programs of space activities undertaken by US military organizations and US intelligence agencies. Generally speaking, the US national intelligence community is comprised of agencies and organizations (whether under the purview of the Department of Defense or not) focused on intelligence collection

key point regarding uses of outer space in the modern era: that the true value of outer space systems from a military perspective was the significant advantage they offered as a means of support for *terrestrial* military forces. As the policy states, "[t]he military space program shall support such functions as command and control, communications, navigation, environmental monitoring, warning, tactical intelligence, targeting, ocean and battlefield surveillance, and space defense."[120] Of these functions, only one—"space defense" (which, as explained later in PD/NSC-37, largely encompassed protecting American space systems from ASATs[121])—could be characterized as a space-specific, non-support function. PD/NSC-37 went on to echo President Ford's NSDM 333: survivability of military space systems was critical, and "an aggressive, long-term program [would] be applied to provide more assured survivability through evolutionary changes to space systems."[122] Survivability would also be critical for national intelligence space systems, as elaborated later in the policy.[123]

President Carter broke with his predecessor, however, on the issue of ASATs—but only to a degree. While President Ford had been adamant that the United States "take immediate steps" to develop an ASAT capability that could attack Soviet space systems via "electronic nullification" or "physical

and use: this includes organizations like the Central Intelligence Agency (CIA), which is separate and distinct from the Department of Defense, and the National Reconnaissance Office (NRO) and National Geospatial-Intelligence Agency (NGA), which are Department of Defense Agencies organized under the Office of the Secretary of Defense, all of which have and continue to operate critical reconnaissance and intelligence-related space systems. True military space activities are those undertaken by the United States' military departments—the Departments of the Air Force, Army, and Navy—for national defense and operational purposes. It should be noted, of course, that the distinction is often blurred; outer space intelligence activities run by the intelligence community (for example, the CIA's 1960s-era CORONA satellite photoreconnaissance program) frequently inform the activities and operations of the military community, and vice versa. This blurring has likely become even more significant over time, as newly-created US intelligence organizations—including the National Security Agency (NSA, 1952) and the Defense Intelligence Agency (DIA, 1961), as well as the NRO (1960) and NGA (1996), previously mentioned—have tended to be organized under the auspices of the Department of Defense.

120 PD/NSC-37, 3.

121 *See* PD/NSC-37, 4. PD/NSC-37 mandated, in its section concerning "Anti-Satellite Capability," that "[t]he space defense program shall include an integrated attack warning, notification, verification, and contingency reaction capability which can effectively detect and react to threats to U.S. space systems."

122 PD/NSC-37, 4.

123 PD/NSC-37, 6.

destruction,"[124] Carter believed that kinetic-kill ASATs were an inherent threat to American interests in outer space and ought to be banned via arms control agreements with the Soviet Union. This was reflected in PD/NSC-37, which mandated that "the United States shall seek a verifiable ban on anti-satellite capabilities, excluding electronic warfare."[125] Despite Carter's desire to resolve the threat of ASATs via diplomatic and international legal initiatives, he understood the risks involved in dealing with the Soviet Union and hedged his bets. Despite its policy preference for arms control negotiations and a binding treaty with the Soviet Union, PD/NSC-37 also required the Department of Defense to "vigorously pursue development of an anti-satellite capability" and stated that annual reviews of the progress of negotiations with the Soviets would help "determine if the U.S. ASAT efforts [were] still adequate."[126] Ultimately, then, Carter was not so different from Ford after all: PD/NSC-37 advanced the proposition that the United States needed to develop a robust ASAT capability, while advocating for a diplomatic solution that would mean the development and deployment of such a capability would never be needed. Unfortunately, Carter's efforts to negotiate an ASAT-banning treaty with the Soviet Union failed: despite several promising bilateral sessions on the issue between the summer of 1978 and the summer of 1979, "the Soviet invasion of Afghanistan in December 1979 and the resultant rupture in East-West relations ... brought to a halt all further progress on ASAT arms control during the Carter Administration."[127] The election of the hawkish Ronald Reagan in 1980 effectively foreclosed further progress on an ASAT-banning treaty with the Soviet Union, and, indeed, the issue of ASATs and the threat they pose to the outer space environment (to say nothing of national security) continue to bedevil US and international space policy-makers to this day.

Extending its previous recognition that space assets are key tools in supporting terrestrial military forces, PD/NSC-37 notes that, while the "foreign intelligence program" will operate its own space systems (independent of the space systems used by the US military and civilian space programs), these systems also play a critical role in supporting the military. Because "[s]upport of military operational requirements is a major space intelligence mission," PD/NSC-37 required "[n]ational space intelligence assets [to] provide appropriate support to deployed military operational forces in balance with their primary

124 NSDM 345.

125 PD/NSC-37, 4.

126 PD/NSC-37, 4.

127 Stares, *The Militarization of Space*, 199.

mission capabilities."[128] In other words, imagery and information from the United States' photoreconnaissance spy satellites, operated by the CIA since the inception of Project Corona during the Eisenhower Administration, must be used, as needed, to support the US military's operations across the globe. It was up to the Secretary of Defense and the Director of the CIA to work together to ensure that this was occurring and that the military and foreign intelligence space programs were not needlessly duplicating programs they could otherwise share.[129]

While President Carter also addressed the civilian space program in PD/NSC-37, the specifics of US civilian space policy, beyond the basic principles and international legal requirements under which it operated, are beyond the scope of this work. Suffice to say, with PD/NSC-37, President Carter accomplished the heady goal laid out in PRM/NSC 23. President Carter had produced the first US National Space Policy since President Eisenhower's dual policies, published two decades earlier. For the most part, little had changed in the basic principles of the two Presidents' approaches to outer space policy. Carter's PD/NSC-37, however, effectively consolidated the previous two decades of American space policy, describing—in a single document—the United States' interpretation of such significant legal principles as the "peaceful use" of outer space, its reiteration of support for certain key international law principles (such as the "non-appropriation," "free use," and "free access" principles of the Outer Space Treaty), and its differentiation of American space programs into three distinct categories ("military," "foreign intelligence," and "civil"). The most significant difference between the policies of Eisenhower and Carter was the evolution of space policy (spurred by both the United States military's insistence that ASATs and, potentially, other space weapons were necessary to match the Soviets, and by President Ford's executive policies on the ASAT issue) toward space-related weaponization. While Carter, like Eisenhower before him, opposed the weaponization of outer space and the deployment of space object-targeting ASAT systems, his continuation of Ford's earlier order that ASATs be developed (with the caveat that they not be put into production if an anti-ASAT treaty was successfully negotiated with the Soviets) allowed weaponization and "space warfare" ideas to gain further ground in official policies.

Although the creation of PD/NSC-37 is not well-known among President Carter's successes, it was a significant development in normalizing the creation

128 PD/NSC-37, 5.

129 *See* PD/NSC-37, 5.

of Presidential national space policies. Since the publication of PD/NSC-37 in 1978, every President save President Joseph Biden (who has been in office for less than two years at the time of this writing and is largely operating under the Trump Administration's NSP) has published his own NSP. Indeed, Carter's successor, President Reagan, would build upon the space policy framework developed in PD/NSC-37, while also furthering the evolution of national security space policy and space weaponization.

3.5 *President Ronald Reagan (1981–1989) and President George H.W. Bush (1989–1993)*

President Ronald Reagan, the vehemently anti-Communist ex-actor and former Governor of California, was voted into office in a landslide election considered to reflect America's discontent with the malaise of the Carter years. Reagan had "run on a platform of redressing a perceived decline in U.S. military capabilities relative to the Soviet Union"[130]—and one of the national security areas in which he would take a particular interest was outer space. As Hall notes in his own extensive examination of Presidential space policies, Reagan "introduced to national space policy more changes than any single President since Dwight Eisenhower."[131] President Reagan would not merely continue the well-trod path of space policy previously constructed by his predecessors: during his presidency, Reagan would tilt the balance of the US space program more firmly toward a focus on national defense, with significant consequences for space weaponization, US-Soviet relations, and perceptions about the need for defensive—and offensive—space systems.

As noted at the end of the previous section, one of the first consequences of President Reagan's election was the end of American efforts to pursue an ASAT arms control treaty with the Soviet Union. Within seven months of his inauguration, in August 1981, Reagan had already rejected a draft treaty on ASAT arms control the Soviets had submitted at the United Nations, and, unlike in previous negotiations involving outer space international law-making, "the US made no effort to make a counter proposal or give any indication that it was interested in resuming bilateral talks" on the subject of ASATs.[132] Instead of continuing the Carter Administration's (to say nothing of previous presidential administrations') reticence concerning ASATs and space weaponry, the Reagan Administration increased emphasis on the significance and benefits of an American ASAT capability and the development of other military

130 Moltz, *Politics of Space Security*, 187.
131 Hall, "The Evolution of U.S. National Security Space Policy," *Journal of Space Law*, 43.
132 Stares, *The Militarization of Space*, 217.

space systems.[133] With the 1982 publication of a Heritage Foundation report by retired Lieutenant General Daniel O. Graham entitled *High Frontier: A New National Strategy* (published the following year as a book with the somewhat more sensationalist title, *High Frontier: A Strategy for National Survival*), the Reagan Administration's interest in ASATS bled into the realm of anti-ballistic missile defense.[134] *High Frontier* advocated—among other militarized uses of outer space—the creation of a "spaceborne ballistic missile defense" system "capable of serious attrition of a Soviet strategic missile attack."[135] This very type of co-orbital missile defense system would shortly become the basis for Reagan's "Strategic Defense Initiative." Given these new priorities, it is no surprise that

> … Reagan's shift in space priorities from civilian to military programs began to be seen in space expenditures. From 1981 to 1983, the defense department's [sic] space budget jumped from $4.8 billion to $8.5 billion, surpassing NASA's budget for the first time since 1960 [internal citations omitted].[136]

In conjunction with its push for increases in national security and military-related defense budgets and rejections of Soviet overtures for space arms control, the Reagan Administration was in the midst of developing its own National Space Policy. This policy, National Security Decision Directive 42, *National Space Policy* (NSDD 42, or, alternatively, the Reagan NSP), would be published on July 4, 1982, and supersede President Carter's previous space policy.[137] NSDD 42 would echo President Carter's PD/NSC-37 in many respects: the two policies' interpretations of permissible "peaceful uses" of outer space, recognition of international outer space law principles, delineation of American space programs into three distinct areas (again, "military," "foreign intelligence," and "civil"), stipulation that these three programs support one another when necessary, and focus on the survivability of US space systems were largely identical.[138] The differences, however, were profound and were largely to be seen in

133 *See* Stares, *The Militarization of Space*, 217.

134 *See* Moltz, *Politics of Space Security*, 188. *See generally* Daniel Graham, *High Frontier: A Strategy for National Survival* (New York: TOR, 1983).

135 Graham, *High Frontier*, 40.

136 Moltz, *Politics of Space Security*, 188.

137 *See* President Ronald Reagan, National Security Decision Directive 42, "National Space Policy," July 4, 1982, available at https://www.reaganlibrary.gov/public/archives/reference/scanned-nsdds/nsdd42.pdf (last visited Apr. 6, 2020) (hereinafter NSDD 42).

138 *Compare* NSDD 42, 2, 6, 7 *with* PD/NSC-37, 2, 3–4, 6.

the Reagan Administration's focus on national defense, weaponization, and military strength.

As an initial matter, the primary goals of the Reagan NSP reflected this change: where PD/NSC-37's most significant goal was framed relatively benignly ("to advance the interests of the United States through the exploration and use of space"[139]), NSDD 42 made no bones about the fact that its primary goal was to "strengthen the security of the United States."[140] Indeed, the Reagan NSP's expanded goals reflected a decidedly more "America first"-style feel. In addition to the focus on strengthening US security, NSDD 42 also sought to "maintain United States space leadership," "obtain [for the United States] economic and scientific benefits from the exploitation of space," and "expand United States private-sector investment and involvement in civil space and space-related activities."[141] NSDD 42 did repeat, as its last-listed (and, thus, presumably, least significant) goal, PD/NSC-37's objective of "cooperat[ing] with other nations in maintaining the freedom of space for all activities which enhance the security and welfare of mankind."[142] The Reagan Administration's goals for US space policy, which, unlike other portions of NSDD 42, were publicly released as part of an unclassified "Fact Sheet" about the policy,[143] could not have been clearer. Far from sugar-coating the United States' renewed focus on outer space security policy, President Reagan—as he would with other key aspects of his outer space policy—made sure the focus on American national security was publicly available for the American people and, perhaps more significantly, the Soviets to see.

The differences between President Reagan's and President Carter's approaches to US space policy were even more starkly apparent in NSDD 42's sections concerning the military space program. Initially, Reagan's NSP echoed key aspects of Carter's, repeating that the "United States will conduct those activities in space that are necessary to national defense."[144] Nearly identical, too, was the list of military support functions with which the military space program was to assist ... with one exception. In addition to "command and control," "communications," "navigation," and the other support functions

139 PD/NSC-37, 1.

140 NSDD 42, 1.

141 NSDD 42, 1.

142 NSDD 42, 1. *See also* PD/NSC-37, 1.

143 *See* Office of the Press Secretary, "Fact Sheet Outlining United States Space Policy," *Ronald Reagan Presidential Library*, July 4, 1982, https://aerospace.csis.org/wp-content/uploads/2019/02/NSDD-42-Reagan-National-Space-Policy.pdf (last visited Apr. 6, 2020).

144 NSDD 42, 6.

previously listed in Carter's NSP, NSDD 42 replaced "space defense" (the final function listed in PD/NSC-37) with a new, more ominous function: "force application."[145] If there were any illusions that this new term was simply different terminology for the same principles underlying "space defense," this was quickly dashed several paragraphs later, when the concept of "Force Application" was specifically addressed:

> The United States will, consistent with treaty obligations: (a) develop and maintain an integrated attack warning, notification, verification, and contingency reaction capability which can *effectively detect and react to threats* to United States space systems; (b) conduct research and planning to be prepared to *develop, acquire, and deploy space weapons systems and to counter adversary space activities*, should national security conditions dictate. These efforts must ensure a reasonable hedge against breakout in space and space-related weapons by any adversary and *should support technology advances that will place the United States in a favorable strategic posture* [emphasis added].[146]

"Force application," then, was directly indicative of the Reagan Administration's new direction. While previous Presidential Administrations had given tacit support to military space projects, including the on-and-off ASAT tests that had occurred since the 1960s, NSDD 42's explicit discussion of not just the testing, but the *deployment* of "space weapons systems" was a radical departure from previous space policy dating back to Eisenhower.[147] Perhaps the closest any previous president had come to such a stance was President Kennedy's more oblique comment concerning how the United States neither "should [n]or will go unprotected against the hostile misuse of space any more than we go unprotected against the hostile use of land or sea"[148]—but Kennedy was speaking before the drafting and ratification of the Outer Space Treaty, the development

145 NSDD 42, 6.

146 NSDD 42, 6.

147 *See* Stares, *The Militarization of Space*, 219 ("Another novel, though less defined, feature of the Reagan Administration's military space policy was the discussion on the projection of force *from* space."). Even the description from part (a) of NSDD 42's "force application" explanation—which, with its references to "warning," "contingency reaction," and "detect[ing] and react[ing] to threats," seems intentionally couched in the language of self-defense—raises problematic implications. NSDD 42, 6. What, after all, is to prevent a system that can "detect and react to threats" from serving, not as a defensive shield, but as an *offensive* weapon?

148 President Kennedy, "Address at Rice University."

of binding international norms regarding outer space access and use, and the administrations of four additional Presidents who had (Ford and Carter's ASAT stances not withstanding) largely stuck with President Eisenhower's initial rejection of space weaponization. Though couched in the language of reaction—the assertion that American space weapons were merely a "hedge against [adversary] breakout in space" and would only be deployed to counter adversary space actions "should national security conditions dictate"[149]—NSDD 42 represented a clear turning point for American space policy with respect to the issue of outer space weapons.

As was to be expected, NSDD 42 also altered course on President Carter's prior policies concerning ASAT development. Gone were references to the United States' desire to pursue an ASAT-banning treaty with the Soviet Union, and gone was President Carter's hedging tactic for the development (but not deployment) of an American ASAT capability. President Reagan would prove to be even more vehement about ASAT development than President Ford: NSDD 42 mandated that "[t]he United States *will* develop and deploy an ASAT capability to *achieve an operational system at the earliest practical date*" [emphasis added].[150] ASATs, according to the new space policy, were essential "to deter threats to space systems of the United States and its Allies" and, "within the limits of international law, to deny any adversary the use of space-based systems that provide support to hostile military forces."[151] ASATs as a method of deterrence and balance between the United States and the Soviet Union was familiar—this was the rationale underlying Ford's and Carter's policies with respect to ASAT development. But as a potentially offensive weapon used to "deny … the use of space-based systems" by potential adversaries? This was a significant expansion of the purposes of the ASAT program, one that, even if the United States had the best of intentions, seemed likely to stoke fears that the United States sought to dominate outer space.[152]

149 NSDD 42, 6.

150 NSDD 42, 6.

151 NSDD 42, 6.

152 Under the Reagan Administration's NSDD 42 policies, the United States military would renew ASAT development and testing. Among the ASAT successes of this period was the ASM-135A, an F-15 fighter jet-launched ASAT missile developed by Vought Aircraft Industries that employed a "miniature homing vehicle" (MHV) to lock onto an orbiting satellite and guide its non-explosive warhead on a collision course with its target. "Vought ASM-135A Anti-Satellite Missile," Fact Sheet, National Museum of the United States Air Force, available at https://www.nationalmuseum.af.mil/Visit/Museum-Exhibits/Fact-Sheets/Display/Article/198034/vought-asm-135a-anti-satellite-missile/ (last visited Mar. 21, 2022). On September 13, 1985, Air Force Major Wilbur D. Pearson, Jr., successfully tested the ASM-135A—destroying Solwind P78-1, a defunct US spectroscopy satellite, and

Finally, NSDD 42 would largely continue the same policies related to the "national foreign intelligence space program" (the photoreconnaissance spy satellite program run by the CIA) as Carter's PD/NSC-37. There was, however, one significant addition to the previous policy. President Reagan's NSP explicitly stated, in a section underlined for emphasis, that "the fact of satellite 'photoreconnaissance' for use in monitoring arms control agreements is UNCLASSIFIED."[153] While NSDD 42 sought to preserve the confidentiality and classification of intelligence-collecting satellite operations, it appears that the Reagan Administration wanted to remind the Soviets—and the rest of the world—that the United States was watching and that, even as the United States began its Reagan-era military revitalization, America's adversaries ought to beware treaty-violating arms build-ups and other bad behavior.

President Reagan's interest in outer space, the publication of NSDD 42, and the Reagan Administration's attentiveness to retired Lieutenant General Graham's *High Frontier* study set the stage for what was to be one of the defining programs of the Reagan Presidency: the Strategic Defense Initiative ("SDI," or, as described by critics, "Star Wars"). On March 23, 1983, President Reagan broadcast a special presidential address to the nation dealing with issues of national defense. Among these national defense issues, one loomed largest: the continuing threat of Soviet nuclear missile attack against the United States. While Reagan recognized that, as under previous Presidential administrations, the United States had to rely on the threat of massive retaliation to deter the Soviets, there was, he told the listening nation, a potentially better, more peaceful way to end the threat of Soviet attack:

> Let me share with you a vision of the future which offers hope. It is that we embark on a program to counter the awesome Soviet missile threat with measures that are defensive. Let us turn to the very strengths in technology that spawned our great industrial base and that have given us the quality of life we enjoy today.
>
> What if free people could live secure in the knowledge that their security did not rest upon the threat of instant U.S. retaliation to deter a Soviet attack, that we could intercept and destroy strategic ballistic missiles before they reached our own soil or that of our allies?

---

becoming "the first [and, to date, the only Air Force] pilot ever to shoot down a space target." Peter Grier, "The Flying Tomato Can," *Air Force Magazine*, Feb. 1, 2009, https://www.airforcemag.com/article/0209tomato/.

153 NSDD 42, 8.

> I know this is a formidable, technical task, one that may not be accomplished before the end of this century. Yet, current technology has attained a level of sophistication where it's reasonable for us to begin this effort. It will take years, probably decades of effort on many fronts. There will be failures and setbacks, just as there will be successes and breakthroughs. And as we proceed, we must remain constant in preserving the nuclear deterrent and maintaining a solid capability for flexible response. But isn't it worth every investment necessary to free the world from the threat of nuclear war? We know it is.
>
> ...
>
> ... I call upon the scientific community in our country, those who gave us nuclear weapons, to turn their great talents now to the cause of mankind and world peace, to give us the means of rendering these nuclear weapons impotent and obsolete.[154]

Reagan's public announcement of SDI was a masterful way of sidestepping critics of the program. With the American public now fully aware of SDI, and, as Reagan characterized it, its potential as a tool to peacefully nullify the Soviet nuclear threat, Congress, the military, and the Executive Agencies of government had little choice but to publicly debate the program, all while the Reagan Administration successfully sought funding for its development.[155] SDI was, in theory, to be a "shield" of orbital missile interceptors à la Graham's *High Frontier*—a comprehensive system that, as Reagan had announced, "could intercept and destroy strategic ballistic missiles" aimed at any location in the United States. While this certainly seemed a noble aim, the problem underlying SDI, which we will examine in greater detail in Chapter 5, was that the entire scheme effectively constituted an anti-ballistic missile system—a system that, despite the machinations of Reagan Administration lawyers, almost certainly violated the 1972 Anti-Ballistic Missile Treaty.

Though (at least to date) the success, indeed even the possible partial success, of SDI and its progeny of similar ballistic missile defense programs remains unclear, Reagan's program would have significant consequences for American space security policy and the global geopolitical landscape. In the

154 President Ronald Reagan, "Address to the Nation on Defense and National Security," Mar. 23, 1983, *Ronald Reagan Presidential Library and Museum*, https://www.reaganlibrary.gov/research/speeches/32383d (last visited Apr. 8, 2020).

155 *See* Moltz, *Politics of Space Security*, 192.

realm of American policy, "SDI … changed views regarding what might be feasible in space, militarily speaking."[156] Describing the advent of SDI as a "psychological freeing-up of the military imagination," Roger Handberg, an expert in outer space policy and former Director of the University of Central Florida's Center for Space Policy & Law, writes:

> What really changed [with the advent of SDI] was the perception that more military space activities might be possible or must be done. Space was moving psychologically from a preserve sheltered from the harsh realities of war to potentially just another theater of operations. Military planners and thinkers could, at one level, return to considering space as merely another battlefield analogous to land, sea, and air.[157]

This change was quickly seen within the military itself. The Air Force had, in June 1982 (and, thus, prior to President Reagan's announcement of the SDI program) announced the creation of Air Force Space Command (AFSPC), a new major command (MAJCOM) that "was expected to form the core of an increasingly unified military space program."[158] AFSPC was activated on September 1, 1982, with missions focused (in line with NSDD 42's military space functions) "on missile warning, launch operations, satellite control, space surveillance and command and control for national leadership."[159] After the SDI announcement, however, space operations quickly became an all-service military effort: on the advice of key Air Force officials and the Joint Chiefs of Staff, United States Space Command, a new functional combatant command[160] that would focus on outer space operations, including assisting with SDI and the military space functions described in NSDD 42 (including "developing survivable and enduring space systems, an anti-satellite capability, and means for detecting and reacting to threats against US space systems") was created in 1985.[161] With the significant policy shifts of Reagan's NSP and SDI initiative related to outer

156 Roger Handberg, *Seeking New World Vistas: The Militarization of Space* (Westport, CT: Praeger, 2000), 81.

157 Handberg, *Seeking New World Vistas*, 82.

158 Thomas Karas, *The New High Ground: Strategies and Weapons of Space-Age War* (New York: Simon & Schuster, 1983), 20.

159 Air Force Space Command, "Air Force Space Command History," afspc.af.mil, https://www.afspc.af.mil/About-Us/AFSPC-History/ (last visited Apr. 8, 2020).

160 A combatant command, also called a "unified combatant command," is defined as "a military command which has broad, continuing missions and which is composed of forces from two or more military departments." 10 U.S.C. §161(c)(1).

161 Edward J. Drea et al., *History of the Unified Command Plan 1946–2012* (Washington, D.C.: Joint History Office, Office of the Chairman of the Joint Chiefs of Staff, 2013), 55–56.

space weaponization, as well as the creation of space-focused organizations within the military, it is easy to pinpoint President Reagan's space security policies as the turning point between Eisenhower's non-weaponization policy and the wider acceptance of military-oriented space operations today.[162]

During the last year of Reagan's presidency, in January 1988, an update to the National Space Policy, NSDD 293, was published to reflect minor changes to NSDD 42.[163] As this policy was largely subsumed into President George H.W. Bush's (President Bush 41) own National Space Policy, National Security Directive (NSD) 30/National Space Policy Directive (NSPD) 1 (for simplicity's sake, NSD 30, or, alternatively, the Bush 41 NSP),[164] we shall examine the two space policies simultaneously. Prior to his election in 1988, President Bush 41 had served as Reagan's Vice President for the past eight years; thus, it should come as little surprise that Bush would largely continue the space policies of his predecessor. Though much of NSDD 293 and NSD 30 echoed Reagan's earlier NSDD 42, several changes should be addressed.

First, the goals of the late Reagan and Bush 41 NSPs are subtly different than those of NSDD 42. Although the primary goal, "to strengthen the security of the United States" remained, as well as the "encourage[ment of] continuing United States private sector investment in space,"[165] both the NSDD 293 and

162 President Reagan's perspectives on space weaponization, as well as his strident anti-Communism (which will be discussed at greater length in Chapter 5), may well have played a role in the Soviets' tendency to view even the United States' civil space programs with suspicion during his Administration. Chief among Soviet complaints in this realm was NASA's Space Shuttle, which the Soviets feared to be a secret space weapon, able to "launch [] military satellites, [engage in] space espionage, deploy[] anti-aircraft and antiballistic missile systems, develop[] and test[] new weapons, and ... function as an outer space command center." Stephen R. Burant, "Soviet Perspectives on the Legal Regime in Outer Space: The Problem of Space Demilitarization," *Studies in Comparative Communism*, vol. 19, no. 3/4 (Autumn/Winter 1986), 171.

163 *See* Hall, "The Evolution of U.S. National Security Space Policy," *Journal of Space Law*, 62–70 (citing President Ronald Reagan, NSDD 93, "National Space Policy," Jan. 5, 1988). *See also* "Presidential Directive on National Space Policy," Feb. 11, 1988, *Federation of American Scientists*, https://fas.org/spp/military/docops/national/policy88.htm (last visited Apr. 8, 2020) [hereinafter NSDD 293 Factsheet]. Aside from the selections of NSDD 293 quoted in Hall's article, the unclassified summary of the policy posted by the Federation of American Scientists was the only text or summary of NSDD 293 the author was able to locate, as parts of the policy itself appear to remain classified.

164 *See* President George H.W. Bush, NSD 30/NSPD 1, "National Space Policy," Nov. 2, 1989, *George H.W. Bush Presidential Library & Museum*, https://bush41library.tamu.edu/files/nsd/nsd30.pdf (last visited Apr. 8, 2020) [hereinafter NSD 30]. Note that portions of NSD 30 apparently remain classified and are redacted from this source. *See generally* NSD 30/NSPD 1.

165 NSD 30/NSPD 1, 2; NSDD 293.

NSD 30 replaced the American-centric goals of Reagan's 1982 NSP with more facially internationalist ones. Gone were references to maintaining US space leadership and exploiting space for purely American benefit. The new goals now included "obtain[ing] scientific, technological, and economic benefits for the general population and to improve the quality of life on Earth through space-related activities;" "promot[ing] international cooperative activities taking into account United States national security, foreign policy, scientific, and economic interests;" "cooperat[ing] with other nations in maintaining the freedom of space for all activities that enhance the security and welfare of mankind;" and, finally, "expand[ing] human presence and activity beyond Earth orbit into the solar system."[166] Whether the altered, more inclusive goals were the result of perceived successes in President Reagan's prior, America-centric objectives; a true about-face to more international-oriented American space policy; or simply a recognition that a softer explanation of US goals was required even if, in practice, little real policy change occurred, the more starkly "America First" goals of NSDD 42 were no more.

The text of NSDD 293 and NSD 30, as well as the historical context of the times the policies were published, seem to indicate that American space policy in the late Reagan and Bush 41 Administrations was influenced by the interplay of all three of the factors cited at the end of the previous paragraph. By 1988/1989, it was becoming increasingly clear that dramatic changes in the Soviet Union, especially the Soviets' grip on their Eastern European satellite States behind the "Iron Curtain," were afoot. By the time President Bush 41's NSD 30 was published in November 1989, Poland and Hungary had largely wrested themselves from Soviet domination, and the fall of the Berlin Wall was only a week away. In other words, Reagan and Bush 41 had good reason to feel that (1) their previous national defense policies (not merely in outer space, but also in more traditional, terrestrial areas) had been successful, and (2) with the weakening of the Soviet Union, and the clear international dominance of the United States, America could once again afford to focus not simply on outer space as an arena in which to pursue its own security and prosperity, but as a realm in which greater international cooperation would be beneficial to all.

The decline—and, soon, the fall—of the Soviet Union was not, however, seen as a reason for the United States to change course on its path of increasing military uses of, and operations in, outer space. NSDD 293 and NSD 30 retained much of NSDD 42's language regarding the operation of the military space program, and, indeed, even expanded the military portion of the space policy

166 NSD 30, 2; NSDD 293.

to include new terms and space strategies developed by the Air Force and Department of Defense. Expanding on the basic purposes of the military space program cited in previous space policies, NSDD 293 and NSD 30 both state,

> [t]he United States will conduct those activities in space that are necessary to national defense. Space activities will contribute to national security objectives by 1) deterring, or if necessary, defending against enemy attack; 2) assuring that forces of hostile nations cannot prevent our own use of space; 3) negating, if necessary, hostile space systems; and 4) enhancing operations of United States and Allied forces.[167]

This expanded list of contributions would be further reflected in the section of the two policies entitled "Military Space Sector Guidelines." Here, the now-familiar concepts of force enhancement, force application, survivability, and ASAT capability development (all with definitions and explanations approximating, if not explicitly repeating, those in NSDD 42[168]) were joined by two new concepts for which the military space program was expected to be responsible: "space support" and "space control." Drawn from the US military's newly developed space doctrine, these concepts described requirements for the Department of Defense to maintain primary and contingency launch capabilities in order to quickly launch or replace satellites and other space systems for both itself and the intelligence community ("space support") and the need to achieve and maintain "freedom of action" for the United States military in outer space ("space control"). "Space control," loosely based on the Air Force doctrine of "air superiority," also typically combines the maintenance of American freedom of action and use of space with a corresponding *denial* of the use of space to the United States' potential adversaries. While this is not mentioned in the unclassified Fact Sheet for NSDD 293,[169] there is a conspicuously redacted portion of the "Space Control" section of NSD 30 that may reflect this common corollary.[170] Regardless, the migration of military doctrinal terms into the late Reagan and Bush 41 National Space Policies was a further reflection of both the militarized direction in which American space policy was moving and the growing significance of outer space for the military itself.

---

167 NSD 30, 4; Hall, "The Evolution of U.S. National Security Space Policy," *Journal of Space Law*, 64–65.

168 *Compare* NSD 30, 11–14, *and NSDD 293 Factsheet, with* NSDD 42, 6–7.

169 *See NSDD 293 Factsheet.*

170 *See* NSD 30, 12.

Although the threat from the Soviet Union was rapidly fading, the importance of outer space to military operations would be dramatically demonstrated within fourteen months of the publication of President Bush 41's NSD 30, when Saddam Hussein's invasion of his weaker, oil-rich neighbor, Kuwait, in August 1990 precipitated the first Gulf War. Five months later, in January 1991, President Bush, after cultivating an extensive coalition of international partners, launched Operation Desert Storm to expel the Iraqi military from Kuwait. Desert Storm was a run-away success—thanks, in no small part, to the significant support the Coalition's terrestrial military forces received from the United States' military and intelligence space assets. The United States' satellite-controlled Global Positioning System (GPS) allowed Coalition forces to "coordinate troop movements, mark minefields, and position artillery" in the otherwise featureless and difficult-to-navigate desert battlefields of Kuwait and southern Iraq, as well as "assist[ ] the mid-course guidance of stand-off missiles" launched against Iraqi targets.[171] Satellite communications also allowed rapid reporting from, and guidance to, forces in the field and the use of satellite television to beam images of the war to television viewers in the United States. So great was the contribution of space assets to the American-led Coalition's victory over Saddam Hussein that the Gulf War would be dubbed the "first space war,"[172] the "first satellite war,"[173] and "the coming out party for space support."[174] Had there been any concern that military uses of outer space were becoming outdated with the formerly omnipresent Soviet threat receding, the Gulf War demonstrated the importance of maintaining a robust military space capability. As James Clay Moltz notes, the benefits of space support, particularly in the field of GPS precision targeting, "only further increased the military support value of space and the continued importance of [outer space legal rights such as the] rights of safe passage and noninterference."[175]

The Republican Administrations of President Reagan and President Bush 41 oversaw a turning point in the realm of American space policy. Ford and, subsequently, Carter had flirted with the idea of space weaponization via their ASAT development policies, all the while insisting upon their commitment to President Eisenhower's seemingly inviolate policy against space weaponization. President Reagan, however, openly rejected Eisenhower's policy, making

171 Lambakis, "Space Control in Desert Storm and Beyond," *Orbis*, 419.

172 Bruger, "Not Ready for the First Space War," 73 (citing Covault, "Desert Storm Reinforces Military Space Direction," *Aviation Week & Space Technology*, 4).

173 Burgess, "Satellites' Gaze Provides New Look at War," *Washington Post*.

174 Dolman, *Astropolitik*, 150.

175 Moltz, *Politics of Space Security*, 223–24.

the development and even the deployment of outer space weapons an explicit part of his NSDD 42 National Space Policy. While Reagan's later National Space Policy, shortly thereafter republished by President Bush 41 in a largely similar form, was toned down from NSDD 42's hardline, "America First" policies and goals, for all practical purposes military space-related operations were slated to continue just as they had under Reagan's original policy. President Bush would reap the benefits of these policies with the successful application of space assets in the support of Operation Desert Storm. Although the United States' victory over Iraq would not be enough to win President Bush a second term of office, it would change the course of warfare by unequivocally demonstrating the profound benefits space support could provide to the United States'—or any other nation's—military operations.

3.6 *President William J. "Bill" Clinton (1993–2001)*

President Bill Clinton, entering office in the aftermath of the Cold War and presiding over a period of relative peace and economic prosperity in the United States, would build on the softened tone of the late Reagan and Bush 41 space policies and deemphasize American space militarization to an even greater degree. Indeed, the Clinton Administration, believing that the Reagan/Bush push toward space weapons was a "move[] in the wrong direction," "sought to downgrade the link between national security and civilian space."[176] With the Soviet Union dissolved, the United States was now the world's unrivaled—indeed, to some degree, sole—space power. But space would have to wait. In the aftermath of the Soviet Union's collapse, a host of new problems required the United States' attention: proliferation of arms and certain dangerous technologies (for example, nuclear weapons and information related to their construction and use) from former Soviet satellite nations, and the newly created Russian Federation itself, had to be combatted; issues of international trade had to be addressed; and new enemies, such as the genocidal Serbian nationalist Slobodan Milošević, had to be confronted. Ironically, with respect to space, one of the primary space security issues during the last year of the Bush 41 Administration and the early years of the Clinton Administration was *assisting* the Russians with the remnants of their space program in an attempt to prevent the proliferation of critical technologies—particularly rocket-related technologies, which could be used for the development of ballistic missiles. It would be nearly halfway through his presidency before President Clinton would release his own National Space Policy. Despite more conciliatory, facially

176 Moltz, *Politics of Space Security*, 235.

internationalist language than the policies of his predecessors, from a practical perspective, Clinton's policy would alter very little within the framework of US space policy created under the Reagan Administration.

President Clinton's National Space Policy, PDD/NSC-49, was signed in September 1996. Among its first notable changes from the policies of Reagan and Bush were PDD/NSC-49's altered goals for the US space program. These goals deemphasized national security (by moving it into the second-tier slot in the list of objectives), emphasized the non-military benefits of outer space, and encouraged private sector investment. America's space goals, as described by PDD/NSC-49 were to:

(a) Enhance knowledge of the Earth, the solar system and the universe through human and robotic exploration;
(b) Strengthen and maintain the national security of the United States;
(c) Enhance the economic competitiveness and scientific and technical capabilities of the United States;
(d) Encourage State, local and private sector investment in, and use of, space technologies;
(e) Promote international cooperation to further U.S. domestic, national security and foreign policies.[177]

What is especially interesting about the new first-tier goal of US space program is its entirely novel focus on the collection of information for the enhancement of knowledge. Unlike the Reagan/Bush policies or even Carter's PD/NSC-37, there were no references (oblique or otherwise) to the "benefits" to be gained from this knowledge or to using this information to "advance the interests" of the United States. PDD/NSC-49, perhaps reflecting the peaceful, unipolar moment of its publication, seemed to focus on knowledge for knowledge's sake.

But if the goals of the US space program had changed to reflect the less bellicose mores of a post-Cold War world, the practical applications of space technology and the focus on natural security inherent in the military and foreign intelligence facets of the space program remained largely the same. PDD/NSC-49, like the National Space Policies of the previous three presidential administrations, was blunt about the fact that "[t]he United States [would] conduct those space activities necessary for national security,"[178] and, as has

177 Office of the Press Secretary, "PDD/NSC-49 Fact Sheet National Space Policy," Sept. 19, 1996, at 1, available at https://aerospace.csis.org/wp-content/uploads/2019/02/NSC-49-Clinton-US-National-Space-Policy.pdf (last visited Apr. 9, 2020). Note that this unclassified Fact Sheet is not the complete text of PDD/NSC-49, the full text of which remains classified.

178 "PDD/NSC-49 Fact Sheet National Space Policy," 4.

been previously discussed, continued to maintain that "peaceful" uses of outer space included "defense and intelligence-related activities in pursuit of national security and other goals."[179] In fact, the list of desired contributions to America's national defense by "[n]ational security space activities" was even *more* extensive than those of Reagan's NSDD 293 and Bush 41's NSD 30. In full, these contributions included:

(a) providing support for the United States' inherent right of self-defense and our defense commitments to allies and friends;
(b) deterring, warning, and, if necessary, defending against enemy attack;
(c) assuring that hostile forces cannot prevent our own use of space;
(d) countering, if necessary, space systems and services used for hostile purposes;
(e) enhancing operations of U.S. and allied forces;
(f) ensuring our ability to conduct military and intelligence space-related activities;
(g) satisfying military and intelligence requirements during peace and crisis as well as through all levels of conflict;
(h) supporting the activities of national policy makers, the intelligence community, the National Command Authorities, combatant commanders and military services, other federal officials, and continuity of government operations.[180]

While references to space weapons were nowhere to be found in PDD/NSC-49 and their development seems to be discouraged, whether or not President Clinton's policy actually prohibited the development of such weaponry was unclear. Indeed, PDD/NSC-49 echoed the Reagan/Bush military space policy when it explicitly referenced the key missions the military space program was expected to undertake: "DoD shall maintain the capability to execute the mission areas of space support, force enhancement, space control, and force application."[181] While the unclassified Fact Sheet for PDD/NSC-49 does not provide a definition of "force application," it does, perhaps surprisingly, provide a description of "space control":

> Consistent with treaty obligations, the United States will develop, operate and maintain space control capabilities to ensure freedom of action

179 "PDD/NSC-49 Fact Sheet National Space Policy," 1.
180 "PDD/NSC-49 Fact Sheet National Space Policy," 5.
181 "PDD/NSC-49 Fact Sheet National Space Policy," 5.

> in space and, if directed, deny such freedom of action to adversaries. These capabilities may also be enhanced by diplomatic, legal or military measures to preclude an adversary's hostile use of space systems and services.[182]

PDD/NSC-49's retention of all four primary military space missions from Reagan's NSDD 293 and Bush 41's NSD 30, along with its similar (possibly expanded) description of space control and correspondingly similar sections related to support and force enhancement, seems to indicate that Clinton's space policy was not, from a military perspective, significantly different from those of his predecessors.

3.7 *President George W. Bush* (*2001–2009*)[183]

President George W. Bush's presidency was largely defined by the terrorist attacks of September 11, 2001, the ensuing invasion of Afghanistan and beginning of the "Global War on Terror," and the war in Iraq. Less well-known, but, perhaps in the long run, no less significant, was the shift in American outer space policy that occurred during his Presidency. In the decade prior to the 9/11 attacks, the implosion of the Soviet Union and the struggles of the Russian space program in the economically decrepit Russian Federation had inaugurated an age in which the United States was the world's preeminent space power. Far from reassuring some policy-makers and strategic thinkers, however, the United States' primacy in outer space caused new concerns. Given the significant national security applications of US outer space assets (which had been demonstrated to great effect during the 1991 Gulf War), and considering the fact that other nations, as well as both international and domestic private corporations, sought their own access to outer space for national or commercial purposes, some believed it was only a matter of time before the United States was challenged in outer space.

In response to this concern, Congress, in the National Defense Authorization Act for Fiscal Year 2000, authorized the establishment of the Commission to Assess United States National Security Space Management and Organization (the Rumsfeld Space Commission) to investigate various aspects of "the

182 "PDD/NSC-49 Fact Sheet National Space Policy," 6.

183 The sub-sections on Presidents George W. Bush, Barack Obama, and Donald J. Trump have been largely drawn from my previous work, "Grounding the Humā: The Legality of Space Denial and (Potential) American Interference in the Iranian Space Program," which was published in the *Air Force Law Review* in January 2021. *See* Grunert, "Grounding the Humā," *Air Force Law Review*.

organization and management of space activities that support U.S. national security interests."[184] Chaired by soon-to-be Defense Secretary Donald H. Rumsfeld, the Commission published its report in early 2001. Echoing the assessment of military Cassandras dating back to Generals Schriever and Gavin nearly half a century earlier, the Commission believed conflict in outer space was inevitable.[185] The report ominously warned of a "Space Pearl Harbor"—a catastrophic attack on American space assets that would devastate commercial, military, and intelligence activities reliant on space-based platforms.[186] In order to preempt threats to or from space, the Commission recommended the creation of a "national-level" policy establishing "space activity as a fundamental national interest of the United States," the development and deployment of "systems in space to deter attack on and … defend" American interests in space (a euphemistic description of space weaponry), and a number of organizational and structural changes within the Armed Services to better facilitate space security.[187]

Had the Commission been chaired by just about anyone else, it is possible that its final report and recommendations would largely have fallen through the cracks of an American defense establishment thrown onto its back foot by the 9/11 attacks and gearing up for a fight against an enemy (the Afghan Taliban) that barely fielded an air force, much less a space program. (Indeed, the 9/11 attacks were not inconsequential for space security matters: in the organizational shake-up that followed the attacks, the military established United States Northern Command (USNORTHCOM) to focus on homeland protection, while USSPACECOM was disestablished and its duties transferred to US Strategic Command (USSTRATCOM)).[188] With Donald Rumsfeld at the head of the Defense Department, however, the Commission's recommendations influenced American military policy at the highest levels. As Dr. Joan

184 Commission to Assess United States National Security Space Management and Organization, *Report of the Commission to Assess United States National Security Space Management and Organization* (Washington, D.C.: Jan. 11, 2001) 1–2 [hereinafter Rumsfeld Commission Report].

185 "[W]e know from history," the Commission Report states in its concluding paragraphs, "that every medium—air, land, and sea—has seen conflict. Reality indicates that space will be no different." *Rumsfeld Commission Report*, 100.

186 *Rumsfeld Commission Report*, 23.

187 *Rumsfeld Commission Report*, Executive Summary, xxx. It should be noted that while, as we have seen throughout this Chapter, there were at least seven official national space policies published prior to the Commission's report, none of these classified space activity as a "vital" or "fundamental" interest of the United States.

188 Drea et al., *supra* note 141 64–65, 86.

Johnson-Freese notes, the Rumsfeld Space Commission report "became the basis for US space policy."[189] Within the Department of Defense during this time, "[s]pace dominance rhetoric prevailed" and "[could] be traced through a series of [official policy] documents."[190] In August 2002, for instance, the Joint Chiefs of Staff released Joint Publication 3–14, *Joint Doctrine for Space Operations*, which emphasized a number of concepts, such as "space superiority" and "space control,"[191] that built upon the Rumsfeld Space Commission's national security concepts.

It should also be noted that the September 11, 2001, terrorist attacks resulted in another development that would carry space-related repercussions: the death of the 1972 Anti-Ballistic Missile Treaty. In the wake of the attacks, President Bush "concluded the ABM treaty hinder[ed] [the United States] government's ways to protect [its] people from future terrorist or rogue state missile attacks" and initiated the six-month withdrawal procedures provided for under the treaty.[192] Both Russia and China opposed the decision, warning that

---

189 Joan Johnson-Freese, *Space Warfare in the 21st Century: Arming the Heavens* (Abingdon, UK: Routledge, 2017), 58.

190 Johnson-Freese, *Space Warfare in the 21st Century*, 9.

191 "Space superiority" was defined in joint doctrine as "[t]he degree of dominance in space of one force over another that permits the conduct of operations by the former and its related land, sea, air, space, and special operations forces at a given time and place without prohibitive interference by the opposing force." U.S. Department of Defense, Joint Chiefs of Staff, Joint Publication 3–14, "Joint Doctrine for Space Operations," GL-6 (Aug. 9, 2002) [hereinafter JP 3–14 2002]. "Space control" was then defined as "Combat, combat support, and combat service support operations to ensure freedom of action in space for the United States and its allies and, when directed, deny an adversary freedom of action in space. The space control mission area includes: surveillance of space; protection of US and friendly space systems; prevention of an adversary's ability to use space systems and services for purposes hostile to US national security interests; negation of space systems and services used for purposes hostile to US national security interests; and directly supporting battle management, command, control, communications, and intelligence." JP 3–14 2002, GL-6. JP 3–14 has undergone multiple revisions since then, which simplify these definitions but retain the same sense. The current definition of "space superiority" is "[t]he degree of control in space of one force over any others that permits the conduct of its operations at a given time and place without prohibitive interference from terrestrial or space-based threats." U.S. Department of Defense, Joint Chiefs of Staff, Joint Publication 3–14, "Space Operations," GL-6 (Apr. 10, 2018) [hereinafter JP 3–14 2018]. The current definition of "space control" is "Operations to ensure freedom of action in space for the United States and its allies and deny an adversary freedom of action in space." JP 3–14 2018, GL-6.

192 Terence Neilan, "Bush Pulls Out of ABM Treaty; Putin Calls Move a Mistake," *New York Times*, Dec. 13, 2001, https://www.nytimes.com/2001/12/13/international/bush-pulls-out-of-abm-treaty-putin-calls-move-a-mistake.html.

US withdrawal could lead to a renewed international arms race[193]—a warning that was echoed by others, including certain experts who believed the ABM Treaty's demise would lead to renewed militarization of outer space. How the United States' withdrawal from the ABM Treaty affected the outer space environment is hotly debated. Some have argued that the ABM Treaty had "not helped to avert an arms race in outer space" even when it was active, and, thus, that the United States' withdrawal (while unwise) ultimately had *no* effect on outer space militarization or conflict.[194] Others insist the United States sought to eliminate "legal obstacles in developing strategic weapon systems, in particular space-based devices critical to its National Missile Defense program, and American space superiority"—meaning that the ABM Treaty's demise is, perhaps, among the most significant factors contributing to outer space weaponization in the early 20th century.[195] While it is certainly true that the ABM Treaty did not explicitly prohibit the development or stationing of outer space weapons, its likely prohibition on space-based anti-ballistic missile systems (such as President Reagan's Strategic Defense Initiative) can be interpreted as having a deterrent effect on space weaponization by reducing the perception of potential US competitors such as Russia and China that they need to develop space-based weapons to counter such a system. In this sense, it is likely that the United States' withdrawal from the ABM Treaty has, to at least some degree, resulted in increased perceptions by US competitors that space weapons development is necessary to prepare for any potential space-based anti-ballistic missile system the United States might develop in the future.

In August 2006, the Bush Administration released its official National Space Policy (NSP).[196] Consistent with Secretary Rumsfeld's and the Armed Forces' emphasis on the significance of outer space for national security, the NSP struck a nationalistic tone. Chief among the NSP's key principles was that "the

---

193 Neilan, "Bush Pulls Out of ABM Treaty."

194 Wulf von Kries, "The demise of the ABM Treaty and the militarization of outer space," *Space Policy*, 18 (2002), 177. Von Kries argues that, while the ABM Treaty was useful as an instrument for regulating terrestrial anti-ballistic missile systems, the Treaty "not only left the door wide open to ASAT development, testing and deployment; it also confirmed, by virtue of its non-interference clause, the acceptance of the principle and practice of satellite reconnaissance." Von Kries, "The demise of the ABM Treaty," 177.

195 Jackson Nyamuya Maogoto and Steven Freeland, "Space Weaponization and the United Nations Charter Regime on Force: A Thick Legal Fog or a Receding Mist?," *The International Lawyer*, vol. 41, no. 4 (Winter 2007), 1092.

196 United States, NSPD-49, "U.S. National Space Policy," Aug. 31, 2006, https://fas.org/irp/offdocs/nspd/space.pdf.

United States considers space capabilities … vital to its national interests."[197] On this basis, America would:

> preserve its rights, capabilities, and freedom of action in space; dissuade or deter others from either impeding those rights or developing capabilities intended to do so; take those actions necessary to protect its space capabilities; respond to interference; and deny, if necessary, adversaries the use of space capabilities hostile to U.S. national interests.[198]

Further, the NSP interpreted the Outer Space Treaty's "peaceful purposes" language, as we have seen in Chapter 2, above, to "allow U.S. defense and intelligence-related activities in pursuit of national interests" and soundly "reject[ed] any limitations on the fundamental right of the United States to operate in and acquire data from space."[199] Indeed, the Bush Administration explicitly "oppose[d] the development of new legal regimes or other restrictions that [sought] to prohibit or limit U.S. access to or use of space."[200] With the publication of the NSP, the Bush Administration had fully realized one of the primary recommendations of the Rumsfeld Space Commission and made its other underlying goals the United States' national policy. The 2006 NSP made official a shift in American outer space policy from caution and international regulation (a policy regime that had been viewed as largely necessary during the Cold War to prevent a dangerous and expensive arms race with the Soviet Union in outer space) to one of American supremacy and "space nationalism."

3.8 *President Barack Obama (2009–2017)*

The election of President Barack Obama in 2008 seemed as though it might bring about a return to more traditional American attitudes in the realm of outer space policy. While he had not focused much on space during his election campaign,[201] Obama's attitude toward international law and partnerships provided a basis for expectations of such a realignment. It would be a year and half after President Obama's inauguration, in June 2010, that the Obama Administration released its own National Space Policy (the Obama NSP). True to form, the Obama NSP struck a more internationalist tone than that of the

197 NSPD-49, para. 2.
198 NSPD-49, para. 2.
199 NSPD-49, para. 2.
200 NSPD-49, para. 2.
201 *See* Moltz, *Politics of Space Security*, 308.

Bush Administration. "It is the shared interest of all nations," begins the NSP's first listed principle, "to act responsibly in space to help prevent mishaps, misperceptions, and mistrust."[202] In a similar vein, the Obama NSP, echoing the Outer Space Treaty, reiterates that "[a]ll nations have the right to explore and use space for peaceful purposes, and for the benefit of all humanity, in accordance with international law."[203] The NSP also contains an entire subsection on "International Cooperation," which includes instructions for US departments and agencies to "[d]emonstrate U.S. leadership in space-related fora and activities" (presumably a reference to international bodies like COPUOS) and calls for the development of both bi- and multi-lateral "transparency and confidence-building measures" in order to "encourage responsible actions in, and the peaceful use of, space."[204]

Despite its conciliatory, internationalist tone, whether the Obama NSP is truly a departure from the space policies of the Bush Administration is hotly debated. Expanding on the Bush-era policy, Obama's NSP explicitly identifies "the sustainability, stability, and free access to, and use of, space" as vital national interests of the United States.[205] The Obama NSP also echoes the previous Bush NSP's characterization of the Outer Space Treaty's "peaceful purposes" language, declaring that the use of space "for national and homeland security activities" falls within the lawful umbrella of "peaceful purposes."[206] But it is in a subsection entitled "National Security Space Guidelines" that the similarities are most notable. In this section, the Secretary of Defense and the Director of National Intelligence are instructed to (1) "[d]evelop, acquire, and operate space systems and supporting information systems and networks to support U.S. national security and enable defense and intelligence operations during times of peace, crisis, and conflict;" (2) "[e]nsure cost-effective survivability of space capabilities ...;" (3) "[i]mprove, develop, and demonstrate ... the ability to rapidly detect, warn, characterize, and attribute natural and man-made disturbances to space systems of U.S. interest;" and, perhaps most significantly of all, (4) "[d]evelop and apply advanced technologies and capabilities that respond to changes to the threat environment."[207] These instructions seem to anticipate both defensive and offensive requirements for

202 United States, "National Space Policy of the United States of America," June 28, 2010, 3 (hereinafter, "2010 NSP").

203 2010 NSP, 3.

204 2010 NSP, 6, 7.

205 2010 NSP, 3.

206 2010 NSP, 3.

207 2010 NSP, 13–14.

outer space-related national defense policy. Such instructions would not be out of place in the Bush Administration's NSP, or as recommendations in the Rumsfeld Space Commission report.

Finally, the Obama NSP contains a concept wholly absent from the previous Bush Administration policy: the idea of "responsibility" in outer space.[208] While this may be no more than a linguistic descriptor, the terms "responsible" and "responsibility" occur with such frequency in the Obama NSP that to consider their use unintended or inconsequential seems unlikely. Indeed, the NSP contains a number of directives emphasizing the importance of the concept. The United States, for instance, "will employ a variety of measures to help assure the use of space for all *responsible parties*," will promote space stability via "domestic and international measures to promote safe and *responsible* operations in space," and will "[l]ead in the enhancement of security, stability, and *responsible* behavior in space" (emphases added).[209] Conversely, the United States frowns upon irresponsible behavior in outer space: "[t]he now-ubiquitous and interconnected nature of space capabilities and the world's growing dependence on them mean that *irresponsible acts* in space can have damaging consequences for all of us" (emphasis added).[210] Although nowhere in the NSP does the Obama Administration elaborate on how such "irresponsible acts" will be dealt with, the implication seems to be that the United States may take undefined steps to discourage irresponsible parties from accessing, or irresponsible acts from occurring in, outer space.

Following up on the Obama Administration's release of the NSP, the Department of Defense and Office of the Director of National Intelligence released the National Security Space Strategy (NSSS) in January 2011.[211] The NSSS builds upon the Obama NSP from the standpoint of national defense, stating that American "national security objectives" rely on a number of strategies, including "[p]romot[ing] responsible, peaceful, and safe use[s] of space;" "[p]revent[ing] and deter[ring] aggression against space infrastructure that supports U.S. national security," and "[p]repar[ing] to defeat attacks and to operate in a degraded environment."[212] The NSSS further echoes the NSP, including its emphasis on "responsibility," in its Strategic Objectives:

---

208 Note that this is a very different concept than the international law concept of "international responsibility" cited in the Outer Space Treaty. In the Obama NSP, "responsibility" refers to the dictionary definition of the word—that is, that States' actions in outer space be trustworthy, good, moral, and taken with due care.

209 2010 NSP, 3, 4, and 6.

210 2010 NSP, 1.

211 "2011 National Security Space Strategy."

212 "2011 National Security Space Strategy," 5.

> We seek a safe space environment in which all can operate with minimal risk of accidents, breakups, and purposeful interference. We seek a stable space environment in which nations exercise shared responsibility to act as stewards of the space domain and follow norms of behavior. We seek a secure space environment in which responsible nations have access to space and the benefits of space operations without need to exercise their inherent right of self-defense.[213]

Again, despite references to international cooperation (a "safe space environment in which all can operate" and a "stable space environment in which nations exercise shared responsibility"), the caveat in the final sentence of the above paragraph regarding "responsible nations" seems to imply that there exists a subset of "irresponsible" nations which the United States would *not* want to "have access to space and the benefits of space operations." This point, of course, is unstated, and the NSSS goes to great lengths—even in the sections concerning "Preventing and Deterring Aggression against Space Infrastructure" and "Preparing to Defeat Attacks and Operate in a Degraded Environment"—to avoid any direct references to the development of space-based weapons systems or offensive capabilities in outer space.[214] Instead, the NSSS simply reiterates the United States' standard declaration that it "will retain the right and capabilities to respond in self-defense" to any attack.[215]

3.9 *President Donald Trump (2017–2021)*

The wild-card election of President Donald Trump in November 2016 initially raised questions about the direction in which American space policy would turn—and, indeed, whether the new President would even make space activities a priority during his presidency at all. On the one hand, in the run-up to the 2016 election, Candidate Trump had deemphasized American space activities (or, at least, civilian space activities) multiple times.[216] On the other hand, at a campaign stop in Florida just two weeks before the November 8 Presidential Election, Candidate Trump seemed to have altered his views. Critiquing the

---

213 "2011 National Security Space Strategy," 4.
214 See "2011 National Security Space Strategy," 10–11.
215 "2011 National Security Space Strategy," 10.
216 In one instance, Trump responded to a question about NASA from a 10-year-old boy by stating, "Right now, we have bigger problems [than NASA.] We've got to fix our potholes. You know, we don't exactly have a lot of money." Jenna Johnson, "Donald Trump tells 10-year-old that 'space is terrific' but potholes are more important," *Washington Post*, Nov. 11, 2015, https://www.washingtonpost.com/news/post-politics/wp/2015/11/11/donald-trump-tells-10-year-old-that-space-is-terrific-but-potholes-are-more-important/.

Obama Administration for having "undermined [the] space program tremendously," Trump claimed that, if elected President, his space policies would "substantially expand public private partnerships to maximize the amount of investment and funding that is available for space exploration and development."[217] Even more ambitiously, Trump stated he would "free NASA from the restriction of serving primarily as a logistics agency for low earth orbit activity …. Instead we will refocus its mission on space exploration."[218] In the national security realm, Trump policy advisors Robert Walker and Peter Navarro insisted Trump's space security policies would focus on "reduc[ing] our current vulnerabilities and assur[ing] that our military commands have the space tools they need for their missions," developing "emerging technologies that have the potential to revolutionize warfare," and encouraging more extensive military partnerships with the space private sector, which "will reduce costs while accessing new advances on a timeline significantly quicker than current, outdated military procurement procedures."[219]

After his inauguration, President Trump initially moved slowly in the realm of space policy. Five months after his inauguration, he issued an Executive Order to reconstitute the National Space Council (an Executive Branch council, chaired by the Vice President, meant to advise the President on outer space policy and strategy),[220] but, for the bulk of his presidency, President Trump largely operated under the National Space Policy that had been previously issued by the Obama Administration. President Trump's National Space Policy would not be published until the waning day of his Administration; rather than establish his own comprehensive NSP early on, President Trump would issue space policy guidance in the form of a brief "National Space Strategy" and a number of "Space Policy Directives" (SPDs).[221] SPD-1, for example, indicated

217 Marcia Smith, "Trump: 'I Will Free NASA' From Being Just a LEO Space Logistics Agency," *Space Policy Online*, Oct. 25, 2016, https://spacepolicyonline.com/news/trump-i-will-free-nasa-from-being-just-a-leo-space-logistics-agency/#.WA_vvNbDfd8.twitter.

218 Smith, "Trump: 'I Will Free NASA' From Being Just a LEO Space Logistics Agency."

219 Robert S. Walker and Peter Navarro, "Op-ed | Donald Trump's 'peace through strength' space vision," *Space News*, Oct. 24, 2016, https://spacenews.com/op-ed-donald-trumps-peace-through-strength-space-doctrine/.

220 President Donald J. Trump, "Presidential Executive Order on Reviving the National Space Council," WhiteHouse.gov, June 30, 2017, https://trumpwhitehouse.archives.gov/presidential-actions/presidential-executive-order-reviving-national-space-council/.

221 *See* U.S. Office of Space Commerce, "Space Policies," https://www.space.commerce.gov/policy/ (last visited Sept. 17, 2021).

the Trump Administration's early adoption of the overarching policies of the Obama Administration by amending a single paragraph from the 2010 NSP.[222]

Of the six additional SPDs President Trump promulgated during his time in office, five were largely subject-matter specific policies. SPD-2, "Streamlining Regulations on Commercial Use of Space," focused (as its name suggests) on streamlining licensing regulations for private space operations, as well as revising regulations related to commercial remote sensing and radio frequency spectrum use in ways more conducive to private enterprises.[223] With the goal of "creating the conditions for a safe, stable, and operationally sustainable space environment," SPD-3, "National Space Traffic Management Policy," elaborated on policies to increase the United States' ability to track and share data about objects in outer space.[224] SPD-5, "Cybersecurity Principles for Space Systems," encouraged space system operators to develop more robust cybersecurity systems for their space objects to "mitigate evolving malicious cyber activities."[225] SPD-6, "National Strategy for Space Nuclear Power and Propulsion," took up the issue of nuclear energy as a means of propulsion for space vehicles—ultimately elaborating an American goal of developing and using safe, sustainable nuclear technology to power future space missions.[226] Finally, SPD-7, "The United States Space-Based Positioning, Navigation, and Timing Policy," which was issued by President Trump just five days prior to leaving office, directs continued "sustainment and modernization" of the

222 President Donald J. Trump, "Presidential Memorandum on Reinvigorating America's Human Space Exploration Program," WhiteHouse.gov, Dec. 11, 2017, https://trumpwhitehouse.archives.gov//presidential-actions/presidential-memorandum-reinvigorating-americas-human-space-exploration-program/.

223 President Donald J. Trump, "Space Policy Directive-2, Streamlining Regulations on Commercial Use of Space," Trump White House Archives, May 24, 2018, https://trumpwhitehouse.archives.gov/presidential-actions/space-policy-directive-2-streamlining-regulations-commercial-use-space/.

224 President Donald J. Trump, "Space Policy Directive-3, National Space Traffic Management Policy," Trump White House Archives, Jun. 18, 2018, https://trumpwhitehouse.archives.gov/presidential-actions/space-policy-directive-3-national-space-traffic-management-policy/.

225 President Donald J. Trump, "Memorandum on Space Policy Directive-5—Cybersecurity Principles for Space Systems," Trump White House Archives, Sept. 4, 2020, https://trumpwhitehouse.archives.gov/presidential-actions/memorandum-space-policy-directive-5-cybersecurity-principles-space-systems/.

226 President Donald J. Trump, "Memorandum on the National Strategy for Space Nuclear Power and Propulsion (Space Policy Directive-6)," Trump White House Archives, Dec. 16, 2020, https://trumpwhitehouse.archives.gov/presidential-actions/memorandum-national-strategy-space-nuclear-power-propulsion-space-policy-directive-6/.

United States' Global Positioning System and the development of capabilities to protect GPS assets from interference.[227]

From a national security perspective, however, the most significant space policies of the Trump Administration can be found in the "National Space Strategy," in a December 2018 memorandum directing the resurrection of US Space Command, and in SPD-4, which ultimately led to the creation of the United States Space Force (USSF). More so than either the Bush or Obama Administrations' National Space Policies, or, indeed, the 2011 National Security Space Strategy issued by the Department of Defense and the Office of the Director of National Intelligence (see above), President Trump's National Space Strategy orients US national security in outer space firmly in a nationalistic and competitive direction. The Strategy emphasizes the principles of "America First Among the Stars" (a more intergalactic application of President Trump's "America First" perspective) and "Space Preeminence Through the American Spirit."[228] Even more significant, the Strategy "recognizes that [America's] competitors and adversaries have turned space into a warfighting domain," and that the United States will "emphasize peace through strength" and "seek to deter, counter, and defeat threats in the space domain that are hostile to the national interests of the United States and our allies."[229] While the National Space Strategy's four "pillars"—(1) "[t]ransform[ing] to more resilient space architectures," (2) "[s]trengthen[ing] deterrence and warfighting options," (3) "[i]mprov[ing] foundational capabilities, structures, and processes," and (4) "[f]oster[ing] conducive domestic and international environments"—are not a far cry from the strategies described in previous administrations' NSPs,[230] the nationalistic and bellicose undertones of the rest of the Strategy demonstrate an overt acceptance of outer space as a zone of conflict and competition that previous administrations had avoided.

---

227 President Donald J. Trump, "Memorandum on Space Policy Directive 7," Trump White House Archives, Jan. 15, 2021, https://trumpwhitehouse.archives.gov/presidential-actions/memorandum-space-policy-directive-7/.

228 "President Donald J. Trump is Unveiling an America First National Space Strategy," *WhiteHouse.gov* (Mar. 23, 2018), https://trumpwhitehouse.archives.gov/briefings-statements/president-donald-j-trump-unveiling-america-first-national-space-strategy/.

229 "President Donald J. Trump is Unveiling an America First National Space Strategy," *WhiteHouse.gov* (Mar. 23, 2018), https://trumpwhitehouse.archives.gov/briefings-statements/president-donald-j-trump-unveiling-america-first-national-space-strategy/.

230 "President Donald J. Trump is Unveiling an America First National Space Strategy," *WhiteHouse.gov* (Mar. 23, 2018), https://trumpwhitehouse.archives.gov/briefings-statements/president-donald-j-trump-unveiling-america-first-national-space-strategy/.

Building upon the space strategy's focus on space-related national security threats, President Trump issued a memorandum to Secretary of Defense James Mattis in December 2018 directing the establishment of a new functional combatant command: United States Space Command (USSPACECOM).[231] As we have seen above, the "new" USSPACECOM would actually be a resurrection of the previous USSPACECOM, originally created during the Reagan Administration and disestablished during the Bush 43 Administration in the aftermath of the 9/11 attacks. President Trump's memorandum reversed the 2002 merger of USSPACECOM with US Strategic Command (USSTRATCOM), assigning USSPACECOM "(1) all the general responsibilities of a Unified Combatant Command; (2) the space-related responsibilities previously assigned to the Commander, United States Strategic Command; and (3) the responsibilities of Joint Force Provider and Joint Force Trainer for Space Operations Forces."[232] USSPACECOM was formally reestablished on August 29, 2019, under the command of Air Force General John Raymond.[233]

231 *See* President Donald J. Trump, "Text of a Memorandum from the President to the Secretary of Defense Regarding the Establishment of the United States Space Command," *WhiteHouse.gov* (Dec. 18, 2018), https://trumpwhitehouse.archives.gov/briefings-statements/text-memorandum-president-secretary-defense-regarding-establishment-united-states-space-command/. It should be noted that President Trump's decision to reestablish USSPACECOM was by no means a surprise. The resurrection of Space Command had been recommended in an August 2018 report on the "Organizational and Management Structure" of the DoD's outer space components, which had been directed in the previous year's National Defense Appropriations Act ("NDAA"). *See* Department of Defense, *Final Report on Organizational and Management Structure for the National Security Space Components of the Department of Defense*, Report to Congressional Defense Committees (Aug. 9, 2018), available at https://media.defense.gov/2018/Aug/09/2001952764/-1/-1/1/ORGANIZATIONAL-MANAGEMENT-STRUCTURE-DOD-NATIONAL-SECURITY-SPACE-COMPONENTS.PDF. Additionally, Congress had already been working to re-establish Space Command (though as a subordinate unified command under USSTRATCOM), and, at the time of President Trump's memorandum, had already passed legislation (the Fiscal Year 2019 NDAA) to this effect. *See* John S. McCain National Defense Authorization Act for Fiscal Year 2019, Pub. L. No. 115–232, § 1601, 132 Stat. 2101–04 (2018), https://www.congress.gov/115/plaws/publ232/PLAW-115publ232.pdf.

232 President Donald J. Trump, "Text of a Memorandum from the President to the Secretary of Defense Regarding the Establishment of the United States Space Command," *WhiteHouse.gov* (Dec. 18, 2018), https://trumpwhitehouse.archives.gov/briefings-statements/text-memorandum-president-secretary-defense-regarding-establishment-united-states-space-command/.

233 *See* Sandra Erwin, *Trump formally reestablishes U.S. Space Command at White House ceremony*, *SpaceNews.com*, Aug. 29, 2019, https://spacenews.com/usspacecom-officially-re-established-with-a-focus-on-defending-satellites-and-deterring-conflict/.

In what may be the culmination of military- and national defense-oriented thinking about outer space, President Trump's SPD-4, issued in February 2019, directed the creation of a Space Force "as a sixth branch of the United States Armed Forces within the Department of the Air Force."[234] On the basis of SPD-4, the Department of Defense developed a legislative proposal for the organization of the USSF passed by Congress as part of the National Defense Authorization Act for Fiscal Year 2020 (2020 NDAA), and signed into law by President Trump on December 20, 2019.[235] Pursuant to the 2020 NDAA, the USSF would be established within the Department of the Air Force—essentially by re-designating Air Force Space Command as the USSF and transforming it into an independent service[236]—and its duties would include: "protect the interests of the United States in space;" "deter aggression in, from, and to space"; and "conduct space operations."[237] General Raymond, already the USSPACECOM Commander, was sworn in as the USSF's first Chief of Space Operations (the senior-ranking USSF officer, who will become a member of the Joint Chiefs of Staff) on January 14, 2020.[238] Since that time, General Raymond, the USAF, and the USSF have been working to build the new service's organization and force structure, matters that were initially discussed in an early February 2020 report providing additional details regarding the new service's organization and operations, and that, as we will discuss further in Chapter 4, have continued to develop ever since.[239] While the final form, organization, and mission of the USSF continue to develop, the Trump Administration's creation of this new military branch tracks with the space nationalist viewpoint originally proposed by the Rumsfeld Space Commission report and molded in both the Bush- and Obama-era policies related to space security.

234 President Donald J. Trump, "Text of Space Policy Directive-4: Establishment of the United States Space Force," Trump White House Archives, Feb. 19, 2019, https://trumpwhitehouse.archives.gov/presidential-actions/text-space-policy-directive-4-establishment-united-states-space-force/.

235 National Defense Authorization Act for Fiscal Year 2020, S. 1790, 116th Cong. §§ 951–61 (2019), https://www.govinfo.gov/content/pkg/BILLS-116s1790enr/pdf/BILLS-116s1790enr.pdf.

236 NDAA 2020 § 952(a).

237 NDAA 2020 § 952(b)(4) (10 U.S.C. § 9081(d), amended).

238 *See* Rachel S. Cohen, "Raymond Sworn In as First Space Force Chief," *Air Force Magazine* (Jan. 14, 2020), https://www.airforcemag.com/raymond-sworn-in-as-first-space-force-chief/.

239 *See generally* U.S. Department of the Air Force, *Comprehensive Plan for the Organizational Structure of the U.S. Space Force*, Report to Congressional Committees, Feb. 2020, https://www.airforcemag.com/app/uploads/2020/02/Comprehensive-Plan-for-the-Organizational-Struccture-of-the-USSF_Feb-2020.pdf.

As noted earlier in this section, the Trump Administration operated under President Obama's previous, 2010 NSP for the majority of its time in office. It was not until December 9, 2020, during the "lame duck" period after the 2020 election, that President Trump's National Space Policy was finally released. Unlike the more nationalistic National Space Strategy, Trump's NSP is a return to the more internationally-oriented language of the Obama Administration's 2010 NSP. Like President Obama's NSP, Trump's 2020 NSP emphasizes key principles of the United States' space policy and operations consistent with international space law, including that "[a]ll nations have the right to explore and to use space for peaceful purposes and for the benefit of all humanity;" that "space systems of all nations to have the right to pass through and conduct operations in space without interference;" and that "outer space … is not subject to national appropriation by claim of sovereignty, by means of use or occupation, or by any other means."[240]

Far more surprising than the (as we have seen above) fairly standard recitation of key space law principles is a dramatic shift in President Trump's NSP from those of his predecessors in the Policy's willingness to encourage the development of standards of responsible behavior in outer space. Where President Bush had advocated freezing the existing framework of binding and non-binding international space law and President Obama had shifted his NSP's emphasis to the importance of responsible behavior in outer space operations, President Trump's 2020 NSP actually advocates the creation of new voluntary legal frameworks. The United States should, for example:

> *Lead* the enhancement of safety, stability, security, and long-term sustainability in space by *promoting a framework* for responsible behavior in outer space, including the pursuit and *effective implementation* of best practices, standards, and norms of behavior …. [emphasis added].[241]

Deeper in the NSP, the Secretary of State is directed to "[c]ooperate with like-minded international partners to establish standards of safe and responsible behavior,"[242] and, deeper still, the Policy directs the United States to "demonstrate responsible behaviors" even in its national security-related space

240 National Space Policy of the United States of America, Trump White House Archive, Dec. 9, 2020, https://trumpwhitehouse.archives.gov/wp-content/uploads/2020/12/National-Space-Policy.pdf, at 3 (hereinafter "2020 National Space Policy").

241 2020 National Space Policy, 12.

242 2020 National Space Policy, 14.

operations.[243] (As we will shortly see, the actualization of this emphasis on "responsible behaviors" would be carried over into the Biden Administration).

The 2020 National Space Policy proved to be a curious—and welcome—way for President Trump and his Administration to conclude their development of US space policy. Unlike so many of President Trump's public pronouncements, the National Space Policy is a measured policy document that contemplates the necessity of a larger, international effort on the part of the United States and its allies to create and maintain a "safe, stable, secure, and sustainable environment for space activities."[244] Its release in the waning days of the Trump Administration provided a solid framework on which the Biden Administration could build.

3.10 *President Joseph R. Biden, Jr. (2021–Present)*

When President Joseph Biden, Jr. took office on January 20, 2021, some questioned whether he would continue to support President Trump's space policies, particularly the creation of the Space Force as the sixth branch of the US Armed Forces. To date, however, there has been far more consensus between the Trump Administration and the Biden Administration on outer space issues than might have been expected. Within two weeks of his inauguration, President Biden had voiced his "full support" for the Space Force, with White House Press Secretary Jen Psaki stating unequivocally that the Biden Administration would not be "revisiting the decision to establish the Space Force."[245] The Biden Administration has also maintained support for the National Space Council,[246] reestablished by President Trump in June 2017, as well as NASA's Artemis Program—a civil space Trump Administration program aimed at returning American astronauts to the Moon by 2024.[247] Indeed, so closely have the space policies of the two Administrations aligned, that outer

243 2020 National Space Policy, 27.

244 2020 National Space Policy, 5.

245 Sandra Erwin, "White House: Space Force 'absolutely has the full support of the Biden administration,'" *Space News*, Feb. 3, 2021, https://spacenews.com/white-house-space-force-absolutely-has-the-full-support-of-the-biden-administration/.

246 Sandra Erwin, "Biden administration to continue the National Space Council," *Space News*, Mar. 29, 2021, https://spacenews.com/biden-administration-to-continue-the-national-space-council/.

247 Christian Davenport, "The Biden administration has set out to dismantle Trump's legacy, except in one area: Space," *Washington Post*, Mar. 2, 2021, https://www.washingtonpost.com/technology/2021/03/02/biden-space-artemis-moon-trump/.

space is one of the few areas in which the Biden White House is willing to recognize its general agreement with the Trump Administration.[248]

In addition to his continued support for Trump's flagship space programs, President Biden has also continued the previous Obama and Trump Administrations' push to develop a clearer framework related to responsible behavior in outer space. The Biden Administration's Secretary of Defense, Lloyd Austin, promulgated a memorandum in July 2021 establishing five tenets of responsible behavior by which Department of Defense components would need to abide in their space activities. These tenets include: (1) "Operat[ing] in, from, to, and through space with due regard to others and in a professional manner; (2) "Limit[ing] the generation of long-lived debris;" (3) "Avoid[ing] the creation of harmful interference;" (4) "Maintain[ing] safe separation and safe trajectory;" and (5) "Communicat[ing] and mak[ing] notifications to enhance the safety and stability of the [space] domain."[249]

Domestic policies like the Tenets of Responsible Behavior have been further supplemented by action on the international stage. Carrying over a pattern of support for international efforts toward establishing norms and principles of responsible behavior from the Trump Administration, the United States co-sponsored a draft resolution on responsible behavior put forward by the United Kingdom at the United Nations' First Committee in early September 2021.[250] The British proposal called for the establishment of an open-ended UN working group tasked with:

> (a) Tak[ing] stock of the existing international legal and other normative frameworks concerning threats arising from State behaviours with respect to outer space;
> (b) Consider[ing] current and future threats by States to space systems, and actions, activities and omissions that could be considered irresponsible;
> (c) Mak[ing] recommendations on possible norms, rules and principles of responsible behaviours relating to threats by States to space systems, including, as appropriate, how they would contribute to

248 C-SPAN, "White House Daily Briefing," Mar. 30, 2021, https://www.c-span.org/video/?510369-1/white-house-press-secretary-covid-19-report-lacks-crucial-data.

249 Secretary of Defense Lloyd Austin, "Memorandum: Tenets of Responsible Behavior in Space," Media.Defense.Gov, July 7, 2021, https://media.defense.gov/2021/Jul/23/2002809598/-1/-1/0/TENETS-OF-RESPONSIBLE-BEHAVIOR-IN-SPACE.PDF.

250 Theresa Hitchens, "Exclusive: UK Pushes New UN Accord On Military Space Norms," *Breaking Defense*, Sept. 13, 2021, https://breakingdefense.com/2021/09/exclusive-uk-pushes-new-un-accord-on-military-space-norms/.

the negotiation of legally binding instruments, including on the prevention of an arms race in outer space; [and,]

(d) Submit[ing] a report to the General Assembly at its seventy-eighth session[.][251]

On November 1, 2021, the US-backed British proposal was approved by the First Committee by an overwhelming margin—163 votes in favor, against eight votes against and nine abstentions—and, at the time of this writing, is likely to be approved in a vote of the full General Assembly later this year. This international effort by the United Kingdom, the United States, and a number of their Western allies is indicative of the wider international support for clearer principles of responsible behavior in space—the development of which the United States intends to continue to lead.

The Biden Administration's early successes in outer space, particularly with respect to the further development of norms of responsible behavior, have not been without challenges. The United States' international competitors have continued to oppose American efforts to solidify norms of space behavior. Both the Russian Federation and the Peoples' Republic of China voted against the United Kingdom's UN proposal for the establishment of the open-ended working group on responsible behavior in outer space. Given the requirement that the working group operate on the basis of consensus, it remains unclear whether continued opposition by Russia and China will stymy the group's operations, similar to the ways in which previous lack of consensus has obstructed progress on space-related issues at the UN Conference on Disarmament or, looking back even further, COPUOS during its early years of Soviet non-cooperation.

Perhaps even more significant than political maneuvering at the United Nations, on November 15, 2021, the Russian Federation conducted a direct-ascent, kinetic-kill ASAT test, destroying COSMOS 1408, a defunct Russian electronic/signals intelligence satellite.[252] The Russian ASAT test created over

251 "Agenda item 98 (d) Prevention of an arms race in outer space: reducing space threats through norms, rules and principles of responsible behaviours," U.N. General Assembly, 76th Sess., U.N. Doc. A/C.1/76/L.52, Oct. 14, 2021.

252 Antony J. Blinken, U.S. Secretary of State, "Press Statement: Russia Conducts Destructive Anti-Satellite Missile Test," U.S. Department of State, Nov. 15, 2021, available at https://www.state.gov/russia-conducts-destructive-anti-satellite-missile-test/. *See also* David Todd, "ISS alarm caused by threatening debris cloud which Russia created via an Anti-Satellite (ASAT) missile strike on dead Cosmos 1408 satellite (Updated)," *Seradata Space Intelligence*, Nov. 15, 2021, https://www.seradata.com/iss-alarm-caused-by-threatening-debris-cloud-which-russia-may-have-created-via-an-anti-satellite-asat-missile-strike-on-dead-cosmos-1408-satellite/.

1,500 new pieces of trackable space debris, and unknown amounts of smaller, un-trackable debris fragments, which, at the time of this writing, have already required the astronauts and cosmonauts on the International Space Station to activate their "safe haven" protocols under the threat of potential space debris impacts to the ISS.[253] Russia's motivations in conducting the test remain unclear, but given the ASAT test's proximity to the UN First Committee vote and the Biden Administration's stated policy goals of encouraging responsible behavior in outer space, it is difficult to interpret the test as anything other than political statement by Russia that it does not intend to comply with American and Western proposals for "responsible" behavior in outer space.

As President Biden and his Administration continue to develop American space policy and press for new and expanded legal principles governing outer space behavior on the international stage, the challenges posed by Russia, China, and other US competitors will have to be addressed. Whether these States can be convinced to adhere to standards of "responsible" behavior will almost certainly play a significant role in how the United States itself conducts its activities in outer space—and how willing the United States may be to bind itself to otherwise non-binding norms of behavior.

3.11 *US Domestic Space Legislation in the Security Context: A Brief Note*

The majority of this Chapter has addressed the United States' space policies—and, primarily, the United States' space *security* policies—largely from the perspective of the *executive* branch of the US Government. This executive perspective, derived from the statements, policy goals, strategy documents, and National Space Policies of the post-*Sputnik* American Presidential Administrations (and their principal security-oriented executive agency, the US Department of Defense) provides a critical window into the United States' overarching outlook on issues of outer space use and interpretations of key elements of the international space law regime. As we have seen, this was a legal regime that the United States played a key role in developing, and few would deny that US policy, for example President Eisenhower's stated policy goals from NSC 5520 concerning the development of "Freedom of Space" and overflight rights in the space domain, contributed to the development of international legal requirements in a significant way.

---

253 Todd, "ISS alarm caused by threatening debris cloud which Russia created via an Anti-Satellite (ASAT) missile strike on dead Cosmos 1408 satellite (Updated)," *Seradata Space Intelligence*, Nov. 15, 2021, https://www.seradata.com/iss-alarm-caused-by-threatening-debris-cloud-which-russia-may-have-created-via-an-anti-satellite-asat-missile-strike-on-dead-cosmos-1408-satellite/.

That said, the distinction between policy and law is a complicated one. This may be particularly true in the modern United States, which, while ostensibly constrained by the Constitutionally mandated "separation of powers" between the executive, legislative, and judicial branches of the US Government, has seen an increased blending of the lawmaking function between the branches—as well as within federal administrative agencies, which are sometimes posited to be a "fourth" branch of the government.[254] Given the significant role that policy plays in developing practical Government behavior and action, both within and beyond executive government agencies, some legal theorists have posited that there is no longer a meaningful difference between Government policy (as articulated primarily by the executive branch and administrative agencies, but also, to some degree, in the pronouncements of members of other branches of government) and law (which, traditionally, would be promulgated by the legislative branch and interpreted, or further expounded upon, by the judicial branch).[255] It should also be noted that the President's Constitutional role as the Commander in Chief of the Armed Forces[256] provides the US executive branch with wide-ranging authority over military activities—which, for the purposes of our present discussion, would include military space activities and may also include interpretations of how and when formal international legal

254 This viewpoint regarding administrative agencies has been advocated by any number of commentators and legal scholars, but for two examples, one earlier and one more recent, see: Kevin B. Smith and Michael J. Licari, *Public Administration: Power and Politics in the Fourth Branch of Government* (Oxford: Oxford University Press, 2006); Peter L. Strauss, "The Place of Agencies in Government: Separation of Powers and the Fourth Branch," *Columbia Law Review*, vol. 84, no. 3 (1984), pp. 574–669.

255 A fascinating discussion of the law/policy dichotomy can be found in Professor Theodore J. Lowi's keynote address to the November 2002 *Cornell Journal of Law & Public Policy* Symposium, which was later published in the journal as Theodore J. Lowi, "Law vs. Public Policy: A Critical Exploration," *Cornell Journal of Law & Public Policy*, vol. 12:493 (Summer 2003). In discussing the evolution of concepts of "law," "policy," and "administration," Lowi states "[i]n effect, "policies," defined as "expressions of state will," was essentially a definition of "policy," as a description of "what legislators do," followed by "administration" as "what governments do." As the twentieth century wore on, and governments, especially the national government, grew larger and more highly differentiated, there were two parallel developments of relevance: (1) the politics/administration dichotomy was rejected in favor of a sustained political process, a "seamless web," with law (or policy) being made at every step of the way; and (2) the law/policy divide was also erased, with the two, for all practical purposes, becoming synonymous." Lowi, "Law vs. Public Policy," *Cornell Journal of Law & Public Policy*, p. 496. While Lowi's discussion.

256 US Constitution, art. II, sec. 2 ("The President shall be Commander in Chief of the Army and Navy of the United States, and of the militia of the several States, when called into the actual service of the United States").

obligations would affect those activities—even though this authority is traditionally not thought of as "law-making" or as being legislative in nature. The extent, then, to which all of the executive policies discussed over the course of this Chapter constitute "law" in any traditional sense is extremely nebulous, though, to the extent these Presidential policies and directives have contributed to actual behavior/action by the United States in or relating to outer space, it is certainly true that they are contributing to US "state practice"—that critical component of international customary law that can, along with *opinio juris*, ultimately contribute to the creation of new legal obligations.

Part of the reason executive policy related to outer space security issues is so important in the American context is that the United States' domestic space *laws*—those legislative acts that have traversed the full federal gamut of Congressional (legislative) enactment and President (executive) approval—and *regulations*—those enactments, primarily by administrative agencies, governing practical of implementing laws or legislation—have comparatively little to say about critical space security issues or interpretations of international space law. As we have seen, the United States' inaugural space-related domestic legislation, the National Aeronautics and Space Act of 1958, stated "that it is the policy of the United States that activities in space should be devoted to peaceful purposes for the benefit of all mankind"[257] and cited the language of "peaceful" use or "peaceful purposes" several additional times in its text. A mere paragraph later in the policy and purpose section of the Act, however, Congress stated that "the general welfare and security of the United States require that adequate provision be made for aeronautical and space activities" and that "activities peculiar to or primarily associated with the development of weapons systems, military operations, or the defense of the United States ... shall be the responsibility of, and shall be directed by, the Department of Defense."[258] In other words, in almost the same breath in which Congress recognized the "peaceful purposes" principles, it was contemplating "military operations" and even the "development of weapons systems" in the space environment! Thus, while the meaning of the term "peaceful purposes" and the full extent of Congress's intent with respect to the United States' *military* space activities remained unclear, there was a decided—indeed, practically explicit—recognition that the United States would use outer space for national security and even military purposes. Whatever Congress's ultimate intent was with respect to the "peaceful purposes" versus national security distinction,

---

257 National Aeronautics & Space Act of 1958, § 102(a).

258 National Aeronautics & Space Act of 1958, § 102(b).

from a practical perspective, neither the Eisenhower Administration nor subsequent Presidential Administration were meaningfully constrained in their space military activities by the National Aeronautics and Space Act's language. The fact that Congress has not clarified its intent with respect to "peaceful" use in its subsequent amendments to the Act, nor has passed additional legislation to constrain executive or military action in this regard, is likely indicative of Congressional approval of such activity.[259] While few of the United States' subsequent domestic space laws and regulations address space security issues, or US interpretations of international space law terms like the "peaceful use"/ "peaceful purposes" language, several that have potential implications in this area are discussed below.

Much of the United States' domestic space legislation has involved commercial uses of outer space. Some of the key legislative activities involving commercial space activities include the original Commercial Space Launch Act of 1984 (Public Law 98–575) and its 1988 Amendments (Public Law 100–657),[260] the Commercial Space Act of 1998 (Public Law 105–303),[261] and the Commercial Space Launch Competitiveness Act of 2015 (Public Law 114–90)—all of which have become part of Title 51 of the United States Code, "National and Commercial Space Programs." (The National Aeronautics and Space Act, as amended in its various amendments since 1958, is also now codified in Title 51).[262] The provisions of these domestic space laws serve as expressions of the United States' obligation under Article VI of the Outer Space Treaty to authorize and continuously supervise the space activities of non-governmental entities. However, again, they offer almost no elaboration of broader security-related or military issues of outer space. The one possible, though tangential, exception to this is the provision in the comparatively recent Commercial Space Launch Competitiveness Act of 2015 that grants US citizens the right "to possess, own, transport, use, and sell" any asteroid or space resource.[263] Though this provision grants rights only for *commercial* recovery of space resources, the broader questions related to national appropriation under Article II of the Outer Space Treaty, not merely for the extracted resources but, potentially, for the area of

259 Congressional action has, in fact, tended to sanction executive branch interpretations of space security-related international law when legislation directly pertinent to space security issues—for example the 2020 National Defense Authorization Act, which created the Space Force and which we will discuss at greater length in Chapter 4—is enacted.

260 Now largely contained in 51 USC §§ 50901–50923.

261 51 USC §§ 50101–50134 (with minor amendments from original act).

262 51 USC §§ 20101–20164.

263 51 USC § 51303.

mining operations that ultimately allows such resource extraction to occur in the first place, implicate issues of State control over resource-rich areas of outer space. Such issues of State control could, ultimately, involve States' desire—or even need—to protect space mining/resource extraction operations with military force. Perhaps more significantly, the resource extraction provisions of the Commercial Space Launch Competitiveness Act of 2015 also demonstrate the United States' willingness to interpret undefined or undeveloped aspects of the Outer Space Treaty in ways that benefit its perceived national interests—just as the United States, and other States, have generally done with respect to military-oriented space issues under international space law.

An example of a set of US domestic laws *and* regulations that is more relevant to outer space military use and "peaceful purposes" issues is the International Traffic in Arms Regulations (or ITAR) regime. The ITAR regime is governed under a combination of US federal legislation, specifically 22 USC § 2778 of the Arms Export Control Act of 1976 (Public Law 94–329),[264] and Presidential Executive Order, President Obama's 2013 Executive Order 13637.[265] In brief, ITAR allows the President to control and restrict the export and import of "defense articles and defense services"—items or services the export of which to certain foreign States could be harmful to the national security interests of the United States.[266] Such designated "defense articles" and "defense services" are included on the US Munitions List, contained in 22 CFR Part 121. Among the items on the Munitions List are certain spacecraft and related outer space technologies: the List's "Category XV" describes

(a) Spacecraft, including satellites and space vehicles, whether designated developmental, experimental, research, or scientific, or having a commercial, civil, or military end-use, that:
  (1) Are specially designed to mitigate effects (e.g., scintillation) of or for detection of a nuclear detonation;
  (2) Autonomously detect and track moving ground, airborne, missile, or space objects other than celestial bodies, in real-time using imaging, infrared, radar, or laser systems;
  (3) Conduct signals intelligence (SIGINT) or measurement and signatures intelligence (MASINT);

264 22 USC § 2778.

265 Barack Obama, "Executive Order 13637—Administration of Reformed Export Controls," Mar. 8, 2013, available at https://www.govinfo.gov/content/pkg/DCPD-201300143/pdf/DCPD-201300143.pdf.

266 *See* 22 CFR § 120.1.

(4) Are specially designed to be used in a constellation or formation that when operated together, in essence or effect, form a virtual satellite (e.g., functioning as if one satellite) with the characteristics or functions of other items [described in this subparagraph (a)];
(5) Are anti-satellite or anti-spacecraft (e.g., kinetic, RF, laser, charged particle);
(6) Have space-to-ground weapons systems (e.g., kinetic or directed energy); [or]
(7) Have any of [a wide range of additionally described] electro-optical remote sensing capabilities or characteristics [...][267]

as restricted defense articles. Much has been written elsewhere on the relative wisdom and effectiveness of the ITAR regime as it applies to outer space technologies. The point here, however, is that the US Munitions List provides a window into the United States' perception of what sorts of military or defense-oriented technologies are *lawful for its own private companies or government research laboratories to develop*. To limit, or, at least, strictly control, the export of such space technologies as "anti-satellite" or "anti-spacecraft" systems of various types, or "space-to-ground weapons systems," seems to presuppose that such technologies are being—or, at least, could *lawfully* be—developed by American engineers and scientists. This at least implies that during the legislative and regulatory development of ITAR there was an understanding that a number of fairly significant military-oriented, if not outright weaponized, technologies were permissible under the United States' perceptions of international outer space law. While there is no broader discussion of space law or the "peaceful use"/"peaceful purposes" principle in the Arms Export Control Act or President Obama's Executive Order 13637, it seems that the United States' conception of the broad permissibility of military uses of outer space informed the inclusion of such wide-ranging, military-oriented space technologies on the Munitions List.

As noted at the beginning of this section, US domestic space *law* is an area that has largely shied away from direct discussion or regulation of the United States' military uses of outer space. To the extent that US law has discussed the "peaceful purposes" principles that have characterized US political leaders' (and organizations like the US Department of Defense's) consistent descriptions of American policy with respect to uses of outer space (primarily, for

267 22 CFR § 121.1, "Category XV."

example, in the National Aeronautics and Space Act of 1958), those principles remain largely undefined and have not provided meaningful restrictions on the United States' military-oriented space activities. Other US domestic space law (such as the space-related provisions and export limitations of the ITAR regime) may not explicitly discuss or reference the United States' underlying perceptions of its international space law obligations, but seem, nevertheless, to recognize and support the United States' general perception of a largely permissive military space environment and the "non-aggressive" interpretation of "peaceful use"/"peaceful purposes" that has characterized US action on military space issues since the 1960s.

4 Conclusion

The "Space Age"—generally considered to be the period of time between the Soviets' *Sputnik* launch and the present day—has seen more than its fair share of world-altering events. With the opening of outer space to human use and exploration, and the radical new possibilities that mankind's ability to access and use space created, it is little surprise that outer space and outer space security played a significant role in the relationship between the United States and the Soviet Union. This chapter has shown that the United States, or, at least, the United States military, recognized the possibilities and promises of outer space shortly after the end of World War II, but that official, national American policies with respect to the use of outer space would not be formulated until nearly a decade later. The architect of these policies was President Eisenhower, who—contrary to public perception at the time—had begun formulating United States space policy even before the *Sputnik* launch. We have seen how the Soviets' historical satellite launch spurred the Eisenhower Administration to further develop its outer space policies, ultimately resulting, on the international level, in the creation of a United Nations organization (COPUOS) meant to guide the development of international outer space policy, and, on the national level, in the production of multiple national space policy documents that would shape the framework of American space policy—and space security policy—for decades to come.

During the course of the rest of the Cold War, United States space policy would walk this dual track of national and international efforts to preserve its interests, and ensure its security, with respect to outer space. National and international activities can be seen as a spectrum—one on which American space policy has, to a significant degree, moved persistently toward the national end over time. Particularly at the very beginning of the Space Age, with President Eisenhower's and Ambassador Henry Cabot Lodge's efforts at the United Nations, American policy tilted more toward the internationalist side of the spectrum. At others times, the United States seemed to pursue both national and international tracks, in equal measure, simultaneously. This was particularly apparent during the Kennedy and Johnson Administrations, when the United States was "racing" the Soviets in outer space, with the goal of a manned Moon landing, for the purpose of reestablishing national confidence and pride, while also working toward—and achieving—international consensus on the basic legal principles that ought to govern human and State activity in outer space. By the end of the 1960s, the United States had achieved successes in both tracks: the approval and ratification of the Outer Space Treaty and the successful, manned Apollo 11 mission to the Moon. As international outer space law solidified with the approval of the additional outer space treaties (the Rescue and Return Agreement, the Liability Convention, and the Registration Convention) in the late 1960s and early 1970s, and as policies of détente with the Soviet Union began to break down during the Ford Administration, American outer space policy began to take a nationalist turn. Despite tentative efforts by later Presidents (President Carter's pursuit of an ASAT treaty, for instance, and President Obama's return to more internationalist language in his Administration's space policies), this is a trend from which the United States' space policies have not significantly deviated ever since. In this context, President Reagan's push toward the development of space weapons and more militarized uses of outer space, while certainly a significant shift from what had been "traditional" American space policy up to that point, represented the result of what until that point had been incremental shifts that had been occurring in American space policy during every presidential administration since President Eisenhower. Despite the brief lull that the end of the Cold War provided, the trend toward more nationalist space policies continued during the second Bush Administration. This trend appeared to reach its pinnacle with the Trump Administration's creation of the new United States Space Force. While President Trump's public rhetoric related to the Space Force was nationalistic and, at times, emphasized the "space dominance" theories popular among many military theorists, the underlying policy promulgated by the Trump Administration was decidedly more measured—emphasizing responsible behavior, the importance of international cooperation, and the need for a greater degree of collaboration among responsible space actors to preserve the outer space environment for productive use. Strangely, then, at the same time the United States Space Force's creation appeared to confirm critics' worst fears about the United States' intentions to weaponize and dominate outer space, the United States Government—beginning with the Obama Administration and continuing through the Trump and, now, Biden Administrations—was recognizing the dangers posed by the laissez faire space environment that had existed since the ratification of the Outer Space Treaty in 1967. This recognition has been accompanied by earnest efforts on the part of the United States to develop clearer norms and principles of responsible behavior to govern State action in outer space. During the Trump and Biden Administrations, these efforts began to bear fruit, with updated US policy documents and, even more significantly, international action aimed at the creation of such norms. The United States has been joined in this effort by a wide range of its international allies, but, with continued opposition by Russia and China—two of the most significant spacefaring States—it remains to be seen whether the United States' and its allies' efforts will ultimately be successful.

CHAPTER 4

The United States Space Force: Organization, Mission, and Legal Implications

1 Introduction

As discussed in this book's introduction and in the previous chapter, among the most significant recent developments in the United States' 21st-century space policy has been the creation of the United States Space Force. The first new military service created in the United States since the formation of the US Air Force in 1947, the Space Force was born in controversy because of its primary patron, President Donald Trump. As we learned in Chapter 1, however, President Trump was by no means a visionary with respect to a space-oriented military service: military theorists and academics, particularly at the United States' military academies and schools of higher education, had been examining the potential need for a Space Force or Space Corps[1] for almost three decades prior to President Trump's promulgation of Space Policy Directive-4. (A bibliography of publications and papers examining the need for a space-oriented military service can be found in Appendix C of this book). Indeed, the eventual language in the National Defense Appropriation Act (NDAA) of 2020 that created the Space Force was not measurably different than a similar Congressional proposal directing the creation of a "Space Corps" within the Department of the Air Force that was passed with bipartisan support in the House of Representatives and included in the House version of the 2018 NDAA.[2] While that provision was eventually pared out of the final version of

1 As previously noted in Chapter 1, the organizational difference between these two concepts within the US military system, is that a 'corps' is a subdivision of a larger organization—as the US Marine Corps is a 'service' within the Department of the Navy. A 'force' would (generally…) be an independent military branch with its own separate military Department. Until 2019, the United States Air Force, organized as an independent military branch within the Department of the Air Force, was a prime example of this concept. As we will see below, however, with the creation of the Space Force in 2019, the distinction between the 'corps' and 'force' concepts is largely immaterial, as the Space Force is largely operating within the Department of the Air Force as the Marine Corps operates in the Department of the Navy.

2 *See* H.R. 2810, 115th Cong., 1st Sess., §1601, July 6, 2017, available at https://www.congress.gov/115/bills/hr2810/BILLS-115hr2810rh.pdf. The House proposal organized the Space Force within "the executive part of the Department of the Air Force" and provided for the creation of a "Chief of Staff of the Space Corps," who would direct the operations of the Corps in

 DOI:10.1163/9789004524064_005

the 2018 NDAA, it demonstrates that the Space Force's creation was not the absurd fancy of a flippant President, but, rather, the culmination of a largely-bipartisan push for greater American action in space that preexisted President Trump's interest in establishing a new military force.

In the two years since its creation, the United States Space Force has grown well beyond the farcical organization mocked in pop-culture offerings like Netflix's *Space Force* series (in which Steve Carrell stars as a hapless Air Force General unwillingly put in charge of the new space organization). The newest military branch has developed a new rank structure, uniforms/insignia, and organizational structure, as well as wrested control of a number of space-focused military bases from the United States Air Force. This chapter will describe the current state of the Space Force, as of the beginning of 2022, starting with its legal underpinnings and then breaking down its organization and structure; its current manpower, missions, and basing elements; and its doctrine.

2 Space Policy Directive-4 and the 2020 NDAA: Creating the Space Force

Any examination of the US Space Force must begin with a discussion of the legal and policy actions underpinning its creation as an independent military service, beginning, generally speaking, with President Trump's SPD-4. President Trump's Space Policy Directive was followed by the Department of Defense proposal that eventually made its way into the 2020 NDAA. Both will be discussed below.

---

conjunction with the Secretary of the Air Force. H.R. 2810 described the duties of the Space Corps as follows:

(1) protecting the interests of the United States in space;

(2) deterring aggression in, from, and through space;

(3) providing combat-ready space forces that enable the commanders of the combatant commands to fight and win wars;

(4) organizing, training, and equipping space forces; and

(5) conducting space operations of the Space Corps under the command of the Commander of the United States Space Command.

While the House bill followed these duties with a much more detailed examination of what the Space Corps would, theoretically, do than would later be written into the 2020 NDAA creating the actual Space Force, these duties are not, as we shall see, significantly different than those which the Space Force was directed to undertake.

2.1 *Space Policy Directive-4: Directing the Creation of the Space Force*

As noted in this book's introduction, the first time most of the American public heard about President Trump's intention to create a Space Force was during the signing of SPD-3 in the summer of 2018. It would be another eight months until SPD-4, "Establishment of the United States Space Force," was promulgated by the Trump Administration and gave some semblance of (potential) structure to the new organization. Some of the SPD-4's specifications—for instance, that the Space Force be "initially placed by statute in the Department of the Air Force"—were reflected in the later NDAA legislation; others, including the establishment of a full "Department of the Space Force" on par with the other military department (the Departments of the Air Force, Army, and Navy) within the Department of Defense, have not yet come to pass.[3] Overarchingly, however, SPD-4 provided an initial model for the new Space Force on which Department of Defense policymakers and Congressional lawmakers could build.

The introduction to SPD-4 explains President Trump's rationale—which, again, was influenced by a much longer history of advocacy in favor of a space-oriented military branch—for directing the creation of the Space Force. "Space," it proclaims, "is integral to [the United States'] way of life, [] national security, and modern warfare."[4] While the United States has "historically maintained a technological advantage over … potential adversaries," advances in the capabilities of the United States' global rivals pose an increasing threat to this traditional superiority. Indeed, the United States' rivals are "actively developing ways to deny [US] use of space in a crisis or conflict."[5] In order to address this growing threat, SPD-4 directs the creation of the Space Force as the method by which the Department of Defense can "marshal its space resources to deter and counter threats in space;" "ensure unfettered access to, and freedom to operate in, space;" and "provide vital capabilities to joint and coalition forces in peacetime and across the spectrum of conflict."[6]

After extolling the importance of outer space and elaborating the threats the Trump Administration believed warrant the creation of a Space Force, Space Policy Directive-4 turns to the practical matters of definitions and legislative

3 President Donald J. Trump, "Text of Space Policy Directive-4: Establishment of the United States Space Force," *WhiteHouse.gov* (Feb. 19, 2019), https://trumpwhitehouse.archives.gov/presidential-actions/text-space-policy-directive-4-establishment-united-states-space-force/ [hereinafter "SPD-4"].

4 Trump, SPD-4, sec. 1.

5 Trump, SPD-4, sec. 1.

6 Trump, SPD-4, sec. 1.

directions. As noted at the beginning of this section, the Directive envisions the Space Force as, at least initially, a subordinate military branch within the Department of the Air Force—much like the Marine Corps, for example, is an independent military service organized under the control of the Department of the Navy. SPD-4, however, posits the eventual creation of a Department of the Space Force: a future independent military department "that will be responsible for organizing, training, and equipping the United States Space Force."[7]

The real action in SPD-4 is located in Section 3, "Legislative Proposal and Purpose." Here, President Trump specifically directs the Secretary of Defense to submit a legislative proposal to establish the Space Force "as a new armed service within the Department of the Air Force."[8] While the specifics of this legislation are not elaborated in SPD-4, the Directive does offer some guidance as to the President's underlying intentions with respect to the Space Force. The Space Force, for example, should include "both combat and combat support functions" that will "enable prompt and sustained offensive and defensive space operations, and joint operations in all domains."[9] As envisioned in SPD-4, then, the Space Force is a multipurpose service. Its operations are not confined to simply attacking the space capabilities of potential adversaries and defending US space assets from attack or interference; instead, the service's role is much broader and includes the provision of needed space services to the United States' joint military forces and allies. Additionally, President Trump details six key priorities that the Space Force must be equipped to meet, specifically:

(a) Protecting the Nation's interests in space and the peaceful use of space for all responsible actors, consistent with applicable law, including international law;
(b) Ensuring unfettered use of space for United States national security purposes, the United States economy, and United States persons, partners, and allies;
(c) Deterring aggression and defending the Nation, United States allies, and United States interests from hostile acts in and from space;
(d) Ensuring that needed space capabilities are integrated and available to all United States Combatant Commands;
(e) Projecting military power in, from, and to space in support of our Nation's interests; and

7 Trump, SPD-4, sec. 2(b).
8 Trump, SPD-4, sec. 3.
9 Trump, SPD-4, sec. 3.

(f) Developing, maintaining, and improving a community of professionals focused on the national security demands of the space domain.[10]

While these priorities heavily emphasize American space superiority—and, to many, will smack of the nationalistic space "dominance" attitudes criticized by Dr. Johnson-Freese and others—there remains a dedication to the outer space legal framework; to the concept of "responsible" use of outer space described in, for example, President Obama's 2010 National Space Policy; and to an internationalization of outer space activities involving not just the United States, but also its "partners" and "allies." Much like previous American space policies, there appears to be a balance, or, at least, a tension, in SPD-4 between the national security and military uses of outer space the United States deems to be critical to its overall security and the need to work with the international community to maintain a free and open space environment characterized by responsible behavior. Additionally, a key aspect of section 3 is the requirement for Congressional approval of the Space Force; given the necessity of Congressional funding for the new organization, the language of SPD-4 is couched in the caveat that the Space Force will be equipped to meet these priorities ... if it is, in fact, so enacted by Congress.

The remainder of SPD-4 provides general, non-specific directions concerning various aspects of the new Space Force. Tying in the initial justifications provided in the Directive's introductory section, section 4, "Scope," directs the consolidation of existing space-related military forces and space activities within the new Space Force in order to reduce bureaucracy and "minimize duplication of effort." It specifically excludes the non-military space organizations of the United States Government—the National Aeronautics and Space Administration (NASA), the National Oceanic and Atmospheric Administration (NOAA), and the National Reconnaissance Office (NRO)—from the Space Force's purview. Budgetary and leadership concerns are briefly addressed, but largely deferred to future legislative and budget proposals. Perhaps most significantly, SPD-4 describes, in a limited way, the relationship between the proposed Space Force and other military and national security organizations. Chief among these is United States Space Command (USSPACECOM), the US military combatant command focused on space-related matters President Trump had ordered be reestablished in December 2018 (see Chapter 3, above).[11] While the Space Force would have authority in the space

10 Trump, SPD-4, sec. 3.

11 *See* Chapter 3, pp. 113–115.

domain in the same way the Navy oversaw the naval domain and the Air Force the air domain, USSPACECOM would take the lead as the primary joint organization and be in charge of "lead[ing] space warfighting [for the joint force] through global space operations that may occur in the space domain, the terrestrial domains, or through the electromagnetic spectrum."[12] In times of conflict involving the need for joint force operations in, from, or to outer space, the Space Force would coordinate with USSPACECOM in the same way as its sister-services, though with broader input given its unique space-specific expertise.

Overall, President Trump's Space Policy Directive-4 provided both the underlying policy direction of the proposed US Space Force and a skeletal framework for its creation. Though key details remained to be fleshed out in the proposed legislation the Secretary of Defense was directed to provide to Congress, the SPD's proposed structure of initially organizing the Space Force under the auspices of the Department of the Air Force, with possible future expansion into its own independent Department, was one that would be followed closely in the legislative proposal eventually approved by Congress. This legislation will be examined in the following section, but it was SPD-4 that provided the Presidential direction to the Department of Defense to create the organization for which President Trump had voiced his support in June 2018. Indeed, it would be a mere ten months after SPD-4's promulgation—approximately 18 months after President Trump's initial surprise announcement concerning the Space Force during the signing of SPD-3—that President Trump would sign the National Defense Appropriation Act for 2020 and officially bring the US Space Force into being.

2.2 *NDAA 2020: The Official Birth of the Space Force*

In the wake of President Trump's SPD-4, the Department of Defense wasted little time in formulating proposals related to establishing the Space Force. By the end of February 2019, a mere nine days after SPD-4's publication, the Department of Defense had already released a 20-page strategic overview of its plans for the new service.[13] As SPD-4 had suggested, this primarily involved the initial establishment of the Space Force as a military service organized under the Department of the Air Force. The possibility of a future independent Department of the Space Force, however, was not discounted; indeed, the strategic planning document stated that "[t]he long-term vision of the DoD is

12 Trump, SPD-4, sec. 7(a).

13 U.S. Department of Defense, "United States Space Force," February 2019, available at https://media.defense.gov/2019/Mar/01/2002095012/-1/-1/1/UNITED-STATES-SPACE-FORCE-STRATEGIC-OVERVIEW.PDF.

to create a new Military Department for space."[14] The six priorities described in SPD-4 were reiterated, as was the Directive's proposal that the majority of the military's space-related activities be consolidated within the Space Force.

Despite its similarities to SPD-4, however, the Department of Defense's strategic overview offered a greater degree of detail on certain aspects of the future Space Force. In order to meet President Trump's stated priorities, for example, the overview notes that the Space Force will develop forces in a wide range of critical space-related areas. These include:

> space situational awareness; satellite operations and global, integrated, command and control of military space forces; global and theater military space operations to enable joint campaigns (to include missile warning); space support to land, air, naval, and cyber forces; spacelift and space range operations; space-based nuclear detonation detection; and prompt and sustained offensive and defensive space operations to achieve space superiority.[15]

Additionally, more specific proposals for staffing and personnel-related matters related to the Space Force's creation were proposed. Interestingly, as we shall see below, while the strategic overview foresaw the need for the Space Force to assume the functions of existing space-focused organizations within the military—most specifically Air Force Space Command, which had traditionally been the leading military space organization in areas such as space situational awareness, space support, space operations, and others—it did not specifically advocate for retrofitting these organizations into the Space Force immediately. Instead, a five-year transition period for the creation of the Space Force was proposed, during which the Secretary of Defense would work with the individual military departments to "determine which existing space forces would transfer into the Space Force" and undertake these transfers "in a manner that avoids disrupting current missions and acquisition programs or adversely impacting military and civilian personnel."[16] These sorts of inter-service transfers of, potentially, entire space-related units from existing services would be but the most extreme method of outfitting the new Space Force with missions and personnel. Other, more traditional, methods of personnel acquisition—such as direct officer commissioning from the civilian world, initial lateral entry (another method of direct hiring, somewhat similar

14 Department of Defense, "United States Space Force," 3.
15 Department of Defense, "United States Space Force," 4.
16 Department of Defense, "United States Space Force," 8.

to that in the civilian educational world), and the use of incentive pay, retention bonuses, and accession waivers to draw in both enlisted members and officers—would also be used.

While the Department of Defense's strategic overview document was neither then, nor is it now, the fixed law and policy related to the Space Force's establishment, this section opened with a brief discussion of that document to demonstrate the general thinking concerning the Space Force which would carry over into the Congressional legislation that would soon create the new service. By early June, an initial version of that legislation had been included in the Senate's initial version of the National Defense Authorization Act for 2020, which was passed by that body on June 27, 2019.[17] The House of Representatives' engrossed amendment version of the NDAA, passed by that body on September 17, 2019, likewise contained a series of provisions creating the new, space-oriented service directed by SPD-4.[18] In the House version, however, this service was referred to as the "Space Corps." While both the Senate and House versions of the legislation nestled the new space service within the Department of the Air Force, the House bill contained a greater degree of detail concerning personnel-related matters associated with the new Space Corps' acquisition of current military personnel and, comparatively, less detail than the Senate's version with respect to issues such as space acquisitions and new roles within the Department of Defense associated with the new service.[19] The differences between the House and Senate versions of the 2020 NDAA were ironed out over the following two and a half months, and the enrolled version of the bill was passed in identical form by both the House and Senate on December 17, 2019.

Ultimately, the section of the 2020 NDAA related to the Space Force, passed by Congress on December 17 and then subsequently signed into law by President Trump on December 20, 2019, can be found in Subtitle D, the

---

17 United States Senate, "Roll Call Vote 116th Congress—1st Session: On Passage of the Bill (S. 1790, As Amended," June 27, 2019, available at https://www.senate.gov/legislative/LIS/roll_call_votes/vote1161/vote_116_1_00188.htm (last visited Dec 21, 2021).

18 Congress.gov, *S.1790—National Defense Authorization Act for Fiscal Year 2020*, "Text: S.1790—116th Congress (2019–2020): Engrossed Amendment House (09/17/2019)," available at https://www.congress.gov/bill/116th-congress/senate-bill/1790/text/eah (last visited Dec. 21, 2021).

19 *See S.1790—National Defense Authorization Act for Fiscal Year 2020*, "Text: S.1790—116th Congress (2019–2020): Engrossed Amendment House (09/17/2019)," at Subtitle C, §§ 921–24.

"United States Space Force Act" (the Space Force Act).[20] The initial language of the Act both settled the issue of the name of the new service (ultimately the "Space Force" specified in SPD-4 and the Senate version of the NDAA, rather than the "Space Corps" proposed in the House version) and solved the initial problem of how best to stand up the new organization. Rather than the multi-year timeline of selective transfers proposed by the Department of Defense's strategic overview document (see above), the Act kickstarted the Space Force by simply re-designating "[t]he Air Force Space Command … as the United States Space Force."[21] While, perhaps, more prompt than the strategy proposed by the Department of Defense in its February strategic overview, this wholesale transformation of the Air Force's 35-year-old space component into the new service tracked with the Department's expectations concerning the Space Force's assumption of Air Force Space Command's duties and mission-set.

The 2020 NDAA/Space Force Act went on to describe the functions and duties of the new Space Force as follows. First, the Space Force would be "organized, trained, and equipped" to undertake two essential functions: the provision of "freedom of operation for the United States in, from, and to space," and the provision of "prompt and sustained space operations."[22] It's duties would include "protect[ing] the interests of the United States in space;" "deter[ring] aggression in, from, and to space;" and "conduct[ing] space operations."[23] These functions and duties reflected, as we have seen in the course of our discussion of American space policy in Chapter 3, the United States' traditional interests in both freedom of action in outer space and in the maintenance of a safe space environment for its operations. Both the functions and the duties described in the Space Force Act are vague—the six priorities elaborated by President Trump in SPD-4 are recognized only in broad strokes, and the more specific missions and skill-sets described in the Department of Defense's strategic overview document are wholly absent. Such lack of specific detail in Congressional legislation is not, however, uncommon; such broad descriptions leave open a wide range of action for implementation by Executive Branch agencies, such as the Department of Defense, within the intent of Congress.

The remainder of the Space Force Act within the 2020 NDAA addressed issues of service leadership, Air Force/Space Force acquisitions, and space

20 National Defense Authorization Act for Fiscal Year 2020, S. 1790, 116th Cong. §§ 951–61 (2019), available at https://www.govinfo.gov/content/pkg/BILLS-116s1790enr/pdf/BILLS-116s1790enr.pdf (last visited Dec. 21, 2021).

21 2020 NDAA § 952.

22 2020 NDAA § 952 (the newly-inserted 10 U.S.C. § 9081).

23 2020 NDAA § 952 (the newly-inserted 10 U.S.C. § 9081).

policy-related representation within the Department of Defense. With respect to leadership within the Space Force, section 953 described the role of the "Chief of Space Operations"—the commanding General of the new service. Appointed by the President for a four-year term (which can be extended an additional four year in a time of war or national emergency declared by Congress), the Chief of Space Operations is directly responsible to the Secretary of the Air Force in the same manner as the Chief of Staff of the Air Force (the senior Active Duty officer in the US Air Force, who serves as the principal advisor to the Secretary of the Air Force and represents the Air Force as a member of the US Joint Chiefs of Staff).[24] In this role, the Chief of Space Operations advises the Secretary of the Air Force on matters related to outer space and the activities/operations of the Space Force, and also

> exercise[s] supervision, consistent with the authority assigned to commanders of unified or specified combatant commands ... over such of the members and organizations of the Space Force as the Secretary determines; and ... perform such other military duties, not otherwise assigned by law, as are assigned to the Chief by the President, the Secretary of Defense, or the Secretary of the Air Force.[25]

General John Raymond, who had been serving as the Commander of USSPACECOM during the summer of 2019, was appointed to the position of Chief of Space Operations on January 14, 2020.[26] At the time of this writing (December 2021), General Raymond remains in this position and is approximately halfway through his four-year tenure as the United States Space Force's first Chief of Space Operations.

Section 954 of the Space Force Act established a "Space Force Acquisitions Council" within the Office of the Secretary of the Air Force. This Council—which the Act envisioned being chaired by the Assistant Secretary of the Air Force for Space Acquisition and Integration, with an additional membership comprised of the Under Secretary of the Air Force, the Assistant Secretary of Defense for Space Policy, the Director of the National Reconnaissance Office, the Chief of Space Operations, and the Commander of the United States Space

24 2020 NDAA § 953.

25 2020 NDAA § 953.

26 Charles Pope, "Raymond sworn in as first Chief of Space Operations at White House event," *United States Space Force: Space Force News*, Jan. 14, 2020, https://www.spaceforce.mil/News/Article/2057219/raymond-sworn-in-as-first-chief-of-space-operations-at-white-house-event/.

Command—was/is to oversee and manage "the acquisition and integration of the Air Force for space systems and programs in order to ensure integration across the national security space enterprise."[27]

As the later sections of this chapter will not specifically address the Space Force Acquisitions Council, it should be noted here that space-related acquisitions remain a contentious issue in the United States two years after the Space Force's creation. Little information about the activities of the Space Force Acquisitions Council is publicly available, and, whether due to the ongoing COVID-19 pandemic or for other reasons, it is unclear whether the Council has met consistently since April 2020.[28] As recently as the summer of 2021, the House of Representatives Appropriations Committee expressed concern

> that the Air Force has not taken more aggressive action in addressing longstanding space acquisition issues and has made little progress in defining what the Space Force will be doing that is fundamentally different than when it was a component of the Air Force.[29]

The Department of the Air Force and the Space Force itself have undertaken a number of efforts to address these concerns, including the re-designation and moderate restructuring of the long-established Air Force Space Command Space and Missile Systems Center into the new "Space Systems Command" (SSC).[30] The SSC's operations will, allegedly, better integrate space acquisitions among US military and intelligence communities, and improve the resiliency of critical American space systems by focusing on "designing and building out a more distributed [space] architecture."[31] Additionally, as of early December 2021, a nominee for the position of Assistant Secretary of the Air Force for

---

27 2020 NDAA § 954 (2019).

28 *See* Secretary of the Air Force Public Affairs, "Space Force Acquisition Council looks to safeguard space industrial base from COVID-19 impacts," *United States Space Force: Space Force News*, Apr. 29, 2020, https://www.spaceforce.mil/News/Article/2168917/space-force-acquisition-council-looks-to-safeguard-space-industrial-base-from-c/.

29 U.S. House of Representatives, "Report of the Committee on Appropriations Together With Minority Views," Department of Defense Appropriations Bill, 2022, Report 117–88, 117th Cong., July 15, 2021, pg. 300, available at https://www.congress.gov/congressional-report/117th-congress/house-report/88 (last visited Dec. 21, 2021).

30 Nathan Strout, "Space Systems Command is more than a name change, says new commander," *C4ISRNet.com*, Aug. 25, 2021, https://www.c4isrnet.com/smr/space-competition/2021/08/25/space-systems-command-is-more-than-a-name-change-says-new-commander/.

31 Strout, "Space Systems Command is more than a name change, says new commander," *C4ISRNet.com*.

Space Acquisition and Integration (which, as one may recall from the previous paragraph, is meant to be the position chairing the Space Force Acquisition Council) has finally been identified and put forward for Congressional confirmation.[32] Whether these efforts will ultimately result in improvements to the space-related acquisitions process remains to be seen.

3 Making It So: The US Space Force's Organization

No military service can exist without the personnel and materiel to carry out its assigned missions. The US Space Force is no exception. As discussed above, the creation of the Space Force did not require the United States Government to create and provision a military service from scratch. Instead, the transition of the US Air Force's Space Command from a subordinate command of the Air Force to its new role as a full-fledged service (though one, as noted, that remained under the control of the Department of the Air Force) made the initial development of the Space Force seem little more than the stroke of a Congressional pen. The conceptual ease of this transition, however, concealed the reality that forming a new military service is a complex endeavor—even when the backbone of the new organization is drawn wholesale from an existing service. This section details the evolution of the Space Force from the theoretical organization described in the 2020 NDAA to the active, though still developing, service branch it is today.

3.1 *Personnel and Organization*

With his appointment by President Trump in December 2019, General John Raymond became not just the Space Force's first Chief of Space Operations; he became the Space Force's first official member.[33] For approximately three months, General Raymond remained the new service's *only* member. This changed in early April 2020, when Air Force Chief Master Sergeant Roger Towberman was sworn in as the Chief Master Sergeant of the Space

32 Sandra Erwin, "Changes ahead for Space Force procurement organizations," *SpaceNews.com*, Dec. 3, 2021, https://spacenews.com/change-is-coming-for-space-force-procurement-organizations/. It should be noted that the 2020 NDAA did not require that the Assistant Secretary of the Air Force for Space Acquisition and Integration to take charge of acquisitions for space systems and programs until October 2022. *See* 2020 NDAA § 956.

33 Ryan Browne, "With a signature, Trump brings Space Force into being," *CNN.com*, Dec. 20, 2019, https://www.cnn.com/2019/12/20/politics/trump-creates-space-force/index.html.

Force—the new service's ranking enlisted member.[34] In the following months, as plans within the Department of the Air Force with respect to the transfer of Air Force Space Command units and personnel to the Space Force continued to develop, membership in the Space Force grew slowly. By the end of the 2020 Fiscal Year (the Department of Defense's Fiscal Years do not follow the calendar year, but, instead, begin on October 1st and end on September 30th each year), membership in the new service had grown to 85 members.[35] By this time, however, the plans for unit transitions had largely been finalized: the fall of 2020 saw the start of these transfers, and, by the end of 2020, membership in the Space Force had grown to over 2,400.[36] Transfers of additional Air

34 Sandra Erwin, "Top enlisted leader Towberman officially joins the U.S. Space Force," *SpaceNews.com*, Apr. 2, 2020, https://spacenews.com/top-enlisted-leader-towberman-to-officially-join-the-u-s-space-force/. Shortly before Chief Master Sergeant Towberman's swearing-in ceremony, General Raymond quipped, "Today, there's one person in the United States Space Force, and that's me. We've identified the second airman that will be, and that's Chief Master Sergeant Towberman." Erwin, "Top enlisted leader Towberman officially joins the U.S. Space Force," *SpaceNews.com*.

35 Office of the Undersecretary of Defense (Comptroller)/Chief Financial Officer, "Defense Budget Overview—United States Department of Defense Fiscal Year 2022 Budget Request," May 2021, p. 4–11, available at https://comptroller.defense.gov/Portals/45/Documents/defbudget/FY2022/FY2022_Budget_Request_Overview_Book.pdf (last visited Dec. 28, 2021).

36 *See* Mark F. Cancian, "U.S. Military Forces in FY 2021: Space, SOF, Civilians, and Contractors," *Center for Strategic and International Studies*, Jan. 8, 2021, https://www.csis.org/analysis/us-military-forces-fy-2021-space-sof-civilians-and-contractors, and Meghann Myers, "Space Force is looking for a few good soldiers, sailors," *Military Times*, Feb. 3, 2021, https://www.militarytimes.com/news/your-military/2021/02/03/space-force-is-looking-for-a-few-good-soldiers-sailors/. Transfers of units and personnel to the Space Force from the other service branches have not been entirely uncontroversial. The US Army has been particularly hesitant to give up certain space assets—missile defense and warning operations, for example, were described by one Pentagon official as "the biggest single open festering wound" in force transfers to the Space Force. Abraham Mahshie, "The Asset Transfer Fight," *Air Force Magazine*, Aug. 27, 2021, https://www.airforcemag.com/article/the-asset-transfer-fight/. Eventually, while a number of Army units and personnel were (or are scheduled to be) transferred, the Department of Defense allowed the Army to retain its coded space operations officers, as well as its "GPS maneuvering and space missile defense capabilities[.]" Abraham Mahshie, "Why the Army Clings to Its Space Troops: 'Translating Geek to Grunt,'" *Air Force Magazine*, Oct. 13, 2021, https://www.airforcemag.com/army-clings-to-space-troops-translating-geek-to-grunt/. Similarly, while the US Navy's contribution to the Space Force was always expected to be fairly modest, it, too, has attempted to retain at least some independent space operability. The Navy has, for example, recently created a new space-oriented career specialty, the Maritime Space Operator. These "MSOs" will serve as "the maritime space integration and planning professionals of the Navy." Diana Stancy Correll, "Navy forges maritime space officer designator,"

Force space-related units—as well as a number of US Army and Navy units involved in satellite operations and signals intelligence—grew the total number of Space Force personnel to approximately 6,434 by the end of September 2021, with the Department of Defense's budget requests for Fiscal Year 2022 anticipating the Space Force growing by an additional 2,000 members by the end of September 2022.[37] In December 2020, the Space Force announced that its members would be referred to as "Guardians."[38]

As membership in the Space Force grew and the transfer of previously existing military units to its control continued, decisions had to be made about the Space Force's organizational structure. Military services, like all government organizations, cannot perform effectively or efficiently without structure and hierarchy—indeed, the structure and interplay of the various components in a military or intelligence organization can be the difference between successful, orderly operations and dramatic failures that threaten national security. By June 2020, the initial plan for the Space Force's organizational structure had been finalized, and the new service announced that it would be organized into three major commands: Space Operations Command, Space Systems Command, and Space Training and Readiness Command. In order to increase efficiency and reduce bureaucracy at the lower levels of command, the Space Force compressed traditional military structures at that level; rather than having multiple lower-level commands (the US Air Force, for example, is organized into "Wings"—generally led by "Wing Commanders" with the rank of Colonel or General—which oversee "Groups"), the Space Force has organized its lower-level commands into "Deltas," which are organized directly under the major commands.[39]

Navy Times, Sept. 2, 2021, https://www.navytimes.com/news/your-navy/2021/09/02/navy-forges-maritime-space-officer-designator/. Despite these personnel and transfer squabbles, however, by the end of 2021, there were at least eleven Army and four Navy organizations scheduled for transfer to the Space Force. Sandra Erwin, "Space Force reveals which Army and Navy units are moving to the space branch," *Space News*, Sept. 21, 2021, https://spacenews.com/space-force-reveals-which-army-and-navy-units-are-moving-to-the-space-branch/.

37 Office of the Undersecretary of Defense (Comptroller)/Chief Financial Officer, "Defense Budget Overview." *See also* "2021 USAF & USSF Almanac: Personnel," *Air Force Magazine*, June 30, 2021, https://www.airforcemag.com/article/2021-usaf-ussf-almanac-people/.

38 Secretary of the Air Force Public Affairs, "U.S. Space Force unveils name of space professionals," *Space Force News*, Dec. 18, 2020, https://www.spaceforce.mil/News/Article/2452593/us-space-force-unveils-name-of-space-professionals/.

39 Sandra Erwin, "Space Force to stand up three major commands, lower echelons to be called 'deltas,'" *SpaceNews.com*, June 30, 2020, https://spacenews.com/space-force-to-stand-up-three-major-commands-lower-echelons-to-be-called-deltas/.

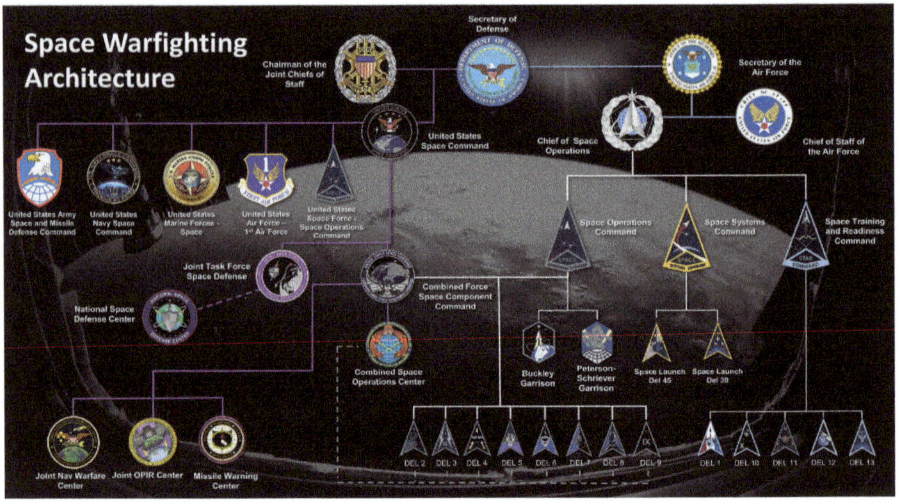

FIGURE 1 US Department of Defense Space Force and Space Command Organization, as of April 2022
IMAGE REPRODUCED WITH PERMISSION FROM THE AIR & SPACE FORCES INTELLECTUAL PROPERTY MANAGEMENT OFFICE, AIR FORCE PUBLIC AFFAIRS AGENCY

As of the end of 2021, the organizational structure of the Space Force's Commands and Deltas is as follows:

Space Operations Command (SpOC): SpOC is the action arm of the Space Force, responsible for space operations and the actual projection of combat power in, from, and to space. The Command "[g]enerates, presents, and sustains combat-ready intelligence, cyber, space and combat support forces" and also serves as the Space Force's "service component" to United States Space Command.[40] SpOC currently controls the following eight Deltas:

Space Delta 2—Space Domain Awareness: Delta 2 "prepares, and presents assigned and attached forces for the purpose of executing combat-ready Space Domain Awareness (SDA) operations" in order to "deter aggression and, if necessary, fight to protect and defend the U.S. and [U.S.] allies from attack in, through and from space."[41]

40 Space Operations Command (SPOC), "About Space Operations Command," spoc.spaceforce.mil, https://www.spoc.spaceforce.mil/About-Us/About-Space-Operations-Command (last visited Dec. 28, 2021).

41 Space Operations Command (SPOC), "Fact Sheets—Space Delta 2," spoc.spaceforce.mil, July 24, 2020, https://www.spoc.spaceforce.mil/About-Us/Fact-Sheets/Display/Article/2334029/space-delta-2 (last visited Dec. 28, 2021).

Space Delta 3—Space Electronic Warfare: Delta 3 "operates electronic attack, protection, and support capabilities to protect and defend the space domain."[42]

Space Delta 4—Missile Warning: Delta 4 "operates and supports three constellations of Overhead Persistent Infrared (OPIR) satellites and two types of Ground-Based Radars (GBRS) for the purpose of conducting strategic and theater missile warning."[43]

Space Delta 5—Command and Control: Delta 5 "[m]aintains global awareness of operational environments and space forces to enable data-driven decisions."[44]

Space Delta 6—Cyber Operations: Delta 6 "[e]xecutes cyber operations to protect space operations, networks, and communications"[45] and "provides assured access to space through the ... Air Force Satellite Control Network and defensive cyberspace capabilities for space mission systems."[46] The Delta also "plans, programs, integrates, operates and maintains command and control and common-user systems in support of U.S. Space Command, U.S. Air Force Warfare Center and the Missile Defense Agency."[47]

Space Delta 7—Intelligence, Surveillance, and Reconnaissance: Delta 7 "provides critical, time sensitive and actionable intelligence for space domain operations to allow for the detection, characterization and targeting of adversary space capabilities."[48]

---

42 Space Operations Command (SPOC), "Fact Sheets—Space Operations Command," spoc.spaceforce.mil, Mar. 25, 2021, https://www.spoc.spaceforce.mil/About-Us/Fact-Sheets/Display/Article/2550627/space-operations-command (last visited Dec. 28, 2021).

43 Space Operations Command (SPOC), "Fact Sheets—Space Delta 4," spoc.spaceforce.mil, July 2020, https://www.spoc.spaceforce.mil/About-Us/Fact-Sheets/Display/Article/2334034/space-delta-4 (last visited Dec. 28, 2021).

44 Space Operations Command (SPOC), "Fact Sheets—Space Operations Command."

45 Space Operations Command (SPOC), "Fact Sheets—Space Operations Command."

46 Space Operations Command (SPOC), "Fact Sheets—Space Delta 6," spoc.spaceforce.mil, July 2020, https://www.spoc.spaceforce.mil/About-Us/Fact-Sheets/Display/Article/2334044/space-delta-6 (last visited Dec. 28, 2021).

47 Space Operations Command (SPOC), "Fact Sheets—Space Delta 6."

48 Space Operations Command (SPOC), "Fact Sheets—Space Delta 7," spoc.spaceforce.mil, July 2020, https://www.spoc.spaceforce.mil/About-Us/Fact-Sheets/Display/Article/2334032/space-delta-7 (last visited Dec. 28, 2021).

Space Delta 8—Satellite Communications & Navigational Warfare: Delta 8 "provides position, navigation, timing and satellite communications to U.S. military, coalition [and] ... interagency partners, and commercial / civilian users."[49] The Delta "executes command and control of the [the United States' Military Satellite Communications] and Global Positioning System (GPS) constellations" and "delivers capabilities through 24/7 crew operations."[50]

Space Delta 9—Orbital Warfare: Delta 9 "conduct[s] protect and defend operations and provid[es] national decision authorities with response options to deter and, when necessary, defeat orbital threats." The Delta also "supports Space Domain Awareness by conducting space-based battlespace characterization operations" and "conducts on-orbit experimentation and technology demonstrations" on behalf of the Space Force.[51]

Space Training & Readiness Command (STARCOM): STARCOM is in charge of the Space Force's education, training, and doctrine-development efforts, as well as the development and application of military exercises for the purpose of training the new service's members. Its self-described mission is to "prepare the USSF to prevail in competition and conflict through innovative education, training, doctrine, and test."[52] STARCOM currently controls the following five Deltas:

Space Delta 1—Training: Delta 1 is the STARCOM Delta specifically devoted to training. It "provides initial skills training, specialized warfighter follow-on training, and advanced training events and courses in order to prepare USSF forces, and designated joint and allied partners, to prevail in a contested, degraded, operationally-limited, all-domain environment."[53]

---

49 Space Operations Command (SPOC), "Fact Sheets—Space Operations Command."

50 Space Operations Command (SPOC), "Fact Sheets—Space Delta 8," spoc.spaceforce.mil, July 2020, https://www.spoc.spaceforce.mil/About-Us/Fact-Sheets/Display/Article/2334040/space-delta-8 (last visited Dec. 28, 2021).

51 Space Operations Command (SPOC), "Fact Sheets—Space Delta 9," spoc.spaceforce.mil, Sept. 2020, https://www.spoc.spaceforce.mil/About-Us/Fact-Sheets/Display/Article/2550598/space-delta-9 (last visited Dec. 28, 2021).

52 Space Training and Readiness Command (STARCOM), "What We Do," starcom.spaceforce.mil, https://www.starcom.spaceforce.mil/About-Us/What-We-Do/ (last visited Dec. 28, 2021).

53 Space Training and Readiness Command (STARCOM), "Space Delta 1—Training," Aug. 2021, starcom.spaceforce.mil, https://www.starcom.spaceforce.mil/About-Us/How-We-Do-It/Space-Delta-1-Training/ (last visited Dec. 28, 2021).

Space Delta 10—Space Doctrine, Tactics, Lessons Learned, and Wargaming: Delta 10 is in charge of "develop[ing] USSF doctrine and tactics," "conduct[ing] the USSF Lessons Learned Program," and "execut[ing] and support[ing] wargames" to prepare US military space forces and allies to operate successfully in the outer space environment.[54]

Space Delta 11—Range and Aggressors: Delta 11 serves as the Space Force's training "Red Team," an imaginary adversary that provides "professional adversary support" for training and exercises. The Delta also "conducts Space Range operations for test and training requirements."[55]

Space Delta 12—Test and Evaluation: Delta 12 "prepares USSF forces to prevail in a contested, degraded, and operationally-limited environment" via "independent test and evaluation of USSF capabilities," as well as the "delivery of timely, accurate, and expert information in support of weapon system acquisition, operational acceptance, and readiness decisions."[56]

Space Delta 13—Education: Delta 13 "delivers institutional developmental education, develops U.S. Space Force officer accessions and executes advanced education programs."[57]

Space Systems Command (SSC): SSC, as its name implies, is the Space Force Command primarily responsible for acquiring, operating, and maintaining the physical space systems and objects used by the Space Force to accomplish its missions. In its own words, the SSC is "responsible for developing, acquiring, equipping, fielding, and sustaining lethal and resilient space capabilities for

54 Space Training and Readiness Command (STARCOM), "Space Delta 10—Doctrine and Wargaming," Aug. 2021, starcom.spaceforce.mil, https://www.starcom.spaceforce.mil/About-Us/How-We-Do-It/Space-Delta-10-Doctrine-Wargaming/ (last visited Dec. 28, 2021).

55 Space Training and Readiness Command (STARCOM), "Space Delta 11—Range and Aggressors," Aug. 2021, starcom.spaceforce.mil, https://www.starcom.spaceforce.mil/About-Us/How-We-Do-It/Space-Delta-11-Range-Aggressors/ (last visited Dec. 28, 2021).

56 Space Training and Readiness Command (STARCOM), "Space Delta 12—Test and Evaluation," Aug. 2021, starcom.spaceforce.mil, https://www.starcom.spaceforce.mil/About-Us/How-We-Do-It/Space-Delta-12-Test-and-Evaluation/ (last visited Dec. 28, 2021).

57 Space Training and Readiness Command (STARCOM), "Space Delta 13—Education," Aug. 2021, starcom.spaceforce.mil, https://www.starcom.spaceforce.mil/About-Us/How-We-Do-It/Space-Delta-13-Education/ (last visited Dec. 28, 2021).

warfighters."[58] This includes control of a number of critical activities, including "launch operations," "developmental testing," and the "sustainment and maintenance of military satellite constellations and other Department of Defense space systems."[59] SSC currently controls the following two Deltas:

> *Space Launch Delta 30*: Based out of Vandenberg Space Force Base in Santa Barbara County, California (see below), Delta 30 "manage[s] Department of Defense space and missile testing [and] range operations," and also "provides the installation infrastructure necessary to place satellites into polar orbit using both expendable and reusable space lift boosters."[60] It also "support[s] Minuteman III Intercontinental Ballistic Missile Force Development Evaluation programs" and "provides safe launch and range capabilities ... to fulfill commercial and government customer requirements."[61]

> *Space Launch Delta 45*: Based out of Patrick Space Force Base in Brevard County, Florida (see below), Delta 45 controls the Eastern Range—a massive space launch range along the southeastern coast of the United States that extends into the south Atlantic Ocean. The Range includes the famous space launch facility at Cape Canaveral, now Cape Canaveral Space Force Station (see below). Delta 45 provides "radar, telemetry and communications instrumentation support" for the launch of "[DoD] National Security Space, [NASA], [NOAA], commercial, and Naval Ordnance Test Unit's support to the Navy's Strategic Systems Programs missions."[62] The Delta controls the four active launch complexes on the Eastern Range, describes itself as the Space Force's "premier launch delta [sic]," and conducted 39 launch missions in 2020.[63]

While the creation or consolidation of new Deltas or Commands is possible in the future, for now the Space Force's three major commands and 15 Deltas

58 Space Systems Command, "About Space Systems Command," ssc.spaceforce.mil, https://www.ssc.spaceforce.mil/About-Us/About-Space-Systems-Command (last visited Dec. 28, 2021).

59 Space Systems Command, "About Space Systems Command."

60 Vandenberg Space Force Base, "History," Vandenberg.spaceforce.mil, https://www.vandenberg.spaceforce.mil/About-Us/History/ (last visited Dec. 28, 2021).

61 Vandenberg Space Force Base, "History."

62 Space Launch Delta 45, "Space Launch Delta 45 History," patrick.spaceforce.mil, https://www.patrick.spaceforce.mil/history/ (last visited Dec. 28, 2021).

63 Space Launch Delta 45, "Space Launch Delta 45 History."

provide the new service with a wide range of space missions and activities to control and enhance as it continues to develop.

3.2 *Basing*

As personnel transfers from other services proceeded through 2020, one of the other major components of establishing the new service—designating Space Force-specific bases for the operations and missions of the Force—was also underway. The 2020 NDAA had specified that the Space Force Act did not "require the relocation of any facility, infrastructure, or military installation of the Air Force" to the control of the Space Force;[64] however, both the mandated re-designation of Air Force Space Command and the planned or expected transfer of additional space-oriented units from the Air Force, Army, and Navy seemed to necessitate that the Space Force have physical jurisdiction over the bases and facilities necessary to carry out its missions. The transfer of existing bases/facilities to the Space Force was scheduled to begin early in 2020, but was delayed due to the global COVID-19 pandemic. Ultimately, the first official transfers would not occur until the end of that year when, in December 2020, Cape Canaveral Air Force Station and Patrick Air Force Base (both located in Florida) were re-named the Cape Canaveral Space Force Station and Patrick Space Force Base to reflect their transfer to the Space Force.[65]

In the months following the transfer of Patrick and Cape Canaveral, a number of other space-focused military installations, primarily controlled by the Air Force, were transferred to the Space Force's jurisdiction. Vandenberg Air Force Base, a key space-launch and missile testing facility located near the town of Lompoc on the coast of California, was officially transferred to the Space Force in May 2021.[66] Buckley Air Force Base in Aurora, Colorado, was transferred and re-named in June,[67] with the Air Force's other space-focused Colorado bases—Peterson Air Force Base, Schriever Air Force Base, and the Cheyenne Mountain Air Force Station, all located in or around Colorado

64 2020 NDAA § 959.

65 Rachel S. Cohen, "Cape Canaveral, Patrick Named First Space Force Installations," *Air Force Magazine*, Dec. 9, 2020, https://www.airforcemag.com/cape-canaveral-patrick-named-first-space-force-installations/.

66 Michael Peterson, "Vandenberg AFB gets new U.S. Space Force name," *Vandenberg Space Force Base*, May 14, 2021, https://www.vandenberg.spaceforce.mil/News/Article-Display/Article/2607448/vandenberg-afb-gets-new-us-space-force-name/.

67 Buckley Garrison Public Affairs, "Buckley receives new name, commander," *Buckley Space Force Base*, June 4, 2021, https://www.buckley.spaceforce.mil/News/Article-Display/Article/2646938/buckley-receives-new-name-commander/.

Springs—following in July.[68] As of the end of December 2021, due to the transfer of units, personnel, and facilities, the Space Force controls the following fourteen installations around the world:

1. Buckley Space Force Base (Aurora, Colorado)
2. Cape Canaveral Space Force Station (Cape Canaveral, Florida)
3. Cape Cod Space Force Station (Bourne, Massachusetts)
4. Cavalier Space Force Station (Cavalier, North Dakota)
5. Cheyenne Mountain Space Force Station (Colorado Springs, Colorado)
6. Clear Space Force Station (Clear, Alaska)
7. Ka'ena Point Space Force Station (Honolulu County, Hawaii)
8. Los Angeles Air Force Base (Los Angeles, California)
9. New Boston Space Force Station (New Boston, New Hampshire)
10. Patrick Space Force Base (Brevard County, Florida)
11. Peterson Space Force Base (Colorado Springs, Colorado)
12. Schriever Space Force Base (Colorado Springs, Colorado)
13. Thule Air Base (Qaanaaq, Greenland)
14. Vandenberg Space Force Base (Santa Barbara County, California)

It should be noted that Peterson Space Force Base and Schriever Space Force Base have, despite their modest geographic separation, been combined to form the Peterson-Schriever Garrison—a combined garrison sharing key facilities and services, headquartered at Peterson Space Force Base.[69] Additionally, most of the smaller facilities in the above list are controlled and operated by units attached to the larger bases. For example, the Cheyenne Mountain, Ka'ena Point, and New Boston Space Force Stations and the Thule Air Base are operated and controlled by units attached to the Peterson-Schriever Garrison.[70] Similarly, the Cape Cod,[71] Cavalier,[72] and

---

68 Angela Case, "Colorado Springs Air Force bases to be renamed for Space Force," *Fox 21 News*, July 22, 2021, https://www.fox21news.com/news/local/colorado-springs-air-force-bases-to-be-renamed-for-space-force/.

69 "Fact Sheet: Peterson-Schriever Garrison," *Schriever Space Force Base*, July 24, 2020, https://www.schriever.spaceforce.mil/About-Us/Fact-Sheets/Display/Article/2287613/peterson-schriever-garrison/ (last visited Dec. 22, 2021).

70 "Fact Sheet: Peterson-Schriever Garrison," *Schriever Space Force Base*.

71 "Fact Sheet: 6th Space Warning Squadron," *Buckley Space Force Base*, https://www.buckley.spaceforce.mil/About-Us/Fact-Sheets/Article/2575788/6th-space-warning-squadron/ (last visited Dec. 22, 2021).

72 "Fact Sheet: 10th Space Warning Squadron," *Buckley Space Force Base*, https://www.buckley.spaceforce.mil/About-Us/Fact-Sheets/Article/2291696/10th-space-warning-squadron/ (last visited Dec. 22, 2021).

Clear[73] Space Force Stations are operated and controlled by units attached to Buckley Space Force Base.

4 *Semper Supra*: The US Space Force's Doctrine

Previous chapters have described some of the historical development of aerospace and space doctrine within the context of the US Air Force's activities related to the space domain—and, most specifically, in reference to the American military's perceptions of the "peaceful purposes" language that has characterized the United States' policies with respect to space.[74] The Air Force's publication of its first space doctrine document, Air Force Manual 1–6, in 1982 began what is now a four-decade development of military space doctrine. Ultimately, the historical development of Air Force space doctrine has carried over to influence the new Space Force's doctrine, just as the Air Force's previous space-related missions have either directly carried over to the new service or have / will influence its mission sets. The Space Force's new motto, the Latin phrase *Semper Supra* (meaning "always above") was supposedly selected to represent "the [new] service's role in establishing, maintaining and preserving U.S. freedom of operations in the ultimate high ground"[75]—operational concepts requiring a basis in military doctrine. How, then, does this motto, and its implication that the USSF will be "always above" to protect US space interests, translate to the new service's doctrine?

In June 2020, the Space Force released a "Space Capstone Document" entitled *Spacepower: Doctrine for Space Forces* that, in the words of General Raymond, the Chief of Space Operations, "represents [the Space Force's] first articulation of an independent theory of spacepower."[76] To date, the 65-page Capstone Document remains not just the first, but the only doctrine document

73 Julie Avey, "Clear Air Force Station renamed as Clear Space Force Station," *168th Wing Air National Guard*, June 16, 2021, https://www.168wg.ang.af.mil/News/Article/2661327/clear-air-force-station-renamed-as-clear-space-force-station/.

74 *See infra* Chapter 2, pp. 40–44.

75 Sandra Erwin, "Space Force unveils logo, 'Semper Supra' motto," *Space News*, July 22, 2020, https://spacenews.com/space-force-unveils-logo-semper-supra-motto/#:~:text=USSF%20vertical%20logo.-,The%20Space%20Force%20motto%20%E2%80%9CSemper%20Supra%E2%80%9D%20means%20%E2%80%9Calways%20above,Air%20Force's%20advertising%20agency%20GSD%26M.

76 United States Space Force, *Spacepower: Doctrine for Space Forces*, "Space Capstone Document," p. iii, available at https://www.spaceforce.mil/Portals/1/Space%20Capstone%20Publication_10%20Aug%202020.pdf (last visited Dec. 27, 2021).

published by the new service. This is likely to change in the future—the Space Force has, for instance, created Space Delta 10, a Delta (see "Organization," above) devoted to developing Space Force doctrine and tactics, examining "lessons learned" as the new service continues to develop, and executing/supporting space-related wargames.[77] For the moment, however, *Spacepower* provides the doctrinal overview necessary to understand how the US military and the Space Force itself view the functions of the new service.

Spacepower provides a comprehensive, but brief, discussion of a number of critical topics, including descriptions of the outer space domain itself. While its first chapter, devoted to the outer space environment, descriptions of orbits, the hazards of orbital space, and other physical and environment factors, contains important information for space operators seeking to understand the outer space environment, we need not devote significant time or space to the chapter from a military doctrine standpoint. Chapter 2, "National Spacepower," devotes its introductory paragraphs to fairly basic discussions of national power generally, the role of politics and policy within the international system, and other generalized international relations theory-type information (such as the famous "DIME" formulation of national power instruments—diplomatic power, information power, military power, and economic power). However, the chapter also discusses and defines two key concepts that play an overarching role in how the Space Force fits into the United States' overall national efforts in outer space. First, the concept of "national spacepower" is defined as "the totality of a nation's ability to exploit the space domain in pursuit of prosperity and security."[78] This ability is "comparatively assessed" based on a nation's ability to leverage the space domain within the DIME framework.[79] Second is the concept of "unified space action," which "synchronizes all components of national spacepower, achieving unity of effort in support of national interests."[80] The role of the Space Force (an organization in the "military power" category), for example, contributes to unified space action by providing military protection to critical national and commercial American satellites and space systems ("space-based sources of economic power") and, as a result of both its space-based military strength and its protection of these systems, enhancing American diplomatic power on the international stage.

77 Space Training and Readiness Command, "Space Delta 10—Space Doctrine, Tactics, Lessons Learned, and Wargaming," Aug. 2021, https://www.starcom.spaceforce.mil/About-Us/How-We-Do-It/Space-Delta-10-Doctrine-Wargaming/.

78 USSF, *Spacepower*, 13.

79 USSF, *Spacepower*, 13.

80 USSF, *Spacepower*, 13.

Within the true military doctrinal context,[81] *Spacepower* organizes the Space Force's doctrinal elements into three nesting categories. The first and most significant of these categories, "Cornerstone Responsibilities," are the three critical responsibilities that "define the vital contributions of military spacepower" and are "the core purpose[s] of the United States Space Force."[82] These Cornerstone Responsibilities are:

1. *Preserving Freedom of Action in the Space Domain*: The preservation of the United States' freedom of action in outer space has been recognized as a critical component of US space doctrine for decades—though only comparatively recently has the "unfettered access to, and freedom to operate in, space" been defined as a vital national interest.[83] It should come as little surprise, then, that preserving this freedom of action is a cornerstone responsibility of military space forces. Indeed, as *Spacepower* notes, "[m]ilitary space forces fundamentally exist to protect, defend, and preserve this freedom of action."[84] The description of this Cornerstone Responsibility in many ways serves as a response to previous criticisms of Air Force space doctrine's emphasis on "space superiority"—while *Spacepower* recognizes and describes the importances of "space parity," "space superiority," and "space supremacy" within the context of preserving freedom of action in the space domain, the Space Force's doctrine recognizes these as situational conditions that may or may not be desirable in a given context.[85]

---

81 The RAND Corporation defines military doctrine as "the fundamental set of principles that guides military forces as they pursue national security objectives." RAND Corporation, "Military Doctrine," 2021, https://www.rand.org/topics/military-doctrine.html (last visited Dec. 27, 2021).

82 USSF, *Spacepower*, 28.

83 National Space Policy of the United States of America, Trump White House Archive, Dec. 9, 2020, https://trumpwhitehouse.archives.gov/wp-content/uploads/2020/12/National-Space-Policy.pdf, at 1.

84 USSF, *Spacepower*, 29.

85 USSF, *Spacepower*, 30. "Space parity" is defined as "any condition where no force derives a relative advantage over another at a given time;" "space superiority" as "a relative degree of control in space of one force over another that would permit the conduct of its operations without prohibitive interference from the adversary while simultaneously denying their opponent freedom of action in the domain at a given time;" and "space supremacy" as a condition implying "that one side could conduct operations with relative impunity while denying space domain freedom of action to an adversary." USSF, *Spacepower*, 30. In what appears to be almost a direct response to the criticisms leveled at "space superiority" doctrine/theory by academics such as Dr. Joan Johnson-Freese, *Spacepower* notes that "[s]pace supremacy is not always desirable, or attainable against a peer adversary, and should not be the unconditional goal of military spacepower." USSF, *Spacepower*, 30.

2. *Enabling Joint Lethality and Effectiveness*: As noted earlier in this work, Desert Storm demonstrated the critical role space power played as a force multiplier in terrestrial conflict. In the thirty years following the United States-led coalition's expulsion of Saddam Hussein's military from Kuwait, outer space and space systems have grown to play an even larger role in the joint operations of the US military. This Cornerstone Responsibility recognizes that "[s]pace capabilities strengthen operations in the other domains of warfare and reinforce every Joint function" and that "the US does not"—and, in the present day, potentially even *cannot*—"project or employ power without space."[86] As such, the Space Force and other US military space organizations, such as USSPACECOM, must "comprehensively and effectively integrate space capabilities into Joint training, planning, and operations" and "operate as part of the closely integrated Joint Force across the entire conflict continuum in support of the full range of military operations."[87]
3. *Providing Independent Options In, From, and To Space*: While the application of US spacepower is meant to enhance the Joint Force, this does not mean that all space operations will be joint or aimed specifically at contributing directly to operations in another operational domain (such as land, sea, or air). Because "[m]ilitary space forces achieve national objectives by projecting power in, from, to space," it is no less critical for the Space Force to have the ability to undertake operations in, from, and to outer space in order to "independently achieve strategic effects" and "provide a diverse set of options" to US civilian and military leadership.[88]

Again, the three Cornerstone Responsibilities represent the primary, overarching goals of the Space Force as an organization in its role within the United States' larger structure of military power.

The Cornerstone Responsibilities are fed by five "Core Competencies"—which "represent the broad portfolio of capabilities military space forces need to provide successfully or [sic] efficiently to the [United States]."[89] These five Core Competencies are:

1. *Space Security*: The competency of Space Security protects American prosperity and economic interests, as well as the interests and safety of the United States' international allies "by establishing conditions for the safe and secure access to space for civil, commercial, Intelligence

---

86 USSF, *Spacepower*, 29.
87 USSF, *Spacepower*, 29, 31.
88 USSF, *Spacepower*, 31–32.
89 USSF, *Spacepower*, 33.

Community (IC), and multinational partners."[90] Space security involves the interplay of military organizations such as the Space Force with civilian, commercial, and international partners to promote cooperation and coordination among all relevant space actors and to address activities that threaten their interests.

2. *Combat Power Projection*: Combat power projection involves the ability of the Space Force and other US military space forces to project combat power (defined as "the force available and, when necessary, employed to protect, defend, or defeat threats") in either defensive or offensive space operations. Defensive space operations, which "protect and preserve friendly space capabilities before, during, or after an attack," can be categorized as either "active" or "passive." Active defensive operations seek to "destroy, nullify, or reduce the effectiveness" of adversary threats, whereas passive defensive operations aim "to improve survivability through system and architectural attributes" (for instance, the "hardening" of satellites to protect them from cyber or certain electronic spectrum attacks, etcetera).[91] Offensive space operations, on the other hand, seize the initiative "to target an adversary's space and counterspace capabilities, reducing the effectiveness and lethality of adversary forces across all domains."[92] *Spacepower* dictates that defensive and offensive space operations are effects- or outcome-based—they must be employed in conjunction to both protect US/allied space architecture in particular way or to harm/impact adversary space capabilities in particular ways.

3. *Space Mobility and Logistics* (*SML*): SML is "the movement and support of military equipment and personnel into the space domain, from the space domain back to Earth, and through the space domain."[93] This competency is critical to the first Cornerstone Responsibility of preserving freedom of action within the space domain. SML can involve the (comparatively) simple capability of launch operations to place satellites, other space systems/hardware, or personnel in orbit; however, it can also involve the much more complex activities of orbital sustainment (the continued provision of fuel or supplies to on-orbit stations or hardware) and orbital recovery (the ability to recover personnel or equipment from the space domain).[94]

---

90 USSF, *Spacepower*, 35.
91 USSF, *Spacepower*, 36.
92 USSF, *Spacepower*, 36.
93 USSF, *Spacepower*, 37.
94 USSF, *Spacepower*, 37.

4. *Information Mobility*: Information mobility is defined as "the timely, rapid, and reliable collection and transportation of data across the range of military operations in support of tactical, operational, and strategic decision making."[95] Information mobility encompasses many of the activities that have been critical to the United States since the earliest days of US space operations. Satellite reconnaissance work, long since rolled into the combined "intelligence, surveillance, and reconnaissance" (ISR) system of integrated information acquisition, is but one of the key technologies involved in the information mobility effort. This competency also encompasses "point-to-point communications; broadcast communications;" "long-haul communication links;" "protected strategic communications;" "machine-to-machine interfaces;" "position, navigation and timing;" "nuclear detonation detection;" and "missile warning."[96]
5. *Space Domain Awareness* (*SDA*): SDA "encompasses the effective identification, characterization, and understanding of any factor associated with the space domain that could affect space operations."[97] This competency involves an incredible amount of data acquisition and analysis—not just about the physical environment of space and the presence of space systems/debris in particular locations on-orbit (this tracking and analysis of physical objects in the space domain is also frequently referred to as Space Situational Awareness, or SSA), but also about the "network" and "cognitive" dimensions of space operations.[98] Network dimensions involve physical nodes/orbits in space, combined with non-physical information of the movement and effects of waves and frequencies along the electromagnetic spectrum; these elements work together to contribute to US military space forces' ability to ensure lines of communication, command and control, and other critical operational elements. Cognitive dimensions are those involving the "decision-making processes, biases, cultural values, and psychological tendencies" of those—both friend and foe—who operate space systems.[99] The ultimate purpose of SDA is to "predict future outcomes and conditions, which [will] in turn drive[] future requirements for domain awareness."[100]

95 USSF, *Spacepower*, 38.
96 USSF, *Spacepower*, 38.
97 USSF, *Spacepower*, 38.
98 USSF, *Spacepower*, 39.
99 USSF, *Spacepower*, 39.
100 USSF, *Spacepower*, 40.

These five Core Competencies, taken in the aggregate, are the methods by which the Space Force seeks to achieve its Cornerstone Responsibilities.

Finally, in order to successfully execute the Core Competencies, certain specializations within the Space Force are required. These specializations are described in seven "Spacepower Disciplines," the descriptions of which, provided below, are taken wholesale (with the additional insertion of numbering) from the *Spacepower* Capstone Document:

1. *Orbital Warfare*: Knowledge of orbital maneuver as well as offensive and defensive fires to preserve freedom of access to the domain. Skill to ensure United States and coalition space forces can continue to provide capability to the Joint Force while denying that same advantage to the adversary.
2. *Space Electromagnetic Warfare*: Knowledge of spectrum awareness, maneuver within the spectrum, and non-kinetic fires within the spectrum to deny adversary use of vital links. Skill to manipulate physical access to communication pathways and awareness of how those pathways contribute to enemy advantage.
3. *Space Battle Management*: Knowledge of how to orient to the space domain and skill in making decisions to preserve mission, deny adversary access, and ultimately ensure mission accomplishment. Ability to identify hostile actions and entities, conduct combat identification, target, and direct action in response to an evolving threat environment.
4. *Space Access and Sustainment*: Knowledge of processes, support, and logistics required to maintain and prolong operations in the space domain. Ability to resource, apply, and leverage spacepower in, from, and to the space domain.
5. *Military Intelligence*: Knowledge to conduct intelligence-led, threat-focused operations based on the insights. Ability to leverage the broader Intelligence Community to ensure military spacepower has the ISR capabilities needed to defend the space domain.
6. *Engineering and Acquisition*: Knowledge that ensures military spacepower has the best capabilities in the world to defend the space domain. Ability to form science, technology, and acquisition partnerships with other national security space organizations, commercial entities, Allies, and academia to ensure the warfighters are properly equipped.
7. *Cyber Operations*: Knowledge to defend the global networks upon which military spacepower is vitally dependent. Ability to employ cyber

security and cyber defense of critical space networks and systems. Skill to employ future offensive capabilities.[101]

The "combined integration" of these spacepower disciplines provides the Space Force and other US military space forces "with the intellectual framework required to perform [the] core competencies" and, thus, achieve the Cornerstone Responsibilities.[102]

A discussion of the Space Force's current doctrine would not be complete without at least some examination of the influence and effect of space law on the doctrine's tenets. As we have previously seen in discussions of prior Air Force and Joint space doctrine in Chapters 2 and 3, space law principles, and, particularly, the US Government's consistent policy that space be used for "peaceful purposes," have played a significant role in many of the doctrine documents of the 1980s and 1990s. References to international space law and international law generally are not wholly absent from the Space Force's doctrine; however, as with many of the later Air Force and Joint doctrine documents, the emphasis of the *Spacepower* doctrine document is largely concerned with more operational matters. Within the 65-page document, there are several references to international law in relation to the Space Force's operations. Some are simple statements of traditional space law principles. In the document's section on orbital attributes, for example, there is a brief reference to international space law's "freedom of space" and the fact that remote sensing by satellite has traditionally been recognized as a legal activity.[103] Others are more prescriptive. In the introductory preface, *Spacepower* notes that the Space Force's application of spacepower in, from, and to the space domain "necessitates close collaboration and cooperation with the U.S. Government, Allies, and partners and in accordance with domestic and international law."[104] At this point, there is no elaboration of *how* the Space Force must operate under domestic and international law, or how these laws will affect the operations of the United States' military space forces.

Some explanation occurs later in the document, in *Spacepower's* sections concerning the nature of war. Here, again, we have doctrinal mention of the "peaceful use/purposes" language of the Outer Space Treaty's introduction—although in a way that seem to *misstate* international law. "In keeping with international law," *Spacepower* states in its discussion on the enduring nature of war in different environment, "the United States *acknowledges that the use of*

101 USSF, *Spacepower*, 51–52.
102 USSF, *Spacepower*, 50.
103 USSF, *Spacepower*, 3.
104 USSF, *Spacepower*, vi.

space is for peaceful purposes, while preparing for the reality that space must be defended from those who will seek to undermine our goals in space [emphasis added]."[105] While the stated policy of the doctrine document (namely, that the United States' interpretation of "peaceful purposes" allows Space Force and other military space forces' "preparation" for the reality of orbital conflict) is consistent with the United States' traditional policies on this matter going back to the 1960s, we have previously seen that there is *not,* in fact, an explicit international space law requirement that uses of outer space be "peaceful." It is unclear whether *Spacepower's* characterization of the "peaceful purposes" language as a requirement "[i]n keeping with international law" was simply an in-artful formulation of the United States' longstanding policy related to "peaceful use/purposes" or whether this language reflects some new intention or interpretation of international space law by the Department of Defense. The former, however, is probably more likely; despite the diplomatic and international push for tenets of "responsible behavior" in outer space and the general encouragement of "peaceful use" of outer space in recent Presidential National Space Policies, the author is aware of no other official US Government document stating the "peaceful use"/"use of outer space for peaceful purposes" is an explicit requirement under international law.

Perhaps the most detailed references to international law in *Spacepower* can be found in the Capstone Document's section discussing military space forces as "Stewards of the [Outer Space] Domain." Here, *Spacepower* makes broad references to the international laws and legal principles that ought to govern the Space Force's activities in outer space:

> Military space forces must be responsible stewards of the space domain. When designing missions, training, and performing end of life operations, military space forces should make every effort to promote responsible norms of behavior that perpetuate space as a safe and open environment in accordance with the Laws of Armed Conflict, the Outer Space Treaty, and international law, as well as U.S. Government and DoD policy. Just like all forms of warfare, the prosecution of space warfare and the potential generation of collateral damage is judged against the principles of military necessity, distinction, and proportionality. Through this approach, military space forces balance our responsibilities for operational readiness with the safety and sustainability of the space environment for use by future generations.[106]

105 USSF, *Spacepower*, 17.
106 USSF, *Spacepower*, 43.

Again, little specificity is offered in the text of the doctrine document. References to the Laws of Armed Conflict (what the United States military now generally refers to as the "Law of War"[107]) and its key principles of distinction (the principle that a military engaged in armed conflict may only target military objectives, which excludes civilians and civilian objects), military necessity (the principle that a military action must serve some military purpose—providing either a distinct advantage to the acting side, or, alternatively, denying a military advantage to an adversary), and proportionality (the principle that any damage to civilian objects or injury/death of civilians as a result of an otherwise lawful military action be proportionate to the military advantage gained) recognize the application of these legal requirements to the space domain, but provide little practical discussion of how or when they would apply. Similarly, the passing reference to the Outer Space Treaty provides an acknowledgment, as in previous Air Force and Joint doctrine documents, that international space law will govern—and, to some extent, constrain—the Space Force's activities. As with the Law of Armed Conflict, however, how the broad principles and legal requirements outlined in the Outer Space Treaty and other international space law treaties will affect Space Force operations is left largely unexamined.

5 Conclusion and Legal Implications

Despite the derisive response President Trump's initial Space Force announcement in June 2018 received from some quarters, the creation of the Space Force was a bipartisan effort that built upon previous Congressional proposals for a space-oriented military service. As we saw in Chapter 3, with President Biden's support for the Space Force and its operations, the new service has also maintained approval from the Executive Branch through the transition from the Trump to the Biden Administration. While some Space Force detractors in the US government remain (Representative Jared Huffman, a California Democratic, has, for example, introduced a bill in the US House of Representatives to abolish the Space Force), the widespread support the Space Force continues to receive from both US political parties seems sufficient to

107 See, for example, the 2015/2016 *Department of Defense Law of War Manual*, available at https://dod.defense.gov/Portals/1/Documents/pubs/DoD%20Law%20of%20War%20Manual%20-%20June%202015%20Updated%20Dec%202016.pdf?ver=2016-12-13-172036-190.

ensure the continued development of the service.[108] From its fledgling beginnings in late 2019 and early 2020, when General Raymond remained the service's sole official member for several months, the Space Force has grown from a force of one to a 6,400+ member military service, complete with physical bases, 15 Deltas with specialized missions, and control over what is arguably the most complex and expansive military space apparatus in the world. The Space Force may not yet have developed into its final form, but the fact that it exists at all is a testament to the theorists, politicians, and military tacticians who have been advocating for the creation of such a service since the mid-1990s.

From a legal and policy standpoint, however, not everyone is convinced the creation of the Space Force is a positive development. Doctor Joan Johnson-Freese, who has been referenced previously in this book in other, similar contexts, has stated that "[f]or military, political, organizational, and budgetary reasons, the creation of a space force [sic] is a bad idea."[109] Citing comments from President Trump emphasizing the need for American space dominance, Dr. Johnson-Freese views the Space Force's creation as an extension of the worst impulses of US military space policy (impulses she previously criticized in her books *Heavenly Ambitions: America's Quest to Dominate Space* and *Space Warfare in the 21st Century: Arming the Heavens*)—indeed, as an "overt[] mov[e] from the militarization of space that occurred in the 1940s to the weaponization of space."[110] She also surmised that standing up the Space Force would result in bureaucratic chaos within the Department of Defense, stove-piped and inefficient space efforts, and radical budgetary costs. Similarly, Dr. Laura Grego, an expert on orbital and astrophysics, space security matters, and missile defense who is currently a Stanton Nuclear Security Fellow at the Massachusetts Institute of Technology, has also argued that a Space Force is "likely to make space a more contentious and dangerous environment," at least in part because it will "create incentives within the national security bureaucracy to hype the threat of space weapons, and to then build new weapons

108 Tom Roeder, "Space Force abolished? House bill would do just that," *The Gazette*, Oct. 18, 2021, https://gazette.com/military/space-force-abolished-house-bill-would-do-just-that/article_7589e9f6-1bd5-11ec-9112-0f98af62e60b.html.

109 Joan Johnson-Freese, "Prompt Essay: One Good Reason for Creating a Space Force," in Texas National Security Review, "Policy Roundtable: Does America Need a Space Force?," Sept. 18, 2018, available at https://tnsr.org/roundtable/policy-roundtable-does-america-need-a-space-force/ (last visited Dec. 29, 2021).

110 Johnson-Freese, "Prompt Essay: One Good Reason for Creating a Space Force."

to counter them."[111] Dr. Grego contrasts what she considers to be the wasteful, dangerous creation of a Space Force to what she views as a more sensible path: for the United States "to vigorously pursue … negotiated constraints" on space weapons and harmful space activity with its potential international rivals.[112] The critiques of Dr. Johnson-Freese, Dr. Grego, and others making similar points track the line of tension that has existed in American space policy (and, to some extent, law) from the earliest days of the Space Age: what is the proper balance between negotiated rules governing the space environment versus the development of military capabilities to exert some degree of control over that environment, given the potential risks of an adversary fielding military space systems of its own?

Though critics like Dr. Johnson-Freese, Dr. Grego, and others—and even some proponents of the new service[113]—believe the creation of the Space Force will lead to greater militarization and weaponization of outer space, most Space Force operations are not notably different than the things the United States has been doing, or building toward, for years. The Space Force, as noted above, has assumed the functions previously accomplished by Air Force Space Command, including critical space traffic management and transparency operations. Indeed, the Space Force "shares information on [the] location of objects in space with more than 100 governmental, academic and commercial partner organizations from 25 nations through formal data sharing agreements, and is steadily adding more parties to the list of users."[114] It is also engaged in a wide range of non-weaponized missions, including the development of more resilient outer space infrastructure through both the disaggregation of space capabilities among multiple systems (or wide-ranging constellations of satellites) and the improvement of security/survivability of other space systems.[115]

111 Laura Grego, "The New U.S. Space Force Will Make Space More Dangerous, Not Less," *World Political Review*, Jan. 8, 2020, https://www.worldpoliticsreview.com/articles/28452/why-the-trump-space-force-will-make-space-more-dangerous (last visited Dec. 29, 2021).

112 Grego, "The New U.S. Space Force Will Make Space More Dangerous, Not Less," *World Political Review*.

113 *See* Henry Olsen, "Opinion: The U.S. Space Force is preparing to militarize space. Good.," *Washington Post*, Mar. 17, 2022, https://www.washingtonpost.com/opinions/2022/03/17/space-force-militarizing-good-thing/.

114 John Lauder, Frank G. Klotz, William Courtney, "How to avoid a space arms race," *The Hill*, Oct. 24, 2020, https://thehill.com/opinion/national-security/522512-space-arms-control-small-steps-can-begin-to-overcome-the-obstacles.

115 Courtney Albon, "US Space Force aims for more resilient architecture by 2026," *C4ISRNet*, Feb. 17, 2022, https://www.c4isrnet.com/battlefield-tech/space/2022/02/17/us-space-force-aims-for-more-resilient-architecture-by-2026/.

Even in the realm of weaponization, while there is no denying the Space Force's partial focus on orbital warfare, this component of the new service's operations is both an outgrowth of previous US military space weapons research (which, as we have seen, can be traced back at least to the Reagan Administration's significant shift in US space policy during the 1980s, if not even farther back in history) and a response to the outer space weaponization activities of potential US competitors. Russia, for example, has been developing a new co-orbital ASAT—a satellite capable of tracking and, based on a July 2020 orbital test that was observed and criticized by the US military space community, attacking another satellite[116]—since 2011.[117] China, meanwhile, has been developing both kinetic and non-kinetic methods of attacking or jamming satellites for some time,[118] and has, more recently, tested orbital hypersonic weapons.[119] Both countries, as we will see below, had also developed space-focused military organizations prior to the creation of the Space Force. All this is not to argue reductionist points of cause-and-effect in a search to determine the ultimate progenitor of space weaponization, but, rather, to describe the international threat environment that contributed to the creation of the Space Force. These facts also raise questions about the viability of the alternative solutions proposed by Space Force critics like Dr. Grego: how serious, for example, are Russian and Chinese proposals for space weapons restrictions when both States are either actively developing the very weapons they claim to oppose or are developing alternative space-based or space-targeting systems that are not restricted by their proposed space arms control mechanisms?

At this point, the primary criticisms of the Space Force have come from a policy perspective—that the new service will increase international tensions, cost precious budgetary dollars that could be better spent in other areas, harm or complicate an already largely inefficient government bureaucracy, and other, similar criticisms. From a legal perspective, however, the creation of a

116 Rachel S. Cohen, "SPACECOM Calls Out Apparent Russian Space Weapon Test," *Air Force Magazine*, July 23, 2020, https://www.airforcemag.com/spacecom-calls-out-apparent-russian-space-weapon-test/.

117 Theresa Hitchens, "Russia Builds New Co-Orbital Satellite: SWF, CSIS Say," *Breaking Defense*, Apr. 4, 2019, https://breakingdefense.com/2019/04/russia-builds-new-co-orbital-satellite-swf-csis-say/.

118 Todd Harrison, Kaitlyn Johnson, and Thomas G. Roberts, *Space Threat Assessment 2018*, Center for Strategic and International Studies, April 2018, 8–11.

119 International Institute for Strategic Studies, "China's 2021 orbital-weapon tests," *Strategic Comments*, Feb. 2022, available at https://www.iiss.org/~/publication/48752548-58b3-4e97-9ac7-4df48de5373d/chinas-2021-orbital-weapon-tests.pdf.

Space Force certainly violates no existing national or international space laws. As we saw in Chapter 2, the Outer Space Treaty may prohibit the placement of nuclear weapons or weapons of mass destruction in outer space, and completely bans military activity on celestial bodies, nothing in the treaty prohibits military uses of interplanetary space (or "outer space void"), nor even the placement or use of conventional weapons in outer space. While Space Force operations could certainly implicate other legal principles or requirements established in the four primary outer space treaties—for example, principles related to international responsibility (Article VI of the Outer Space Treaty); liability (Article VII of the Outer Space Treaty and the whole of the Liability Convention); and largely undefined concepts of " principles of co-operation and mutual assistance," "due regard," and "harmful interference" (Article IX of the Outer Space Treaty)—whether or not the Space Force will run afoul of these requirements in any true legal sense will likely be a case-by-case determination. This will also be influenced, of course, by whatever progress (or lack thereof) is made at the international level with respect to developing non-binding principles/norms or customary rules concerning "responsible" behavior in outer space.

Additionally, the United States is not alone in developing a space-oriented military service. After the break-up of the Soviet Union in 1992, the Russian Federation established its first largely independent "Space Forces" to oversee the control of the former Soviet Union's military satellites and missiles (though it should be noted that the Space Forces were later incorporated as a sub-branch of the Russian Aerospace Forces, a position the organization still shares with the Russian Air Force and Air, or Aerospace, Defense Forces).[120] While the People's Republic of China may not have as extensive a history of space activity as Russia, the country's rapid rise as a premier space power influenced its thinking in the military realm as well. In a series of military reforms undertaken in 2015, the People's Republic of China created the Strategic Support Force, an independent service within the People's Liberation Army focused entirely on space, cyber, and information warfare.[121] China's potential South-Asian rival India has also determined that a more significant degree of military-oriented

120 *See* Ministry of Defence of the Russian Federation, "Aerospace Forces," https://eng.mil.ru/en/structure/forces/type/vks.htm (last visited Dec. 29, 2021) (English Links to Russian Military Sites Defunct Post-2022 Ukraine Invasion).

121 John Costello and Joe McReynolds, "China's Strategic Support Force: A Force for a New Era," *China Perspectives*, Institute for National Strategic Studies (Washington, D.C.: National Defense University Press, December 2018), available at https://ndupress.ndu.edu/Portals/68/Documents/stratperspective/china/china-perspectives_13.pdf.

space activity is necessary to protect its international interests; over the past several years, India has both tested an anti-satellite (ASAT) missile[122] and has established a joint military organization, the Defense Space Agency, devoted to space warfare and satellite intelligence.[123] Even France, recognizing the national security issues associated with outer space systems and activities, has taken steps to enhance its military space readiness by creating a Space Military Command within the French Air Force, which, as of September 2020, had been renamed the French "Air and Space Force."[124]

To relate these developments back to our overarching discussion of international law and wider questions related to military uses of outer space and the "peaceful purposes" principle, the increased willingness by spacefaring States to develop space-oriented military organizations and to engage in more significant military uses of the space domain may be contributing to the establishment of State practice under international law. Persistent State practice is a critical component (along with *opinio juris*, or the belief that a particular act, behavior, or situation under international law actually imposes legal rights or obligations) of the development of customary international law. Even if the original intent of the States involved in creating the Outer Space Treaty and the international outer space law regime tilted toward a non-military, exclusively peaceful understandings of the law's components,[125] the actual practice of an increasing number of States toward more military-oriented uses of space and, specifically, the development of military organizations devoted to outer space affairs could eventually alter those original perceptions. As we have seen, however, the Outer Space Treaty is already largely permissive with respect to military activities conducted by States in interplanetary space—with the exception of the stationing of weapons of mass destruction or nuclear weapons on orbit.

122 *See generally* Shounak Set, "India's Space Power: Revisiting the Anti-Satellite Test," Carnegie India, Carnegie Endowment for International Peace, September 2019, available at https://carnegieendowment.org/files/7-30-19_Set_India_ASAT_Test.pdf.

123 Asian News International, "Defence Space Research Agency: Modi govt approves new body to develop space warfare weapon systems," *India Today*, June 11, 2019, https://www.indiatoday.in/india/story/defence-space-research-agency-modi-govt-approves-new-body-to-develop-space-warfare-weapon-systems-1546951-2019-06-11.

124 *See* Jean-Claude Vecchiatto, "The latest developments of the French Space Military Command," *Bird & Bird*, Jan. 2021, https://www.twobirds.com/en/news/articles/2021/france/the-latest-developments-of-the-french-space-military-command (last visited Dec. 29, 2021); News Wires, "Macron announces creation of French space force," *France 24*, July 13, 2019, https://www.france24.com/en/20190713-macron-france-space-force.

125 As we have seen, some States' interpretations or beliefs regarding critical space law principles *did* tilt in this direction, even if the understandings of those principles by the United States and Soviet Union, the two primary spacefaring powers of the time, did not.

The increased number of States pursuing military space programs, therefore, is both a reflection of that permissive legal environment (an environment informed and shaped, it should be added, by the increasingly widely-accepted "non-aggressive" interpretation of the Outer Space Treaty's "peaceful purposes language) *and* a mechanism by which persistent State practice among a growing number of States is contributing to further solidification of the legality of such military space programs under international law.

All this is to say that, regardless of whether the increased military use of outer space by larger numbers of State actors is good or bad as a matter of international *policy*, the military actions States have undertaken in outer space up to this time have been largely, if not entirely, within the bounds of legal behavior under the existing space law regime. (There have, on occasion, been accusation of violations of outer space law on the basis of military activities conducted in space—for example, the 2007 Chinese ASAT test that will be discussed in greater detail in Chapter 5; however, such allegations have generally *not* centered on violations of the Outer Space Treaty's Article IV "peaceful purposes" and military use provisions). From a policy perspective, there are certainly grave consequences to increased space militarization and weaponization. Critics like Dr. Johnson-Freese and Dr. Grego may be correct that the development of a new, space-focused military service by the United States contributes to the risk that outer space may become a theater for conflict or armament competition. The general recognition by space-faring States that outer space cannot be ignored from a military perspective, however, begs the question of whether the United States is causing the militarization of space or merely responding, along with other actors within the international system, to a natural—though tragic—development of a new domain.

CHAPTER 5

Outer Space Policy and the "Security Dilemma": Is America Destined for Space Conflict?

1 Introduction

Among the most prominent criticisms of the United States' 21st-century space policies—particularly those involving the American military—is that a focus on space security, characterized by a pursuit of "space control" or "space dominance," is unlikely to make the United States safer. Indeed, critics argue, such policies are far more likely to trigger unintended reactions by other members of the international community, *increasing* the number, and the strength, of the United States' adversaries in outer space and, ultimately, making the United States *less* safe. Former editor of *The Bulletin of the Atomic Scientists* and Independent Institute Research Fellow Mike Moore, for instance, makes this argument a central pillar of his 2008 book, *Twilight War: The Folly of U.S. Space Dominance*. "There is," he writes in his introduction, "a certain circular truth to [the belief that conflict in space is inevitable]: If the United States acts as if conflict in space is inevitable, it will be. It will be a self-fulfilling prophecy."[1] More recently, Dr. Joan Johnson-Freese, a National Security Affairs professor at the US Naval War College, makes the same point: "The inevitability of conflict in space has been widely assumed and accepted by the military. That assumption, however, increasingly seems to be creating a self-fulfilling prophecy."[2] "[C]urrent US emphasis on war plans, dominance, and control," she later concludes, "are only provoking potential adversaries and making a first-strike option on US space assets—assets the United States is more reliant on than their [sic] adversaries are—a compelling option to strive toward."[3]

This chapter will examine whether these critics' claims are correct. Is the United States, particularly now with the creation of the Space Force, a military branch solely devoted to outer space security operations, creating a more unstable space environment? Like Casaubon and his friends in *Foucault's*

1 Mike Moore, *Twilight War: The Folly of U.S. Space Dominance* (Oakland, CA: Independent Institute, 2008), xvi.

2 Joan Johnson-Freese, *Space Warfare in the 21st Century: Arming the Heavens* (Abingdon, UK: Routledge, 2017), 74.

3 Johnson-Freese, *Space Warfare in the 21st Century*, 166.

 | DOI:10.1163/9789004524064_006

Pendulum, did the United States imagine an outer space environment that didn't exist—a threatening environment in which potential adversaries lurk, seeking to surpass the United States' space capabilities or undermine its valuable space systems—and then inadvertently *create* such an environment by acting as if it did? Or do the more alarmist Cassandras—the James Gavins, Bernard Schrievers, Ronald Reagans, Donald Rumsfelds, and, more recently, as we shall see, Steven Kwasts of space security policy—have the right of it when they argue it is sheer naivety to believe space can be anything other than another domain which will be exploited for military purposes, and that if the United States is unwilling to engage in such exploitation, its adversaries will surely step into the breach? Beginning with an overview of the international relations theory of the "security dilemma," this chapter will investigate whether American space security policies truly conform to the classic "security dilemma" paradigm. Even if they do not, there may still be significant risks related to extraterrestrial one-upsmanship between the United States and its potential adversaries that must be considered and addressed.

2 The Security Dilemma in International Relations Theory

For Moore, Johnson-Freese, and other scholars concerned about the direction of American space policy, the context of the United States' behavior, and, especially, military behavior, in outer space is a classic "security dilemma." The security dilemma model, which has achieved a prominent place in theories of international relations, posits that conflict between States can occur on the basis of a paradox: a State, having no aggressive intent and seeking solely to ensure its own security, takes certain steps or engages in certain actions, which, triggering a fear reaction in another State, cause that State to take its own steps to preserve *its* own security from the perceived threat of the first. As John H. Herz, who coined the term "security dilemma" to describe the phenomenon, puts it:

> Groups or individuals ... must be, and usually are, concerned about their security from being attacked, subjected, dominated, or annihilated by other groups and individuals. Striving to attain security from such attack, they are driven to acquire more and more power in order to escape the impact of the power of others. This, in turn, renders the others more insecure and compels them to prepare for the worst. Since none can ever feel

> entirely secure in such a world of competing units, power competition ensues, and the vicious circle of security and power accumulation is on.[4]

The paradox, or dilemma, ultimately leads to war not because any State fervently desires war or conflict with any other State, but because at least one State determines that confronting its rival is the only way to stop its rival's accumulation of power and ensure its own security.

Herbert Butterfield, another early theorist of the "security dilemma" model, posited that conflicts resulting from a security dilemma scenario would be even more acrimonious than those that occurred for other reasons due to the fear and self-righteousness felt by the participants:

> [N]ot only could the greatest war in history be produced between two Powers both of which were moderately virtuous and desperately anxious to prevent a conflict, but such a struggle, far from being a nice, quiet, and reasonable affair, would be imbittered by the heat of moral indignation on both sides, just because each was so conscious of its own rectitude, so enraged with the other for leaving it without any alternative to war. It is the peculiar characteristic of the situation I am describing—the situation of what I should call Hobbesian fear—that you yourself may vividly feel the terrible fear that you have of the other party, but you cannot enter into the other man's counter-fear, or even understand why he should be particularly nervous. For you know that you yourself mean him no harm, and that you want nothing from him save guarantees for your own safety; and it is never possible for you to realise or remember properly that since he cannot see the inside of your mind, he can never have the same assurance of your intentions that you have. As this operates on both sides the Chinese puzzle is complete in all its interlockings—and neither party sees the nature of the predicament he is in, for each only imagines the other party is being hostile and unreasonable.[5]

Fear and misperception, then, lie at the heart of the security dilemma theory. While Butterfield, Herz, and other security dilemma theorists (including Columbia University Professor Robert Jervis), proffer slightly different elements that make up a typical security dilemma scenario, all agree on this point,

4 John H. Herz, "Idealist Internationalism and the Security Dilemma," 2 *World Politics* 2, 157 (Jan. 1950).

5 Herbert Butterfield, *History and Human Relations* (New York: Macmillan, 1951), 21.

and on the fact that States' fears and misunderstandings, if left unchecked, can lead to disaster.[6]

In 2009, Dr. Shiping Tang, a professor of international relations at Fudan University in Shanghai, China, undertook an updated examination of the security dilemma theory that is useful in both its elemental factors and its posited scenarios. Digging down into the earlier theories of Butterfield, Herz, and Jervis, Tang establishes eight factors that, he argues, characterize true security dilemmas: (1) *international anarchy* (the "source of the security dilemma is the anarchic nature of international politics"[7]); (2) *uncertainty/fear* (within an anarchic system, "[S]tates cannot be certain about each other's present and future intentions" and "[a]s a result, ... tend to fear each other"[8]); (3) *unintentionality/ lack of malign intentions* (a true security dilemma is "unintentional in origin"—that is, both sides in the dilemma are "defensive realist [S]tates," which Tang defines as "[S]tates that merely want security without intending to threaten ... other [States]"[9]); (4) *power accumulation* ("[b]ecause of the uncertainty about each other's intentions ... and fear, [S]tates resort to the accumulation of power or capabilities as a means of defense, and these capabilities inevitably contain some offensive capabilities"[10]); (5) *self-reinforcement* ("[t]he dynamics of the security dilemma are self-reinforcing and often lead to (unintended and bad) spirals such as the worsening of relationships and arms races"[11]); (6) *self-defeating behavior by participants* ("[t]he dynamics of the security dilemma tends to make some measures for increasing security ... self-defeating: more power but less security"[12]); (7) *tragic results* ("[t]he vicious cycle derived from the security dilemma can lead to tragic results, such as unnecessary or avoidable wars"[13]); and, finally, (8) *severity regulation* ("[t]he severity of the security dilemma can be regulated by both material factors and psychological factors"[14]). Tang's factors provide an amalgamation of Butterfield's, Herz's, and Jervis's theories regarding the security dilemma. Again, the key factors that trigger the dilemma are the fear and uncertainty each party feels as it watches the other accumulate power and capability.

---

6 *See* Shiping Tang, "The Security Dilemma: A Conceptual Analysis," 18 *Security Studies* 3, 589–593 (2009).

7 Tang, "The Security Dilemma," 18 *Security Studies* 3, 594.

8 Tang, "The Security Dilemma," 18 *Security Studies* 3, 594.

9 Tang, "The Security Dilemma," 18 *Security Studies* 3, 594.

10 Tang, "The Security Dilemma," 18 *Security Studies* 3, 595.

11 Tang, "The Security Dilemma," 18 *Security Studies* 3, 595.

12 Tang, "The Security Dilemma," 18 *Security Studies* 3, 595.

13 Tang, "The Security Dilemma," 18 *Security Studies* 3, 595.

14 Tang, "The Security Dilemma," 18 *Security Studies* 3, 595.

In addition to providing a concise explanation of the security dilemma's central features, Tang explores a number of scenarios in which the security dilemma may apply. He takes as his starting point the idea of conflicts of interest between States—since, after all, States must disagree about something if conflict or war between them is to take place. Tang divides possible conflicts of interests into two categories: those that are "objectively illusory," that is, those that are *perceived* by the States involved to be conflicts of interest even though they are not, and those that are "objectively genuine," true conflicts of interest between the States involved.[15] These two categories of conflicts of interest are further subdivided based on whether the States involved *believe* a conflict of interest can be resolved via international cooperation, bilateral interaction, or some other non-violent method, and whether the conflict of interest *actually can be*—that is, whether the conflict of interest is objectively and subjectively "reconcilable."[16]

Tang posits that, in situations involving a genuine conflict of interest that is objectively irreconcilable, true security dilemmas typically do not occur, because one or both parties acknowledge the irreconcilability of the conflict.[17] In these cases, any action one State takes to strengthen its position with respect to the conflict of interest is necessarily malign: the acting State *knows* its behavior is taken to the detriment of the other party—that is, in fact, the point. It is, according to Tang, in the realms of illusory conflicts of interest and objectively reconcilable, genuine conflicts that the risks of misperception, the effects of fear and uncertainty, and the missteps of the States involved can trigger security dilemma scenarios. This is particularly the case where one or both States *perceive* an illusory conflict of interest, or an objectively reconcilable, genuine conflict of interest, to be irreconcilable.

3 American Space Security Policy and the International Community

3.1 *True Security Dilemma?*

Given the criticisms of the United States' space security policy—particularly the idea that American emphasis on military uses of space creates a "self-fulfilling prophecy" of instability and threat in outer space—the million-dollar question is straightforward: does the United States' approach to outer space, and other States' responses to this approach, represent a true security

15 Tang, "The Security Dilemma," 18 *Security Studies* 3, 600.
16 Tang, "The Security Dilemma," 18 *Security Studies* 3, 600.
17 Tang, "The Security Dilemma," 18 *Security Studies* 3, 600, 602.

dilemma? As we have seen, a number of authors and critics of the United States' policies seem to answer this question with an unequivocal "yes." It is fairly simple, however, to play the game of spotting actions and reactions (particularly with the benefit of hindsight), and speculation concerning the future is nearly as easy—after all, if things don't turn out as expected, there are innumerable variables and factors to which a would-be prophet can point to explain the reasons their prediction failed to pan out. Theories related to "self-fulfilling prophecies" are only useful if there is some objective way to analyze whether the United States is, or has previously found itself, in a "security dilemma." Tang's eight-factor analysis of true "security dilemma" scenarios provides an excellent starting point for examining this. If the arena of space security constitutes a true security dilemma, conclusions can certainly be drawn with respect to which State is most at fault for triggering the scenario, but, far more importantly, we can work to develop policies designed to halt the self-sustaining nature of such a scenario and, hopefully, avert conflict. If space security is *not* a true security dilemma, this may not entirely nullify the threat of conflict or competition in space, but may provide different avenues for addressing possible space conflict.

It should also be noted that a "security dilemma" between two or more States is unlikely to involve just one arena, or domain, of potential conflict. In a "security dilemma" scenario involving, say, the United States and China, outer space would constitute just one aspect of an overarching, multi-domain confrontation. The two sides' outer space policies and activities would join a host of other factors—terrestrial and naval military movements, economic policies, political maneuvers, and so on—that could either contribute to perpetuating, or help to dissipate, a "security dilemma." Due to the complexity of examining every potential military, political, diplomatic, national, and international facet contributing to the security situation between two or more States, this chapter will focus its analysis of the "security dilemma" squarely within the outer space realm.

An additional difficulty in reaching a clear answer to the "security dilemma" question is that, in the context of international relations, American space policy can be divided into at least two distinct historical periods, which, in another several years, will be approximately equal in length. The first of these periods, the Cold War Era of American space security policy, extended from the mid-1950s (though potentially, as noted at the beginning of Chapter 3, as early as the mid- to late-1940s) to the dissolution of the Soviet Union in 1991. This period was characterized by bipolar competition, though never direct conflict, in outer space between the United States and the Soviet Union. The second is the Post-Cold War Era, which began in 1991 and continues through the present day. Despite a brief period during the 1990s during which the United States enjoyed unipolar space dominance, this period has been characterized by expanding access to outer space by both national and private space actors, ultimately resulting in a multipolar space environment—though one in which the United States still maintains a predominant position. Each of these periods will be examined using three factors of Tang's "security dilemma" rubric—international anarchy, fear/uncertainty, and power accumulation—in order to tease out their potential implications for American space security policy. These three factors were chosen because (1) in this author's view, they represent the core factors that must exist for a "security dilemma" to be possible; and (2) because the Cold War did not ultimately result in a self-reinforcing conflict between the United States and the Soviet Union, and because current outer space relations between the United States and other countries have not resulted in such a conflict either, there is little to substantially examine with respect to Tang's other "security dilemma" factors. Tang's self-reinforcement, self-defeating behavior, tragic results, and severity regulation factors all pertain to a "security dilemma" in progress; these factors can only come into play if international anarchy, fear/uncertainty between two or more countries, and power accumulation between those countries push them into a "security dilemma" scenario. Finally, Tang's third factor, unintentionality/lack of malign intentions, has not been examined because, in this author's view, *none* of the States examined—including the United States—can truly be considered "defensive Realist States" that are concerned solely with their own security.

While the parameters described in the previous paragraph may preclude us from determining that a true "security dilemma" exists (at least, under the holistic "security dilemma" theory described by Tang), examining Tang's factors of international anarchy, fear/uncertainty, and power accumulation provides significant insights into State behavior during and after the Cold War. What we will find may sound simplistic, but it has significant implications for future action in the outer space realm: while no international relations theory (realism, liberalism, institutionalism, or others) can be objectively proven to be true or untrue, the extent to which these theories influence State action depends on a number of factors—and, chief among these, as Casaubon and his friends realized to their cost in *Foucault's Pendulum*, is perception.

3.2 *Cold War Era American Space Security Policy*

As described in Chapter 3, the United States military had begun considering the possible uses of orbital satellites in the mid-1940s, shortly after the end of World War II. The first national US policies related to outer space security, however, weren't released until almost a decade later, starting with President

Eisenhower's NSC 5520, and continuing, after the *Sputnik* launch, with NSC 5814/1 and NSC 5918. *Sputnik* unequivocally triggered the beginning of the United States' Cold War Era space security policies, spurring the United States to redouble its outer space efforts for fear of being permanently outpaced by the Soviet Union. While the Cold War, at least initially, appeared to present factors, and to take place in an international environment, conforming to realist "security dilemma" theory, the United States and the Soviet Union successfully navigated their low-level, approximately 45-year conflict without a deadly slide into the self-reinforcing conflict cycle predicted by "security dilemma" theorists. Why? This section examines three of Tang's factors—international anarchy, fear/uncertainty, and power accumulation—to show that, even if the international environment and the bilateral interactions between the United States and the Soviet Union initially resembled the world portrayed by "security dilemma" theorists, the two sides were able to find internationalist methods of reducing conflict, that, as we will see in our upcoming discussion of international relations theory, implicitly—if not *explicitly*—undermined key assumptions of "security dilemma" theory.[18]

3.2.1 International Anarchy

The first factor of Tang's "security dilemma" analysis—and, indeed, a key factor in all iterations of "security dilemma" theory from Herz to Tang—is international anarchy. Of all the elements of the "security dilemma," this may be the most difficult to examine, as the question of whether the international system *is*, in fact, anarchic is one that lies at the very heart of international relations theory itself. International theorists and political philosophers have argued for centuries, if not millennia, about this question. Thucydides, the 5th century BC Greek historian, general, and author of the *History of the Peloponnesian War*, was among the first to articulate a theory of international anarchy. In Thucydides' Melian Dialogue, the Athenians seek to explain their subjugation of the island of Melos to its populace, not with reference to traditional

---

18 It should be noted that supporters of the "security dilemma" theory may point to Tang's eighth factor, "severity regulation," to explain how the United States and the Soviet Union were able to avoid conflict. *See* Tang, "The Security Dilemma," 18 *Security Studies 3*, 595. There are at least two counter-points to such an argument. First, it assumes that a "security dilemma" does, in fact, exist—meaning that the rest of Tang's and other theorists' factors must exist—and that it is only the severity of the active "security dilemma" that is mitigated rather than the existence of the "dilemma" itself. The second, related point is that such an argument rests on certain international relations theory assumptions that, as we will see below, *infra* notes 27–67, are not present in interactions between the United States and Soviet Union during the Cold War.

justifications based on international rights, morality, or legality, but purely with reference to their own power and ability to conquer:

> For ourselves, we shall not trouble you with specious pretenses—either of how we might have a right to our empire because we overthrew the Mede, or are now attacking you because of wrong that you have done us—and make a long speech which would not be believed … since you know as well as we do that right, as the world goes, is only in question between equals in power, while the strong do what they will and the weak suffer what they must.[19]

Thucydides' articulation of the Athenians' words has the dramatic, and even poetic, ring of classical history, but the sentiments it expresses have changed little in the 2500 years since the *History of the Peloponnesian War* was written. Kenneth Waltz, for instance, reiterated Thucydides' point more academically in his classic work of political theory, *Man, the State, and War*, published in 1959:

> With many sovereign states, with no system of law enforceable among them, with each state judging its grievances and ambitions according to the dictates of its own reason or desire—conflict, sometimes leading to war, is bound to occur. To achieve a favorable outcome from such a conflict a state has to rely on its own devices, the relative efficiency of which must be its constant concern.[20]

Waltz may lack the poetry of Thucydides, but the connotation is the same. Similarly, though more concisely, former National Security Advisor and international stateman Henry Kissinger (himself no stranger to Great Power politics, including in the outer space realm) described 19th century *realpolitik*, a political theory to which he himself largely subscribes, as "foreign policy based on calculations of power and national interest."[21]

Thucydides, Waltz, and Kissinger are all representatives of the "realist" school of international politics. While all but a rudimentary examination of realist theory is impossible in this work, suffice to say that realism "emphasizes

19 Robert B. Strassler, ed., *The Landmark Thucydides* (New York: Free Press/Simon & Schuster, 1996), 352.

20 Kenneth N. Waltz, *Man, the State and War: A Theoretical Analysis* (New York: Columbia University Press, 1959), 159.

21 Henry Kissinger, *Diplomacy* (New York: Simon & Schuster, 1994), 137.

the constraints on politics imposed by human nature and the absence of international government."[22] Realist theory characterizes the international system as "a realm of power and interest," in which States are the primary players, pursuing their real (or perceived) interests to the best of their abilities in an otherwise anarchic environment.[23] From this description and our previous discussion of the "security dilemma," it should be obvious that the theory of the "security dilemma" itself is nested squarely in the more comprehensive theory of international realism. While the two theories do not necessarily rise or fall together (it is possible to imagine a scenario in which the overarching theory of realism accurately describes the international system, but the "security dilemma" theory is inaccurate), if the international system is *not* anarchic—or is not *perceived* to be anarchic by States acting within the system—then neither realism nor the "security dilemma" can accurately describe or predict State behavior.

There are a number of alternatives to realist international relations theory that posit a different interpretation of the international system: one based not on anarchy and self-interest, but on interdependence. Overarchingly, these theories of international relations are subsumed under the umbrella of "idealism," which posits that, because States are interdependent with one another within the international system, constraints on State action through international law, norms, or institutions result in greater benefit and prosperity for all.[24] Cooperation, not competition, is the primary fixation of idealism. Under the idealist worldview are a number of theories, or sub-theories, emphasizing various aspects of these overarching concepts. "Liberalism," for example, (which is sometimes considered to be synonymous with "idealism") posits that "individuals, organizations, and groups" are also critical actors in international relations and that States behavior is influenced by these subsidiary actors.[25]

22 Jack Donnelly, *Realism and International Relations* (Cambridge: Cambridge University Press, 2000), 9.

23 Donnelly, *Realism and International Relations*, 9.

24 *See* "Political Realism in International Relations," *Stanford Encyclopedia of Philosophy*, May 24, 2017, https://plato.stanford.edu/entries/realism-intl-relations/.

25 Thanh Phan, "Article: Realism and International Cooperation in Competition Law," *Houston Journal of International Law*, 40:297, 307 (Fall 2017). For similar arguments related to the "bottom-up" nature of "liberal" international relations theory, see Harvard University Professor Andrew Moravcsik's discussion of "domestic society"—that is, "rational individual and private groups" within a State—as being the primary drivers of State action in international affairs. Andrew Moravcsik, "Liberal International Relations Theory: A Social Scientific Assessment," Paper No. 01–02, Weatherhead Center for International Affairs, Harvard University, April 2001, available at https://datascience.iq.harvard.edu/files/wcfia/files/607_moravscik.pdf.

Another key aspect of liberalism is economic interdependence between States—one reason why "Liberals" are traditionally thought to favor free trade and open markets.[26] Another sub-theory of "idealism" is "institutionalism," sometimes referred to as "neo-liberal institutionalism" or "liberal institutionalism."[27] In contrast to realism's characterization of the international environment as wholly anarchic, institutionalism posits that "domestic and international institutions play central roles in facilitating cooperation and peace between nation-states."[28] Under institutionalist theory, international institutions facilitate the creation of "[r]ules, norms, principles, and decision-making procedures" that "reduce transaction costs ... [and] promote cooperation between and among states."[29] The idea underlying institutionalism,

26 *See* Phan, "Realism and International Cooperation," *Houston Journal of International Law*, 306–307.

27 *See* Stephen McGlinchey, Rosie Walters & Christian Scheinpflug, eds., *International Relations Theory* (Bristol, England: E-International Relations Publishing, 2017), 25; Anne-Marie Slaughter, "Liberal International Relations Theory and International Economic Law," 10 *American University Journal of International Law and Policy* 2, 724 (1995). Indeed, whether institutionalism is a distinct international relations theory or merely a subset of "liberalism" is hotly debated. "Liberalism" has, at least traditionally, been the primary contrast to realism. As noted above, liberal theory posits that international affairs have a moral dimension: that the rights of individuals matter, that people—and States—can live together harmoniously if certain conditions (notably, the existence of "liberal" or democratic governance in a majority of States) are met, and national and international institutions can constrain political power among States and protect individual rights. *See* McGlinchey, Walters & Scheinpflug, eds., *International Relations Theory*, 4, 22. This last element of liberal thought is similar to the theory of institutionalism. To the extent a difference exists between liberalism and institutionalism, it is that institutionalism, like realism, views States as the primary actors on the international stage, and their own interests as the primary motivators for States' actions (as noted above, this is in contrast to liberal perceptions, as explained by Phan and Moravcsik, that individuals and groups within civil society are the primary motivators of State interest and action)—institutions simply alter States' perceptions of their interests by providing benefits, or imposing costs, for State actions within the international system. *See* Slaughter, "Liberal International Relations Theory and International Economic Law," 10 *American University Journal of International Law and Policy* 2, 724–27.

28 Tana Johnson & Andrew Heiss, "Liberal Institutionalism" in Thomas G. Weiss and Rorden Wilkinson, eds., *International Organization and Global Governance* (London: Routledge, 2018), 2nd ed., 123.

29 Slaughter, "Liberal International Relations Theory and International Economic Law," 10 *American University Journal of International Law and Policy* 2, 725. As Slaughter further explains "International regimes also enhance compliance with international agreements in a variety of ways. They reduce incentives to cheat, enhance the value of reputation, establish 'legitimate standards of behavior for states to follow,' and facilitate monitoring. In this way they create 'the basis for decentralized enforcement founded on the principle of reciprocity.'" Slaughter, "Liberal International Relations Theory and International

then, is that States can become interdependent on one another via the benefits and stability international agreements, and the international institutions facilitating or overseeing such agreements, provide. Much of the discussion throughout the rest of this chapter will discuss and contrast institutional or international constraints (through, for example, international space law as passed by the United Nations) on State action in outer space with possible realist activities in that domain. For this reason, the term "institutionalism" will be used throughout in discussing the contrast between realist and institutionalist activities in outer space in the context of the security dilemma.

All this is a lengthy background to the factor of Tang's "security dilemma" theory we are currently examining: whether the relationship between the United States and the Soviet Union vis-à-vis their outer space programs more closely reflected the anarchic, power-and-interest theory of realism, or the more constrained, even utopian, theory of institutionalism. The perhaps unsatisfying answer seems to be that, at different times during the Cold War, this relationship resembled *both* international relations theories. While the Cold War space security era was bookended by periods of realist posturing, for the majority of the Cold War institutionalism largely prevailed. This may be part of the reason why outer space, though certainly an area of competition, never became a domain of conflict during the Cold War.

At the time of the *Sputnik* launch, the United Nations was little more than a decade old, the world was locked in a largely binary ideological conflict between the United States and the Soviet Union, and the nascent postwar international legal framework had been unable to prevent major wars in Korea, Israel/Palestine, Indochina, and other areas; Communist aggression in Eastern Europe; or capitalist/imperialist meddling in Iran, the Suez, and Africa. Perhaps worst of all from an American perspective, the United Nations (largely due to Soviet intransigence) had failed to prevent both the Soviet development of nuclear weapons and the rapidly advancing Soviet ballistic missile/rocketry program. Finally, due to the novelty of previously unimaginable outer space activities, no international law or policy on the subject existed outside of a handful of academic papers theorizing about abstract future space law principles.[30] In this context, there was next to nothing from an institutionalist standpoint that could prevent, or impose international costs for, Soviet outer

---

Economic Law," 10 *American University Journal of International Law and Policy* 2, 725 (citing Robert O. Keohane, *After Hegemony: Cooperation and Discord in the World Political Economy* (Princeton, NJ: Princeton University Press, 1984), 244).

30 *See* Stephen E. Doyle, "Nandasiri Jasentuliyana Keynote Address on Space Law: A Concise History of Space Law," *International Institute of Space Law* (2010), 1–6.

space activity. Despite the existence of an international forum like the United Nations, the outer space realm—if not the entire sphere of terrestrial international politics—resembled the anarchic environment posited by realist political theory.

Additionally, the Soviet space program was driven by the Soviet Union's perceived international interests. Throughout the 1950s, the Soviets pursued their ICBM program full-tilt to counter what they perceived as threatening encirclement by the United States and its allies: by 1957, thanks to the extensive network of post-WWII military bases the United States was able to install in Europe, a significant number of "medium-range missiles and bombers [were] deployed around the Soviet periphery."[31] Soviet leaders certainly did not believe international institutions would be sufficient to prevent a military attack by the United States. In the months prior to the *Sputnik* launch, particularly after the Soviets' successful test of the R-7 ICBM in August 1957, Soviet First Secretary Nikita Khrushchev made a point of boasting about the Soviet Union's missile capabilities—a bluff (since, despite their success with the R-7, the Soviets had no significant missile stockpile at the time) designed to deter American military action.[32] The *Sputnik* launch itself was a dramatic advancement of Soviet interests in at least three ways. First, it enhanced Soviet prestige and, domestically, Soviet citizens' faith in the supremacy of their country's Communist ideology. Second, it demonstrated unequivocally that the Soviet Union had sufficient rocketry capabilities to launch objects outside of the Earth's atmosphere, thus lending credence to Khrushchev's boasts concerning the Soviet Union's missile superiority over the United States. Third, it was a major international propaganda coup, shaking the confidence of the United States and its Western allies, impressing non-aligned States, and electrifying its Soviet bloc allies. The Soviet Union's development of outer space-capable missiles based on their perceived State interests (notably, fear of the United States, as will be discussed further below) in an international system largely incapable of imposing any costs or consequences tracks quite closely with what we would expect in the anarchic international system realism and the "security dilemma" describe.

It may be curious, then, to consider the response of the United States to the *Sputnik* launch and the reality of Soviet missile development. In a purely anarchic system, the United States would have been expected to engage in "self-help"—developing its own missiles, space systems, and military weaponry;

31 Moltz, *Politics of Space Security*, 91.
32 Moltz, *Politics of Space Security*, 90–91.

confronting the Soviet threat through espionage, sabotage, or military means; and crafting alliances with other States to "balance" the Soviet threat. And the United States did, to one degree or another, do all of these things. We have previously seen how, in the outer space realm specifically, *Sputnik* resulted in the development of official national space policy and a renewed urgency in the ongoing development of American photoreconnaissance spy satellites, and, although it is beyond the scope of this work, the United States also redoubled its ICBM efforts and nuclear testing (see also, below, in the section on "Uncertainty, Fear, and Power Accumulation"). But if the United States pursued a realist policy in its technological and national policy development, it struck on a decidedly different strategy at the international level: rather than eschewing international organizations and international law in favor of self-help and balance-of-power politics, the United States turned to the United Nations and made a concerted effort to mold an international framework and create organizational safeguards for the outer space domain.

The United States had been pressing the United Nations for international regulations related to outer space since even before the *Sputnik* launch. Henry Cabot Lodge, the American ambassador to the United Nations, had linked outer space technology development to international arms control as early as January 1957, nine months before *Sputnik*, and suggested to the General Assembly that the testing of outer space technology be subject to international inspection.[33] Lodge renewed this call with greater urgency in the immediate aftermath of *Sputnik*, calling again for international inspection of space objects, this time by a "technical committee" that would guarantee "exclusively peaceful use of outer space."[34] The Soviets rejected Lodge's proposal, but the United States, even as it moved ahead with its own satellite and rocket development, did not give up on the idea of using international institutions to regulate outer space. In September 1958, Lodge was back with a new proposal: the creation of a "programme for international co-operation in the field of outer space," which would involve the formation of an ad hoc committee "to make … studies and recommendations as to what specific steps the [UN General] Assembly might take to further man's progress in this field [that is, the peaceful use of outer space] and to assure that outer space will be used solely for the benefit of all mankind."[35]

---

33 *See* Henry Cabot Lodge, "Statement by Ambassador Lodge, January 14" in *U.S. Department of State, The Department of State Bulletin*, Vol XXXVI, No. 920, 227 (Feb. 11, 1957).

34 Lodge Speech, 25.

35 Lodge Speech, 25.

As previously explored in Chapter 2, here, at last, US efforts gained traction, ultimately resulting in first an ad hoc, and then a permanent, Committee on the Peaceful Uses of Outer Space.[36] There is no need for lengthy repetition of what has been previously written about COPUOS and its role in developing the international legal regime for outer space. It is enough to reiterate here that COPUOS *did*, in fact, contribute immeasurably to the development of this regime, first through the early discussions and debates between its members, then via the non-binding Declaration of Legal Principles Governing the Activities of States in the Exploration and Use of Outer Space, and, finally, through the binding international treaties—the Outer Space Treaty, Rescue and Return Agreement, Liability Convention, and Registration Convention—it helped to develop and approve. With the international consensus reached on many of the outer space-related issues of concern to the United States and the Soviet Union (particularly with respect to the weaponization of space), COPUOS and the international outer space treaties to which it contributed represented a resounding victory of international institutionalism over international anarchy. As James Clay Moltz notes, the trust, restraint, and budding cooperation engendered by the United States' and the Soviet Union's "effort to build institutionalized, multilateral framework for space security" would prove to have "major 'spin-off' value" by contributing to the eventual signing of the Anti-Ballistic Missile Treaty and the Strategic Arms Control Limitation Agreement.[37]

The United States' successful effort to create an international sub-organization like COPUOS, to engage in the development of international

36 *See* Chapter 2, pp. 12–13.

37 Moltz, *Politics of Space Security*, 125. The Anti-Ballistic Missile Treaty, negotiated between the United States and the Soviet Union and signed in May 1972, limited the parties' ability to develop and deploy anti-ballistic missile systems. Treaty on the Limitation of Anti-Ballistic Missile Systems, May 26, 1972, U.S.-U.S.S.R., 23 U.S.T. 3435, T.I.A.S. No. 7503 [hereafter Anti-Ballistic Missile Treaty]. The United States later withdrew from the Treaty in December 2001, in the aftermath of the September 11, 2001, terrorist attacks, with President George W. Bush citing the risk "from future terrorist or rogue-state missile attacks" as a key motivation for the withdrawal. "U.S. Withdrawal From the ABM Treaty: President Bush's Remarks and U.S. Diplomatic Notes," Dec. 13, 2001, Arms Control Association, https://www.armscontrol.org/act/2002-01/us-withdrawal-abm-treaty-president-bush%E2%80%99s-remarks-us-diplomatic-notes. The Anti-Ballistic Missile Treaty was part of the larger Strategic Arms Limitation Talks (or SALT negotiations). The SALT negotiations took place in two stages between 1969 and 1979, and eventually resulted in the Strategic Arms Control Limitation Agreement (or SALT II Treaty). Treaty Between the United States and the Union of Soviet Socialist Republics on the Limitation of Strategic Offensive Arms, June 18, 1979, 79 *Department of State Bulletin* 24 (1979).

legal principles related to outer space, and, perhaps, most significantly of all, to bring the Soviet Union and its allies to the table and convince them of the importance of international norms for outer space activities is puzzling if viewed through the realist lens of a Thucydides, Waltz, or Kissinger. Why would the United States seek to develop international regulations for outer space, pinning its hopes for peace on the compliance of the untrustworthy Soviets? The only explanation from a realist perspective is a cynical one: that the United States sought some kind of international legal framework conducive to its own interests so as to bolster its international image, or give its own actions a veneer of legality, at the expense of their Soviet rivals. Such a theory builds off realist interpretations of State posturing and justification, since, as international law Professors Jack Goldsmith and Eric Posner point out, it is often the case that States

> … provide legal or moral justifications for their actions, no matter how transparently self-interested their actions are. Their legal or moral justifications cleave to their interests, and so when interests change, so do the rationalizations. At the same time, states frequently accuse other [S]tates of violating international law and norms, as though to discredit them.[38]

While few would argue with the idea that States frequently behave in the manner described by Goldsmith and Posner, seeking to bend or twist various justifications to suit their interests, a realist interpretation of the US push for international outer space law suffers from a number of deficiencies. First, the reasoning underlying the theory is convoluted, even from a realist perspective. After all, if international law or a State's reputation within international organizations matter, doesn't this alone provide a significant blow to realism's key assumptions concerning the primacy of States, the insignificance of international organizations, and the anarchic nature of the international system? Second, even from a realist perspective, a policy of pursuing not just the creation of an international legal regime, but the creation of an *entirely new international sub-organization* that would contribute to the creation of this regime, seems extremely impractical—a great deal of work and effort, spread over a significant period of time, for comparatively little pay-off. Finally, how to explain the significant confluence of American and Soviet beliefs about outer space law, and the two sides' willingness to reflect these beliefs first in

38 Jack L. Goldsmith & Eric A. Posner, *The Limits of International Law* (Oxford: Oxford University Press, 2005), 169.

the Declaration of Legal Principles and then in the Outer Space Treaty and subsequent international conventions? A happy accident?

Considering all this, and despite US policy-makers' hedging with additional missile and outer space development, it makes a good deal more sense to place American—and, once COPUOS had been established, Soviet and, even more broadly, international—actions from the late 1950s through the mid-1970s squarely within an institutionalist international relations framework. Yes, the United States continued the development of nuclear-armed ICBMs, the development and launch of photoreconnaissance spy satellites, and, until the Partial Test-Ban Treaty of 1963, orbital nuclear weapons testing, as well as limited anti-satellite and other military space system development. But American efforts to develop the international law of outer space cannot be considered anything but sincere. The United States' push to form COPUOS and subsequent years of work to develop, in partnership with the Soviet Union (and, to a more limited degree, the other nations represented on COPUOS), international outer space law, reflected a deep-seated belief on the American side—extending all the way back to the Truman Administration's post-war proposal of the "Baruch Plan" for international regulation of nuclear weapons[39]—that international legal frameworks and organizations were the best way to prevent a repetition of the horrors of World War II. American faith in the international order was not misplaced: outer space never became a battlefield of the Cold War, and the international legal framework that the United States, the Soviet Union, and COPUOS created has been among the most enduring and widely-accepted in

39 The Baruch Plan, presented to the United Nations in June 1946, "attempted to create an international organisation that could effectively manage the development of atomic energy for the international community under the auspices of the United Nations." David W. Kearn, "The Baruch Plan and the Quest for Atomic Disarmament," *Diplomacy & Statecraft* 21:41–67, 42 (2010). It represented a radical—and, from a realist perspective, unthinkable—offer by the United States, which, at the time, was the only State to have developed nuclear weapons. Under the Baruch Plan, the US would agree to give up its nuclear weapons in return for the creation of a supranational organization that would "polic[e] against potential defection" from a global framework mandating the peaceful use of atomic energy; sanction States that *did* violate this framework; and also "actively work[] with nations to develop peaceful civilian atomic capabilities." Kearn, "The Baruch Plan and the Quest for Atomic Disarmament," *Diplomacy & Statecraft* 21:41–67, 50. While the Baruch Plan ultimately failed due to opposition from the Soviet Union (which was in the process of developing its own nuclear weapon), it provides a clear example of American faith in the post-war international order and the importance the United States' placed on international law and international organizations in contrast to naked self-interest.

international law.[40] The United States may have hedged its bets by continuing its development of outer space technology (both military and civilian), but for the majority of the Cold War—from President Eisenhower's initial refusal to militarize space, through President Kennedy's and President Johnson's push toward the development of legal principles and formal treaties related to outer space; President Nixon's approval of the Liability Convention, his Administration's support for the drafting of the Moon Agreement, and his outer space partnerships with the Soviet Union itself; and, despite their broadening of American ASAT development, President Ford's and President Carter's continued pursuit of international agreement and cooperation (including the Registration Convention and Carter's failed proposal for an ASAT treaty) in the outer space realm—internationalist policies and a steadfast belief in the enduring strength of international and bilateral agreements governed American space policy.[41]

It would be over twenty years after the founding of COPUOS and the beginnings of international outer space law development that the Reagan Administration would alter American space security policies and move the United States away from its previous, internationalist perspective. Reagan, as noted above in Chapter 3, emphasized the military and security aspects of outer space in his National Space Policy, proposing the development of outer space weapons, the potential projection of military force from outer space, and the deployment (rather than merely the development) of operational ASAT systems.[42] These policies, in addition to the proposed orbital anti-missile platforms of the Strategic Defense Initiative—the development and testing of which, despite the legal gymnastics of Administration lawyers, were widely criticized by international legal scholars, domestic critics of the Reagan Administration, and Soviet diplomats as a violation of the Anti-Ballistic Missile Treaty[43]—sounded the death-knell of President Eisenhower's goal of

---

40 Indeed, States continue to accede to the Outer Space Treaty and the other four space-related international conventions to this day. *See* COPUOS Legal Subcommittee., *Status of International Agreements relating to activities in outer space as at 1 January 2019*, 58th Sess., U.N. Doc. A/AC.105/C.2/2019/CRP.3 (Apr. 1, 2019).

41 *See* Chapter 3, pp. 55–87.

42 *See* Chapter 3, pp. 87–99.

43 *See* John E. Parkerson, Jr., "International Legal Implications of the Strategic Defense Initiative," 116 *Military Law Review* 67, 96–129 (Spring 1987). The primary debate between proponents and opponents of SDI was whether the Anti-Ballistic Missile Treaty's prohibitions actually applied to SDI, which, at least theoretically, was proposed as a laser- or beam-based weapons system—a system that would not have the "interceptor missiles" or "launchers" described by Article II of the Treaty's definitions of an "ABM system." *See* Parkerson, "International Legal Implications," 99–100; Anti-Ballistic Missile Treaty,

preventing the weaponization and militarization of space. In contrast to his predecessors, President Reagan's outer space policy was decidedly realist: by scuttling the efforts initiated by the Carter Administration for an ASAT treaty, pursuing SDI, and altering the United States' space security policies in the ways previously described, the Reagan Administration demonstrated an unequivocal preference for nationalist, self-help policies over internationalist, institutionalist ones. Reagan's policies are curious because, while realist and anti-internationalist, they stemmed from the President's decidedly idealist—even Wilsonian—beliefs concerning the superiority of American democracy as a government system and the evil and backwardness of Communism. Reagan believed that the Soviet Union was an "evil empire," whose very ideology mandated deception in the pursuit of their goals:

> … Soviet leaders have openly and publicly declared that the only morality they recognize is that which will further their cause, which is world revolution …. Morality is entirely subordinate to the interests of class war. And everything is moral that is necessary for the annihilation of the old, exploiting social order and for uniting the proletariat.
>
> Well, I think the refusal of many influential people to accept this elementary fact of Soviet doctrine illustrates an historical reluctance to see totalitarian powers for what they are. We saw this phenomenon in the 1930's. We see it too often today.
>
> …
>
> It was C. S. Lewis who, in his unforgettable "Screwtape Letters," wrote: "The greatest evil is not done now in those sordid 'dens of crime' that Dickens loved to paint. It is not even done in concentration camps and labor camps. In those we see its final result. But it is conceived and ordered (moved, seconded, carried and minuted) in clear, carpeted, warmed, and well-lighted offices, by quiet men with white collars and cut fingernails and smooth-shaven cheeks who do not need to raise their voice."

---

art. II. The Anti-Ballistic Missile Treaty's Article III prohibition on anything more than two ground-based ABM sites, however, was considered a significant limitation on the orbital deployment of the proposed SDI system. *See* Parkerson, "International Legal Implications," 100–107; Anti-Ballistic Missile Treaty, art. III.

> Well, because these "quiet men" do not "raise their voices," because they sometimes speak in soothing tones of brotherhood and peace, because, like other dictators before them, they're always making "their final territorial demand," some would have us accept them at their word and accommodate ourselves to their aggressive impulses. But if history teaches anything, it teaches that simple-minded appeasement or wishful thinking about our adversaries is folly. It means the betrayal of our past, the squandering of our freedom.[44]

Consequently, although Reagan never explicitly described the international system as anarchic, he was firm in his belief that the Soviet Union could not be constrained by international law or the reputational checks of international institutions, and any protestations by Soviet leaders to the contrary could not be trusted.[45] Reagan's realist perspective guided not just his approach to outer space policy, but a wide range of his Administration's policies concerning the

---

44 Ronald Reagan, "Remarks at the Annual Convention of the National Association of Evangelicals in Orlando, Florida," *Reagan Foundation*, Mar. 8, 1983, available at https://www.reaganfoundation.org/media/50919/remarks_annual_convention_national_association_evangelicals_030883.pdf (last visited Apr. 26, 2020).

45 Another example of Reagan's unabashed realist perspective can be found in the introduction of his address to the UN General Assembly on the 40th anniversary of the UN's founding: "Mr. President, Mr. Secretary General, honored guests, and distinguished delegates, thank you for the honor of permitting me to speak on this anniversary for the United Nations. Forty years ago, the world awoke daring to believe hatred's unyielding grip had finally been broken, daring to believe the torch of peace would be protected in liberty's firm grasp. Forty years ago, the world yearned to dream again innocent dreams, to believe in ideals with innocent trust. Dreams of trust are worthy, but in these 40 years too many dreams have been shattered, too many promises have been broken, too many lives have been lost. *The painful truth is that the use of violence to take, to exercise, and to preserve power remains a persistent reality in much of the world.* The vision of the U.N. Charter—to spare succeeding generations this scourge of war—remains real. It still stirs our soul and warms our hearts, *but it also demands of us a realism that is rockhard, clear-eyed, steady, and sure—a realism that understands the nations of the United Nations are not united*" [emphasis added]. Ronald Reagan, "Address to the 40th Session of the United Nations General Assembly in New York, New York," *Reagan Foundation*, Oct. 24, 1985, https://www.reaganfoundation.org/media/128611/assembly.pdf (last visited Dec. 30, 2021). It should be noted that although Reagan uses the term "realism" several times in this passage, it is likely he is using the term in its traditional sense—i.e. seeing and accepting a thing or situation as it really is—rather than in its more specialized definition under international relations theory. Even so, Reagan's recognition of international disunity among nations, their failure to be constrained by the supposedly supranational UN, and the all too frequent use of might-makes-right ("the use of violence to take, to exercise, and to preserve power") places his thinking firmly in line with realist international relations principles.

Soviet Union, including arming the Afghan Mujahideen and the Nicaraguan Contras; supporting the anti-Communist Solidarity movement in Poland; and building up the United States' military.

Whether Reagan's perception of the Soviet Union (at least, with respect to international relations theory) was correct and the extent to which his Administration's actions—particularly the pursuit of SDI—contributed to the United States' ultimate victory in the Cold War continue to be topics of debate. What *is* clear, however, is that the realist policies resulting from Reagan's perception of the international environment and his belief that international law was insufficient to prevent Soviet aggression have had far-reaching consequences. Key aspects of the United States' space security policy during the Reagan Administration—notably a greater willingness to develop and even deploy space weapons, the creation of military commands devoted to space-related military matters, and the perception of outer space as a "war-fighting domain"—have become permanent fixtures of American space policy. We have seen how Reagan's presidency marked a turning point in outer space security policy, and how, particularly after the publication of once-and-future Defense Secretary Donald Rumsfeld's 2001 Space Commission report, Reagan-esque views of space came to be solidified in modern American national space policy.

Even given President Reagan's more realist view of the world, the case for a more anarchic international order near the end of the Cold War should not be overstated. Despite Soviet aggression in Afghanistan and President Reagan's more confrontational anti-Soviet policies—including his space security policies, and his pursuit of SDI, in arguable contravention of the Anti-Ballistic Missile Treaty—neither the United States nor the Soviet Union wholly abandoned international law, international agreements, or the use of international systems. During the first year of his presidency, Reagan continued treaty negotiations with the Soviets for strategic arms reductions, particularly on intermediate-range ballistic missiles, that had originally begun near the end of the Carter Presidency. On the same subject, Reagan agreed—despite loathing the agreement—to abide by the nuclear arms limitations contained in the unratified SALT II treaty, at least until its expiration in December 1985.[46] President Carter had withdrawn SALT II from consideration by the Senate in

46 The SALT II Treaty, mentioned above in footnote 37, imposed requirements for reductions in nuclear armaments and limitations on the development of new missile systems and programs. Treaty Between the United States and the Union of Soviet Socialist Republics on the Limitation of Strategic Offensive Arms, June 18, 1979, 79 *Department of State Bulletin* 24 (1979).

response to the Soviet Union's invasion of Afghanistan, but the Soviets had nevertheless agreed to abide by its terms. There was strong domestic and international pressure behind Reagan's decision to do likewise. Further, though President Reagan was highly critical of the United Nations, he did not hesitate to use the bully-pulpit it provided to contrast the United States and the Soviet Union and to attempt to subject the Soviets to international scrutiny.[47] Though Reagan may not have had faith in the ability of international law to constrain Soviet action, he was also unwilling for the United States to fully cede the moral high ground that abiding by international law provided: even for SDI, Reagan attempted to balance international law with the almost self-evident violation of the spirit (if not the text) of the ABM Treaty that SDI represented, by (perhaps self-contradictorily) mandating that development of the SDI system "be carried out in a manner consistent with our obligations under the ABM Treaty."[48]

47 President Reagan's first address before the UN General Assembly, for instance, focused heavily on the strategic arms reduction negotiations with the Soviet Union (a new round of which was about to begin), emphasizing the United States' willingness to reduce its military armaments and its numerous attempts at proposing disarmament solutions: "Over the past seven months, the United States has put forward a broad-based, comprehensive series of proposals to reduce the risk of war. We have proposed four major points as an agenda for peace: elimination of land-based, intermediate-range missiles; a one-third reduction in strategic ballistic missile warheads; a substantial reduction in NATO and Warsaw Pact ground and air forces; and new safeguards to reduce the risk of accidental war. We urge the Soviet Union today to join with us in this quest. We must act not for ourselves alone, but for all mankind. / On November 18th of last year, I announced United States objectives in arms control agreements. They must be equitable and militarily significant. They must stabilize forces at lower levels, and they must be verifiable. The United States and its allies have made specific, reasonable, and equitable proposals. / In February, our negotiating team in Geneva offered the Soviet Union a draft treaty on intermediate-range nuclear forces. We offered to cancel deployment of our Pershing II ballistic missiles and ground-launched cruise missiles in exchange for Soviet elimination of the SS—20, SS—4, and SS—5 missiles. This proposal would eliminate with one stroke those systems about which both sides have expressed the greatest concern. / The United States is also looking forward to beginning negotiations on strategic arms reductions with the Soviet Union in less than 2 weeks. We will work hard to make these talks an opportunity for real progress in our quest for peace." / Ronald Reagan, "Remarks in New York, New York, Before the United Nations General Assembly Special Session Devoted to Disarmament," *Reagan Library*, June 17, 1982, https://www.reaganlibrary.gov/research/speeches/61782a (last visited Dec. 30, 2021).

48 Ronald Reagan, NSDD-85, *Eliminating the Threat from Ballistic Missiles*, Mar. 25, 1983, available at https://aerospace.csis.org/wp-content/uploads/2019/02/NSDD-85-Eliminating-the-Threat-From-Ballisitc-Missiles.pdf (last visited June 15, 2022).

Additionally, and, perhaps most importantly of all given our current discussion, President Reagan made no attempt to withdraw from or significantly alter the international outer space legal framework. Both of Reagan's National Space Policies, the more aggressive NSDD 42 and the (slightly) more conciliatory NSDD 293, recognized key principles of international outer space law, as well as repeated earlier American policy references to ideas like the use of outer space for "peaceful purposes," which were traditionally understood as being part of the international space law framework. While NSDD 42 was certainly a sea-change in American policy concerning the development and potential use of outer space weapons, none of its proposed policies actually violated the Outer Space Treaty or other international outer space law. Even SDI (had it been successfully developed and leaving aside issues of its likely violation of the ABM Treaty) would likely not have been contrary to the outer space legal regime: assuming the SDI system's orbital anti-missile platforms were not armed with nuclear weapons or "weapons of mass destruction," their stationing in orbit would be perfectly legal, as our previous discussion of the arms control provisions of Article IV of the Outer Space Treaty shows.[49]

49 This assumption, it should be noted, rests on the traditional understanding of the term "weapons of mass destruction" (largely drawn from other areas of international law) as meaning "nuclear, chemical, biological, or radiological weapons capable of causing indiscriminate death to masses of people, or devastation to large areas of property." Parkerson, "International Legal Implications," *Military Law Review*, 87 (internal citations omitted). As Major John Parkerson explains, this understanding of the term "weapons of mass destruction" tracks with the perceptions of several key American political leaders—specifically, Deputy Secretary of Defense Cyrus Vance and US Ambassador to the United Nations Arthur Goldberg—during the ratification hearings of the Outer Space Treaty. *See* Parkerson, "International Legal Implications," 86–87. Both Vance and Goldberg, however, cited the possibility of weapons with capabilities of destruction similar to those of nuclear weapons potentially qualifying as "weapons of mass destruction." Because the SDI orbital platforms were, at least theoretically, not envisioned as being nuclear-armed or employing other chemical, biological, or radiological weapons, they would likely be considered conventional weapons under Article IV of the Outer Space Treaty. This was the conclusion of not just Major Parkerson, but also a number of other American legal researchers examining the issue. *See generally* George Bernhardt, Sandra M. Gresko, and Thomas R. Merry, "Star Wars versus Star Laws: Does SDI Conform to Outer Space Law; The Reagan Legacy and the Strategic Defense Initiative: Note," *Journal of Legislation*, vol. 15, iss. 2 (1989), pp. 251–73. That said, considering the potentially wide-ranging effects of the orbital debris (at least theoretically) created through the use of SDI's destruction of intercontinental ballistic missiles during their on-orbit travel to intended targets, the question of whether possible multi-order effects of a "successful" SDI defensive strike could qualify as resulting in level of destruction similar to a nuclear weapon is an open one. The United States' STARFISH PRIME on-orbit nuclear test in July 1962, for example, resulted in the premature "loss of seven satellites within months after the test" through their increased

Further, even the military policies related to outer space that were drafted during the Reagan Administration, most notably the Air Force's AFM 6–1, *Military Space Doctrine*, make explicit reference to the provisions of the Outer Space Treaty and other international space law.[50] These facts are indicative of the United States' continued acceptance of outer space law as it had been understood since at least the ratification of the Outer Space Treaty, and its belief that its actions (even its new willingness to expand military—and even weaponized—uses of outer space) fell squarely within the acceptable bounds the international outer space law framework.

All this is to say that, while Ronald Reagan's Presidency was characterized by an increased amount of realist-inspired thinking and realist-style confrontation with the Soviet Union, there was hardly a full-scale abandonment of internationalist, institutionalist principles during the last years of the Cold War. Bilateral negotiations, interaction with and use of international organizations, compliance with (or justification under) international law, and a continued adherence to the international outer space legal framework all continued through the end of the Reagan Administration. Reagan's successor, President George H.W. Bush, exhibited an even greater acceptance of internationalism—an acceptance demonstrated by his stringent efforts to build an international coalition for military operations in the Persian Gulf War and his management, through both US and international efforts, of the disintegration of the Soviet Union. From the days of US-Soviet competition under President Eisenhower through the Soviet Union's collapse under President Bush I, the international system was more than the simple, anarchic system posited by realist theory. Far from being a Hobbesian arena in which either side could do whatever it

---

exposure to ionizing radiation. Epaminondas G. Stassinopoulos, "The STARFISH Exo-atmospheric, High-altitude Nuclear Weapons Test," Supplemental Speaker Notes, Hardened Electronics and Radiation Technology (HEART) 2015 Conference, Chantilly, VA, April 22, 2015, available at https://nepp.nasa.gov/files/26652/2015-561-Stassinopoulos-Final-Paper-Web-HEART2015-STARFISH-supplemental-TN26292.pdf. Should orbital weapons, like those proposed for the SDI program, be considered "weapons of mass destruction"—regardless of their traditional, terrestrial status as "conventional" (non-chemical, non-biological, non-nuclear, and non-radiological) weapons—if their on-orbit results are as destructive or dangerous (particularly over the long term, considering the length of time debris can persist in orbit) to other space objects and the orbital environment as those of a nuclear weapon? This is a question that remains to be answered.

50 Section 1–9 of AFM 6–1, entitled "International Law," contains ten sub-paragraphs describing key legal principles from the Outer Space Treaty, the PTBT, the ABM Treaty, and the UN Charter; while the three latter international documents are explicitly referenced, the Outer Space Treaty is not, but is included in the "Selected Bibliography for Military Space Doctrine" at the end of the document. *See* AFM 1–6, *Military Space Doctrine*, 3–4, 12.

pleased, the international system contained certain checks and balances that constrained—however slightly, at times—State behavior. Even during periods when the Cold War was at its most realist points, such as the *Sputnik* launch and beginning of true Soviet missile development and the more significant international confrontation occurring during the 1980s, the post-World War II international framework, and, in the realm of outer space, the space law framework developed in the Outer Space Treaty and other international space law instruments remained.

3.2.2 Uncertainty, Fear, and Power Accumulation

We have already seen, in our examination of "international anarchy," above, that outer space relations between the United States and the Soviet Union during the Cold War are unlikely to fit the "security dilemma" theory—and not just because American-Soviet relations never devolved into the self-reinforcing conflict cycle that is the unfortunate consequence of true "security dilemmas." Still, even if the "international anarchy" required for a true "security dilemma" is lacking, it remains an importance intellectual exercise to examine at least two additional factors of Tang's "security dilemma" analysis—that States in a "security dilemma" scenario fear one another due to uncertainty about one another's actions and intentions, and, consequently, that the States in question seek to accumulate power and capability to increase their own security. Even outside a truly anarchic international system, these two factors can contribute to significant conflict between States—including arms races and conflict cycles that may be "security dilemma"-esque, even if they fail to fulfill all of the factors described by Tang and other "security dilemma" theorists. As these two factors—fear/uncertainty and power accumulation—relate closely to each other, they will be examined together. While there may be a serious question concerning the nature of the international system and whether Cold War space policy did, in fact, represent action-and-reaction in an anarchic international environment, there is little doubt that uncertainty and even fear existed on both the American and Soviet sides over one another's space programs. The extent to which this uncertainty and fear resulted in policies directed toward increasing or improving outer space capabilities (whether photoreconnaissance satellite capabilities, or more directly military space capabilities) varied by Presidential Administration, but increasing the robustness of American space capabilities and American space security was, as we have seen, a continuous policy from the Eisenhower Presidency through the modern day.

The *Sputnik* launch brought home to large numbers of Americans that the Soviet Union was a technologically capable foe—one that could, as Soviet politicians had already boasted, use its rocket technology to launch warheads at the United States rather than satellites into space. Though *Sputnik* itself posed no direct military threat to the United States, the satellite launch rocked American public perception: General James Gavin, the World War II hero and former commanding general of the 82nd Airborne Division, characterized the *Sputnik* launch as "a technological Pearl Harbor,"[51] while President Eisenhower (who had likely been forewarned about the *Sputnik* launch and was also confident that then-existing American advancements in space technology were more than a match for the Soviets' capabilities) later acknowledged that

> [i]n the weeks and months after Sputnik many Americans seemed to be seized not only with a sudden worry that our defenses had crumbled, but also with an equally unjustified alarm that our entire education system was defective. The Soviets, some suspected, would soon surpass us intellectually, if indeed they had not already done so.[52]

Less than ten days after the launch, the media had already coined the term "Sputnik diplomacy" to describe the Soviet Union's efforts to use *Sputnik* as a propaganda tool to attract non-aligned nations into the Soviet camp—and as a technological cudgel to bully its enemies.[53] Even worse, the perception of the United States among its European allies was significantly affected by *Sputnik*: "[t]he result of public opinion polls in Western Europe following the Soviets' *Sputnik* flight showed that by a large margin the French, Italian, German, and even British populations had become convinced of Soviet superiority over the United States in scientific development" and "rated the Soviet Union ahead [of the United States] in overall military power, albeit by a lesser margin."[54]

---

51 Gavin, *War and Peace in the Space Age* 16.

52 Dwight D. Eisenhower, *The White House Years: Waging Peace 1956–1961* (Garden City, NY: Doubleday, 1965), 216.

53 *See* Associated Press, "Sputnik Diplomacy," *New York Times* (Oct. 13, 1957), available at https://timesmachine.nytimes.com/timesmachine/1957/10/13/96960759.html?pageNumber=190 (last visited Apr. 21, 2020). Vehemently editorializing on what the author perceived to be Soviet bullying in the aftermath of *Sputnik*, one article on so-called "Sputnik diplomacy" snarled, "[i]f the spirit of arrogance and vindictiveness were [sic] not already in the Russian Communists the sputnik helped put it there. If that spirit were already in them the sputnik did not weaken or remove it." Associated Press, "Sputnik Diplomacy," *New York Times* (Oct. 13, 1957).

54 Moltz, *Politics of Space Security*, 92 (citing Dodd L. Harvey & Linda C. Ciccoritti, *U.S.-Soviet Cooperation in Space* (Washington: Center For Advanced International Studies, University Of Miami, 1974), 49–50; Walter A. McDougall, … *the Heavens and the Earth: A Political History of the Space Age* 2nd ed. (Baltimore, MD: Johns Hopkins University Press, 1997), 240–41).

The fearful reaction of the American and global public was exacerbated when Eisenhower's Democratic political rivals—most notably then-Senate Majority Leader Lyndon Johnson, who initiated a Congressional Committee to investigate how the Soviets were able to surpass the United States' space efforts—seized upon the *Sputnik* launch as evidence of Republican failures to protect US national security.

Despite the public reaction to *Sputnik* and the alarmist accusations of unpreparedness Eisenhower's Democratic rivals sought to turn to their political advantage, the US government's reaction to *Sputnik* was surprisingly calm. President Eisenhower, fully aware of the American military's multiple rocket and satellite projects, downplayed *Sputnik* as "one small ball in the air" that posed neither a military nor an intelligence threat to the United States.[55] Indeed, as we have seen, in some ways the Eisenhower Administration was privately pleased the Soviets had launched first, as it made Eisenhower's goal of free passage overflight rights in space effectively a fait accompli.[56] Secretary of Defense Charles Wilson described the Soviets' launch as a little more than a "neat scientific trick" and reassured Americans that "nobody is going to drop anything down on you from a satellite while you're asleep, so don't worry about it."[57] Even Air Force General Curtis LeMay, the Commander of Strategic Air Command and not a man known for his tolerance of Soviet military power, dismissed *Sputnik* as "just a hunk of iron"[58] and (apparently independently of President Eisenhower, who agreed with his position) rejected calls from the Air Force staff to protest *Sputnik's* overflight of the United States.[59]

This is not to say, of course, that *Sputnik* and the Soviet space and rocketry program did not contribute to development of the American space program or that the United States as a whole was unconcerned about the Soviets'

55 Delbert R. Terrill, Jr., *The Air Force Role in Developing International Outer Space Law* (Maxwell Air Force Base, AL: Air University Press, 1999), 29–30, available at https://media.defense.gov/2010/Sep/22/2001330058/-1/-1/0/AFD-100922-019.pdf (last visited Apr. 24, 2020).

56 *See* Chapter 3, pp. 54–55.

57 U.S. House of Representatives, *Toward the Endless Frontier: History of the Committee on Science and Technology, 1959–79* (Washington, D.C.: U.S. Government Printing Office, 1980), 4–5.

58 Sharon Weinberger, *The Imagineers of War: The Untold History of DARPA, the Pentagon Agency that Changed the World* (New York: Knopf, 2017), 33.

59 *See* Terrill, *The Air Force Role in Developing International Outer Space Law*, 29. When LeMay was asked by members of the Air Staff "whether the US should protest given that by Sputnik's overflight of the United States the Soviets had violated US sovereignty," LeMay bluntly refused, responding, "We were going to orbit their country weren't we?" Terrill, *The Air Force Role in Developing International Outer Space Law*, 29.

successful space launch. Public perception, both from the American citizenry and the United States' international allies, mandated an American response. Recognizing this, Eisenhower sought to bolster both the nation's military and civilian space programs, transferring responsibility for the United States' first satellite launch to the Army (which accomplished this goal with the launch of *Explorer 1* on a modified Jupiter-C rocket in January 1958) and creating NASA in the National Aeronautics and Space Act in July 1958.[60] He also spurred the Air Force and CIA on with their efforts to development photoreconnaissance spy satellites. This effort, of course, was successful, but did nothing to assuage American or international concern regarding Soviet capabilities because it was highly classified and could not be publicly discussed. Indeed, the election of John F. Kennedy in 1960 could be considered (at least in part) a political victory tracking the fear and uncertainty inherent in security dilemma theory. During his presidential campaign against Richard Nixon, who was then Eisenhower's Vice President, Kennedy took up the national security critiques that Lyndon Johnson had raised in Congress two years earlier, hammering Nixon for the missile and space technology the Soviet Union had been able to develop and the resulting "missile gap" the Eisenhower Administration had failed to close. Nixon could do little to counter Kennedy's accusations; even though he knew that no such "missile gap" existed, he could not say so, as this would reveal the United States' then-secret satellite surveillance capabilities.[61] Kennedy's election, and his Administration's more competitive stance toward overtaking the Soviet Union in outer space, can be seen as a classic example of fear (of Soviet capabilities, a "missile gap," and Soviet domination of space) and uncertainty (the American public having no way of knowing what Eisenhower and Nixon knew, and, thus, of rationally examining the risks associated with their fears) leading to actions to develop or increase a State's own capabilities. Had the Kennedy Administration, and, after Kennedy's assassination, the Johnson Administration, not combined their "Space Race" technological development with additional efforts at the international level, through COPUOS and the

60 *See* Moltz, *Politics of Space Security*, 95–96.

61 James Clay Moltz describes Nixon's dilemma thus: "Nixon knew that these charges [Kennedy's accusations of the development of a "missile gap"] and even some U.S. government statements about Soviet capabilities were false. However, intelligence limitations kept him from revealing that the Soviets had not in fact developed any sizeable missile stockpile. But this *perceived* imbalance in U.S.-Soviet capabilities affected the American political scene greatly and provided Kennedy with a cause célèbre. Nixon attempted to argue that despite operational setbacks, the United States held a lead in space technology. Given the secrecy of the Corona program, however, his line of reasoning proved hard to sell to a now doubtful American public." Moltz, *Politics of Space Security*, 106.

United Nations, to develop outer space law, it may be more likely that a true "security dilemma" would have resulted.

On the Soviet side, distrust and fear of American intentions (and, at least at the beginning of the Space Age, a desire to maintain Soviet technological advantage), drove Soviet decision-making even more than it did on the American side. As Soviet First Secretary Nikita Khrushchev would later write in his memoirs, the Soviets celebrated their successful development of advanced rocket boosters and rockets—which allowed them to develop both ICBMs and outer space launch vehicles—as a necessary deterrent to American "aggression":

> We'd come a long way from the time when Stalin was terrified we would be attacked by our imperialist enemies at any moment. No longer were we contaminated by Stalin's fear; no longer did we look at the world through his eyes. Now it was our enemies who trembled in *their* boots ....
>
> Of course, we tried to derive maximum political advantage from the fact that we were the first to launch our rockets into space. We wanted to exert pressure on American militarists—and also influence the minds of more reasonable politicians—so that the United States would start treating us better.[62]

Stalin's well-known paranoia may have made Soviet fears more extreme than the average State's within the international system, but it is little wonder that the Soviet Union, under both Stalin and Khrushchev, should suffer from fear and distrust of its international enemies. Neither Stalin's trust, nor the Soviet Union's non-aggression pact with Nazi Germany, had prevented Adolf Hitler's armies from invading the Soviet Union in June 1941. Hitler's aggression had resulted in over 23 million Soviet deaths[63] and nearly toppled the Soviet Union. The raw memories of Hitler's betrayal made it perfectly natural that, in the post-war period—with the United States now the Soviet Unions' unequivocal ideological and global adversary and in possession of a devastating new atomic weapon—fear and uncertainty of US intentions would drive the Soviets to develop their own nuclear weapons and means for delivering them.

62 Nikita Sergeevich Khrushchev, *Khrushchev Remembers: The Last Testament* (Boston, MA: Little Brown & Company, 1974), Strobe Talbott, trans. & ed., 53.

63 *See* "World War II Casualties," *Centre Européen Robert Schuman*, http://www.centre-robert-schuman.org/userfiles/files/REPERES%20–%20module%201-2-0%20-%20explanatory%20notes%20–%20World%20War%20II%20casualties%20–%20EN.pdf (last visited Apr. 20, 2020).

As Khrushchev crowed in his memoirs, the Soviet development of intercontinental and outer space-capable missiles threw the United States onto its back foot. We have seen, above, the international political overtures and national military/scientific development that Soviet space and rocketry activities triggered in the United States. But the Soviets, at least initially, would not engage with the United States on the matter of space cooperation. Khrushchev later explained:

> I believe at that time [the first several years after the launch *Sputnik 1*] the US might have been willing to cooperate with us, but we weren't willing to cooperate with them. Why? Because while we might have been ahead of the Americans in space exploration, we were still behind them in nuclear weaponry. The US had more warheads, more air bases, and more bombers ....
>
> ... The Americans were terribly curious about our *Semyorka* [missile] booster. They were obviously interested in space cooperation merely as a pretext for finding out our secret. We knew that if we let them have a look at our rocket, they'd easily be able to copy it. Then, with their mighty industry and superb technology, they'd be able to start producing replicas of our booster and soon have more than we had. That would have been a threat to our security ....
>
> We felt we needed time to test, perfect, produce, and install the boosters by ourselves. Once we got our feet planted firmly on the ground and provided for the defense of our country, *then* we could begin space cooperation with the United States. Such cooperation could be to the benefit of both sides. After all, there's enough outer space for everyone.[64]

Khrushchev's explanation tracks perfectly with the "security dilemma" factors of fear/uncertainty and power accumulation. If, as Khrushchev and other Soviet leaders frequently claimed, the development of nuclear weapons and missile, rocket, and outer space technology was a defensive measure intended solely to protect the Soviet Union from attack, Soviet behavior through the 1950s and into the early 1960s seems to satisfy Tang's two elements.

If the "security dilemma" factors of fear, uncertainty, and power accumulation seemed to be influencers for both American (more minor influence)

64 Khrushchev, *Khrushchev Remembers: The Last Testament*, 54.

and Soviet (significant influence) actions in the early Space Age, however, two key developments would reduce at least uncertainty, if not fear, to more manageable levels. First, the United States' push for the creation of COPUOS and efforts at the United Nations to convince the Soviet Union and its allies to participate in the Committee marked the beginning of what would be a significant shift in the fear/uncertainty factor (at least in terms of outer space activity) between the two sides of the Cold War. By the end of 1962, a number of events—including the hair-trigger Cuban Missile Crisis and multiple high-altitude nuclear tests by both the United States and the Soviet Union, which damaged satellites and interfered with terrestrial radio frequencies—had convinced the belligerents that increased cooperation was necessary if catastrophic nuclear conflict was to be avoided.[65] Further, in the outer space realm, pressure from both the American and Soviet militaries for research and development of space weaponry, especially nuclear weaponry, were causing concern: "[s]pace-based weapons systems … raised the very real specter of an arms race in space, a prospect not attractive for budget reasons and even less desirable due to persistent evaluations that space-based weapons in themselves did not add appreciably" to military deterrence.[66] These events and factors finally tipped the balance toward greater Soviet Bloc participation in COPUOS, which ultimately laid the groundwork for the development of the international outer space legal framework. The coming together of the United States and the Soviet Union through their representatives in COPUOS, and the mutual realization that the two sides shared many key beliefs concerning preferred principals for outer space law, provided a basis for increased trust and cooperation. The resulting development of the Outer Space Treaty and its entrance into force in 1967 with both the United States and the Soviet Union as signatories created clear international limits with respect to the most significant military uses of space, as well as clear (or, at least, clearer) guidelines with respect to State behavior in outer space. This legal framework—supplemented over the next eight years with additional international agreements concerning the protection of astronauts and spacecraft, international liability, and the registration of space objects—helped to minimize uncertainty surrounding States' extraterrestrial behavior and increase trust between the United States and the Soviet Union, thereby decreasing the chances of "security dilemma"-esque escalation or confrontation.

---

65 *See* Moltz, *Politics of Space Security*, 127–42.

66 Handberg, *Seeking New World Vistas: The Militarization of Space*, 58.

Second, the development of first American, and, later, Soviet, photoreconnaissance and other signal- and electronic-intelligence collection satellites[67] provided the Cold War belligerents with almost a "silver bullet" for "security dilemma" uncertainty. With the intelligence satellite imagery could provide, the two sides might not have been able to fathom each other's intentions, but they *could* accurately detect each other's military capabilities, including troop build-ups/movements, military bases, missile silos, and more. Such intelligence was key to reducing political leaders' fears and the risk of counter-productive or escalatory behavior on both sides. President Johnson would, in March 1967, provide a window into the significance of satellite technology in reducing Cold War tensions when he gave a glowing assessment of the Corona Project satellites first developed during the Eisenhower Administration (as well as a belated recognition that Nixon's arguments against Johnson's running-mate, President Kennedy, during the 1960 election had been right all along):

> I wouldn't want to be quoted on this but we've spent 35 or 40 billion dollars on the space program. And if nothing else had come out of it except the knowledge we've gained from space photography, it would be worth ten times what the whole program has cost. Because tonight we know how many missiles the enemy has and, it turned out, our guesses were way off. *We were doing things we didn't need to do. We were building things we didn't need to build. We were harboring fears we didn't need to harbor* [emphasis added].[68]

---

67 The United States' Corona satellite program has been previously discussed; other early American intelligence satellite programs included the Naval Research Laboratory's GRAB ("Galactic Radiation and Background") satellite, also code-named "Tattletale," which was designed to collect Soviet radar signals. *See generally* Robert A. McDonald and Sharon K. Moreno, "Raising the Periscope… Grab and Poppy: America's Early ELINT Satellites," Center for the Study of National Reconnaissance, National Reconnaissance Office, September 2005, available at https://www.nro.gov/Portals/65/documents/history/csnr/programs/docs/prog-hist-03.pdf. On the Soviet side, the Zenit model reconnaissance satellites (which, similar to the Corona satellites, returned capsules of film from orbit) and a number of ELINT satellites fulfilled these functions. *See* Asif A. Siddiqi, "Soviet Space Power During the Cold War" in *Harnessing the Heavens: National Defense through Space*, Paul G. Gillespie and Grant T. Weller, eds. (Chicago: Imprint Publications, 2008), 140–41; National Intelligence Estimate, "Soviet Military Intentions and Capabilities in Space," NIE 11-1-80, August 6, 1980, available at https://www.cia.gov/readingroom/docs/DOC_0000284010.pdf.

68 Peter L. Hays, *Space and Security: A Reference Handbook* (Santa Barbara, CA: ABC-CLIO, 2011), 28 (quoting William E. Burrows, *Deep Black: Space Espionage and National Security* (New York: Berkley Books, 1988), vii).

Johnson's concluding points are indicative of the "security dilemma"-style thinking in which many American political and military leaders—including President Kennedy and Johnson himself—had been engaging during the early 1960s. Just as Tang and other "security dilemma" theorists posit, "fear" had been leading the United States to "do things" and "build things"— seeking to increase its relative power and capabilities in response to the perceived threat posed by the Soviet Union. But this cycle was broken, partially due to the clarity and transparency provided by satellite photoreconnaissance. On the Soviet side, too, development of satellite photoreconnaissance capabilities proved to be critical in convincing Soviet leadership that international agreements with the United States could be independently verified, ultimately resulting in greater willingness by the Soviets to engage in treaty negotiations with the United States.[69]

The vacillations of the Cold War would result in a number of returns to fear/uncertainty and power accumulation behavior. Deteriorating American-Soviet relations during the Ford Administration, as well as a resumption of Soviet ASAT tests during the early 1970s, for instance, triggered the Ford and Carter Administration policies related to the enhancement of the American ASAT program.[70] But, as was the case with his Administration's tilt toward realism in our "international anarchy" discussion, above, it was President Reagan's proposed development of SDI, that represented the sharpest return to action-reaction power accumulation during the Cold War. Reagan's plan, as described in Chapter 3, was to develop a technologically advanced anti-ballistic missile "shield" that would protect the United States from Soviet ICBM attack. The idea of SDI had all the classic characteristics of a "security dilemma"-style technological advance: even if purportedly developed for peaceful, defensive reasons (as Reagan and other SDI proponents claimed), an operational SDI system would present a potential adversary with the unacceptable prospect of facing

69 Describing Khrushchev's first review of Soviet satellite intelligence, James Clay Moltz writes: "In April 1962, the four-camera Zenit 2 system aboard the so-called *Kosmos 4* flight had returned its first images, and by late July, a returning spacecraft delivered the first usable photographs of U.S. sites. While the Soviet satellite system would not have full functionality until 1964, even its initial capability represented a revelation for Khrushchev. Suddenly, he glimpsed what the United States had enjoyed for two years and recognized the potential of photo-reconnaissance to assist in treaty verification over U.S. soil without having to allow prying U.S. inspectors onto Soviet territory." In a secret communication to President Kennedy on September 4 [1962], Khrushchev proposed, "Let us immediately sign an agreement on the cessation of nuclear tests in the atmosphere, outer space and under water." … . [internal citations omitted]. Moltz, *Politics of Space Security*, 129.

70 *See* Chapter 3, pp. 78–86.

an invincible enemy. It should come as no surprise, then, that the Soviet Union reacted vehemently to SDI:

> The first reaction of the Soviet Union to President Reagan's address of 23 March 1983, in which he announced the program that would later become known as the SDI, was resolutely negative. The Soviet leadership immediately accused the United States of attempting to undermine the existing strategic balance by seeking to deny Soviet strategic forces the ability to retaliate effectively to a U.S. first strike [internal citations omitted].[71]

In addition to fears related to the nuclear balance of power, the Soviets were also concerned about SDI as a space-based weapons system that the United States could use to attack the Soviet Union. As historian and University of Southern California history professor Peter J. Westwick notes,

> [t]he Soviets were deeply suspicious of offensive aspects of SDI, and not just in the usually recognized strategic sense of encouraging a first strike with missiles. Rather, they feared a new generation of space-based beam weapons that could instantly strike targets on Soviet territory at any time.[72]

Between their fears of an upset to the nuclear "balance of terror" and their worries about possible space-strike weapons, the Soviets' response to SDI could well have fallen within the action-reaction, power accumulation model.

Classic "security dilemma" theory would posit that the period between the announcement of SDI and its successful implementation and deployment would be extremely dangerous. In the "vicious circle of security and power accumulation" it would represent the window of opportunity before a turning point: if the Soviet Union truly feared that SDI would permanently alter the existing security balance of the Cold War to the advantage of the United States, launching a first strike *before* SDI was operational might have been an attractive option. But the SDI program did not, of course, result in a nuclear holocaust. Despite the perceived threat posed by SDI from a Soviet perspective, Soviet leaders largely resisted a renewed technological race with the United States, and certainly did not take the ultimate step of attempting a

71 Pavel Podvig, "Did Star Wars Help End the Cold War? Soviet Response to the SDI Program," Science & Global Security 25:1, 5 (2017).

72 Peter J. Westwick, "'Space-Strike Weapons' and the Soviet Response to SDI," *Diplomatic History* 32:5, 958 (November 2008).

military strike prior to the deployment of SDI. Indeed, in some ways, the Soviet response to SDI mirrored Eisenhower's response to *Sputnik*, though on a more limited scale: the Soviets pursued a dual-tack of linking SDI to arms control and pushing to address it at the international level, while also pursuing technological development to counter the perceived threats of the SDI system.[73] Ultimately, with Gorbachev's *Perestroika* reforms within the Soviet power structure, a growing belief by the Soviets that SDI was technologically infeasible, additional Soviet arms control concessions, and the end of the Cold War, any potential issues related to Soviet-American confrontation over the issue of SDI were overtaken by events. The Cold War's last potential fear/uncertainty and power accumulation event resulted not in a "security dilemma"-style arms race or a military confrontation, but in limited diplomatic and technological response by the Soviet Union as it slid toward dissolution.

3.2.3 Conclusions Related to American Cold War Space Policy

It should be clear from the preceding discussion that while certain factors of "security dilemma" theory exist in Cold War American-Soviet outer space activities—particularly in terms of the periodic cause-and-effect relationship between fear/uncertainty and scientific or military development—the overarching course of Cold War space security policy fails to conform to Tang's, Herz's, and Butterfield's "security dilemma" theory. Not only did the Cold War itself never devolve into the self-reinforcing conflict cycle characteristic of true "security dilemmas," but neither did American and Soviet interactions in

---

73 The Soviets' international efforts can be seen in their proposal to the United Nations of a treaty prohibiting "the use of force in outer space and from space against the Earth" just a few months after President Reagan's SDI speech, *see* Westwick, "'Space-Strike Weapons' and the Soviet Response to SDI," *Diplomatic History* 32:5, 963 (citing Proposed "Treaty on the Prohibition of the Use of Force in Outer Space and from Space Against the Earth," Aug. 19, 1983), and in their goals at international nuclear and space negotiations. As Westwick notes, "[i]n 1985, the Soviet delegation to the Nuclear and Space Talks in Geneva had three main instructions: ban antisatellite weapons, ban space-based missile defense, and ban weapons 'designed for hitting targets in the atmosphere and on earth from space.'" Westwick, "'Space-Strike Weapons' and the Soviet Response to SDI," *Diplomatic History* 32:5, 963. Similarly, at a bilateral level, SDI became *the* significant sticking point at the Reykjavik Summit between Reagan and Gorbachev—a sticking point that some argue Reagan was able to parlay into additional Soviet concessions in later talks. *See generally* Vivek Viswanathan, "Fallout From Reykjavik: Reagan's Stand and the Fate of Arms Control," *New York History* 87:1, 135–43 (Winter 2006). In the realm of domestic technology development, the Soviet Union continued development and tests of laser weapons, and even at one point conducted a failed test-launch of a potential laser-armed satellite. *See* Westwick, "'Space-Strike Weapons' and the Soviet Response to SDI," *Diplomatic History* 32:5, 972.

the more limited arena of outer space. Contrary to the action-and-reaction, power-oriented, self-help behavior typical of realist and "security dilemma"-style theories of international relations, the United States and the Soviet Union recognized that they both had more to lose from confrontation in outer space than they had to gain. While this realization rarely resulted in true outer space cooperation (the joint Apollo-Soyuz mission planned during the Nixon Administration and accomplished during the Ford Administration being a notable exception), the two sides were willing to work together at the international level to create the outer space legal framework that has survived to the present day. American-Soviet relations also benefitted from the increased bilateral relations made possible by the all-seeing eyes of the superpowers' satellites guaranteeing (at least to some degree) treaty compliance.

While the Cold War Space Race, and American space security policy specifically, never devolved into a "security dilemma"-style confrontation for the reasons described above, one key factor contributing to the trajectory of Cold War-era space security policy cannot be overlooked. That factor is leadership. Nearly thirty years after the dissolution of the Soviet Union, it is easy to view the eventual realization by the United States and the Soviet Union that outer space activities required some degree of cooperation, the development of outer space law, and reduced tensions between the Soviets and the Americans in the outer space realm as historical inevitabilities. But at any point from the late 1950s through the end of the Cold War, different policy decisions by American—or Soviet—leaders could have led to far different results for the use, exploration, and militarization of outer space. Due, in part, to his military experience and familiarity with international coalitions as Supreme Allied Commander during World War II, President Eisenhower, the first president to confront the need for a serious American outer space policy, had strong views regarding the need to preserve outer space as a non-weaponized (though not entirely non-military) arena of international cooperation. We have seen in Chapter 3 how Eisenhower's views have shaped the United States' outer space policies, including outer space security policy, ever since. Had someone other than Eisenhower been President at the time of the *Sputnik* launch, had Eisenhower had different views, or had he been more easily swayed by the proponents of a more militant approach to outer space, like General Schriever or General Gavin, the entire course of American outer space security policy might be far different. Similarly, if President Kennedy, in response to Soviet intransigence and the Cuban missile crisis, had abandoned the international negotiation efforts of COPUOS that the Eisenhower Administration had set in motion, or if President Johnson, perhaps in response to Soviet support to the North Vietnamese, had withheld American support for the Outer Space Treaty, the entire edifice of international outer space law would never have been constructed. The influence of individual leadership can also be seen in President Reagan, who (though building on the deterioration of American-Soviet relations that had begun during the Ford Administration and only grown worse during the Carter Administration) almost single-handedly shifted the United States' space security policies, making them more military- and security-oriented, and potentially even space-weapons-friendly. Indeed, due to Reagan's worldview and strong hatred of Communism, and national policies reflecting his anti-Communist stance including space security policies like the Strategic Defense Initiative, the United States may have come closer to realist-style confrontation with the Soviet Union during the Reagan Administration than at any time since the Cuban Missile Crisis.

In the context of our discussion of the "security dilemma," leadership provides the critical link between what the international environment *is* and what it *could be*. To return to the literary example from *Foucault's Pendulum* cited in Chapter 1, it is the beliefs and perceptions of leaders and policy-makers that, to some degree, shape reality and make the world what it is. While there is certainly truth to the institutionalist view that international organizations and institutions *can* constrain State action, such constraints are largely ineffective if a national leader—an Adolf Hitler, Joseph Stalin, Saddam Hussein, Bashar al-Assad, or Vladimir Putin, say—refuses to recognize them. When this occurs, the international community, or certain members of it, can seek to enforce international mandates through the application of force (as in the case of Saddam Hussein's invasion of Kuwait), or not (as in the Russian Federation's seizure and annexation of Crimea). That international law, and international organizations' ability to constrain State action, is largely dependent on the beliefs of world leaders regarding these laws and organizations is no less true of outer space law than it is of any other international legal principle, such as prohibitions on aggression or illegal war.

3.3 *Post-Cold War Era American Space Security Policy*

With the end of the Cold War and the break-up of the Soviet Union in 1991, the United States suddenly found itself to be the sole Superpower in a now-unipolar world. In outer space, too, the United States was unrivaled. The Soviet space program, already reeling during the late 1980s from expensive technological projects (most notably the Energiya booster and *Buran* space shuttle, meant to surpass the capabilities of NASA's Space Shuttle program[74]), was

74 *See* Moltz, *Politics of Space Security*, 216–18, 226.

thrown into complete disarray by the Soviet Union's dissolution. It only survived, now as the national space program of the new Russian Federation, due, in part, to new national cooperative agreements and private business ventures between the United States and the Russian government.[75] For over a decade, the United States enjoyed a degree of space dominance unlike that enjoyed by any country before or since.

As the United States' old adversary Nikita Khrushchev reflected in his memoirs, however, "[i]t's impossible for one country to maintain its leadership in space exploration forever."[76] For the United States, the virtual monopoly on outer space power it had enjoyed during the 1990s began to change in the early 2000s. A decade after the end of the Cold War, as the United States faced the unexpected threat of transnational Islamist terrorism and the challenges resulting from what would become nearly two decades of foreign wars in the Middle East, outer space was about to be democratized in new ways. Barriers to entry into the space environment, in terms of both cost and the availability of the necessary technology, were falling. Smaller, non-spacefaring States were expanding their access to space through the purchase and operation of telecommunications and remote sensing satellites, and others, including American adversaries like North Korea and Iran, were actively working toward developing space launch capabilities. The so-called "NewSpace" movement—private spaceflight companies with varying business plans for turning space launch, space tourism, satellite operations, on-orbit manufacturing, and other space operations into profitable industries—was gearing up, with a number of its key players incorporating in the early 2000s. But most significantly of all, particularly from a "security dilemma" perspective, was a resurgence of true space competition. Not only was the Russian Federation finding its footing in outer space and beginning to reestablish itself as a space power, but Russia and the United States were soon to be joined by another powerful international competitor: the People's Republic of China.

China has been an outer space power since April 1970, when it successfully launched a satellite into orbit using a domestically-made space launch vehicle, the Long March-1 (utilizing technology derived from China's Dongfeng ICBM systems).[77] Over the next 33 years, China conducted 78 additional satellite

75 *See* Moltz, *Politics of Space Security*, 230–37.

76 Khrushchev, *Khrushchev Remembers: The Last Testament*, 55.

77 Mark A. Stokes with Dean Cheng, *China's Evolving Space Capabilities: Implications for U.S. Interests*, Report Prepared for the U.S.-China Economic & Security Review Commission, Apr. 26, 2012, 14, available at https://www.hsdl.org/?view&did=708400 (last accessed May 5, 2020).

launches, with only 12 of these launches failing to place their satellite payloads into their intended orbits.[78] In October 2003, however, China took a proverbial "great leap forward" when it successfully orbited its first astronaut, Lieutenant Colonel Yang Liwei of the People's Liberation Army (PLA) Air Force.[79] This dramatic achievement made China only the third State (after the Soviet Union and the United States) to conduct crewed space operations.

In the sixteen years since China's first crewed space flight, the space capabilities of the Russians, the Chinese, and other potential American adversaries like Iran and North Korea, have continued to grow. Iran successfully developed its own domestically-produced launch vehicles, the Safir and Simorgh space launch vehicles, using ballistic missile technology obtained from North Korea. North Korea itself launched several small satellites into orbit. Both States have also made advances in jamming and spoofing technology, which can be used to interfere with, alter, or emulate satellite signals. Russia has resurrected its space program, maintaining robust space launch capabilities and developing a range of counter-space capabilities, including electronic warfare, kinetic-kill, and even potentially orbital capabilities.[80] Finally, Chinese space capabilities have developed by leaps and bounds since 2003. In the years since their first manned spaceflight, the Chinese have tested a direct-ascent ASAT system (2007), conducted a number of additional manned spaceflights (2011 and 2016), landed a lunar rover on the far side of the Moon (2019), and plan to operate a permanently-manned space station by 2022 and to conduct a manned Moon-landing by the mid-2030s.

Do the changed circumstances in the post-Cold War world more closely resemble the realist "security dilemma" theories of Tang, Butterfield, and Herz? Has the Soviet Union's demise made the outer space environment—and, perhaps, even the international system as a whole—less stable than it was during the Cold War? In the sub-sections below, Tang's "security dilemma" factors of international anarchy, fear/uncertainty, and power accumulation will be reexamined from a post-Cold War context to determine the answers to these questions—particularly with respect to the so-called "security dilemma" that a number of space security writers have predicted between the United States and China.

78 *See* Marcia S. Smith, Congressional Research Service, *China's Space Program: An Overview* (2003), 1.

79 *See* Joan Johnson-Freese, *Space as a Strategic Asset* (New York: Columbia University Press, 2007) 1, 10.

80 *See* Defense Intelligence Agency, *Challenges to Security in Space*, 23–30.

3.3.1 International Anarchy

In the previous section, we found that the international system during the Cold War operated in far more complex and internationalist ways than traditional realist and "security dilemma" theory describes. This raises a key question: why would the international system be any different in the post-Cold War world? The United Nations is more firmly established than it was at the beginning of the Cold War; economic, educational, and cultural globalization has brought the world together in interconnected and mutually beneficial ways; and, to return to our primary topic, the legal framework of international outer space law remains strong. No State Parties to the four primary outer space treaties—much less any significant spacefaring States—have withdrawn from these international agreements, and even the less popular Moon Agreement (rejected by the major space powers due primarily to its internationalist/communalist provisions concerning resource extraction on celestial bodies) periodically gains new State Party signatories. Given the resiliency and widespread acceptance of the outer space legal framework, isn't the prospect of a more anarchic international system even *less likely* now than it was during the Cold War?

Perhaps. But, as we noted above, the nature of the international system is malleable due to the perceptions and beliefs of participants within the system, and can, to some degree, shift between exhibiting more realist or more internationalist or institutionalist characteristics based on those perceptions and beliefs. Have the various national and international changes in the post-Cold War world resulted in altered perceptions with respect to the international system, particularly with respect to outer space and outer space security? There are at least some indications they have. First, the United States' perceptions of both the outer space and international legal environments changed as a result of its new role as the world's sole superpower. The United States' monopoly on the use of outer space for security purposes—an asymmetrical, space-based advantage over its potential adversaries, first demonstrated during the Persian Gulf War with the significant force-multiplication effects of outer space military support—encouraged the continued development of "space superiority" and "space dominance" theories in American space security policy. Meanwhile, post-Cold War international relations theories emphasizing the conflict-reducing and prosperity-producing effects of liberal democracy, and, particularly in the wake of 9/11, legal theories downplaying the significance of international law, contributed to a growing American distrust of international organizations and unwillingness to be bound by international law. This was further exacerbated by global events that seemed to demonstrate the impotence of international law. Second, the growing multipolarity of the outer space environment in the modern age, which, on the one hand, seems like it would encourage greater international cooperation, somewhat contradictorily *increases* the risks associated with outer space security policy. The international legal framework for outer space was fairly manageable during the Cold War, when only the two Superpowers were engaged in significant outer space operations. As access to space continues to dramatically increase, and activities in space continue to be undertaken not only by significant space powers but also smaller States and private companies, space-object threatening risks (including unintentional damage from space debris or accidental collisions, in addition to intentional, nefarious interference) will proliferate. Finally, the steadily advancing outer space capabilities of China directly threaten the United States' previously unrivaled post-Cold War outer space hegemony. While the American-Chinese rivalry does not necessarily foreordain a radical shift in perceptions of the international environment, increasing worries about Great Power competition, the so-called "Thucydides Trap," and, as we shall see below, the activities in which both sides have engaged to address the fear/uncertainty they feel about each other risks pushing the world in a more anarchic, realist direction—particularly if one or both sides choose to pursue "self-help" methods of balancing the other, rather than emulating the Cold War strategy of using, and building, international frameworks to address contentious outer space issues.

Our discussion of the first point, that the United States' perceptions of the outer space and international legal regimes shifted after the Cold War, can begin with outer space. The Persian Gulf War and its use of space-based navigational, guidance, and communications capabilities to assist the American-led coalition's victory over the Iraqi Army has been previously discussed. Its significance in the development of the United States military's uses of space cannot be overstated. As Dr. Johnson-Freese notes, the Persian Gulf War "was a first step toward much greater reliance and utilization of military space assets in areas such as intelligence, surveillance, and reconnaissance (ISR), communications, and use of precision-guided munitions …."[81] The spectacular results of the Gulf War resulted in continued development of policy and doctrine related to outer space warfare, resulting in a more decisive push by the United States to develop both defensive and offensive outer space weapons. The Air Force's 2004 Air Force Doctrine Document (AFDD) 2-2.1, *Counterspace Operations*, would describe in detail both "Defensive Counterspace (DCS) Operations" (which "preserve US/friendly ability to exploit space to its advantage via active

81 Johnson-Freese, *Space as a Strategic Asset*, 19.

and passive actions to protect friendly space-related capabilities from enemy attack or interference") and "Offensive Counterspace (OCS) Operations" (which "preclude an adversary from exploiting space to their advantage").[82] While not radically different in underlying meaning than previous military space documents, AFDD 2-2.1 communicated "Air Force intentions about protecting US space assets and denying the use of space to potential adversaries … more clearly … than ever before in an unclassified document."[83] In the wake of the Gulf War, the Air Force determined that the radical force-multiplying effects of outer space mandated a key goal in any future conflict: the establishment and maintenance of "space superiority," defined as "[t]he degree of dominance in space of one force over another that permits the conduct of operations by the former and its related land, sea, air, space, and special operations forces at a given time and place without prohibitive interference by the opposing force."[84]

It is clear from our previous examinations of United States national space policy, particularly beginning in the Reagan Administration, that a tilt toward greater acceptance of space weapons began prior to the end of the Cold War. The outer space legal regime did not prohibit weapons in outer space with the exception of nuclear weapons and weapons of mass destruction, and, while the Anti-Ballistic Missile Treaty may—indeed, likely *did*, despite the Reagan Administration's arguments to the contrary—prohibit the stationing of anti-ballistic missile weapons in space, the United States' position was that the development of conventional weapons systems that could be stationed in orbit was permissible. President Reagan certainly held a hard line against the Soviet Union and was devoted to the development of the SDI system; however, the Cold War—and the prospect of an outer space arms race with the Soviets—imposed certain risks on the actual development of space weapons. As the United States surveyed the outer space landscape in the years after its successful war against Saddam Hussein, however, these risks were gone: the Soviet Union dissolved in December 1991, just ten months after the end of the Persian Gulf War; the Russian Federation's inherited Soviet space program was largely crippled by budgetary problems and more pressing national priorities; and no other nations were in a position (at least at that time) to challenge the United States in space. With the significant advantages of space-supported military forces proven, and with a now-permissive international environment,

---

82 Department of the Air Force, Air Force Doctrine Document (AFDD) 2-2.1, *Counterspace Operations*, Aug. 2, 2004, 3, available at https://fas.org/irp/doddir/usaf/afdd2_2-1.pdf (last visited May 12, 2020).

83 Johnson-Freese, *Space as a Strategic Asset*, 19.

84 Department of the Air Force, AFDD 2-2.1, 1, 55.

the United States military's push for enhanced space capabilities is unsurprising. This was not a radical shift in the United States' perception of international outer space law, but it *was* an opportunity for the United States to press its interpretations of the Outer Space Treaty and "peaceful uses" of outer space to the limit without the opportunity costs associated with a powerful rival that could challenge or counter-balance its actions.

The development of shifting perspectives was not confined simply to outer space law and policy, but to the nature of the international system and the role of international law as well. In the aftermath of the Cold War, the United States found itself in an unprecedented role: with the collapse of its arch-rival, the Soviet Union, it was now the sole superpower in a largely unipolar world. The threat of Soviet Communism was defeated; the United States had won. So significant was the dissolution of the Soviet Union that it triggered a reevaluation on the part of American policy-makers of the United States' role in the world, and on the part of academics with respect to theories of international politics. Perhaps most famously (or infamously as the case may be), political scientist Francis Fukuyama argued that the victory of liberal democracy over Soviet communism represented "the end of history"—that is, the "end point of mankind's ideological evolution and the universalization of Western liberal democracy as the final form of human government."[85] While Fukuyama's theory would be heavily criticized, some of his central ideas, including the dusting-off of the "democratic peace theory" (he argued that the "ideal" of liberalism and democracy would "govern the material world in the long run" due to its ability to create economic prosperity and reduce conflict[86]), would come to play a significant role in the development of various strands of American political thought throughout the 1990s—particularly within the neoconservative movement, which came to dominate American politics with the election of George W. Bush to the presidency in 2000.[87] Neoconservatism, that strange hybrid

85 Francis Fukuyama, "The End of History?," *The National Interest*, No. 16, 4 (Summer 1989).

86 Fukuyama, "The End of History?," *The National Interest*, No. 16, 4.

87 The relationship between Fukuyama and neoconservative ideology is extremely complex. It is generally accepted that his end-of-history theories had a direct effect on the development of neoconservative thought. Fukuyama himself associated with prominent neoconservatives and neoconservative organizations, including the Project for a New American Century ("PNAC"), and lent his signature to several PNAC letters to both President Clinton and President Bush II advocating regime change in Iraq. *See* Project for a New American Century, "Open Letter to President George W. Bush," Sept. 20, 2001, available at https://web.archive.org/web/20131018052135/http://www.newamericancentury.org/Bushletter.htm (last visited May 12, 2020); Project for a New American Century, "Open Letter to President William J. Clinton," Jan. 26, 1998, available at https://www.noi.org/wp-content/uploads/2016/01/iraqclintonletter1998-01-26-Copy.pdf (last visited May 12, 2020). As late as 2004,

of realism and idealism, emphasized both the Wilsonian (and Fukuyaman) notions that liberal democracy is the best form of government and democratization will result in reduced international conflict and increased economic prosperity, as well as the realist notions that States—in true neoconservative thought, primarily the United States, as the world's sole superpower—ought to pursue their own national interests.[88] (Indeed, in a curious amalgamation that illustrates the blurred lines between different international relations theories, neoconservatism posits that international democratization, and its attendant

---

Fukuyama stated that he "still consider[ed] [himself] to be a dyed-in-the-wool neoconservative." Nikolas K. Gvosdev & Damjan de Krnjevic-Miskovic, "The Neoconservatism of Francis Fukuyama," *The National Interest*, Aug. 4, 2004, https://nationalinterest.org/article/the-neoconservatism-of-francis-fukuyama-2725. But even then, Fukuyama was having prominent—and public—disagreements with Bush Administration policy and with other neoconservative thinkers. In June 2004, he penned a strident critique of Charles Krauthammer's defense of neoconservatism and the Iraq War (Francis Fukuyama, "The Neoconservative Moment," *The National Interest*, June 1, 2004, https://nationalinterest.org/article/the-neoconservative-moment-811), and by 2006 had largely defected from the movement. It was in March of that year that Fukuyama published *America at the Crossroads: Democracy, Power and the Neoconservative Legacy*, a much more detailed critique of Bush Administration policy, in which he repudiated neoconservatism, at least as it was then understood: "Whatever its complex roots, neoconservatism has now become inevitably linked to concepts like preemption, regime change, unilateralism, and benevolent hegemony as put into practice by the Bush administration. Rather than attempting the feckless task of reclaiming the meaning of the term, it seems to me better to abandon the label and articulate an altogether distinct foreign policy position." Francis Fukuyama, *America at the Crossroads: Democracy, Power and the Neoconservative Legacy* (New Haven, CT: Yale University Press, 2006), 7.

88 Attempting a brief definition of neoconservatism or description of neoconservative thought is difficult, with various sub-strands of the movement laying claim to "true" neoconservatism. Two descriptions are offered here. Fukuyama himself identified "[f]our common principles" characterizing neoconservative thought: "a concern with democracy, human rights, and more generally the internal politics of states; a belief that U.S. power can be used for moral purposes; *a skepticism about the ability of international law and institutions to solve serious problems*; and, finally, a view that ambitious social engineering often leads to unexpected consequences and often undermines its own ends" [emphasis added]. Fukuyama, *America at the Crossroads*, 4–5. Similarly, describing early neoconservative thought and, specifically, the characteristics of neoconservative foreign policy, Dr. Stephen McGlinchey writes "Irving Kristol [one of the neoconservatism's founding intellectuals] describes three central pillars [of neoconservatism]; a strong idea of patriotism, a round rejection of anything resembling or pointing towards a world government, including *round rejection of the United Nations and NATO* ..., and finally the view that statesmen should clearly distinguish friends from enemies. These pillars are fused with a strong Manichean morality that *compels America to use its power for the common good rather than reserve it*" [emphasis added]. Stephen McGlinchey, "Neoconservatism and American Foreign Policy," *Politikon* 16.1, 22 (2010).

benefits, must be pursued *because* it is a direct national interest of the United States[89]—it is, at once, an idealistic and realistic goal). Neoconservative principles would lead the Bush Administration into a number of significant policy decisions that continue to haunt the United States, the Middle East, and South Asia to this day: the decision to undertake a program of nation-building and democratization in Afghanistan after the initial success of the American invasion in October 2001; the decision to invade Iraq in March 2003; and the push for Palestinian elections in 2006.

In conjunction with the international relations theories of "democratic peace theory" and neoconservatism, the two decades after the Cold War saw new legal theories related to the role (and, indeed, in some instances the very existence) of international law on the world stage that shaped the United States' perceptions and attitudes toward its role in the international system. In their book, *The Limits of International Law*, for instance, legal Professors Jack Goldsmith and Eric Posner craft the theory that, in most instances, international law—to the extent it exists at all—plays very little role in the behavior of States in the international system. "Much of customary international law is simply coincidence of interest" between States, and, while bilateral or multilateral treaties may "foster cooperation and coordination more effectively than customary international law," the efficacy of such treaties will depend on "the configuration of state interests, the distribution of state power, the logic of collective action, and asymmetric information."[90] Indeed, "[m]ore often [than not], international legal rhetoric"—that is, States' references to their supposed fulfilment of international obligations or their adversaries' failure to conform to international obligations—"is used to mask or rationalize behavior driven by self-interested factors *that have nothing to do with international law*" (emphasis added).[91] In the introduction to his book critically responding to Goldsmith and Posner, Jens David Ohlin summarizes their argument thus:

> [T]he world community is full of states that act in their own self-interest and essentially ignore international law. When states *appear* to be

89 British conservative/neoconservative columnist Douglas Murray hits on this dichotomy between the global need for democratization and democratization's importance for the safety (i.e. national interests) of existing democratic societies when he writes, concerning neoconservative thought, that "the world is adrift, but for our safety it needs to be moored." Douglas Murray, *Neoconservatism: Why We Need It* (New York: Encounter Books, 2006), 46.

90 Goldsmith & Posner, *The Limits of International Law*, 225.

91 Goldsmith & Posner, *The Limits of International Law*, 226.

> following international law, in most instances, their actions are really motivated by self-interest, not by the idea that international law *needs* to be followed. Much of international law is therefore illusory—it is just self-interested state behavior. And when self-interest conflicts with international law, states have no moral obligation to follow it.[92]

But it is Ohlin's conclusion to this paragraph that is particularly significant: *The Limits of International Law*, he asserts, is essentially "an intellectual manifesto expressing much of the sentiment—and policy—of the Bush administration."[93]

Analyses of the United States' perceptions of international law, and relationship to the international community, under the George W. Bush Administration risk turning us far afield from our discussion of outer space and the "security dilemma" factor of international anarchy. Suffice to say that, in general, the Bush Administration was seen (as Ohlin disapprovingly notes) to be willing to downplay or ignore international law in order to advance what it perceived to be the interests of the United States. In the arena of outer space, this can be seen to some degree in the Bush II National Space Policy. While this NSP did not repudiate the existing international space law regime, it specifically discouraged the development of any new outer space regulations at the international level: in its second paragraph, describing the key principles of American national space policy, the NSP states, "[t]he United States will oppose the development of new legal regimes or other restrictions that seek to prohibit or limit U.S. access to or use of space."[94] In addition to its rejection of new international legal regimes for space, the Bush II NSP frames American space policy through the lens of national interests. The United States government must "[e]nable unhindered U.S. operations in and through space to defend [its] interests there," and even international space cooperation must only be pursued if it is "consistent with U.S. national security interests" and involves space activities that 1) are "of mutual benefit" to the United States and the other States, 2) "further the peaceful exploration and use of space," and, most importantly, 3) "advance [the United States'] national security, homeland security, and foreign policy objectives."[95] In other words, just as Goldsmith and Posner argued, the Bush Administration's space policy appears to have paid a certain degree of lip service to existing international law, while framing the United States' goals

---

92 Jens David Ohlin, *The Assault on International Law* (Oxford: Oxford University Press, 2015), 9–10.

93 Ohlin, *The Assault on International Law*, 10.

94 2006 National Space Policy, 2.

95 2006 National Space Policy, 2, 7.

(and actions) related to outer space in the context of American national interests and repudiating any new attempt to build upon the international space law regime.

While the Obama Administration drew the United States back toward a more traditional acceptance of, and attitude toward, international law, the extent to which this affected American outer space policy was limited—and, indeed, significant global events during President Obama's term of office continued to call the efficacy of international organizations, and international law, into question. President Obama removed much of the Bush Administration's more nationalist language (including the rejection of new international law development for outer space) from his own 2011 National Space Policy, but, as has been previously discussed, the extent to which the Obama NSP represented a significant change from that of the previous Administration is questionable. Additionally, the Obama Administration did not significantly alter the United States' traditional rejection of Prevention of an Arms Race in Outer Space (PAROS) resolutions at the United Nations, nor did it exhibit any greater willingness to engage with Russia and China's proposed space weapons treaty than had previous administrations. Outside of the outer space realm, the Obama years would see grave challenges to international law on the world stage. The impotence of international regimes in the face of the grinding, post-Arab Spring conflict in Syria; waves of refugees from Syria, Iraq, North Africa, and other conflict zones around the world; Russia's initial "hybrid" invasion—and subsequent annexation—of Crimea, and its more recent full-scale invasion of Ukraine; the rise of the barbaric Islamic State in the ruins of eastern Syria and northern Iraq; and China's international law of the sea and public international air law-defying claims over increasingly large swathes of airspace and water in the South China Sea all demonstrate that the post-World War II international order is struggling to face new and shifting threats in the 21st century. It may be little wonder, then, that the Trump Administration has returned to—and perhaps even surpassed—the Bush Administration's suspicion of international law and distrust of international institutions. While the international legal framework that developed in the wake of the Second World War was not always able to prevent conflict or guide the Cold War superpowers toward peaceful coexistence, it is grimly ironic that, in a post-Cold War world that was supposed to be progressing steadily toward the globalization of liberal democracy, the international system actually seems to be more multipolar and anarchic than ever before.

Multipolarity is precisely the second characteristic of the modern, post-Cold War world that may be shifting perceptions of the international outer space environment toward a more anarchic, realist perspective. The introduction to this section described the radically expanding participation in the outer space environment, and the ever-growing outer space capabilities of smaller States and even private entities, that is making outer space (as the United States military describes it) more "congested, contested, and competitive."[96] The Department of Defense's "three C's" may sound pithy, but they are significant for two reasons. First, they—and the language used to describe the concepts they represent—are framed in a realist vein: the relative power of States ("contested" space) or private companies ("competitive" space) are profound concerns, with, of course, a particular emphasis on preserving the relative power and competitiveness of American space power and private industry. While "congestion" is presented, accurately, as being a threat to all users of outer space, it is clear that the underlying concern is its effect on American space operations. Second, as the "congestion" example shows, each of the "three C's" represents a real—and serious—aspect of the modern outer space environment.

Space "congestion," the concept of outer space, particularly specific Earth orbits, simply becoming more crowded with active satellites, rockets, space stations, and associated space debris, may seem absurd to the average person considering the vastness of space. But when space objects are orbiting the Earth at speeds of over 17,000 miles per hour and even an orbiting fleck of paint can damage windows or instruments if it collides with a spacecraft,[97] the risks associated with increased congestion are profound. As the Department of Defense noted in the 2011 National Security Space Strategy,

> there are approximately 60 nations and government consortia that own and operate satellites, in addition to numerous commercial and academic satellite operators .... This congestion—along with the effects of operational use, structural failures, accidents involving space systems, and irresponsible testing or employment of debris-producing destructive ASATs—is complicating space operations for all those that seek to benefit from space.[98]

In 2011, the Department of Defense estimated it was tracking over 22,000 space objects, but that there were potentially hundreds of thousands of pieces of

96 2011 National Security Space Strategy, 1.

97 *See* Mark Garcia, ed., "Space Debris and Human Spacecraft," *NASA*, Sept. 26, 2013, https://www.nasa.gov/mission_pages/station/news/orbital_debris.html.

98 2011 National Security Space Strategy, 2.

space debris too small to track.[99] The amount of space debris has only increased over the past nine years, with the European Space Agency estimating there to be approximately 34,000 space objects larger than 10cm in size, approximately 900,000 objects between 1cm and 10cm in size, and over 120 million objects less than 1cm in size orbiting the Earth.[100] The other two "C's" require little additional explanation. It is almost self-evident, for instance, that "U.S. competitive advantage has decreased as market-entry barriers have lowered" and foreign space companies, manufacturers of space technology, and others push into an increasingly competitive global space industry market (ergo, the space environment is increasingly "competitive").[101] Similarly, it doesn't take a crystal ball—particularly when viewing the outer space environment from a realist perspective—to postulate that "[a]s more nations and non-state actors develop counterspace capabilities over the next decade, threats to U.S. space systems and challenges to the stability and security of the space environment will increase" (meaning the space environment is "contested").[102]

It should come as no surprise that the radical increase in both State and private outer space usage would cause the United States concern from a security perspective. During the Cold War, the United States had only one space competitor. Granted, the Soviet Union was the United States' superpower rival and greatest adversary, but it was still only one State that the United States needed to concern itself with in the space domain. Particularly after the development of photoreconnaissance and other advanced remote sensing satellites (for instance, early warning systems that could detect rocket launches), it was fairly manageable for both the United States and the Soviet Union to keep abreast of what the other was doing with respect to outer space. Now, however, with thousands of active satellites, potentially millions of pieces of space debris, and new launches from almost a dozen countries taking place every year, it is much more difficult for the United States to detect and track potential threats to its space systems. Additionally, there appears to be a growing recognition that the United States' own interpretation of the "peaceful purposes" language of the Outer Space Treaty—and the Outer Space Treaty's permission of conventional, non-nuclear weapons on orbit—is a double-edged sword, one that permits other States to develop their own military space systems and,

99 2011 National Security Space Strategy, 1.

100 European Space Agency, "Space debris by the numbers," *esa.int*, https://www.esa.int/Safety_Security/Space_Debris/Space_debris_by_the_numbers (updated Feb. 2020) (last visited May 13, 2020).

101 2011 National Security Space Strategy, 2.

102 2011 2011 National Security Space Strategy, 2.

potentially, orbital weapons. This may be one reason why, as was discussed in Chapter 3, recent United States space policies, particularly President Obama's 2010 NSP and the 2011 NSSS, began emphasizing the concept of "responsibility" in the permissible use of outer space.[103] Finally, while the outer space legal regime contains prohibitions on interfering with other States' outer space activities, as well as liability regimes for orbital damage or destruction of space objects, the practical difficulties of even identifying the State liable for orbital damage (regardless of whether such damage is intentional or accidental), much less analyzing and attributing fault, present significant difficulties for a State seeking to protect its outer space assets. With the increasing number of space actors and the United States' recognition that it may not be able to rely on the existing international outer space legal framework to protect its space assets, the United States appears to be moving away from reliance on international law and international systems (the outer space legal framework, for instance) toward a more realist, "self-help" strategy emphasizing enhanced military capabilities to both detect and respond to outer space threats. The United States' actions are a direct reflection of its perception that the space environment is growing more anarchic and less susceptible to regulation by the current international legal regime—or, in the words of the United States military, more "congested, contested, and competitive"—all the time.

Finally, as will be further examined below in the section addressing "Fear, Uncertainty, and Power Accumulation," the rise of China as a new Great Power, both terrestrially and in outer space, is affecting American perceptions of the international environment, the United States' role as a superpower, and the limits of international law. As China opened up to the world after the Sino-Soviet Split and President Nixon's visit in the early 1970s, it "has recognized the merits of interdependence and has practiced multilateralism, albeit in its own peculiar way" and some academics have speculated that its "shift toward greater openness has ... been accompanied by an increasing willingness to play by international rules."[104] There is no denying that China reaps great benefits—such as its meteoric rise to the become the world's second largest economy[105]—from the interdependent world system in which it has been playing an increasingly important role over the past several decades. But as China's economic, technological, and, particularly, military clout has grown, it has begun to exhibit a

---

103 *See* Chapter 3, pp. 106–109.

104 Roda Mushkat, "China's Compliance with International Law: What Has Been Learned and the Gaps Remaining," 20 *Pacific Rim Law & Policy Journal* 1, 68 (Jan. 2011).

105 *See* David Barboza, "China Passes Japan as Second-Largest Economy," *New York Times* (Aug. 15, 2010), https://www.nytimes.com/2010/08/16/business/global/16yuan.html.

worrisome disregard for certain international legal norms, seeking to expand its regional power, particularly in the South China Sea, and developing more robust international relations as far afield as Africa and South America. In the South China Sea, China has undertaken questionable—if not internationally illegal—actions like the construction of artificial islands to bolster its territorial claims and seize new swathes of territorial sea and airspace.[106] China's unique interpretation of certain aspects of public international air law, particularly apparent in its creation of an Air Defense Identification Zone (ADIZ) above disputed territories in the East China Sea, has also caused concern.[107] China's domestic human rights abuses, including the detentions of hundreds of thousands of minority Uighur Muslims and crackdowns on pro-democracy protests in Hong Kong; its use of economic coercion and bullying to achieve its diplomatic and foreign policy goals; and, as we shall see, its growing presence in outer space, have all contributed to increasing unease and distrust on the part of the United States toward a growing China.

Exacerbating the distrust and even fear that China's growth and international actions already engender is a return to realist-based international relations theories positing counter-balancing, and even near-inevitable antagonism, between the United States and China. The most representative of such theories is the so-called "Thucydides Trap" thesis of Graham Allison, a political scientist and professor at Harvard's John F. Kennedy School of Government. Thucydides, as we have previously discussed, was among the first political thinkers to articulate a theory of international realism. Allison seizes on Thucydides' realist explanation of the origins of the Peloponnesian War—"[i]t was the rise of Athens, and the *fear that this inspired* in Sparta, that made war inevitable" (emphasis added)—to craft an international relations theory focused on the likelihood of conflict between "rising" and "ruling" powers.[108] Put simply, Allison's theory is that "[w]hen a rising power threatens to displace

106 *See generally* Ben Dolven, et al., Congressional Research Service, *Chinese Land Reclamation in the South China Sea: Implications and Policy Options* (June 18, 2015).

107 *See generally* Edmund J. Burke & Astrid Stuth Cevallos, *In Line or Out of Order? China's Approach to ADIZ in Theory and Practice* (RAND, 2017).

108 Graham Allison, "The Thucydides Trap: Are the U.S. and China Headed for War?," *The Atlantic* (Sept. 24, 2015), https://www.theatlantic.com/international/archive/2015/09/united-states-china-war-thucydides-trap/406756/. *See also* Graham Allison, *Destined for War: Can America and China Escape Thucydides' Trap?* (Boston, MA: Houghton Mifflin Harcourt, 2017). An alternative translation of Allison's formulation of Thucydides' words can be found in *The Landmark Thucydides*: "The growth of the power of Athens, and the alarm which this inspired in Sparta, made war inevitable." Strassler, ed., *The Landmark Thucydides*, 16.

a ruling one, the most likely outcome is war."[109] Allison and his team at the Kennedy School's Belfer Center for Science and International Affairs have collected 16 historical examples they claim offer support for the theory—as well as for its corollary that war between rising and ruling powers is not necessarily inevitable if the parties involved recognize what is happening and engage in "imaginative statecraft" to avert conflict (four of the 16 examples cited by Allison did *not* result in war between the rising and ruling powers).[110] Allison's theory is, in many ways, a slightly altered restatement of the "security dilemma," as "Thucydides Trap" conflicts arise from a spiral of fear (by a "ruling" power) triggered by power accumulation (by a "rising" power).

The application of the "Thucydides Trap" theory to the relationship between the United States and China—both in outer space and in the terrestrial international system more generally—is obvious. China's growth, both economically and militarily, presents a challenge to the United States, the current globally dominant power. In the outer space realm, as Dr. Joan Johnson-Freese notes,

109 Harvard Kennedy School Belfer Center for Science and International Affairs, "Can America and China Escape Thucydides's Trap?—The Book," *Special Initiative: Thucydides's Trap*, belfercenter.org, https://www.belfercenter.org/thucydides-trap/overview-thucydides-trap (last visited May 13, 2020).

110 Harvard Kennedy School Belfer Center for Science and International Affairs, "Can America and China Escape Thucydides's Trap?—The Book," *Special Initiative: Thucydides's Trap*. Allison's examples include the French Revolutionary and Napoleonic Wars (with the United Kingdom serving as the "ruling" power and revolutionary and post-revolutionary France as the "rising" power), the Crimean War (with France and the United Kingdom as "ruling" powers and the Russian Empire as "rising" power), World War I (with the United Kingdom as "ruling" power, supported by France and Russia, and Germany as "rising" power"), and World War II (somewhat inexplicably counted twice, first with the Soviet Union, France, and Britain as "ruling" powers and Germany as "rising" power, and second with the United States as "ruling" power and Japan as "rising" power), among other historical examples. *See* Harvard Kennedy School Belfer Center for Science and International Affairs, "Can America and China Escape Thucydides's Trap?—Case File," *Special Initiative: Thucydides's Trap*. The four examples cited by Allison in which war did *not* result from a rising/ruling power conflict were: the 15th-century rivalry between Portugal and Spain (Portugal as "ruling" power and Spain as "rising" power), the early 20th-century peaceful transition of global naval supremacy between the United Kingdom and the United States (the United Kingdom as "ruling" power and the United States as "rising" power), the Cold War between the United States and the Soviet Union (the United States as "ruling" power and the Soviet Union as "rising" power), and the post-Cold War reunification of Germany and its peaceful integration into the European community (the United Kingdom and France as "ruling" powers and Germany as "rising" power). Harvard Kennedy School Belfer Center for Science and International Affairs, "Can America and China Escape Thucydides's Trap?—Case File," *Special Initiative: Thucydides's Trap*.

> [t]he Thucydides Trap metaphor holds especially true ... because, as Allison points out in his example of Germany challenging Britain's naval power, all that mattered in Britain's assessments was capability, not intentions. Similarly, the US military characterization of space as "congested, contested, and competitive" is based on an assessment of potential competitor capabilities; regarding space, this refers largely to China ....[111]

While a full analysis of the Thucydides Trap is beyond the scope of this work, its significance for our purposes here is primarily ideological. Specifically, its acceptance of international realism, drive toward Great Power competition, and inherently realist balance-and-conflict dynamics reflect a prominent vein of post-Cold War thinking—and its application to Chinese-American relations particularly indicates the shift back toward realist-style thinking in the modern age.

Perceptions concerning the nature of the international system and the relative ability of the outer space legal framework to preserve beneficial, peaceful interactions among spacefaring States may be driving international interactions toward a more realist, less internationalist, approach, particularly with respect to space security. Interestingly, and somewhat ironically, the post-Cold War development of a more multipolar world has increased the perception that the international system is anarchic, that State interests are the dominant motivating factor in international relations, and that States, in Thucydides' words, "do what they will" or "suffer what they must" without significant reference to international law or organizations. While the international system created in the aftermath of World War II remains, and, with concerted effort, could well be used to foster greater international cooperation through institutionalist measures, the factors described in this subsection show that international realism seems to be enjoying a more prominent place in international relations thought now than during the Cold War.

3.3.2 Fear, Uncertainty, and Power Accumulation

In addition to the influence of State perception on the international system itself, reexamining the "security dilemma" factors of fear/uncertainty and power accumulation in the post-Cold War context shows that, even in the absence of a superpower adversary, the United States has, to varying degrees, continued to make space security policy decisions based on uncertainty and fear. Despite the relative space hegemony the United States enjoyed during

---

111 Johnson-Freese, *Space Warfare in the 21st Century*, 57.

the 1990s, fears about the United States being overtaken in space persisted, ultimately resulting in the study of American space security conducted by the Rumsfeld Space Commission and its dire warnings regarding the safety and survivability of American space systems. As we have seen in the previous section, the rise of new outer space powers, particularly China, added additional fuel to the United States' fears. All this contributed to renewed American efforts to maintain superiority in outer space, culminating, most recently, in the creation of the United States Space Force. Meanwhile, across the world, other States watched the United States' efforts in outer space with varying degrees of approval, irritation, and alarm. In response to the United States' efforts and (as the Rumsfeld Commission had noted) its ever-increasing reliance on space systems, the United States' competitors and adversaries began to develop their own means of countering the United States' space systems.

As the Clinton Administration—and the first decade of largely unrivaled American space dominance—drew to a close, the Rumsfeld Commission report represented a clear turn back toward realist assumptions concerning international fear/uncertainty. Emphasizing the United States' reliance on satellites and space-based technology for a wide range of commercial and military activities ("[t]he U.S. is more dependent on space than any other nation"), the Commission noted that "the threat to the U.S. and its allies in and from space does not command the attention it merits from the departments and agencies of the U.S. Government charged with national security responsibilities."[112] If the United States failed to analyze and address potential threats to its space systems, it "could be surprised by the *emergence of new technological capabilities in the hands of potential adversaries*" (emphasis added).[113] The Commission's report elaborated some of these emerging technological threats—including rapidly-improving methods of electronically jamming satellite signals and the potential use of widely-accessible micro-satellite technology to develop inexpensive on-orbit ASAT systems. The possibility of Great Power competition in space was not ignored: "[i]n July 2000," the Commission reports, "the Xinhau news agency reported that China's military is developing methods and strategies for defeating the U.S. military in a high-tech and space-based future war."[114] The United States' complacency in the face of the potential threats to its space systems was extremely dangerous, making it "an attractive candidate for a 'Space Pearl Harbor'"—a catastrophic, surprise attack on American space systems that would lay bare (all too late…) both the criticality of outer space

112 *Rumsfeld Commission Report*, 18.
113 *Rumsfeld Commission Report*, 18.
114 *Rumsfeld Commission Report*, 22.

capabilities to American society and the vulnerability of the United States' outer space infrastructure. The worst part, from the Commission's perspective, was that the warning signs of threats to the United States' space systems (from both States and even potentially non-state actors), and the realist recognition that the United States could not hope to maintain a preeminent role in space without other States or parties seeking to challenge it, were readily apparent. The Commission's own unclassified report demonstrated that one did not even need a security clearance to recognize such threats. "We are on notice" of the risks and threats to American space systems, the Commission darkly warned, but it is apparent from the United States government's lack of action on the issue that "we have not noticed."[115]

With its stark warnings about threats to space systems, technological outpacing by potential adversaries, and even a possible "Space Pearl Harbor," the Rumsfeld Commission report returned the "security dilemma" factor of fear/uncertainty to the forefront of United States space security policy in the post-Cold War world. Even a State as unrivaled in outer space as the United States risked falling victim to the shifting tides of realist balance-of-power theory if it failed to continue its own power/capability accumulation to preserve its superior position. To this end, the Rumsfeld Commission offered a number of recommendations it believed would assist in addressing the weakness it noted in the United States' approach to outer space and in maintaining the United States' superiority in the space domain. Three of these recommendations deserve examination here. First, and most significantly from a "security dilemma" perspective, the Commission recognized the United States military's oft-repeated assertion that outer space—like the domains of land, air, and sea—was, or would soon become, a war-fighting domain.[116] To address this unfortunate reality, the Commission believed "[t]he United States must develop, deploy and maintain the means to deter attack on and to defend vulnerable space capabilities," to include the development of "weapons systems that operate in space and that can defend assets in orbit and augment air, land and sea forces."[117] Second, though in a similar vein, the Commission recommended a reorganization within the Department of Defense, including a realignment of Air Force "headquarters and field commands," to "more effectively organize, train and equip for prompt and sustained space operations."[118] The Commission did not discount the possibility that a space-oriented military service branch would

115 *Rumsfeld Commission Report*, 25.

116 *Rumsfeld Commission Report*, x, 13, 28–33, & 100.

117 *Rumsfeld Commission Report*, 28.

118 *Rumsfeld Commission Report*, 89.

be needed at some point in the future,[119] but expressed greater support for incremental steps in this direction, beginning with the realignment of space operations within the Air Force: "once the realignment in the Air Force is complete, a logical step toward a Space Department could be to transition from the new Air Force Space Command to a Space Corps within the Air Force."[120] Finally, returning to the issue of direct technological/military advancement, the Commission stated that, if the United States "is to remain the world's leading space-faring nation," it must invest in the sciences, technologies, and, most importantly of all, the education of an innovative workforce, that will drive the development and production of outer space products and capabilities.[121] These recommendations demonstrate that, while the Rumsfeld Commission did not single out any specific State as a key threat to American outer space superiority, fear and uncertainty over the intentions and technological developments of other States (and, again, even private entities and non-state actors) were driving the Commission's beliefs concerning the need for more significant power accumulation—space weapons development, greater attention to space-related activities within the national defense establishment, more significant investment in advanced technologies, and other, similar policies—on the part of the United States. The Rumsfeld Commission report and, to the extent its recommendations were implemented, the American outer space policies it engendered are representative of a significant return to "security dilemma"-style thinking, even in the absence of a clear adversary threatening the United States in the space domain.

While the recommendations of the Rumsfeld Commission, and, to some extent, United States space security in general, were forced to take a backseat to the War on Terror in the aftermath of 9/11 (see Chapter 3), warnings concerning the importance of, risks associated with, and need for continued American

119 On the issue of a United States Space Force, or, as its report calls it, a "Space Department," the Rumsfeld Commission had this to say: "The use of space in defense of U.S. interests may require the creation of a military department for space at some future date. A Space Department would provide strong advocacy for space and a single organization with the primary mission of providing forces for conducting both military and intelligence space operations. However, the Commission believes that the disadvantages of creating a department today outweigh the advantages for a number of reasons, including that there is not yet a critical mass of qualified personnel, budget, requirements or missions sufficient to establish a new department. Meanwhile, near- and mid-term organizational adjustments should be fashioned so as to not preclude eventual evolution toward a Space Department if that proves desirable." *Rumsfeld Commission Report*, 80.

120 *Rumsfeld Commission Report*, 93.

121 *Rumsfeld Commission Report*, 100.

technological advancement in outer space persisted from the highest levels of the Defense Department. In March 2004, for instance, Vice Admiral Arthur K. Cebrowski, who was then the Director of Force Transformation in the Office of the Secretary of Defense, provided a statement to the US Senate Armed Services Committee's Subcommittee on Strategic Forces advocating a "new and complementary [outer space] business model" (called "Operationally Responsive Space") that would improve and increase military space operations while reducing costs.[122] Describing outer space capabilities as "a prominent feature of the global advantage [the United States] currently enjoy[s]," Admiral Cebrowski went on to warn of the dangers posed by the United States' reliance on outer space systems and, particularly as access to space increases, by other nations seeking to displace the United States in outer space:

> One may ask, why we need a new model [for outer space]; given the success of our existing force. From all indications our space forces are providing us with an asymmetric advantage that no adversary currently enjoys. Although that is clearly true, *evidence suggests that our space supremacy is not guaranteed. An adversary might turn our asymmetric advantage into an asymmetric vulnerability if we cannot maintain space supremacy*. The United States is the most heavily space dependent nation in the world and that holds true for our joint military forces—this will continue to hold true for the foreseeable future.
>
> Alfred Thayer Mahan, a prominent naval historian and strategist, described the oceans as a Great Common. Today, space and cyberspace must be added to the list of commons that must be controlled. One of the recognized barriers to becoming a hegemonic power is the ability to operate in and control the commons. Therefore, *we can expect nations with hegemonic aspirations to try to erode our ability to operate effectively in the commons and to achieve the ability to control the commons for their own use.*
>
> The barriers to entry into space, which were so high during the Cold War, have eroded. *No longer is space reserved for great power nations alone.*

122 Arthur K. Cebrowski, *Statement of the Director of Force Transformation Office of the Secretary of Defense Before the Subcommittee on Strategic Forces*, U.S. Senate Armed Services Committee, Mar. 25, 2004, at available at https://fas.org/irp/congress/2004_hr/032504cebrowski.pdf (last visited May 7, 2020).

> *Space has become much more common, and today a nation needs not be a space power to employ space power* [emphasis added].[123]

In addition to reiterating the Rumsfeld Commission's warnings, Cebrowski criticized "[t]he Cold War attributes of [the United States'] existing space program" for "limit[ing] [the United States'] ability to maintain space superiority required by today's rapidly changing strategic environment."[124] But in recommending his proposed solution—"Operationally Responsive Space," a space business model designed to increase responsiveness of military space operations and take advantage of technological developments in small satellite technology—Cebrowski made a curious comment with profound implications from a "security dilemma" perspective. "Sound space science and technology stewardship," he told the Subcommittee, "*requires that the sole superpower* [i.e. the United States] *compete with itself to avoid stagnation*" (emphasis added).[125]

In "security dilemma" theory, a State typically accumulates power in response to a perceived threat posed by a real or perceived adversary. Under Cebrowski's formulation, however, it appears that the United States must *preemptively* react not merely to perceived current threats but also to *theoretical* future ones. Cebrowski seemed to confirm this when he noted that "[s]tagnation of institutional learning [in the space environment] comes at the expense of creating future advantage" and that the cost of ossified organization and thinking in military space affairs "is likely to be technological surprise that works to our disadvantage in future conflicts."[126] While it certainly makes sense for a State, particularly one driven by private industry and entrepreneurship like the United States, to seek constant improvement (no one would deny that consumers, both in the private and public sectors, crave cheaper, faster, better technologies and products), the sort of self-competition described by Cebrowski carries with it significant geopolitical risks. First, it exponentially increases the fear/uncertainty inherent in "security dilemma" thinking. While the "fear" in this situation is largely imaginary (after all, if a State is competing

---

123 Cebrowski, *Statement of the Director of Force Transformation Office of the Secretary of Defense Before the Subcommittee on Strategic Forces*, 5–6. As an aside, it is little surprise that a naval officer like Cebrowski would cite Mahan, who is among the most highly regarded American naval strategists—and one whose observations concerning naval strategy are frequently analogized to describe the outer space environment.

124 Cebrowski, *Statement of the Director of Force Transformation Office of the Secretary of Defense Before the Subcommittee on Strategic Forces*, 7.

125 Cebrowski, *Statement of the Director of Force Transformation Office of the Secretary of Defense Before the Subcommittee on Strategic Forces*, 12.

126 Cebrowski, *Statement of the Director of Force Transformation Office of the Secretary of Defense Before the Subcommittee on Strategic Forces*, 11.

with itself there is no actual external threat to be faced), the type and number of theoretical threats for a State to be "afraid" of, and, thus, prepare for, are limited only by the imaginations of its strategic planners. This leads to a second risk: that, in its quest for constant improvement, a State may focus on the development of capabilities or technologies that, however advanced, fail to address the *actual* threats posed by its real-world adversaries. Finally, and most significantly of all, the "self-competition" of a hegemonic State like the United States is unlikely to be perceived positively by other States, and certainly not by its adversaries. Particularly with respect to outer space capabilities—an area in which, as Cebrowski himself admitted, the United States already overshadows the rest of the world—the United States would likely have a difficult time convincing other States that its actions were purely defensive. Instead, the rest of the world is likely to view such self-competition as additional evidence of American intentions to dominate the space domain—a view which, in "security dilemma" fashion, could spur other States' development of their own outer space capabilities.

While the Rumsfeld Commission report and Department of Defense officials like Vice Admiral Cebrowski pressed for action against theoretical threats, the falling costs of outer space access, the proliferation of rocket and other outer space technology, and the drive of foreign States towards expanding their outer space capabilities all began to propel such theoretical threats closer to reality. China's manned space flight in late 2003 and its continuing space technology advancement, including its testing of a kinetic-kill ASAT system in January 2007 (see below); the development of increasingly sophisticated "jamming" and "spoofing" techniques by Iran, North Korea, and other States; Iran's successful development of indigenous space launch capabilities; North Korea's progressing pursuit of ballistic missiles (some of which have been used for North Korean satellite launches); and Russia's pursuit of counter-space capabilities have all contributed to the United States' perception that international actors "are seeking ways to deny [its] effectiveness" in outer space.[127] Of all the growing threats—or perceived threats—to American outer space activities, however, none engender as much fear, uncertainty, and calls for action from American officials as those of China.

Chinese space activities, perhaps more so than those of any other State, have contributed to the United States' current space security trajectory. While some references to Chinese activities are veiled in official United States policy

---

127 Defense Intelligence Agency, *Challenges to Security in Space*, 7. For a more in-depth description of the worrisome space and counter-space capabilities of China, Russia, Iran, and North Korea, *see generally id.*

documents (for instance, President Obama's National Security Space Strategy emphasizes the importance of outer space security because "[p]otential adversaries are seeking to exploit perceived space vulnerabilities,"[128] and President Trump's National Space Strategy claims the United States' "competitors and adversaries have turned space into a warfighting domain"),[129] other references to American fear and reaction to Chinese behavior are more explicit. The Defense Intelligence Agency has listed China (in an ignominious distinction it shares with Russia, Iran, and North Korea) as one the key threats to security in outer space.[130] Further, in August 2018, Secretary of Defense James Mattis, explaining that the development of a Space Force was necessary to confront the space threats posed by China and Russia, directly referenced China's ASAT test as a key motivator for the United States' increased interest in outer space security.[131] Mattis again referenced the Chinese ASAT test in an interview later that year, describing the importance of defending American space capabilities (and, potentially, employing offensive space weapons) and stating that outer space "is not an area that we want to be second place in."[132]

But perhaps no high-ranking American official demonstrates fear-and-power-accumulation "security dilemma"-style thinking concerning Chinese space activities as profoundly as now-retired Air Force Lieutenant General Steven A. Kwast. Kwast, who served as Commander of the USAF's Air Education and Training Command prior to his retirement in September 2019, is an outspoken advocate of a more robust American military presence in space—primarily, as numerous op-eds, speeches, and articles he has written both before and after his retirement show, due to what he perceives to be the threat of China outpacing the United States.[133] Characterizing outer space as "critical

128 *See* 2011 National Security Space Strategy, 3.

129 "President Donald J. Trump is Unveiling an America First National Space Strategy," *WhiteHouse.gov* (Mar. 23, 2018), https://trumpwhitehouse.archives.gov/briefings-statements/president-donald-j-trump-unveiling-america-first-national-space-strategy/.

130 *See generally* Defense Intelligence Agency, *Challenges to Security in Space*.

131 Robert Burns, Associate Press, "Mattis: US needs Space Force to counter Russia, China," *Military Times* (Aug. 14, 2018), https://www.militarytimes.com/news/your-military/2018/08/14/mattis-us-needs-space-force-to-counter-russia-china/.

132 James N. Mattis & Stephen Hadley, "Secretary Mattis Remarks on the National Defense Strategy in Conversation with the United States Institute for Peace," *defense.gov* (Oct. 30, 2018), https://www.defense.gov/Newsroom/Transcripts/Transcript/Article/1678512/secretary-mattis-remarks-on-the-national-defense-strategy-in-conversation-with/.

133 *See* Steve Kwast, "Where the Space Force must go," *Politico* (Jan. 17, 2020), https://www.politico.com/news/2020/01/17/where-the-space-force-must-go-098884; Steven Kwast, "The Urgent Need for a U.S. Space Force," Speech at Hillsdale College, Washington, D.C., Nov. 20, 2019, available at https://www.youtube.com/watch?v=KsPLmb6gAdw&feature=emb_title; Steve Kwast, "The Real Stakes in the New Space Race," *War on the Rocks* (Aug.

to [humanity's] future" and "a *multi*-trillion-dollar market that will disproportionately benefit the first great power that builds a vibrant infrastructure there" (emphasis in the original), Kwast darkly warns that if the United States does not take steps to more dramatically exploit emerging technologies, "the values that determine the future will be those of the Chinese Communist Party rather than democratic ideals of the United States."[134] Kwast frequently emphasizes China's "superior strategy" for outer space dominance, pointing to its bold initiatives for outer space activities—including plans for lunar and Martian laboratories, advanced space shuttles, and even a space-based solar power station.[135] Most ominously of all, Kwast asserts that China is "building a navy in space, with the equivalent of battleships and destroyers that can move fast and kill."[136] It is not difficult to see the "security dilemma" factors of fear/uncertainty and power accumulation in Kwast's thinking; indeed, Kwast himself portrays his worldview in the starkly realist terms of great power competition:

> America has become complacent and mistakes its rapidly dissipating economic and military advantages as rights. The United States is making the same mistake that other fallen great powers have made. Namely, it is doubling down on the approach that made America successful in previous generations and discounting rising powers taking new approaches.[137]

For Kwast, the only way to prevent a future in which China dominates outer space, and, consequently, the world, is for the United States to radically expand the Space Force's mission, militarizing it into a "guardian force" that can enforce "rule of law"—and American dominance—in outer space.[138]

As we have previously seen in Chapter 3, Lieutenant General Kwast's views fit neatly into a long tradition of American military officers predicting dire consequences if the United States fails to control the "ultimate high ground" of outer space. But whether they are representative of the views of a majority of American policy-makers, or, indeed, even the majority of American military

---

19, 2019), https://warontherocks.com/2019/08/the-real-stakes-in-the-new-space-race/; Steve Kwast, "OPINION: 'There won't be many prizes for second place,'" *Politico* (Aug. 10, 2018), https://www.politico.com/story/2018/08/10/space-race-kwast-768751.

134 Kwast, "The Real Stakes in the New Space Race," *War on the Rocks*.

135 *See* Kwast, "Where the Space Force must go," *Politico*; Kwast, "The Urgent Need for a U.S. Space Force," Speech at Hillsdale College; Kwast, "The Real Stakes in the New Space Race," *War on the Rocks*.

136 Kwast, "Where the Space Force must go," *Politico*.

137 Kwast, "The Real Stakes in the New Space Race," *War on the Rocks*.

138 Kwast, "Where the Space Force must go," *Politico*.

officers, is less clear. There is a persistent rumor that senior Air Force officials forced Kwast into premature retirement due to his outspoken views on outer space policy—although it should be noted that even if this were true, it may not reflect disagreement with Kwast's perspective, but, rather, displeasure at the fact he was publicly expressing it in apparent contravention of "a service-wide gag order regarding space issues."[139] Despite Kwast's exit from active duty service, however, it is clear that his views *do* have significant support among certain sectors of the military, particularly among current and former space policy academics at the Air Force's Air University (several of whom drafted op-eds advocating for Kwast to be promoted to four-star General and installed as the first commander of the Space Force).[140] Indeed, Kwast's admonition that "[f]inishing second in this [new space] race means accepting defeat," sounds eerily similar to Mattis's comment that outer space is "not an area we want to be second place in."[141] All this is to say that, if Kwast and his supporters are any indication, there is a widespread belief within at least certain sectors of the United States military, if not the United States government at large, that United States space activities vis-à-vis China are inherently competitive and that the potential threats posed by Chinese space activities requires a robust accumulation of power by the United States.

Let us now turn away from the United States and view the "security dilemma" factors of fear/uncertainty and power accumulation from the Chinese perspective. The extent to which China is developing outer space and military capabilities in a fear/uncertainty response to the perceived threat of American outer space capabilities or space strategy concepts is somewhat unclear. As Dr. Joan Johnson-Freese notes, "[i]t is more clearly known *what* China has done to build its space capabilities than *why*."[142] Even so, Johnson-Freese herself describes the Gulf War as China's "'ahooga moment' [i.e. the sound of a klaxon going off warning of an emergency] … regarding the advantages of military space capabilities, and the technology gap developing between the United States and

139 Oriana Pawlyk, "Air Force General's Supporters Mount Campaign to Make Him Leader of Space Force," *military.com* (Aug. 8, 2019), https://www.military.com/daily-news/2019/08/08/air-force-generals-supporters-mount-campaign-make-him-leader-space-force.html.

140 *See* Peter Garretson, "Air Force Suppressed Space Force Debate; Lt. Gen. Kwast Spoke Truth To Power," *Breaking Defense* (Aug. 8, 2019), https://breakingdefense.com/2019/08/air-force-suppressed-space-force-debate-lt-gen-kwast-spoke-truth-to-power/; Brent D. Ziarnick, "The commander the Space Force needs," *The Hill* (Aug. 6, 2019), https://thehill.com/opinion/national-security/456400-the-commander-the-space-force-needs; Pawlyk, *supra* note 133.

141 *Compare* Kwast, *supra* note 133, *with* Mattis & Hadley, *supra* note 132.

142 Johnson-Freese, *Space Warfare in the 21st Century*, 71.

other countries."[143] The ease with which the United States' space-supported coalition was able to defeat Saddam Hussein, she argues, influenced China to modernize, focusing on technological and "informationized" warfare, rather than a reliance on "troop size as its primary strength."[144] In an example of classic realist behavior, China's fear of potential military disadvantage seems to have driven it to develop new methods and strategies of warfare.

At the international level, China has publicly articulated concerns about American intentions in outer space—particularly in the realm of space weaponization—since at least the early 2000s. In April 2002, for example, China's Vice Foreign Minister, Zonghuai Qiao,[145] offered a warning concerning space weaponization at a China/UN Disarmament Conference:

> Considerable progress has been made in outer space-related weapons research and military technology. It will not take long before drawings of space weapons and weapon systems [are] turned into lethal combat instruments in outer space. Meanwhile, military doctrines and [concepts] such as "control of space" and "ensuring space superiority" have been unveiled successively, and space operation [command] headquarters and combatant troops are in the making. *If we should remain indifferent to the above-mentioned developments, an arms race would very likely emerge in outer space in the foreseeable future. Outer space would eventually become the fourth battlefield besides land, sea and air*. If such a scenario should become reality it would be virtually impossible for mankind to continue their anticipated exploration, development and utilization of outer space, and all economic, cultural and social activities in connection with the utilization of outer space would be severely interrupted [emphasis added].[146]

143 Johnson-Freese, *Space Warfare in the 21st Century*, 68.

144 Johnson-Freese, *Space Warfare in the 21st Century*, 71.

145 It should be noted that in most English-language articles and diplomatic materials, Qiao's name will be written as "Qiao Zonghuai" following traditional Chinese conventions of address in which a person's surname precedes their given name. Qiao's name is presented here in the Western style of given name followed by surname.

146 Hui Zhang, "Chinese Perspectives on Space Weapons" in Pavel Podvig & Hui Zhang, *Russian and Chinese Responses to U.S. Military Plans in Space* (Cambridge, MA: American Academy of Arts & Sciences, 2008), 31 (citing Qiao Zonghuai, "An Effective Way to Prevent an Arms Race in Outer Space The Early Negotiation and Conclusion of an International Legal Instrument," Speech Presented at the China/UN Disarmament Conference, Apr. 3, 2002, http://www3.fmprc.gov.cn/eng/29794.html [link defunct]).

While Qiao did not explicitly single out the United States, it is impossible to mistake the country that he believes to be the primary driver of space weaponization—and, as such, the biggest threat to mankind's "exploration, development and utilization of outer space." His references to military space doctrine theories ("control of space" and "ensuring space superiority") and to space-centric military organizations ("space operation [command] headquarters") are, of course, critiques of then-current, and continuing, United States military space policy and organization. The Chinese ultimately fear a number of potential disadvantages from American militarization/weaponization of space, including an arms race in outer space (as noted by Qiao, who implicitly indicated China would not sit idly by while another country developed a space weapons advantage), threats to China's traditional nuclear deterrent, threats to China's civilian and commercial space activities, decreased international stability from the effects of space weaponization on international arms control agreements, and an increase in dangerous space debris.[147]

From China's perspective, the most significant of these threats—and, viewed through a "security dilemma" lens, the one most likely to engender fear and uncertainty that would lead to Chinese action—is that posed to China's nuclear deterrent. As of 2008, China was estimated to have approximately 20 nuclear ICBMs capable of reaching the United States (although this has likely grown in the previous decade). Hui Zhang explains Chinese nuclear strategy, and the perceived threat to this strategy posed by American outer space activities thus:

> ... China's nuclear deterrence is based on the retaliatory capability it retains after absorbing a nuclear attack. Unless it could confidently eliminate China's twenty ICBMs in an initial strike, the United States would in theory be deterred from initiating a nuclear attack. If the United States were to deploy missile defense systems, this situation would change completely. A space-based, boost-phase defense would be particularly threatening.
>
> Within China, it is widely believed that U.S. missile defense and space planning targets China. Many Chinese are skeptical of U.S. statements that the purpose of missile defense is to protect against "rogue" states .... From China's perspective, it seems untenable that the United States would expend massive resources on a system that has only "rogue" states in mind.

---

147 *See* Podvig & Zhang, *Russian and Chinese Responses to U.S. Military Plans in Space*, 39–48.

> Some missile defense advocates in the United States have not minced their words about the utility of the system for addressing Chinese capabilities .... As [China's] Ambassador [for Disarmament Affairs at the United Nations Office in Geneva] Sha Zukang said, "Though the U.S. government has publicly denied that China is a major target of its NMD program, the history of missile defense programs and the acknowledged design capabilities of NMD show that the proposed system can be directed against China and can seriously affect China's limited nuclear capability."
>
> ...
>
> ... China worries that U.S. space weapons and its missile defense system could subject China to political or strategic blackmail and infringe on China's sovereignty. These capabilities would free the United States to intervene much more in China's affairs, including efforts at reunification with Taiwan.[148]

This may be one reason why China has sought to modernize, expand, and diversify its nuclear arsenal. In a May 2019 address to the Hudson Institute, Lt. Gen. Robert P. Ashley, Jr., the Director of the Defense Intelligence Agency, noted that, in addition to developing new capabilities in all three prongs of its traditional nuclear "triad"—including "a new road-mobile ICBM," "a new multi-warhead version of its silo-based ICBM," "a new submarine-launched ballistic missile," and "a new nuclear-capable strategic bomber"—China is "likely to at least double the size of its nuclear stockpile" over the next decade.[149] Chinese officials claim that China's push to modernize its nuclear arsenal is designed to preserve a credible second-strike capability and does not represent a shift to a more expansive or ambitious nuclear strategy. This seems to imply a perception by the Chinese government that changes to the international balance of power—perhaps, as Zhang notes, caused in no small part by American security activities in outer space—require a power accumulation strategy (modernizing and expanding its nuclear arsenal) to maintain stability. If this is so, the United States-Chinese interactions seem to be exhibiting classic "security dilemma" fear/uncertainty and power accumulation characteristics: American

---

148 Podvig & Zhang, *Russian and Chinese Responses to U.S. Military Plans in Space*, 41–43.

149 Robert P. Ashley, Jr., "Russian and Chinese Nuclear Modernization Trends," Remarks at the Hudson Institute, DIA.GOV (May 29, 2019), https://www.dia.mil/Articles/Speeches-and-Testimonies/Article/1859890/russian-and-chinese-nuclear-modernization-trends/ (last visited July 20, 2022).

space activities are perceived to alter the relative balance of power between the United States and China, resulting, due to China's fear of a permanent imbalance to its detriment, in Chinese nuclear modernization activities to restore relative stability. It is easy to see how, pursuant to "security dilemma" theory, the spiral could continue, with new Chinese nuclear capabilities alarming the United States, resulting in additional military, space, or missile defense activities, triggering additional responses from China, and so on.

Perhaps the most oft-cited example of Chinese power accumulation behavior related directly to American outer space activities is China's successful kinetic-kill ASAT test, conducted in January 2007. In the United States, both military and non-military sources characterize this test as both a Chinese reaction to American activities in outer space and as an attempt to send a message—or, even more ominously, a warning—to a United States supposedly hellbent on increasing its military and security-related outer space activities. Then-Secretary of Defense James Mattis characterized China's ASAT test in this manner in comments related to the creation of the Space Force: "We understand the message that China was sending [with their ASAT test]—that they could take out a satellite in space."[150] Similarly, as one officer wrote in a master's thesis for the US Air Force's School of Advanced Air and Space Studies:

> China's emerging space doctrine is the driving force behind its efforts to develop antisatellite weapons. The PLA, as well as its closely associated research and development academies, perceive a significant advantage in developing the capabilities to conduct space warfare. *ASATs represent a relatively simple, cost-effective option to counter what Chinese military leaders describe as an expanding US space hegemony*—a perception that pervades Chinese strategy circles. Hegemonic powers in any domain constitute a real threat toward China's long-term vision.
>
> Strategically, China's military planners and strategists believe ASATs are a critical element of a robust space deterrent that can further protect China's nuclear and conventional deterrents against emerging threats like US ballistic missile defense programs. Doctrinally, China places a premium on deterrence strategies and will relentlessly pursue the requisite capabilities to protect it from coercion or blackmail. *The anti-satellite test communicated, unequivocally, that China has a direct-ascent antisatellite*

150 Burns, Associate Press, "Mattis: US needs Space Force to counter Russia, China," *Military Times*.

> *capability and is willing to use it—fulfilling all the criteria for a credible deterrent strategy* [emphasis added].[151]

Mike Moore, writing in *Twilight War*, also characterizes the Chinese test as a message, positing it was an extreme (and likely counter-productive) way for China to signal "that it was time for the United States to begin serious, good faith negotiations that might lead to a new space treaty."[152]

Whether China truly developed an ASAT capability in response to perceived threats from American space technology or space security policy is unknown—the Chinese Government has not provided any official explanation as to why the 2007 ASAT test was conducted, and there are few English-language articles conveying Chinese perspectives regarding ASATs. In a journal article on China's ASAT test for *The Nonproliferation Review*, Gregory Kulacki, the China Project Manager for the Union of Concerned Scientists, and Jeffrey G. Lewis, the Director of the East Asia Nonproliferation Program at the James Martin Center for Nonproliferation Studies (a subsidiary program of the Middlebury Institute of International Studies at Monterey, Middlebury, Vermont), interviewed a number of Chinese sources off the record about the 2007 test and China's ASAT development more generally.[153] Their sources claimed that China began its research and development of ASAT technology in the 1980s, not because it had any "specific military mission or objective in mind," but, rather, simply due to the fact that the Soviet Union and the United States were both developing and testing such technology.[154] In a similarly non-bellicose explanation of the test itself, Kulacki and Lewis's sources claimed that the 2007 ASAT test was "not determined by any particular external event or series of events, but by the maturity of the technology" and "pressure to show that [the project] had produced something that worked."[155] These off-the-record observations, particularly those related to the development of China's ASAT program, generally track with available open-source literature;[156] indeed, the fact that Chinese

151 Anthony J. Mastalir, *The US Response to China's ASAT Test: An International Security Space Alliance for the Future*, Drew Paper No. 8 (Maxwell Air Force Base, AL: Air University Press, 2009), 4.

152 Moore, *Twilight War: The Folly of U.S. Space Dominance*, xix.

153 Gregory Kulacki & Jeffrey G. Lewis, "Understanding China's Antisatellite Test," *Nonproliferation Review* 15, No. 2, 336 (July 2008).

154 Kulacki & Lewis, "Understanding China's Antisatellite Test," *Nonproliferation Review* 15, No. 2, 336.

155 Kulacki & Lewis, "Understanding China's Antisatellite Test," *Nonproliferation Review* 15, No. 2, 337.

156 *See* Kulacki & Lewis, "Understanding China's Antisatellite Test," *Nonproliferation Review* 15, No. 2, 336–37.

ASAT efforts began in the 1980s seems to indicate that it was not simply rivalry with the United States that initially drove Chinese ASAT development. By the beginning of 2007, however, the United States would have been the only space power with which China would have been competing. While certainly not outside the realm of possibility, that China would have undertaken its ASAT test for no other reason than to internally prove its program was viable without significant thought about how such a test would be perceived internationally (or, if Kulacki and Lewis's sources are to be believed, an overly optimistic opinion concerning the test's debris creation and effect on the international community[157]) seems far-fetched. It may, therefore, not be unreasonable to agree with Mattis, Moore, and others that the Chinese intended to send the United States a message regarding its space capabilities.

As a brief aside from our discussion of the security dilemma, the Chinese ASAT test also presented serious questions related to international space law. Even beyond the security- and weaponization-related issues associated with such a test (for example, is a terrestrially-launched ASAT missile that creates significant clouds of potentially harmful space debris a "weapon of mass destruction" subject to the prohibition contained in Article IV of the Outer Space Treaty?), China's intentional destruction of its satellite implicates a number of other space law provisions. Some of these are relatively straightforward: China's liability for damage caused to other satellites or space objects by pieces of debris from its satellite or the ASAT missile itself would be determined under the provisions of the Liability Convention related to damage caused "elsewhere than on the surface of the earth" or in terrestrial airspace (provisions, which, themselves, built on Article VII of the Outer Space Treaty).[158] Others, however, are more nebulous—though potentially no less important. What, for example, of the requirement, under Article IX of the Outer Space Treaty, that States "conduct all their activities in outer space ... with due regard to the corresponding interests of all other States" that are party to the treaty?[159] Or the requirement for international consultation when a State "has reason to believe that an activity or experiment planned by it or its nationals in outer space ... would cause potentially harmful interference" with the space activities of other States?[160]

157 *See* Kulacki & Lewis, "Understanding China's Antisatellite Test," *Nonproliferation Review* 15, No. 2, 337–338.

158 Liability Convention, art. III.

159 Outer Space Treaty, art. IX.

160 Outer Space Treaty, art. IX.

China undertook no "international consultations" with other spacefaring States in advance of its ASAT test, an omission that would arguably violate Article IX given the risk of harmful interference that could be caused to other States' space objects or activities by the resultant debris. With respect to the question of "due regard," the meaning of the phrase is not explicitly defined.[161] That China failed to act with "due regard" in undertaking its ASAT test is not an unreasonable interpretation, given possible duties of care with respect to outer space activities and the reasonably foreseeable risk of harm potentially caused by such an action. In the aftermath of the test, however, only Japan asserted that China's actions were a violation of the Outer Space Treaty and, even then, without reference to an explicit treaty provision allegedly violated.[162] No State explicitly accused China of violating the "due regard" principle; a pattern that has recently been repeated with Russia after its November 2021 ASAT test.[163]

This reticence concerning the "due regard" principle has interesting implications. While the United States and a number of other States are encouraging

161 Sergio Marchisio, in his commentary on Article IX in the seminal *Cologne Commentary on Space Law*, describes the "due regard" principle as follows: "In Article IX of the Outer Space Treaty, 'due regard' refers to the performance of an act with a certain standard of care, attention or observance. The requirement of 'due regard' is indeed a qualification of the rights of States in exercising the freedoms in outer space, the Moon and celestial bodies. The State must prove beyond a reasonable doubt that everything possible was undertaken to prevent a harmful act from occurring. The 'due regard' principle is to be interpreted according to the particular facts and circumstances of the case." Marchisio, "Article IX," *Cologne Commentary on Space Law, Volume 1: Outer Space Treaty* (Stephan Hobe, et al, eds.,Cologne: Carl Heymanns Verlag, 2009). While this is certainly helpful, the case-specific nature of the application of the principle, as well as the nature and extent of the "standard of care, attention, or observance" required in a given set of circumstances, makes "due regard" a difficult principle to apply in practice.

162 Carin Zissis, "China's Anti-Satellite Test," *Council on Foreign Relations*, Feb. 22, 2007, https://www.cfr.org/backgrounder/chinas-anti-satellite-test.

163 A number of States criticized the Russian ASAT test as "irresponsible behavior that undermines sustainable and stable use of outer space" (Japan), as a "provocative and dangerous act" (Australia), and as evidence of the continuing need for "all nations to act responsibly in space to ensure peaceful and sustainable use of space" (South Korea). Chelsea Gohd, "Russian anti-satellite missile test draws condemnation from space companies and countries," *Space.com*, Nov. 22, 2021, https://www.space.com/crussian-anti-satellite-missile-test-world-condemnation. The United States presented among the most strident criticisms, calling the Russian test "dangerous and irresponsible" and describing Russia itself as being engaged in "reckless and irresponsible behavior." Antony J. Blinken, "Russia Conducts Destructive Anti-Satellite Missile Test," US Department of State, Press Statement, Nov. 15, 2021, available at https://www.state.gov/russia-conducts-destructive-anti-satellite-missile-test/. However, again, none of these States directly accused Russia of having violated Article IX's "due regard" provision.

the development of principles, regulations, or norms of "responsible behavior" at the international level, is the unwillingness of States to label ASAT activity—or, at least, irresponsibly-conducted tests creating significant amounts of harmful space debris—as a violation of "due regard" contributing to the development of State practice that such activity does *not* violate the principle? It may be too early, with too few States engaged in ASAT-related activities or too few believing themselves to be in a position to speak out about them, to know for sure. Continued reluctance by States to label ASAT tests like those conducted by China and Russia under the terms or definitions of binding space law agreements, however, risks the development of consistent State practice and, potentially with time, the development of a customary legal understanding that such behavior *does not* violate the Outer Space Treaty.

3.3.3 Conclusions Related to Post-Cold War American Space Policy

The preceding discussion indicates that, in certain respects, the international and outer space environments of the post-Cold War world present more significant challenges to the United States than its Cold War confrontation with Soviet Union. Despite the utopian theories of late Cold War, and early post-Cold War, political scientists, the United States has not been able to parlay its "sole superpower" status into a stable, liberal democratic world. Instead, a series of unexpected events—the 9/11 terrorist attacks; the difficult American wars in Iraq and Afghanistan; the destabilization of the Middle East due to the Arab Spring and Syrian Civil War; the continued threat of transnational Islamist terrorism; the flow of refugees to Western countries from conflict zones in the Middle East and Africa and the attendant rise of anti-immigrant, right-wing populism; and significant political turns toward nationalism over internationalism in several significant Western countries, including the United States and the United Kingdom—threatened global confidence in the post-World War II international system and the ability of international law to prevent, or even to alleviate the effects of, violent conflict. At the same time, a resurgent, predatory Russian Federation and a steadily rising China portend a return to a more multipolar world in which the United States cannot maintain its status as global superpower. All these factors contribute to a perception that, as the US National Defense Strategy states, the United States is facing "increased global disorder, characterized by decline in the long-standing rules-based international order;" "overt challenges to the free and open international order;" and "the re-emergence of long-term, strategic competition between nations."[164]

164 U.S. Department of Defense, "Summary of the 2018 National Defense Strategy of the United States of America: Sharpening the American Military's Competitive Edge," Jan.

Indeed, some have even theorized that Russia and China are seeking to use the ongoing coronavirus pandemic as a springboard for the dissolution of the "liberal world order" and for their ascendance as the world's leading powers.[165] In stark contrast to the bipolar system of the Cold War, in which the world was largely aligned into pro-American and pro-Soviet blocs, the new, multi-polar international system presents new and myriad dangers—particularly as confidence in international institutions and the ability of international law to regulate and prevent conflict wavers.

In the outer space realm, too, the drive toward multipolarity is becoming a reality. With both technological and cost barriers to entry falling, and with increasing numbers of both States and private entities engaging in space launches and the operation of space objects, space is becoming, in the words of the United States military, more "congested, contested, and competitive." As we have seen, the radical increase in outer space users is a matter of significant concern to the United States: it means there are more potential risks (from both unintentional collisions and intentional nefarious acts) to American space systems and even greater difficulty in both tracking such risks and in attributing blame when damage occurs. At the same time, traditional American interpretations of key outer space legal provisions—including the meaning of using space for "peaceful purposes" and the legality of placing traditional, non-nuclear weapons in orbit—have become a "double-edged sword" of sorts. Now that a greater number of States actually have the technological capability to produce their own space weapons and utilize outer space for military purposes, any foreign military use of space is viewed as decreasing the relative power of the United States' space assets (in other words, turning space into a "contested" arena). This perception falls squarely within the realm of zero-sum, realist thinking, with the attendant risk that, in response to outer space "threats," the United States and others will engage in power accumulation competition—always seeking to maintain their technological or military "edge" over the other.

Particularly with respect to the relationship between the United States and China, the post-Cold War international and outer space environments exhibit characteristics that track much more closely with the "international anarchy,"

2018, 1, 2, available at https://dod.defense.gov/Portals/1/Documents/pubs/2018-National-Defense-Strategy-Summary.pdf (last visited Dec. 30, 2021).

165 *See* Sergey Sukhankin, "COVID-19 as a Tool of Information Confrontation: Russia's Approach," *University of Calgary SPP Communiqué*, 13:3, 1, 4 (April 2020), available at https://www.policyschool.ca/wp-content/uploads/2020/03/COVID-19-Tool-of-Information-Sukhankin.pdf (last visited July 20, 2022).

"fear/uncertainty," and "power accumulation" factors of "security dilemma" theory than the Cold War environment exhibited. So common has realist-style thinking become that it is even the basis of "new" theories of international relations, such as Graham Allison's "Thucydides Trap," that seek to explain—and, as Allison claims, to prevent—a likely coming conflict between the United States and China. Despite the fact that perceptions of the current international environment seem to be trending more toward realism than institutionalism, however, it is hardly inevitable that there will be conflict between the United States and China either terrestrially or in outer space. International institutions, despite the difficulties they have faced in recent years, still provide a forum for communication and negotiation. At least at present, the United States' traditional alliances—with NATO, individual European countries, Japan, and South Korea—remain strong, and, as former Air Force intelligence officer and Ph.D. candidate Aaron Bateman has recently written, the time is ripe for extending such alliances into outer space:

> … the United States has allies who are eager to create a more robust network for monitoring adversary activity on orbit and to establish a unified space doctrine to achieve a resilient space security framework. Washington can build a coalition with its spacefaring allies to effectively prepare for and win a war that extends into outer space. Indeed, the United States should leverage its allies to build a more robust network to monitor and track activities in space. While doing so, Washington should lead its allies and the world to develop norms and practices that prevent destabilizing military activities in space.[166]

Finally, despite the significant challenges presented by the multipolar post-Cold War world, the threat of a superpower nuclear confrontation no longer looms as the ultimate risk from international disagreements. In this sense, while the multipolar world may present a larger *number* of threats or risks to the United States than did the bipolar Cold War world, the *stakes* are, at least at the moment, much lower. If the United States and the Soviet Union were able to agree to binding principles of outer space law and even to non-binding norms of behavior in outer space under the real and constant threat of each others' nuclear arsenals, is it so difficult to believe that the nations of the world

---

166 Aaron Bateman, *America Needs a Coalition to Win a Space War*, WAR ON THE ROCKS (Apr. 29, 2020), https://warontherocks.com/2020/04/america-needs-a-coalition-to-win-a-space-war/.

could not similarly negotiate new frameworks for outer space activity and behavior without the serious, Cold War fears of nuclear annihilation?

4 Conclusion: The United States Space Force and the "Security Dilemma"

The preceding discussion has largely left one question unexamined: what role does the creation of the United States Space Force play in contributing to, or detracting from, a "security dilemma"-style situation in the modern, post-Cold War world? In other words, is the United States' creation of a military organization devoted to outer space affairs a result and response to "security dilemma" factors of international anarchy, fear/uncertainty, and power accumulation? And is the Space Force's creation likely to trigger additional fear, uncertainty, and power accumulation responses on the part of the United States' international competitors—responses that would ultimately increase the likelihood of conflict on orbit?

Examining the creation of the Space Force in isolation might tempt one to answer that the United States' action were the result of "security dilemma" style fears. Among the justifications for developing a Space Force cited in the introduction to President Trump's Space Policy Directive-4, for example, is that "potential [US] adversaries are now advancing their space capabilities and actively developing ways to deny our use of space in a crisis or conflict."[167] The restructuring of the American military to include a Space Force, as well as an increased focus on outer space more generally, will, in turn, "deter aggression and protect [US] interests."[168] These sorts of justifications and pronouncements certainly seem to fit the "fear/uncertainty" and "power accumulation" factors of the traditional "security dilemma" analysis: the United States' fear of the space power and capabilities of potential international rivals has caused an attempt to defend against this potential threat, and increase its own power, via the creation of the Space Force. The statements of certain government officials from the United States' potential competitors also appear, at first glance, to follow the "security dilemma" playbook. Several spokespeople for China's Foreign Ministry, for example, have criticized the creation of the Space Force

167 President Donald J. Trump, "Text of Space Policy Directive-4: Establishment of the United States Space Force," Trump White House Archives, Feb. 19, 2019, https://trumpwhitehouse.archives.gov/presidential-actions/text-space-policy-directive-4-establishment-united-states-space-force/.

168 Trump, "Text of Space Policy Directive-4."

as dangerous and destabilizing. One, Shuang Geng, described the United States' decision to develop the Space Force as "undermin[ing] global strategic balance and stability, and pos[ing] a direct threat to outer space peace and security,"[169] while another argued that the creation of the Space Force "makes it more likely … the risks of weaponizing outer space and making it a battlefield [will become a reality.]"[170] The implication of such statements seems to be that China will not stand idly by and allow its own security interests to be threatened by American action and, thus, may take further action of its own to counter the perceived threat—precisely as "security dilemma" theory would predict. It is, perhaps, no surprise that certain space experts like Dr. Laura Grego and Dr. Joan Johnson-Freese criticize the Space Force for making outer space more "contentious," "dangerous," and "weapon[ized]."

That said, a number of factors cut against the idea that the Space Force contributes to the actualization of a "security dilemma" in space. Not least of these is that the Space Force's creation *cannot* be viewed in isolation: it is both the product of a long history of policy, law, theory, and activity (a history extending back at least to the beginning of the Space Age) and only one piece of a multifaceted strategy by the United States Government to influence the future of outer space. Since at least the Obama Administration, the United States has recognized the need to encourage "responsible" behavior in space, and the Obama, Trump, and now Biden Administrations have not merely paid lip service to this idea. Instead, each successive Administration has worked, in both the domestic and international spheres, to make the concept of "responsible behavior" a reality. This includes, as we have noted in Chapter 3, both partnering with international allies at the United Nations to encourage the development of international, non-binding rules of responsible behavior and creating domestic, binding policies for US space organizations. Perhaps the most important of these is the Department of Defense's "Tenets of Responsible Behavior" in outer space, issued by Secretary of Defense Lloyd Austin in July 2021, which mandates all US military organizations, including the new Space Force, to comply with its five titular tenets.[171] Far from being an example of

---

169 Associated Press, "China attacks US Space Force as threat to peace," *Air Force Times*, Dec. 23, 2019, https://www.airforcetimes.com/news/your-military/2019/12/23/china-attacks-us-space-force-as-threat-to-peace/.

170 "Foreign Ministry Spokesperson Hua Chunying's Regular Press Conference on February 12, 2019," Consulate General of the People's Republic of China in Mumbai, Feb. 12, 2019, https://www.fmprc.gov.cn/ce/cgmb/eng/fyrth/t1637290.htm.

171 *See* Secretary of Defense Lloyd Austin, "Memorandum: Tenets of Responsible Behavior in Space," Media.Defense.Gov, July 7, 2021, https://media.defense.gov/2021/Jul/23/2002809598/-1/-1/0/TENETS-OF-RESPONSIBLE-BEHAVIOR-IN-SPACE.PDF.

naked militarization and "power accumulation," the creation of the US Space Force seems to be yet another example of the United States jointly pursuing both realist military space operations and the institutional development of the international space law regime—a strategy it has employed since the launch of *Sputnik* in 1957.

Further, examining the "fear/uncertainty" element of the "security dilemma," it is by no means clear that either fear or uncertainty were the motivating factors underlying the United States' decision to create the Space Force. American space situational awareness has long been considered the best in the world; indeed, the Department of Defense has been characterized as "the only entity able to technically support a global space safety frame-work" due to its advanced capabilities in the space surveillance and situational awareness realms.[172] While the full extent of the United States' capabilities remains unknown (it is likely highly classified), the United States is capable of tracking a significant number of space objects and debris on-orbit, as well as gathering intelligence concerning potential competitor activity on-orbit. This is clear from publicly-released material, including the Defense Intelligence Agency's unclassified "Challenges to Security in Space" publication, which was originally published in 2019 and which has recently been updated in April 2022.[173] This publication details a wide range of technologies and capabilities either actively employed, or under development, by American competitors. Considering the United States' significant intelligence collection and space situational awareness capabilities, the extent to which "fear" and "uncertainty" ultimately contributed to its decision to create the Space Force seems less significant than the public policy justifications contained in SPD-4 might suggest.

It should also be noted that, to trigger a "security dilemma" situation, the Space Force would need to trigger a corresponding fear, uncertainty, and power accumulation response by US competitors like Russia and China. One of the goals of American military leaders in the Space Force and in the Department of Defense more broadly seems to be to prevent this from occurring by making the Space Force more transparent, and its activities and operations to some degree more publicly accessible. General Raymond, the Space Force's Chief of

172 Quentin Verspieren, "The United States Department of Defense space situational awareness sharing program: Origins, development and drive towards transparency," *Journal of Space Safety Engineering*, 8:1 (March 2021), 86.

173 *See* Defense Intelligence Agency, "Challenges to Security in Space: Space Reliance in an Era of Competition and Expansion," April 2022, available at https://www.dia.mil/Portals/110/Documents/News/Military_Power_Publications/Challenges_Security_Space_2022.pdf.

Space Operations, has noted that over-classification of space activities "limits [the United States'] ability to deter conflict" with potential competitors in outer space and has characterized reducing classification as a "requirement" for "changing the deterrent calculus … of [potential] adversary[ies]," as well as increasing cooperation between the United States' and its allies.[174] Raymond's opinion has been echoed by Barbara Barrett, at the time the Secretary of the Air Force, and by members of Congress.[175] Ultimately, Congress included a provision in the 2022 National Defense Authorization Act mandating the review of "each classified program managed under the authority of the Space Force" in order to determine whether each program's "level of classification … could be changed to a lower level" or whether certain programs could be de-classified entirely.[176]

With its efforts to encourage "responsible behavior" in outer space being taken in conjunction with actions to make its military operations in the domain more transparent, the United States seems to be taking steps to directly address the potential "security dilemma" risks of its outer space activities and its new Space Force. Though the full extent of the Space Force's de-classification plans remains to be seen, the United States appears to be completely in earnest in its stated intent to increase transparency and to increase its international cooperation with allies and partners. Such efforts are all the more important in an international system that seems to be growing increasingly anarchic and multipolar—with recent events like the Russian Federation's February 2022 invasion of Ukraine providing stark reminders of the importance of international partnerships and strategic alliances. Indeed, should the United States successfully navigate and synchronize its multiple outer space-related lines of effort—in the international law-making arena, in the domestic policy arena, and in its military activities and partnerships—it may not be an exaggeration to say that US activities will actually enhance the safety, viability, and sustainability of the space environment.

174 Nathan Strout, "Space Force chief says he's working on a declassification strategy, but offers scant details," *C4ISRNet*, Mar. 3, 2021, https://www.c4isrnet.com/battlefield-tech/space/2021/03/03/space-force-chief-says-hes-working-on-a-declassification-strategy-but-offers-scant-details/.

175 Nathan Strout, "Barrett, Rogers consider declassifying secretive space programs," *Defense News*, Dec. 7, 2019, https://www.defensenews.com/smr/reagan-defense-forum/2019/12/08/barrett-rogers-plan-to-declassify-black-space-programs/.

176 National Defense Authorization Act for Fiscal Year 2022, Public Law 117–81, 117th Cong., § 1609 (2020), available at https://www.congress.gov/117/plaws/publ81/PLAW-117publ81.pdf.

CHAPTER 6

Conclusion: The Future of American Space Policy and Legal Development in a Post-USSF World

1 Introduction

The creation of the Space Force in December 2019 represents a new chapter in United States' space security policy. As this work has discussed, and as has been lost in the public critiques and mockery surrounding President Trump's decision to create this new, sixth branch of the armed forces, the Space Force is a culmination of over fifty years of American space security policies pursued over twelve presidential administrations and overseen by both American political parties. Over this long history, not every President, or political party, has necessarily behaved as modern Americans might expect. There have been Republican outer space "doves" (Eisenhower and, to a degree, Nixon) and Democratic "hawks" (Kennedy), and even the most liberal administrations either contributed to the advancement of outer space for military and security purposes (the Carter Administration) or left the basic space security framework intact, even while paying lip-service to more internationalist ideals of non-weaponization (the Obama Administration). The recognition of the importance of outer space by the United States' political and military leaders, particularly after key developments such as the invention of photo-reconnaissance satellites or the radical demonstration of space-support provided by the Persian Gulf War, has been largely bipartisan, even if much of the American public remains unaware of the profound significance of outer space-based assets to the United States' economic wellbeing and physical security. As General John Raymond, the Commander of United States Space Command and now the Space Force's Chief of Space Operations, has bluntly stated, "[t]he average American needs to understand just how reliant their life is on space. Space fuels the American way of life. Space also fuels our American way of war."[1]

---

1 Charles Pope, *Barrett, Raymond discuss Space Force's status and future; debut new recruiting ad*, SPACEFORCE.MIL (May 6, 2020), https://www.spaceforce.mil/News/Article/2178584/barrett-raymond-discuss-space-forces-status-and-future-debut-new-recruiting-ad. *See also* Jim Garamone, *Leaders Chart the Course as U.S. Space Force Launches*, DEFENSE.GOV (May

 DOI:10.1163/9789004524064_007

This book has sought to examine the principles of international outer space law, the US contribution to the development of the outer space legal regime, and the history of American space security policy, all in order to frame and contextualize the recent creation of the United States Space Force. This brief conclusion will offer closing remarks with respect to the interplay of outer space law with the creation of the Space Force and the future direction of US space security policy.

2 Outer Space Law and the United States Space Force

This work has examined the basic framework of outer space law, particularly as it relates to security and military-oriented uses of outer space (Chapter 2), as well as the historical development of the United States' domestic space security policies over time (Chapter 3). While the previous section shows how the Space Force is an incremental step in the United States' domestic space security policies, how does the Space Force fit into outer space law more generally? Although this question will probably be broad enough to serve as the subject of whole books in the future, after the Space Force has become more fully established and undertaken a more significant number of military space-related missions, this section will offer a succinct set of observations regarding the Space Force and its operations in the context of international law.

Nothing in existing outer space law prohibits the development of a national military organization focusing on outer space operations. The debates concerning the meaning and extent of the Outer Space Treaty's "peaceful purposes" language have been previously examined in Chapter 2: as we saw, despite some disagreement with respect to whether outer space must be used exclusively for "peaceful purposes," the plain language of the Treaty, and air and space law expert Bin Cheng (among others), make a persuasive argument that no requirement to use outer space void (the expanses of space between celestial bodies) for exclusively "peaceful purposes" exists. If this is the case, the only significant limits on military activity in outer space void are the nuclear weapons/weapons of mass destruction prohibitions contained in Article IV of the Outer Space Treaty and the general international law rules (applicable to outer space due to Article III) concerning aggression, lawful conflict, and self-defense.

6, 2020), https://www.defense.gov/Explore/News/Article/Article/2177974/leaders-chart-the-course-as-us-space-force-launches/.

The Space Force as an organization does not violate any of the provisions or principles of the Outer Space Treaty, nor any other instrument of international outer space law. Neither the Space Force, nor its predecessor, the Air Force's Space Command, has ever had any serious plans to station nuclear weapons or other weapons of mass destruction in orbit. Indeed, most of the Space Force's current missions are decidedly technical and, in many ways, even non-military. Those missions that potentially have a military force-projection, or even kinetic, component ("Space Superiority" and "Offensive and Defensive Space Control") are generally conceived to take place in the context of operations in orbit around the Earth—that is, outer space void, rather than on the surface of other celestial bodies. Even without reference to the United States' current (and historic) understanding of the "peaceful use" and "peaceful purposes" language of the Outer Space Treaty, the Space Force is, at least at the moment, framed squarely within the limits of existing international outer space law.

3 The Future of United States Space Security Policy

It is clear from the incremental steps the Department of Defense is taking in the development of the Space Force that the United States is not planning a radical expansion of its military activities in outer space. Despite the increased focus on outer space as a "warfighting domain" and an arena of potential Great Power conflict, the practical changes to American space operations caused by the Space Force's creation are, at least in the near term, fairly minimal. Indeed, with SPD-4's and the Department of Defense's focus on "consolidation"—the "vision to consolidate the operational and combat support capabilities of space units from across DoD under the banner of a single institution"—it may, in fact, be the case that American military space activities will decrease somewhat in the short term as military space projects among the separate services are consolidated under the Space Force.[2] Indeed, because "the fragmented decision processes for DoD space architecture planning and acquisition represent the greatest impediment to keeping pace with the growing threats posed by America's adversaries in the [space] domain," a certain restriction in military space activities seems likely as the Space Force determines what space

2 U.S. Dept. of the Air Force, *Comprehensive Plan for the Organizational Structure of the U.S. Space Force*, 12.

missions, operational capabilities, and acquisitions best serve the United States' national security goals.[3]

What the founding of the Space Force will mean for United States space security policy in the long term remains to be seen. However, as this work has attempted to show, particularly through Chapter 3's exploration of the history of American space security policy, the United States has seen an increasing acceptance of more military-oriented, and even weaponized, uses of outer space since at least the early 1980s. While every president since Eisenhower contributed (some more, some less) to a greater acceptance of military uses of space, President Reagan's Cold War military build-up, support for SDI, and, particularly, his push for outer space weapons (clearly articulated in his National Space Policy, NSDD 42[4]) represented a clear sea-change in American space security policy. The Persian Gulf War's profound demonstration of the benefits of space-support to terrestrial military forces further encouraged the continued tilt toward more military-oriented uses of space, despite the Cold War's end and the United States' assumption of a "sole superpower" status in both the international system and the outer space domain. With the risks to American space systems described in the Rumsfeld Commission report of 2001, the continued development of space-based support for terrestrial military forces during the wars in Afghanistan and Iraq, and the proliferation of outer space access and rise of new space powers, the creation of a military department like the Space Force seems a logical culmination of a trend that has been proceeding largely unabated for nearly forty years.

Should this trend concern us? Is the United States' trajectory pushing the rest of the world, and, particularly, rival powers like Russia and China, toward their own more militant uses of space—uses that will lead, inexorably, to conflict with the United States? The history of American space security policy development and our examination of how the United States' averted "security dilemma"-style conflict with the Soviet Union during the Cold War demonstrate that conflict is by no means inevitable. The post-Cold War world may be more multipolar and, in some ways, more threatening than the bipolar Cold War, but it is by no means as dangerous. Globalization, economic codependence, and enhanced (though admittedly shaky, particularly in the aftermath of the global coronavirus pandemic) international relationships between China—the United States' most likely Great Power competitor—and the rest of the world make the threat of nuclear war far less likely than during the Cold

3 U.S. Dept. of the Air Force, *Comprehensive Plan for the Organizational Structure of the U.S. Space Force*, 12.

4 *See* Chapter 3, pp. 89–91.

War period. While conflict is not impossible (indeed, if theorists like Graham Allison are to be believed, conflict between China and the United States is likely), whether in space or more generally, the United States and the world system as a whole have a number of significant advantages that were not present during the Cold War—particularly with respect to issues related to outer space. If the United States and the Soviet Union were able to create a workable legal and international policy framework for outer space at the height of the Cold War, surely conflict in outer space could continue to be averted in the more interconnected, globalized world of the 21st century!

With respect to the question of cause-and-effect, and the "security dilemma" quotation from *Foucault's Pendulum* that inaugurated this work, our discussion of history, of international law, and of international relations makes clear that the question of whether the United States is propelling the world toward a space-based "security dilemma" is a murky one. Unlike Casaubon and his friends, the United States did not "make up" its outer space security concerns—the potential threats posed by Soviet outer space technology, and, even more significantly, by the rocket technology used by the Soviets to propel *Sputnik* into orbit were neither imaginary, nor even merely theoretical. Particularly in the context of the Cold War, the Soviets' scientific advancement could not go unanswered. The United States' dual-track response, however, set the stage for fairly measured outer space relations between the two Cold War Superpowers and, as seen in Chapter 2, led to the development of international outer space law. The United States' Cold War experience was certainly dissimilar to the cycle of fantastical invention, followed by a deadly, self-defeating destruction experienced by Casaubon and his friends.

The full history of the United States' space security policies—particularly, their development in response to real and potential threats from a technologically-advanced Superpower rival—seems to be largely forgotten when characterizing the United States as the primary driver of outer space insecurity in the post-Cold War world. The United States' Cold War space architecture, built up in response to the perceived threats from the Soviet Union, was already robust as the Cold War drew to a close. Particularly after the Persian Gulf War, when space support for the United States' and its allies' war effort proved decisive, there was little chance that the United States would abandon its space-based technology—particularly since so much of it, including meteorological, geo-positioning, and communications satellite technology, had civilian as well as military uses. That the United States' Gulf War success, and the clear benefits of space-based support systems, would be an "ahooga moment" for China or other States (leading them, potentially, to take steps to utilize space systems themselves or work to develop means to counter them) makes sense, particularly from a realist international relations perspective. Still, that the United States developed such systems in response to the Soviet threat and would seek to retain and protect such systems in the post-Cold War environment is hardly an indictment of the United States.

Ultimately, perceptions of the United States as an outer space hegemon bent on even further space dominance could affect the behaviors of its allies and adversaries. This may not lead to realist confrontation or "security dilemma"-style conflict, but the cause-and-effect relationship between the United States' perceived desires in outer space and other States' reactions should not be discounted, either. As the United States takes steps—through the creation of the United States Space Force and through other means—to protect its outer space infrastructure and the critical terrestrial services this infrastructure provides, policy-makers and military leaders should reflect on the United States' previous space policy actions. Increased weaponization and brute force will not necessarily protect the United States' interests in outer space. Creative, institutionalist solutions to outer space-related competition prevented significant confrontation during the Cold War; might similar institutionalist engagement do so again?

As the United States navigates the tensions between protecting its national security, encouraging outer space commercial endeavors, and "help[ing] assure the use of space for all responsible parties," the activities of the United States Space Force will contribute significantly to the future of the outer space security environment. Should the current Biden Administration and future American political leaders successfully balance these tensions, the United States' efforts to develop frameworks for outer space behavior while, at the same time, ensuring the protection of American and allied space assets via the work of the Space Force, may largely preserve the freedoms of use and access to outer space and the wider aspirations of cooperation, international partnership, and international law enshrined in the Outer Space Treaty. And, perhaps, if the United States and its allies are successful in their endeavors to codify responsible behavior, this will allow the nations of the world to, in the words of the HAL 9000 supercomputer from *2001: A Space Odyssey*, finally put outer space to its "fullest possible use."

Appendices

APPENDIX A

Treaty on Principles Governing the Activities of States in the Exploration and Use of Outer Space, including the Moon and Other Celestial Bodies

The States Parties to this Treaty,

Inspired by the great prospects opening up before mankind as a result of man's entry into outer space,

Recognizing the common interest of all mankind in the progress of the exploration and use of outer space for peaceful purposes,

Believing that the exploration and use of outer space should be carried on for the benefit of all peoples irrespective of the degree of their economic or scientific development,

Desiring to contribute to broad international co-operation in the scientific as well as the legal aspects of the exploration and use of outer space for peaceful purposes,

Believing that such co-operation will contribute to the development of mutual understanding and to the strengthening of friendly relations between States and peoples,

Recalling resolution 1962 (XVIII), entitled "Declaration of Legal Principles Governing the Activities of States in the Exploration and Use of Outer Space", which was adopted unanimously by the United Nations General Assembly on 13 December 1963,

Recalling resolution 1884 (XVIII), calling upon States to refrain from placing in orbit around the earth any objects carrying nuclear weapons or any other kinds of weapons of mass destruction or from installing such weapons on celestial bodies, which was adopted unanimously by the United Nations General Assembly on 17 October 1963,

Taking account of United Nations General Assembly resolution 110 (II) of 3 November 1947, which condemned propaganda designed or likely to provoke or encourage any threat to the peace, breach of the peace or act of aggression, and considering that the aforementioned resolution is applicable to outer space,

Convinced that a Treaty on Principles Governing the Activities of States in the Exploration and Use of Outer Space, including the Moon and Other Celestial Bodies, will further the purposes and principles of the Charter of the United Nations,

Have agreed on the following:

ARTICLE I

The exploration and use of outer space, including the moon and other celestial bodies, shall be carried out for the benefit and in the interests of all countries, irrespective of their degree of economic or scientific development, and shall be the province of all mankind.

 | DOI:10.1163/9789004524064_008

Outer space, including the moon and other celestial bodies, shall be free for exploration and use by all States without discrimination of any kind, on a basis of equality and in accordance with international law, and there shall be free access to all areas of celestial bodies.

There shall be freedom of scientific investigation in outer space, including the moon and other celestial bodies, and States shall facilitate and encourage international co-operation in such investigation.

ARTICLE II

Outer space, including the moon and other celestial bodies, is not subject to national appropriation by claim of sovereignty, by means of use or occupation, or by any other means.

ARTICLE III

States Parties to the Treaty shall carry on activities in the exploration and use of outer space, including the moon and other celestial bodies, in accordance with international law, including the Charter of the United Nations, in the interest of maintaining international peace and security and promoting international co-operation and understanding.

ARTICLE IV

States Parties to the Treaty undertake not to place in orbit around the earth any objects carrying nuclear weapons or any other kinds of weapons of mass destruction, install such weapons on celestial bodies, or station such weapons in outer space in any other manner.

The moon and other celestial bodies shall be used by all States Parties to the Treaty exclusively for peaceful purposes. The establishment of military bases, installations and fortifications, the testing of any type of weapons and the conduct of military manoeuvres on celestial bodies shall be forbidden. The use of military personnel for scientific research or for any other peaceful purposes shall not be prohibited. The use of any equipment or facility necessary for peaceful exploration of the moon and other celestial bodies shall also not be prohibited.

ARTICLE V

States Parties to the Treaty shall regard astronauts as envoys of mankind in outer space and shall render to them all possible assistance in the event of accident, distress, or emergency landing on the territory of another State Party or on the high seas. When astronauts make such a landing, they shall be safely and promptly returned to the State of registry of their space vehicle.

In carrying on activities in outer space and on celestial bodies, the astronauts of one State Party shall render all possible assistance to the astronauts of other States Parties.

States Parties to the Treaty shall immediately inform the other States Parties to the Treaty or the Secretary-General of the United Nations of any phenomena they discover in outer space, including the moon and other celestial bodies, which could constitute a danger to the life or health of astronauts.

ARTICLE VI

States Parties to the Treaty shall bear international responsibility for national activities in outer space, including the moon and other celestial bodies, whether such activities are carried on by governmental agencies or by non-governmental entities, and for assuring that national activities are carried out in conformity with the provisions set forth in the present Treaty. The activities of non-governmental entities in outer space, including the moon and other celestial bodies, shall require authorization and continuing supervision by the appropriate State Party to the Treaty. When activities are carried on in outer space, including the moon and other celestial bodies, by an international organization, responsibility for compliance with this Treaty shall be borne both by the international organization and by the States Parties to the Treaty participating in such organization.

ARTICLE VII

Each State Party to the Treaty that launches or procures the launching of an object into outer space, including the moon and other celestial bodies, and each State Party from whose territory or facility an object is launched, is internationally liable for damage to another State Party to the Treaty or to its natural or juridical persons by such object or its component parts on the Earth, in air or in outer space, including the moon and other celestial bodies.

ARTICLE VIII

A State Party to the Treaty on whose registry an object launched into outer space is carried shall retain jurisdiction and control over such object, and over any personnel thereof, while in outer space or on a celestial body. Ownership of objects launched into outer space, including objects landed or constructed on a celestial body, and of their component parts, is not affected by their presence in outer space or on a celestial body or by their return to the Earth. Such objects or component parts found beyond the limits of the State Party to the Treaty on whose registry they are carried shall be returned to that State Party, which shall, upon request, furnish identifying data prior to their return.

ARTICLE IX

In the exploration and use of outer space, including the moon and other celestial bodies, States Parties to the Treaty shall be guided by the principle of co-operation and mutual assistance and shall conduct all their activities in outer space, including the moon and other celestial bodies, with due regard to the corresponding interests of all other States Parties to the Treaty. States Parties to the Treaty shall pursue studies of outer space, including the moon and other celestial bodies, and conduct exploration of them so as to avoid their harmful contamination and also adverse changes in the environment of the Earth resulting from the introduction of extraterrestrial matter and, where necessary, shall adopt appropriate measures for this purpose. If a State Party to the Treaty has reason to believe that an activity or experiment planned by it or its nationals in outer space, including the moon and other celestial bodies, would cause potentially harmful interference with activities of other States Parties in the peaceful exploration and use of outer space, including the moon and other celestial bodies, it shall undertake appropriate international consultations before proceeding with any such activity or experiment. A State Party to the Treaty which has reason to believe that an activity or experiment planned by another State Party in outer space, including the moon and other celestial bodies, would cause potentially harmful interference with activities in the peaceful exploration and use of outer space, including the moon and other celestial bodies, may request consultation concerning the activity or experiment.

ARTICLE X

In order to promote international co-operation in the exploration and use of outer space, including the moon and other celestial bodies, in conformity with the purposes of this Treaty, the States Parties to the Treaty shall consider on a basis of equality any requests by other States Parties to the Treaty to be afforded an opportunity to observe the flight of space objects launched by those States. The nature of such an opportunity for observation and the conditions under which it could be afforded shall be determined by agreement between the States concerned.

ARTICLE XI

In order to promote international co-operation in the peaceful exploration and use of outer space, States Parties to the Treaty conducting activities in outer space, including the moon and other celestial bodies, agree to inform the Secretary-General of the United Nations as well as the public and the international scientific community, to the greatest extent feasible and practicable, of the nature, conduct, locations and results of such activities. On receiving the said information, the Secretary-General of the United Nations should be prepared to disseminate it immediately and effectively.

ARTICLE XII

All stations, installations, equipment and space vehicles on the moon and other celestial bodies shall be open to representatives of other States Parties to the Treaty on a basis of reciprocity. Such representatives shall give reasonable advance notice of a projected visit, in order that appropriate consultations may be held and that maximum precautions may be taken to assure safety and to avoid interference with normal operations in the facility to be visited.

ARTICLE XIII

The provisions of this Treaty shall apply to the activities of States Parties to the Treaty in the exploration and use of outer space, including the moon and other celestial bodies, whether such activities are carried on by a single State Party to the Treaty or jointly with other States, including cases where they are carried on within the framework of international intergovernmental organizations.

Any practical questions arising in connection with activities carried on by international intergovernmental organizations in the exploration and use of outer space, including the moon and other celestial bodies, shall be resolved by the States Parties to the Treaty either with the appropriate international organization or with one or more States members of that international organization, which are Parties to this Treaty.

ARTICLE XIV

1. This Treaty shall be open to all States for signature. Any State which does not sign this Treaty before its entry into force in accordance with paragraph 3 of this article may accede to it at anytime.
2. This Treaty shall be subject to ratification by signatory States. Instruments of ratification and instruments of accession shall be deposited with the Governments of the United Kingdom of Great Britain and Northern Ireland, the Union of Soviet Socialist Republics and the United States of America, which are hereby designated the Depositary Governments.
3. This Treaty shall enter into force upon the deposit of instruments of ratification by five Governments including the Governments designated as Depositary Governments under this Treaty.
4. For States whose instruments of ratification or accession are deposited subsequent to the entry into force of this Treaty, it shall enter into force on the date of the deposit of their instruments of ratification or accession.
5. The Depositary Governments shall promptly inform all signatory and acceding States of the date of each signature, the date of deposit of each instrument of ratification of and accession to this Treaty, the date of its entry into force and other notices.
6. This Treaty shall be registered by the Depositary Governments pursuant to Article 102 of the Charter of the United Nations.

ARTICLE XV

Any State Party to the Treaty may propose amendments to this Treaty. Amendments shall enter into force for each State Party to the Treaty accepting the amendments upon their acceptance by a majority of the States Parties to the Treaty and thereafter for each remaining State Party to the Treaty on the date of acceptance by it.

ARTICLE XVI

Any State Party to the Treaty may give notice of its withdrawal from the Treaty one year after its entry into force by written notification to the Depositary Governments. Such withdrawal shall take effect one year from the date of receipt of this notification.

ARTICLE XVII

This Treaty, of which the English, Russian, French, Spanish and Chinese texts are equally authentic, shall be deposited in the archives of the Depositary Governments.

Duly certified copies of this Treaty shall be transmitted by the Depositary Governments to the Governments of the signatory and acceding States.

IN WITNESS WHEREOF the undersigned, duly authorized, have signed this Treaty.

DONE in triplicate, at the cities of London, Moscow and Washington, the twenty-seventh day of January, one thousand nine hundred and sixty-seven.

APPENDIX B

Text of Space Policy Directive-4, "Establishment of the United States *Space Force" (President Donald J. Trump, February 19, 2019*)

SUBJECT: Establishment of the United States Space Force

Section 1. Introduction. Space is integral to our way of life, our national security, and modern warfare. Although United States space systems have historically maintained a technological advantage over those of our potential adversaries, those potential adversaries are now advancing their space capabilities and actively developing ways to deny our use of space in a crisis or conflict. It is imperative that the United States adapt its national security organizations, policies, doctrine, and capabilities to deter aggression and protect our interests. Toward that end, the Department of Defense shall take actions under existing authority to marshal its space resources to deter and counter threats in space, and to develop a legislative proposal to establish a United States Space Force as a sixth branch of the United States Armed Forces within the Department of the Air Force. This is an important step toward a future military department for space. Under this proposal, the United States Space Force would be authorized to organize, train, and equip military space forces of the United States to ensure unfettered access to, and freedom to operate in, space, and to provide vital capabilities to joint and coalition forces in peacetime and across the spectrum of conflict.

Sec. 2. Definitions. For the purposes of this memorandum and the legislative proposal directed by section 3 of this memorandum, the following definitions shall apply:

(a) The term "United States Space Force" refers to a new branch of the United States Armed Forces to be initially placed by statute within the Department of the Air Force.

(b) The term "Department of the Space Force" refers to a future military department within the Department of Defense that will be responsible for organizing, training, and equipping the United States Space Force.

(c) The term "United States Space Command" refers to a Unified Combatant Command to be established pursuant to the Presidential memorandum of December 18, 2018 (Establishment of United States Space Command as a Unified Combatant Command), that will be responsible for Joint Force space operations as will be assigned in the Unified Command Plan.

Sec. 3. Legislative Proposal and Purpose. The Secretary of Defense shall submit a legislative proposal to the President through the Office of Management and Budget that would establish the United States Space Force as a new armed service within the Department of the Air Force.

The legislative proposal would, if enacted, establish the United States Space Force to organize, train, and equip forces to provide for freedom of operation in, from, and to the space domain; to provide independent military options for national leadership; and to enhance the lethality and effectiveness of the Joint Force. The United States Space Force should include both combat and combat support functions to enable prompt and sustained offensive and defensive space operations, and joint operations in all domains. The United States Space Force shall be organized, trained, and equipped to meet the following priorities:

(a) Protecting the Nation's interests in space and the peaceful use of space for all responsible actors, consistent with applicable law, including international law;
(b) Ensuring unfettered use of space for United States national security purposes, the United States economy, and United States persons, partners, and allies;
(c) Deterring aggression and defending the Nation, United States allies, and United States interests from hostile acts in and from space;
(d) Ensuring that needed space capabilities are integrated and available to all United States Combatant Commands;
(e) Projecting military power in, from, and to space in support of our Nation's interests; and
(f) Developing, maintaining, and improving a community of professionals focused on the national security demands of the space domain.

Sec. 4. Scope.

(a) The legislative proposal required by section 3 of this memorandum shall, in addition to the provisions required under section 3 of this memorandum, include provisions that would, if enacted:
    (i) consolidate existing forces and authorities for military space activities, as appropriate, in order to minimize duplication of effort and eliminate bureaucratic inefficiencies; and
    (ii) not include the National Aeronautics and Space Administration, the National Oceanic and Atmospheric Administration, the National Reconnaissance Office, or other non-military space organizations or missions of the United States Government.
(b) The proposed United States Space Force should:
    (i) include, as determined by the Secretary of Defense in consultation with the Secretaries of the military departments, the uniformed and civilian personnel conducting and directly supporting space operations from all Department of Defense Armed Forces;
    (ii) assume responsibilities for all major military space acquisition programs; and

(iii) create the appropriate career tracks for military and civilian space personnel across all relevant specialties, including operations, intelligence, engineering, science, acquisition, and cyber.

Sec. 5. United States Space Force Budget. In accordance with the Department of Defense budget process, the Secretary of Defense shall submit to the Director of the Office of Management and Budget a proposed budget for the United States Space Force to be included in the President's Fiscal Year 2020 Budget Request.

Sec. 6. United States Space Force Organization and Leadership.

(a) The legislative proposal required by section 3 of this memorandum shall create a civilian Under Secretary of the Air Force for Space, to be known as the Under Secretary for Space, appointed by the President by and with the advice and consent of the Senate.

(b) The legislative proposal shall establish a Chief of Staff of the Space Force, who will be a senior military officer in the grade of General or Admiral, and who shall serve as a member of the Joint Chiefs of Staff.

Sec. 7. Associated Elements.

(a) A Unified Combatant Command for space, to be known as the United States Space Command, will be established consistent with law, as directed on December 18, 2018. This command will have all of the responsibilities of a Unified Combatant Command in addition to the space-related responsibilities previously assigned to United States Strategic Command. It will also have the responsibilities of the Joint Force provider and Joint Force training for space operations forces. Moving expeditiously toward a Unified Combatant Command reflects the importance of warfighting in space to the Joint Force. The commander of this command will lead space warfighting through global space operations that may occur in the space domain, the terrestrial domains, or through the electromagnetic spectrum.

(b) With forces provided by the United States Space Force and other United States Armed Forces, the United States Space Command shall ensure unfettered access to, and freedom to operate in, space and provide vital effects and capabilities to joint and coalition forces during peacetime and across the spectrum of conflict.

Sec. 8. Relationship with National Intelligence. The Secretary of Defense and the Director of National Intelligence shall create and enhance mechanisms for collaboration between the Department of Defense and the United States Intelligence Community in order to increase unity of effort and the effectiveness of space operations. The Secretary of Defense and the Director of National Intelligence shall provide a report to the President within 180 days of the date of this memorandum on steps they have taken and are planning to take toward these ends, including legislative proposals as necessary and appropriate.

Sec. 9. Operational Authorities. In order to ensure that the United States Space Force and United States Space Command have the necessary operational authorities, the National Space Council and the National Security Council shall coordinate an accelerated review of space operational authorities. Within 90 days of the date of this memorandum, the Secretary of Defense shall present to the National Space Council and the National Security Council proposed relevant authority changes for the President's approval. The National Space Council and the National Security Council shall then conduct an interagency review of the Secretary's proposal and make recommendations to the President on appropriate authorities, to be completed no later than 60 days from the date the Secretary of Defense presents his proposal to the councils.

Sec. 10. Periodic Review. As the United States Space Force matures, and as national security requires, it will become necessary to create a separate military department, to be known as the Department of the Space Force. This department will take over some or all responsibilities for the United States Space Force from the Department of the Air Force. The Secretary of Defense will conduct periodic reviews to determine when to recommend that the President seek legislation to establish such a department.

Sec. 11. General Provisions.

(a) Nothing in this memorandum shall be construed to impair or otherwise affect:
   (i) the authority granted by law to an executive department or agency, or the head thereof; or
   (ii) the functions of the Director of the Office of Management and Budget relating to budgetary, administrative, or legislative proposals.

(b) This memorandum shall be implemented consistent with applicable law and United States national and homeland security requirements, and subject to the availability of appropriations.

(c) This memorandum is not intended to, and does not, create any right or benefit, substantive or procedural, enforceable at law or in equity by any party against the United States, its departments, agencies, or entities, its officers, employees, or agents, or any other person.

(d) The Secretary of Defense is authorized and directed to publish this memorandum in the Federal Register.

DONALD J. TRUMP

Publications Examining the Organization of Space Forces or the Creation of a Space-Oriented Military Service Branch (1994–2018)

1994: Major Ricky B. Kelly, "Centralized Control of Space: The Use of Space Forces by a Joint Force Commander," Thesis (Maxwell Air Force Base, AL: School of Advanced Airpower Studies, Sept. 22, 1994), available at https://spp.fas.org/eprint/p187.pdf.

1998: Major Mark Jelonek, "Toward an Air and Space Force: Can We Get There From Here? Naval Aviation and the Implications for Space Power," Thesis (Maxwell Air Force Base, AL: School of Advanced Airpower Studies, Jan. 6, 1998), available at https://apps.dtic.mil/sti/pdfs/ADA391798.pdf.

2000: Colonel Michael Whittington, "A Separate Space Force: An 80-Year-Old Argument," Maxwell Paper No. 20 (Maxwell Air Force Base, AL: Air War College, May 2000), available at https://apps.dtic.mil/sti/pdfs/ADA378853.pdf.

2002: Colonel Kurt Story, "A Separate Space Force: An Old Debate w/ Renewed Relevance," Senior Service College Fellowship Paper (Carlisle, PA: U.S. Army War College, April 9, 2002), available at https://apps.dtic.mil/sti/pdfs/ADA404193.pdf.

2004: Major Franz J. Gayl, "Time for a Military Space Service," *Proceedings*, Vol. 130, No. 7, July 2004, pp. 43–45.

2006: Lieutenant Colonel Mark Harter, "Ten Propositions Regarding Space Power: The Dawn of a Space Force," *Air & Space Power Journal*, Summer 2006, available at https://apps.dtic.mil/sti/pdfs/ADP023961.pdf.

2006: Taylor Dinerman, "United States Space Force: sooner rather than later," *The Space Review*, Feb. 27, 2006, https://www.thespacereview.com/article/565/1.

2012: Lieutenant Colonel John Cinnamon, "US Department of the Space Force: A Necessary Evolution," Thesis (Norfolk, VA: Joint Advanced Warfighting School, Joint Forces Staff College, National Defense University, May 2012), available at https://apps.dtic.mil/sti/pdfs/ADA562163.pdf.

2016: Lieutenant Colonel Peter Norsky, "The United States Space Force: Not If, But When," Thesis (Maxwell Air Force Base, AL: School of Advanced Air and Space Studies, June 2016), available at https://apps.dtic.mil/sti/pdfs/AD1030447.pdf.

 | DOI:10.1163/9789004524064_010

APPENDIX D

Portions of 2020 National Defense Authorization Act Pertaining to the Creation of the United States Space Force

Subtitle D—United States Space Force

SEC. 951. SHORT TITLE.

This subtitle may be cited as the "United States Space Force Act".

SEC. 952. THE SPACE FORCE.

(a) REDESIGNATION.—The Air Force Space Command is hereby redesignated as the United States Space Force (USSF).

(b) AUTHORITY.—Title 10, United States Code, is amended—

(1) in chapter 907 of part I of subtitle D, by redesignating sections 9067, 9069, 9074, 9075, 9081, and 9084 as sections 9063, 9064, 9065, 9066, 9067, and 9068, respectively;

(2) by adding at the end of such part the following new chapter:

Chapter 908—The Space Force

"Sec.

9081. The United States Space Force.

9082. Chief of Space Operations.

9083. Officer career field for space."

(3) by transferring section 2279c to chapter 908, as so added, and redesignating such section as section 9081; and

(4) by amending such section 9081 to read as follows:

"§ 9081. The United States Space Force

"(a) ESTABLISHMENT.—There is established a United States Space Force as an armed force within the Department of the Air Force.

"(b) COMPOSITION.—The Space Force shall be composed of the following:

 | DOI:10.1163/9789004524064_011

"(1) The Chief of Space Operations.

"(2) The space forces and such assets as may be organic therein.

"(c) FUNCTIONS.—The Space Force shall be organized, trained, and equipped to provide—

"(1) freedom of operation for the United States in, from, and to space; and

"(2) prompt and sustained space operations.

"(d) DUTIES.—It shall be the duty of the Space Force to—

"(1) protect the interests of the United States in space;

"(2) deter aggression in, from, and to space; and

"(3) conduct space operations.".

(c) SPACE FORCE AS AN ARMED FORCE.—Section 101(a)(4) of title 10, United States Code, is amended by inserting "Space Force," after "Marine Corps,".

(d) MEMBERS.—

(1) IN GENERAL.—Effective as of the date of the enactment of this Act, there shall be assigned to the Space Force such members of the Air Force as the Secretary of the Air Force shall specify.

(2) NO AUTHORIZATION OF ADDITIONAL MILITARY BILLETS.— The Secretary shall carry out this subsection within military personnel of the Air Force otherwise authorized by this Act. Nothing in this subsection shall be construed to authorize additional military billets for the purposes of, or in connection with, the establishment of the Space Force.

(e) OFFICER CAREER FIELD FOR SPACE.—Section 9068 of title 10, United States Code (as redesignated by subsection (b)(1)), is hereby transferred to the end of chapter 908 of such title (as added by subsection (b)(2)) and redesignated as section 9083.

(f) TABLES OF CHAPTERS.—The tables of chapters at the beginning of subtitle D of title 10, United States Code, and part I of such subtitle are each amended by inserting after the item relating to chapter 907 the following new item:

"908. The Space Force ....9081.".

(g) CONFORMING CLERICAL AMENDMENT TO CHAPTER 907.— The table of sections at the beginning of chapter 907 of title 10, United States Code, is amended by striking the items relating to sections 9067, 9069, 9074, 9075, 9081, and 9084 and inserting the following new items:

"9063. Designation: officers to perform certain professional functions.

"9064. Air Force nurses: Chief; appointment.

"9065. Commands: territorial organization.

"9066. Regular Air Force: composition.

"9067. Assistant Surgeon General for Dental Services.".

Sec. 953. Chief of Space Operations

(a) CHIEF.—Chapter 908 of title 10, United States Code (as added by section 952 of this Act), is amended by inserting after section 9081 the following new section:

"§ 9082. Chief of Space Operations

"(a) APPOINTMENT.—

(1) There is a Chief of Space Operations, appointed by the President, by and with the advice and consent of the Senate, from the general officers of the Air Force. The Chief serves at the pleasure of the President.

"(2) The Chief shall be appointed for a term of four years. In time of war or during a national emergency declared by Congress, the Chief may be reappointed for a term of not more than four years.

"(b) GRADE.—The Chief, while so serving, has the grade of general without vacating the permanent grade of the officer.

"(c) RELATIONSHIP TO THE SECRETARY OF THE AIR FORCE.— Except as otherwise prescribed by law and subject to section 9013(f) of this title, the Chief performs the duties of such position under the authority, direction, and control of the Secretary of the Air Force and is directly responsible to the Secretary.

"(d) DUTIES.—Subject to the authority, direction, and control of the Secretary of the Air Force, the Chief shall—

"(1) preside over the Office of the Chief of Space Operations;

"(2) transmit the plans and recommendations of the Office of the Chief of Space Operations to the Secretary and advise the Secretary with regard to such plans and recommendations;

"(3) after approval of the plans or recommendations of the Office of the Chief of Space Operations by the Secretary, act as the agent of the Secretary in carrying them into effect;

"(4) exercise supervision, consistent with the authority assigned to commanders of unified or specified combatant commands under Chapter 6 of this title, over such of the members and organizations of the Space Force as the Secretary determines; and

"(5) perform such other military duties, not otherwise assigned by law, as are assigned to the Chief by the President, the Secretary of Defense, or the Secretary of the Air Force.

"(e) JOINT CHIEFS OF STAFF.— (1) Commencing one year after the date of the enactment of the United States Space Force Act, the Chief of Space Operations shall be a member of the Joint Chiefs of Staff.

"(2) To the extent that such action does not impair the independence of the Chief in the performance of the duties of the Chief as a member of the Joint Chiefs of Staff pursuant to paragraph (1), the Chief shall inform the Secretary of the Air Force regarding military advice rendered by members of the Joint Chiefs of Staff on matters affecting the Department of the Air Force.

"(3) Subject to the authority, direction, and control of the Secretary of Defense, the Chief shall keep the Secretary of the Air Force fully informed of significant military operations affecting the duties and responsibilities of the Secretary.".

(b) SERVICE.—

(1) INCUMBENT.—The individual serving as Commander of the Air Force Space Command as of the day before the date of the enactment of this Act may serve as the Chief of Space Operations under subsection (a) of section 9082 of title 10, United States Code (as added by subsection (a) of this section), after that date without further appointment as otherwise provided for by subsection (a) of such section 9082.

(2) U.S. SPACE COMMAND.—During the one-year period beginning on the date of the enactment of this Act, the Secretary of Defense may authorize an officer serving as the Chief of Space Operations to serve concurrently as the Commander of the United States Space Command, without further appointment.

(c) JOINT CHIEFS OF STAFF MATTERS.—Effective on the date that is one year after the date of the enactment of this Act, section 151(a) of title 10, United States Code, is amended by adding at the end the following new paragraph:

"(8) The Chief of Space Operations.".

Sec. 954. Space Force Acquisition Council

(a) IN GENERAL.—Chapter 903 of title 10, United States Code, is amended—

(1) by redesignating section 9021 as section 9021a; and

(2) by inserting after section 9020 the following new section 9021:

"§ 9021. Space Force Acquisition Council

"(a) ESTABLISHMENT.—There is in the Office of the Secretary of the Air Force a council to be known as the 'Space Force Acquisition Council' (in this section referred to as the 'Council').

"(b) MEMBERS.—The members of the Council are as follows:

"(1) The Under Secretary of the Air Force.

"(2) The Assistant Secretary of the Air Force for Space Acquisition and Integration, who shall act as chair of the Council.

"(3) The Assistant Secretary of Defense for Space Policy.

"(4) The Director of the National Reconnaissance Office.

"(5) The Chief of Space Operations.

"(6) The Commander of the United States Space Command.

"(c) DUTIES.—The Council shall oversee, direct, and manage acquisition and integration of the Air Force for space systems and programs in order to ensure integration across the national security space enterprise.

"(d) MEETINGS.—The Council shall meet not less frequently than monthly.

"(e) REPORTS.—Not later than 30 days after the end of each calendar year quarter through the first calendar year quarter of 2025, the Council shall submit to the congressional defense committees a report on the activities of the Council during the calendar year quarter preceding the calendar year quarter in which such report is submitted.".

(b) CLERICAL AMENDMENT.—The table of sections at the beginning of chapter 903 of such title is amended by striking the item relating to section 9021 and inserting the following new items:

"9021. Space Force Acquisition Council.

"9021a. Air Force Reserve Forces Policy Committee.".

Sec. 955. Assistant Secretary of Defense for Space Policy

(a) IN GENERAL.—Section 138(b) of title 10, United States Code, is amended by adding at the end the following new paragraph:

"(5) One of the Assistant Secretaries is the Assistant Secretary of Defense for Space Policy. The principal duty of the Assistant Secretary shall be the overall supervision of policy of the Department of Defense for space warfighting.".

(b) ELEMENTS OF OFFICE.—

(1) DEVELOPMENT OF RECOMMENDATIONS.—The Secretary of Defense shall seek to enter into an agreement with a federally funded research and development center on the development of recommendations as to the appropriate elements of the Office of the Assistant Secretary of Defense for Space Policy, including, in particular, whether the elements of the Office should include elements on space that are currently assigned to the Office of the Under Secretary of Defense for Intelligence or the Military Intelligence Program.

(2) TRANSMITTAL.—Not later than 180 days after the date of the enactment of this Act, the Secretary shall transmit to the Committees on Armed Services of the Senate and the House of Representatives the recommendations developed pursuant to paragraph (1), together with an assessment of such recommendations by the Secretary.

Sec. 956. Assistant Secretary of the Air Force for Space Acquisition and Integration

(a) REDESIGNATION OF PRINCIPAL ASSISTANT FOR SPACE AS ASSISTANT SECRETARY FOR SPACE ACQUISITION AND INTEGRATION.—

(1) IN GENERAL.—The Principal Assistant to the Secretary of the Air Force for Space is hereby redesignated as the Assistant Secretary of the Air Force for Space Acquisition and Integration.

(2) REFERENCES.—Any reference to the Principal Assistant to the Secretary of the Air Force for Space in any law, regulation, map, document, record, or other paper of the United States shall be deemed to be a reference to the Assistant Secretary of the Air Force for Space Acquisition and Integration.

(b) CODIFICATION OF POSITION AND RESPONSIBILITIES.—

(1) IN GENERAL.—Section 9016 of title 10, United States Code, as amended by subtitle B of this title, is further amended—

(A) in subsection (a), by striking "four" and inserting "five"; and

(B) in subsection (b), by adding at the end the following new paragraph:

"(6)(A) One of the Assistant Secretaries is the Assistant Secretary of the Air Force for Space Acquisition and Integration.

"(B) Subject to the authority, direction, and control of the Secretary of the Air Force, the Assistant Secretary shall do as follows:

"(i) Be responsible for all architecture and integration of the Air Force for space systems and programs, including in support of the Chief of Space Operations under section 9082 of this title.

"(ii) Act as the chair of the Space Force Acquisition Council under section 9021 of this title.

"(iii) Advise the service acquisition executive of the Air Force with responsibility for space systems and programs (including for all major defense acquisition programs under chapter 144 of this title for space) on the acquisition of such systems and programs by the Air Force.

"(iv) Oversee and direct each of the following:

"(I) The Space Rapid Capabilities Office under section 2273a of this title.

"(II) The Space and Missile Systems Center.

"(III) The Space Development Agency.

"(v) Advise and synchronize acquisition projects for all space systems and programs of the Air Force, including projects for space systems and programs responsibility for which is transferred to the Assistant Secretary pursuant to section 956(b)(3) of the United States Space Force Act.

"(vi) Effective as of October 1, 2022, in accordance with section 957 of that Act, serve as the Service Acquisition Executive of the Department of the Air Force for Space Systems and Programs.".

(2) EXECUTIVE SCHEDULE LEVEL IV.—Section 5315 of title 5, United States Code, is amended by striking the item relating to the Assistant Secretaries of the Air Force and inserting the following new item:
"Assistant Secretaries of the Air Force (5).".

(3) TRANSFER OF ACQUISITION PROJECTS FOR SPACE SYSTEMS AND PROGRAMS.—Effective October 1, 2022, the Secretary of the Air Force shall transfer to the Assistant Secretary of the Air Force for Space Acquisition and Integration under paragraph (6) of section 9016(b) of title 10, United States Code (as added by this subsection), responsibility for architecture and integration of any acquisition projects for space systems and programs of the Air Force that are under the oversight or direction of the Assistant Secretary of the Air Force for Acquisition as of September 30, 2022.

Sec. 957. Service Acquisition Executive of the Department of the Air Force for Space Systems and Programs

(a) IN GENERAL.—Effective October 1, 2022, there shall be within the Department of the Air Force a Service Acquisition Executive of the Department of the Air Force for Space Systems and Programs.

(b) SERVICE.—

(1) IN GENERAL.—Effective as of October 1, 2022, and subject to paragraph (2), the individual serving as Assistant Secretary of the Air Force for Space Acquisition and Integration under paragraph (6) of section 9016(b) of title 10, United States Code (as added by section 1832(b) of this Act), shall also serve as the Service Acquisition Executive for Space Systems and Programs.

(2) INCUMBENT.—The individual serving as Assistant Secretary of the Air Force for Space Acquisition and Integration as of October 1, 2022, may also serve as the Service Acquisition Executive for Space Systems and Programs pursuant to paragraph (1) only if appointed as the Service Acquisition Executive for Space Systems and Programs by the President, by and with the advice and consent of the Senate, pursuant to a nomination submitted to the Senate on or after that date.

(c) AUTHORITIES AND RESPONSIBILITIES.—

(1) IN GENERAL.—The Service Acquisition Executive for Space Systems and Programs shall have within the Department of the Air Force all the authorities and responsibilities of a service acquisition executive under section 1704 of title 10, United States Code, and other applicable law, for the Department of the Air Force with respect to space systems and programs.

(2) SEPARATE SAE WITHIN THE AIR FORCE.—The Service Acquisition Executive for Space Systems and Programs shall be in addition to the service acquisition executive in the Department of the Air Force for all acquisition matters of the Department of the Air Force other than with respect to space systems and programs.

(3) GUIDANCE ON RELATIONSHIP AMONG SAES.—Not later than October 1, 2022, and from time to time thereafter, the Secretary of the Air Force shall issue guidance for the Department of the Air Force on the authorities and responsibilities of the Service Acquisition Executive for Space Systems and Programs and the authorities and responsibilities of the service acquisition executive of the Department for all acquisition matters of the Department other than with respect to space systems and programs.

Sec. 958. Conforming Amendments and Clarification of Authorities

(a) CONFORMING AMENDMENTS.—Title 10, United States Code, is amended as follows:

(1) In section 101(a)(9)(C), by inserting "and the Space Force" before the semicolon.

(2) In section 2273a—

(A) in subsection (a), by striking "Air Force Space Command" and inserting "Space Force"; and

(B) in subsection (b), by striking "Commander of the Air Force Space Command" and inserting "Chief of Space Operations".

(b) CLARIFICATION OF AUTHORITIES.—

(1) IN GENERAL.—Except as specifically provided by this subtitle or the amendments made by this subtitle—
  (A) a member of the Space Force shall be treated as a member of the Air Force for the purpose of the application of any provision of law, including provisions of law relating to pay, benefits, and retirement; and
  (B) a civilian employee of the Space Force shall be treated as a civilian employee of the Air Force for the purpose of the application of any provision of law, including provisions of law relating to pay, benefits, and retirement

(2) APPOINTMENT AND ENLISTMENT.—For purposes of the appointment or enlistment of individuals as members of the Space Force pending the integration of the Space Force into the laws providing for the appointment or enlistment of individuals as members of the Armed Forces, appointments and enlistments of individuals as members of the Armed Forces in the Space Force may be made in the same manner in which appointments and enlistments of individuals as members of the Armed Forces in the other Armed Forces may be made by law.

Sec. 959. Effects on Military Installations

Nothing in this subtitle, or the amendments made by this subtitle, shall be construed to authorize or require the relocation of any facility, infrastructure, or military installation of the Air Force.

Sec. 960. Availability of Funds

(a) IN GENERAL.—Subject to subsection (b), amounts authorized to be appropriated for fiscal year 2020 by this Act and available for the Air Force may be obligated and expended for programs, projects, and activities for space, including personnel and acquisition programs, projects, and activities, for and in connection with the establishment of the Space Force and the discharge of the other requirements of this title and the amendments made by this subtitle.

(b) LIMITATION.—The total amount obligated and expended in fiscal year 2020 from amounts authorized to be appropriated by this Act for and in connection with the establishment of the Space Force and the discharge of the requirements described in subsection (a) may not exceed the total amount requested for the

Space Force in the budget of the President for fiscal year 2020, as submitted to Congress pursuant to section 1105(a) of title 10, United States Code.

Sec. 961. Implementation

(a) REQUIREMENT.—Except as specifically provided by this subtitle, the Secretary of the Air Force shall implement this subtitle, and the amendments made by this subtitle, by not later than 18 months after the date of the enactment of this Act.

(b) BRIEFINGS.—Not later than 60 days after the date of the enactment of this Act, and every 60 days thereafter until March 31, 2023, the Secretary of the Air Force and the Chief of Space

Operations shall jointly provide to the congressional defense committees a briefing on the status of the implementation of the Space Force pursuant to this subtitle and the amendments made by this subtitle. Each briefing shall address the current missions, operations and activities, manpower requirements and status, and budget and funding requirements and status of the Space Force, and such other matters with respect to the implementation and operation of the Space Force as the Secretary and the Chief jointly consider appropriate to keep Congress fully and currently informed on the status of the implementation of the Space Force.

Bibliography

"2021 USAF & USSF Almanac: Personnel." *Air Force Magazine*. June 30, 2021. https://www.airforcemag.com/article/2021-usaf-ussf-almanac-people/.

Act of July 29, 1958 (National Aeronautics and Space Act of 1958), Pub. L. No. 85–568, §102(a), 72 Stat. 426 (1958).

Agreement on the Rescue of Astronauts, the Return of Astronauts and the Return of Objects Launched into Outer Space. April 22, 1968. 19 U.S.T. 7570, 672 U.N.T.S. 119.

Albon, Courtney. "US Space Force aims for more resilient architecture by 2026." *C4ISRNet*. February 17, 2022. https://www.c4isrnet.com/battlefield-tech/space/2022/02/17/us-space-force-aims-for-more-resilient-architecture-by-2026/.

Allison, Graham. "The Thucydides Trap: Are the U.S. and China Headed for War?" *The Atlantic*. September 24, 2015. https://www.theatlantic.com/international/archive/2015/09/united-states-china-war-thucydides-trap/406756/.

Allison, Graham. *Destined for War: Can America and China Escape Thucydides' Trap?* Boston, MA: Houghton Mifflin Harcourt, 2017.

The Antarctic Treaty. December 1, 1959. 12 U.S.T. 794, 402 U.N.T.S. 71.

Armor, Jr., James B. "The Air Force's Other Blind Spot." *The Space Review*. September 15, 2008. https://www.thespacereview.com/article/1213/1.

Ashley, Jr., Robert P. "Remarks at the Hudson Institute—Russian and Chinese Nuclear Modernization Trends." *dia.gov*. May 29, 2019. https://www.dia.mil/News/Speeches-and-Testimonies/Article-View/Article/1859890/russian-and-chinese-nuclear-modernization-trends/ (last visited May 6, 2020).

Associated Press. "China attacks US Space Force as threat to peace." *Air Force Times*. Dec. 23, 2019. https://www.airforcetimes.com/news/your-military/2019/12/23/china-attacks-us-space-force-as-threat-to-peace/.

Associated Press. "Sputnik Diplomacy." *New York Times*. October 13, 1957. Available at https://timesmachine.nytimes.com/timesmachine/1957/10/13/96960759.html?pageNumber=190 (last visited Apr. 21, 2020).

Austin, Lloyd. Secretary of Defense. "Memorandum: Tenets of Responsible Behavior in Space." *Media.Defense.Gov*. July 7, 2021. https://media.defense.gov/2021/Jul/23/2002809598/-1/-1/0/TENETS-OF-RESPONSIBLE-BEHAVIOR-IN-SPACE.PDF.

Avey, Julie. "Clear Air Force Station renamed as Clear Space Force Station." *168th Wing Air National Guard*. June 16, 2021. https://www.168wg.ang.af.mil/News/Article/2661327/clear-air-force-station-renamed-as-clear-space-force-station/.

Barboza, David. "China Passes Japan as Second-Largest Economy." *New York Times*. August 15, 2010. https://www.nytimes.com/2010/08/16/business/global/16yuan.html.

Bateman, Aaron. "America Needs a Coalition to Win a Space War." *War on the Rocks*. April 29, 2020. https://warontherocks.com/2020/04/america-needs-a-coalition-to-win-a-space-war/.

Blinken, Antony J. U.S. Secretary of State. "Press Statement: Russia Conducts Destructive Anti-Satellite Missile Test." U.S. Department of State. November 15, 2021. Available at https://www.state.gov/russia-conducts-destructive-anti-satellite-missile-test/.

Britto, Brittany. "JFK's 1962 moon speech—though deliberate, political—is still inspiring after all these years." *Houston Chronicle*. June 11, 2019. https://www.houstonchronicle.com/local/space/mission-moon/article/JFK-s-1962-moon-speech-though-deliberate-13960428.php.

Browne, Ryan. "With a signature, Trump brings Space Force into being." *CNN.com*. December 20, 2019. https://www.cnn.com/2019/12/20/politics/trump-creates-space-force/index.html.

Bruger, Steven J. "Not Ready for the First Space War: What About the Second?" 48 *Naval War College Review* 1, 73 (Winter 1995).

Buckley Garrison Public Affairs. "Buckley receives new name, commander." *Buckley Space Force Base*. June 4, 2021. https://www.buckley.spaceforce.mil/News/Article-Display/Article/2646938/buckley-receives-new-name-commander/.

Buckley Space Force Base. "Fact Sheet: 6th Space Warning Squadron." *Buckley Space Force Base*. https://www.buckley.spaceforce.mil/About-Us/Fact-Sheets/Article/2575788/6th-space-warning-squadron/.

Buckley Space Force Base. "Fact Sheet: 10th Space Warning Squadron." *Buckley Space Force Base*. https://www.buckley.spaceforce.mil/About-Us/Fact-Sheets/Article/2291696/10th-space-warning-squadron/.

Burant, Stephen R. "Soviet Perspectives on the Legal Regime in Outer Space: The Problem of Space Demilitarization." *Studies in Comparative Communism*. Vol. 19. No. 3/4. (Autumn/Winter 1986).

Burgess, John. "Satellites' Gaze Provides New Look at War." *Washington Post*. February 19, 1991. Available at https://www.washingtonpost.com/archive/politics/1991/02/19/satellites-gaze-provides-new-look-at-war/768b19e4-a1da-4f40-8267-28a5dda48726/.

Burke, Edmund J. & Astrid Stuth Cevallos, *In Line or Out of Order? China's Approach to ADIZ in Theory and Practice* (RAND, 2017).

Burns, Robert. Associate Press. "Mattis: US needs Space Force to counter Russia, China." *Military Times*. August 14, 2018. https://www.militarytimes.com/news/your-military/2018/08/14/mattis-us-needs-space-force-to-counter-russia-china/.

Bush, George H.W. NSD 30/NSPD 1. *National Space Policy*. November 2, 1989. *George H.W. Bush Presidential Library & Museum*. https://bush41library.tamu.edu/files/nsd/nsd30.pdf (last visited Apr. 8, 2020).

Butterfield, Herbert. *History and Human Relations*. New York: Macmillan, 1951.

Cancian, Mark F. "U.S. Military Forces in FY 2021: Space, SOF, Civilians, and Contractors." *Center for Strategic and International Studies*. January 8, 2021. https://www.csis.org/analysis/us-military-forces-fy-2021-space-sof-civilians-and-contractors.

Carter, Jimmy. Presidential Review Memorandum/National Security Council 23, *A Coherent U.S. Space Policy*. March 28, 1977. Available at https://www.jimmycarterlibrary.gov/assets/documents/memorandums/prm23.pdf (last visited Apr. 1, 2020).

Carter, Jimmy. PD/NSC-37, *National Space Policy*. May 11, 1978. Available at https://www.jimmycarterlibrary.gov/assets/documents/directives/pd37.pdf (last visited Apr. 2, 2020).

Case, Angela. "Colorado Springs Air Force bases to be renamed for Space Force." *Fox 21 News*. July 22, 2021. https://www.fox21news.com/news/local/colorado-springs-air-force-bases-to-be-renamed-for-space-force/.

Cebrowski, Arthur K. *Statement of the Director of Force Transformation Office of the Secretary of Defense Before the Subcommittee on Strategic Forces*. United States Senate Armed Services Committee. March 25, 2004. https://fas.org/irp/congress/2004_hr/032504cebrowski.pdf (last visited May 7, 2020).

Centre Européen Robert Schuman. *World War II Casualties*. http://www.centre-robert-schuman.org/userfiles/files/REPERES%20–%20module%201-2-0%20-%20explanatory%20notes%20–%20World%20War%20II%20casualties%20–%20EN.pdf (last visited Apr. 20, 2020).

Cheng, Bin. "The Legal Status of Outer Space Issues: Delimitation of Outer Space and the Definition of Peaceful Use." 11 *Journal of Space Law* 1 & 2, 89 (1983).

Cheng, Bin. "Properly Speaking, Only Celestial Bodies Have Been Reserved for Use Exclusively for Peaceful (Non-Military) Purposes, but not Outer Space Void." *International Across the Spectrum of Conflict: Essays in Honor of L.C. Green on the Occasion of His Eightieth Birthday*. Michael N. Schmidtt, ed. 2000.

Cheng, Bin. *Studies in International Space Law*. Oxford: Oxford University Press, 2004.

Chun, Clayton K. S. "Shooting Down a 'Star': Program 437, the US Nuclear ASAT System and Present-Day Copycat Killers." The Cadre Papers, Cadre Paper #6. Maxwell AFB, AL: Air University Press, 2000.

Cohen, Rachel S. "Cape Canaveral, Patrick Named First Space Force Installations." *Air Force Magazine*. December 9, 2020. https://www.airforcemag.com/cape-canaveral-patrick-named-first-space-force-installations/.

Cohen, Rachel S. "Raymond Sworn In as First Space Force Chief." *Air Force Magazine*. January 14, 2020. https://www.airforcemag.com/raymond-sworn-in-as-first-space-force-chief/.

Cohen, Rachel S. "SPACECOM Calls Out Apparent Russian Space Weapon Test." *Air Force Magazine*. July 23, 2020. https://www.airforcemag.com/spacecom-calls-out-apparent-russian-space-weapon-test/.

Colbert, Stephen. "Mike Pence Tries to Make Space Force Sound Less Dumb." *The Late Show with Stephen Colbert*. YouTube.com. August 9, 2018. https://www.youtube.com/watch?v=7ipwho-kxkI.

Commission to Assess United States National Security Space Management and Organization. *Report of the Commission to Assess United States National Security Space Management and Organization*. Washington, D.C.: January 11, 2001.

Convention on International Liability for Damage Caused by Space Objects. March 29, 1972, 24 U.S.T. 2389, 961 U.N.T.S. 187.

Convention on Registration of Objects Launched into Outer Space. January 14, 1975. 28 U.S.T. 695, 1023 U.N.T.S. 15.

Correll, Diana Stancy. "Navy forges maritime space officer designator." *Navy Times*. September 2, 2021. https://www.navytimes.com/news/your-navy/2021/09/02/navy-forges-maritime-space-officer-designator/.

Costello, John and Joe McReynolds. "China's Strategic Support Force: A Force for a New Era." *China Perspectives*. Institute for National Strategic Studies (Washington, D.C.: National Defense University Press, December 2018). Available at https://ndupress.ndu.edu/Portals/68/Documents/stratperspective/china/china-perspectives_13.pdf.

C-SPAN. "White House Daily Briefing." March 30, 2021. https://www.c-span.org/video/?510369-1/white-house-press-secretary-covid-19-report-lacks-crucial-data.

Davenport, Christian. "The Biden administration has set out to dismantle Trump's legacy, except in one area: Space." *Washington Post*. March 2, 2021. https://www.washingtonpost.com/technology/2021/03/02/biden-space-artemis-moon-trump/.

Dolman, Everett C. *Astropolitik*. London: Frank Cass, 2002.

Dolven, Ben, et al. Congressional Research Service. *Chinese Land Reclamation in the South China Sea: Implications and Policy Options*. June 18, 2015.

Donnelly, Jack. *Realism and International Relations*. 2000.

Dorr, Robert F. "X-20 Dyna-Soar Spaceplane Was Decades Ahead of Its Time." Defense Media Network. September 19, 2018. https://www.defensemedianetwork.com/stories/what-might-have-been-x-20-dyna-soar/.

Doyle, Stephen E. *Nandasiri Jasentuliyana Keynote Address on Space Law: A Concise History of Space Law*. International Institute of Space Law (2010). Available at https://www.iislweb.org/website/docs/2010keynote.pdf.

Drea, Edward J., et al. *History of the Unified Command Plan 1946–2012*. Washington, D.C.: Office of the Chairman of the Joint Chiefs of Staff, Joint History Office, 2013.

Eco, Umberto. *Foucault's Pendulum*. William Weaver, trans. Boston, MA: Mariner Books, 2007.

Eisenhower, Dwight D. *The White House Years: Waging Peace 1956–1961*. Garden City, NY: Doubleday, 1965.

Erwin, Sandra. "Trump formally reestablishes U.S. Space Command at White House ceremony." *SpaceNews.com*. August 29, 2019. https://spacenews.com/usspacecom-officially-re-established-with-a-focus-on-defending-satellites-and-deterring-conflict/.

Erwin, Sandra. "Top enlisted leader Towberman officially joins the U.S. Space Force." *SpaceNews.com*. April 2, 2020. https://spacenews.com/top-enlisted-leader-towberman-to-officially-join-the-u-s-space-force/.

Erwin, Sandra. "Space Force to stand up three major commands, lower echelons to be called 'deltas.'" *SpaceNews.com*. June 30, 2020. https://spacenews.com/space-force-to-stand-up-three-major-commands-lower-echelons-to-be-called-deltas/.

Erwin, Sandra. "White House: Space Force 'absolutely has the full support of the Biden administration.'" *SpaceNews.com*. February 3, 2021. https://spacenews.com/white-house-space-force-absolutely-has-the-full-support-of-the-biden-administration/.

Erwin, Sandra. "Biden administration to continue the National Space Council." *SpaceNews.com*. March 29, 2021. https://spacenews.com/biden-administration-to-continue-the-national-space-council/.

Erwin, Sandra. "Space Force reveals which Army and Navy units are moving to the space branch." *Space News*. September 21, 2021. https://spacenews.com/space-force-reveals-which-army-and-navy-units-are-moving-to-the-space-branch/.

Erwin, Sandra. "Changes ahead for Space Force procurement organizations." *SpaceNews.com*. December 3, 2021. https://spacenews.com/change-is-coming-for-space-force-procurement-organizations/.

European Space Agency. "Space debris by the numbers." *esa.int*. https://www.esa.int/Safety_Security/Space_Debris/Space_debris_by_the_numbers (updated February 2020).

"Foreign Ministry Spokesperson Hua Chunying's Regular Press Conference on February 12, 2019." Consulate General of the People's Republic of China in Mumbai. Feb. 12, 2019. https://www.fmprc.gov.cn/ce/cgmb/eng/fyrth/t1637290.htm.

Frankel, Michael J., James Scouras, & George W. Ullrich. *The Uncertain Consequences of Nuclear Weapons Use*. National Security Report. Johns Hopkins University Applied Physics Laboratory (2015).

Fukuyama, Francis. "The End of History?" *The National Interest*, 16: 4 (Summer 1989).

Fukuyama, Francis. "The Neoconservative Moment." *The National Interest*. June 1, 2004. https://nationalinterest.org/article/the-neoconservative-moment-811.

Fukuyama, Francis. *America at the Crossroads: Democracy, Power and the Neoconservative Legacy*. New Haven, CT: Yale University Press, 2006.

Gaiman, Neil. *The Sandman Omnibus: Volume II*. Burbank, CA: DC Comics/Vertigo, 2013.

Garamone, Jim. "Leaders Chart the Course as U.S. Space Force Launches." *defense.gov*. May 6, 2020. https://www.defense.gov/Explore/News/Article/Article/2177974/leaders-chart-the-course-as-us-space-force-launches/.

Garcia, Mark, ed. "Space Debris and Human Spacecraft." National Aeronautics and Space Administration. *nasa.gov*. September 26, 2013. https://www.nasa.gov/mission_pages/station/news/orbital_debris.html.

Garretson, Peter. "Air Force Suppressed Space Force Debate; Lt. Gen. Kwast Spoke Truth To Power." *Breaking Defense*. August 8, 2019. https://breakingdefense.com/2019/08/air-force-suppressed-space-force-debate-lt-gen-kwast-spoke-truth-to-power/.

Gavin, James M. *War and Peace in the Space Age*. New York: Harper, 1958.

Gayl, Franz J. "Time for a Military Space Service." *Proceedings*, 130:7 (July 2004).

Gleeson, Patrick K. *Legal Aspects of the Use of Force in Outer Space*. A Thesis Submitted to McGill University in partial fulfillment of the requirements for the degree of Master of Laws (LL.M.). McGill University, 2005.

Goldsmith, Jack L. & Eric A. Posner. *The Limits of International Law*. Oxford: Oxford University Press, 2005.

Gonzalez, Sandra. "Sorry, Trump. Netflix is creating its own 'Space Force.'" *CNN.com*. January 17, 2019. https://www.cnn.com/2019/01/16/entertainment/space-force-netflix/index.html.

Gore, Albert. *Letter dated 8 December 1962 from the representative of the United States of America to the Chairman of the First Committee*. U.N. Doc. A/C.1/881 (Dec. 8, 1962).

Graham, Daniel. *High Frontier: A Strategy for National Survival*. New York: TOR, 1983.

Grego, Laura. "The New U.S. Space Force Will Make Space More Dangerous, Not Less." *World Political Review*. January 8, 2020. https://www.worldpoliticsreview.com/articles/28452/why-the-trump-space-force-will-make-space-more-dangerous.

Grier, Peter. "The Flying Tomato Can." *Air Force Magazine*. February 1, 2009. https://www.airforcemag.com/article/0209tomato/.

Grunert, Jeremy. "Grounding the Humā: Space Denial and (Potential) American Interference in the Iranian Space Program." 81 *Air Force Law Review* 75 (2020).

Gvosdev, Nikolas K. & Damjan de Krnjevic-Miskovic. "The Neoconservatism of Francis Fukuyama." *The National Interest*. August 4, 2004. https://nationalinterest.org/article/the-neoconservatism-of-francis-fukuyama-2725.

Hagen, John P. "The Viking and the Vanguard." *Technology and Culture*. Vol. 4. No. 4 (Autumn 1963).

Hall, R. Cargill. "The Evolution of U.S. National Security Space Policy and Its Legal Foundations in the 20th Century." 22 *Journal of Space Law* 1, 1 (2007).

Handberg, Roger. *Seeking New World Vistas: The Militarization of Space*. Westport, CT: Praeger, 2000.

Harrison, Todd, Kaitlyn Johnson, and Thomas G. Roberts. *Space Threat Assessment 2018*. Center for Strategic and International Studies. April 2018.

Harvard Kennedy School Belfer Center for Science and International Affairs. "Can America and China Escape Thucydides's Trap?" *Special Initiative: Thucydides's Trap*.

belfercenter.org. https://www.belfercenter.org/thucydides-trap/overview-thucydides-trap (last visited June 9, 2020).

Hays, Peter L. *Space and Security: A Reference Handbook*. Santa Barbara, CA: ABC-CLIO, 2011.

Herz, John H. "Idealist Internationalism and the Security Dilemma." 2 *World Politics* 2, 157 (January 1950).

Hitchens, Theresa. "Russia Builds New Co-Orbital Satellite: SWF, CSIS Say." *Breaking Defense*. April 4, 2019. https://breakingdefense.com/2019/04/russia-builds-new-co-orbital-satellite-swf-csis-say/.

Hitchens, Theresa. "Exclusive: UK Pushes New UN Accord On Military Space Norms." *Breaking Defense*. September 13, 2021. https://breakingdefense.com/2021/09/exclusive-uk-pushes-new-un-accord-on-military-space-norms/.

Hobe, Stephan; Bernhard Schmidt-Tedd; & Kai-Uwe Schrogl, eds. *Cologne Commentary on Space Law: Volume I Outer Space Treaty*. Cologne: Carl Heymanns Verlag, 2009.

Interim Agreement Between the United States and the Union of Soviet Socialist Republics on Certain Measures with Respect to the Limitation of Strategic Offensive Arms, May 26, 1972, U.S.-U.S.S.R., 23 U.S.T. 3462, T.I.A.S. No. 7504.

International Institute for Strategic Studies. "China's 2021 orbital-weapon tests." *Strategic Comments*. February 2022. Available at https://www.iiss.org/~/publication/48752548-58b3-4e97-9ac7-4df48de5373d/chinas-2021-orbital-weapon-tests.pdf.

John S. McCain National Defense Authorization Act for Fiscal Year 2019. Public Law No. 115–232. 132 Stat. 2101–04. 2018. https://www.congress.gov/115/plaws/publ232/PLAW-115publ232.pdf.

Johnson, Lyndon B. *The Vantage Point: Perspectives on the Presidency, 1963–1969*. New York: Holt, Rinehart and Winston, 1971.

Johnson-Freese, Joan. *Space as a Strategic Asset*. New York: Columbia University Press, 2007.

Johnson-Freese, Joan. *Space Warfare in the 21st Century: Arming the Heavens*. Abingdon, UK: Routledge, 2017.

Johnson-Freese, Joan. "Prompt Essay: One Good Reason for Creating a Space Force." *Policy Roundtable: Does America Need a Space Force?* Texas National Security Review. September 18, 2018. Available at https://tnsr.org/roundtable/policy-roundtable-does-america-need-a-space-force/.

Kalic, Sean N. *US Presidents and the Militarization of Space, 1946–1967*. College Station, TX: Texas A&M University Press, 2012.

Karas, Thomas. *The New High Ground: Strategies and Weapons of Space-Age War*. New York: Simon & Schuster, 1983.

Kearn, David W. "The Baruch Plan and the Quest for Atomic Disarmament." *Diplomacy & Statecraft*, 21:41–67 (2010).

Kennedy, John F. "Address to Joint Session of Congress." May 25, 1961. *John F. Kennedy Library & Museum.* https://www.jfklibrary.org/learn/about-jfk/historic-speeches/address-to-joint-session-of-congress-may-25-1961 (last visited Apr. 11, 2020).

Kennedy, John F. "Address at Rice University, Houston, Texas." 12 September 1962. *John F. Kennedy Presidential Library and Museum.* Available at https://www.jfklibrary.org/asset-viewer/archives/JFKPOF/040/JFKPOF-040-001.

Khrushchev, Nikita Sergeevich. *Khrushchev Remembers: The Last Testament.* Strobe Talbott, trans. & ed. Boston, MA: Little Brown & Company, 1974.

Kissinger, Henry. *Diplomacy.* New York: Simon & Schuster, 1994.

Kulacki, Gregory & Jeffrey G. Lewis. "Understanding China's Antisatellite Test." *Nonproliferation Review* 15, No. 2, 335 (July 2008).

Kwast, Steve. "OPINION: 'There won't be many prizes for second place.'" *Politico.* August 10, 2018. https://www.politico.com/story/2018/08/10/space-race-kwast-768751.

Kwast, Steve. "The Real Stakes in the New Space Race." *Wars on the Rocks.* August 19, 2019. https://warontherocks.com/2019/08/the-real-stakes-in-the-new-space-race/.

Kwast, Steve. "The Urgent Need for a U.S. Space Force." Speech at Hillsdale College. Washington, D.C. November 20, 2019. Available at https://www.youtube.com/watch?v=KsPLmb6gAdw&feature=emb_title.

Kwast, Steve. "Where the Space Force must go." *Politico.* January 17, 2020. https://www.politico.com/news/2020/01/17/where-the-space-force-must-go-098884.

Lachs, Manfred. *The Law of Outer Space: An Experience in Contemporary Lawmaking.* Leiden: Brill Nijhoff, 2010 (originally published 1972).

Lambakis, Steven. "Space Control in Desert Storm and Beyond." 39 *Orbis* 3, 419 (Summer 1995).

Lauder, John, Frank G. Klotz, and William Courtney. "How to avoid a space arms race." *The Hill.* October 24, 2020. https://thehill.com/opinion/national-security/522512-space-arms-control-small-steps-can-begin-to-overcome-the-obstacles.

Lodge, Henry Cabot. *Letter dated 2 Sept. 1958 from the Permanent Representative of the United States of America to the United Nations, addressed to the Secretary-General.* United Nations General Assembly. 13th Session. U.N. Doc A/3902. September 2, 1958.

Lopez, C. Todd. "Shanahan: Space Force to Preserve Margin of Dominance, $19 Trillion Economy." *Defense.gov.* March 20, 2019. https://www.defense.gov/Explore/News/Article/Article/1790830/shanahan-space-force-to-preserve-margin-of-dominance-19-trillion-economy/.

Mahshie, Abraham. "The Asset Transfer Fight." *Air Force Magazine.* Aug. 27, 2021. https://www.airforcemag.com/article/the-asset-transfer-fight/.

Mahshie, Abraham. "Why the Army Clings to Its Space Troops: 'Translating Geek to Grunt.'" *Air Force Magazine.* Oct. 13, 2021. https://www.airforcemag.com/army-clings-to-space-troops-translating-geek-to-grunt/.

Malangone, Abigail. "We Choose to Go to the Moon: The 55th Anniversary of the Rice University Speech." *John F. Kennedy Presidential Library Archives Blog*. September 12, 2017. https://jfk.blogs.archives.gov/2017/09/12/we-choose-to-go-to-the-moon-the-55th-anniversary-of-the-rice-university-speech/.

Maogoto, Jackson Nyamuya, and Steven Freeland. "Space Weaponization and the United Nations Charter Regime on Force: A Thick Legal Fog or a Receding Mist?" *The International Lawyer*. 41, 4. Winter 2007.

Mastalir, Anthony J. *The US Response to China's ASAT Test: An International Security Space Alliance for the Future*. Air University, Drew Paper No. 8. August 2009.

Mattis, James N. & Stephen Hadley. "Secretary Mattis Remarks on the National Defense Strategy in Conversation with the United States Institute for Peace." *defense.gov*. October 30, 2018. https://www.defense.gov/Newsroom/Transcripts/Transcript/Article/1678512/secretary-mattis-remarks-on-the-national-defense-strategy-in-conversation-with/.

McDonald, Robert A. and Sharon K. Moreno. "Raising the Periscope… Grab and Poppy: America's Early ELINT Satellites." Center for the Study of National Reconnaissance. National Reconnaissance Office. September 2005.

McGlinchey, Stephen. "Neoconservatism and American Foreign Policy." *Politikon*, 16:1, 22 (2010).

McGlinchey, Stephen, Rosie Walters & Christian Scheinpflug, eds. *International Relations Theory*. Bristol, England: E-International Relations Publishing, 2017.

Ministry of Defence of the Russian Federation. "Aerospace Forces." https://eng.mil.ru/en/structure/forces/type/vks.htm.

Moltz, James Clay. *The Politics of Space Security: Strategic Restraint and the Pursuit of National Interests*. 3rd Edition. Stanford, CA: Stanford University Press, 2019.

Moore, Mike. *Twilight War: The Folly of U.S. Space Dominance*. Oakland, CA: Independent Institute, 2008.

Moravcsik, Andrew. "Liberal International Relations Theory: A Social Scientific Assessment." Paper No. 01-02. Weatherhead Center for International Affairs, Harvard University, April 2001.

Murray, Douglas. *Neoconservatism: Why We Need It*. New York: Encounter Books, 2006.

Mushkat, Roda. "China's Compliance with International Law: What Has Been Learned and the Gaps Remaining." 20 *Pacific Rim Law & Policy Journal* 1, 68 (Jan. 2011).

Myers, Meghann. "Space Force is looking for a few good soldiers, sailors." *Military Times*. February 3, 2021. https://www.militarytimes.com/news/your-military/2021/02/03/space-force-is-looking-for-a-few-good-soldiers-sailors/.

National Aeronautics & Space Administration. "President Nixon's 1972 Announcement on the Space Shuttle." *history.nasa.gov*. https://history.nasa.gov/stsnixon.htm (last visited Apr. 1, 2020).

National Defense Authorization Act for Fiscal Year 2020. S. 1790. 116th Congress. 2019. https://www.govinfo.gov/content/pkg/BILLS-116s1790enr/pdf/BILLS-116s1790enr.pdf.

National Intelligence Estimate. "Soviet Military Intentions and Capabilities in Space." NIE 11-1-80. August 6, 1980, available at https://www.cia.gov/readingroom/docs/DOC_0000284010.pdf.

National Security Council. NSC 5814/1, *Preliminary U.S. Policy on Outer Space*. August 18, 1958.

National Security Council. NSC 5918, *U.S. Policy on Outer Space*. December 17, 1959.

National Security Council. National Security Decision Memorandum 72, *Exchange of Technical Data Between the United States and the International Space Community*. July 17, 1970. Available at https://aerospace.csis.org/wp-content/uploads/2019/02/NSDM-72-Exchange-of-Technical-Data-between-the-United-States-and-the-International-Space-Community-17-Jul-1970-.pdf.

National Security Council. National Security Decision Memorandum 187, *International Space Cooperation—Technology and Launch Assistance*. August 30, 1972. Available at https://aerospace.csis.org/wp-content/uploads/2019/02/NSDM-187-International-Space-Cooperation-30-Aug-1972-.pdf.

National Security Council. National Security Decision Memorandum 333, *Enhanced Survivability of Critical U.S. Military and Intelligence Space Systems*. July 3, 1976. Available at https://aerospace.csis.org/wp-content/uploads/2019/02/NSDM-333-Enhanced-Survivability-of-Critical-Space-Systems.pdf (last visited May 27, 2020).

National Security Council. National Security Decision Memorandum 345, *U.S. Anti-Satellite Capabilities*. January 18, 1977. Available at https://aerospace.csis.org/wp-content/uploads/2019/02/NSDM-345-US-Anti-Satellite-Capabilities.pdf (last visited May 27, 2020).

National Security Council Planning Board. NSC 5520, *Draft Statement of Policy on U.S. Scientific Satellite Program General Considerations*. Dwight D. Eisenhower Presidential Library and Museum. May 20, 1955. Available at https://aerospace.csis.org/wp-content/uploads/2019/02/NSC-5520-Statement-of-Policy-on-U.S.-Scientific-Satellite-Program-20-May-1955.pdf (last visited May 25, 2020).

Neilan, Terence. "Bush Pulls Out of ABM Treaty; Putin Calls Move a Mistake." *New York Times*. December 13, 2001. https://www.nytimes.com/2001/12/13/international/bush-pulls-out-of-abm-treaty-putin-calls-move-a-mistake.html.

News Wires. "Macron announces creation of French space force." *France 24*. July 13, 2019. https://www.france24.com/en/20190713-macron-france-space-force.

Norsky, Peter C. *The United States Space Force: Not If, But When*. (A Thesis Presented to the Faculty of the School of Advanced Air & Space Studies). Air University. June 2016. Available at https://apps.dtic.mil/dtic/tr/fulltext/u2/1030447.pdf (last visited May 27, 2020).

Office of the Undersecretary of Defense (Comptroller)/Chief Financial Officer. *Defense Budget Overview—United States Department of Defense Fiscal Year 2022 Budget*

Request. May 2021. https://comptroller.defense.gov/Portals/45/Documents/defbudget/FY2022/FY2022_Budget_Request_Overview_Book.pdf.

Office of the White House Press Secretary. "Fact Sheet Outlining United States Space Policy." *Ronald Reagan Presidential Library.* July 4, 1982. Available at https://aerospace.csis.org/wp-content/uploads/2019/02/NSDD-42-Reagan-National-Space-Policy.pdf (last visited Apr. 6, 2020).

Office of the White House Press Secretary. *PDD/NSC-49 Fact Sheet National Space Policy.* September 19, 1996. Available at https://aerospace.csis.org/wp-content/uploads/2019/02/NSC-49-Clinton-US-National-Space-Policy.pdf (last visited Apr. 9, 2020).

Ohlin, Jens David. *The Assault on International Law.* Oxford: Oxford University Press, 2015.

Olsen, Henry. "Opinion: The U.S. Space Force is preparing to militarize space. Good." *Washington Post.* March 17, 2022. https://www.washingtonpost.com/opinions/2022/03/17/space-force-militarizing-good-thing/.

Parkerson, Jr., John E. "International Legal Implications of the Strategic Defense Initiative." 116 *Military Law Review* 67 (Spring 1987).

Pawlyk, Oriana. "Air Force General's Supporters Mount Campaign to Make Him Leader of Space Force." *military.com.* August 8, 2019. https://www.military.com/daily-news/2019/08/08/air-force-generals-supporters-mount-campaign-make-him-leader-space-force.html.

Petras, Christopher M. "'Space Force Alpha': Military Use of the International Space Station and the Concept of 'Peaceful Purposes.'" 53 *Air Force Law Review* 135, 135 (2002).

Pfrang, Kaila, and Brian Weeden. "U.S. Direct Ascent Anti-Satellite Testing." Secure World Foundation. April 2021. Available at https://swfound.org/media/207180/swf_us_da-asat_fact_sheet_apr2021.pdf.

Phan, Thanh. "Article: Realism and International Cooperation in Competition Law." *Houston Journal of International Law*, 40:297, 307 (Fall 2017).

Podvig, Pavel. "Did Star Wars Help End the Cold War? Soviet Response to the SDI Program." *Science & Global Security,* 25:1, 5 (2017).

Podvig, Pavel, & Hui Zhang. *Russian and Chinese Responses to U.S. Military Plans in Space.* Washington, D.C.: American Academy of Arts & Sciences, 2008.

Pope, Charles. "Barrett, Raymond discuss Space Force's status and future; debut new recruiting ad." *spaceforce.mil.* May 6, 2020. https://www.spaceforce.mil/News/Article/2178584/barrett-raymond-discuss-space-forces-status-and-future-debut-new-recruiting-ad.

Pope, Charles. "Raymond sworn in as first Chief of Space Operations at White House event." *spaceforce.mil.* January 14, 2020. https://www.spaceforce.mil/News/Article/2057219/raymond-sworn-in-as-first-chief-of-space-operations-at-white-house-event.

Project for a New American Century. *Open Letter to President William J. Clinton*. January 26, 1998. Available at https://www.noi.org/wp-content/uploads/2016/01/iraqclintonletter1998-01-26-Copy.pdf (last visited May 12, 2020).

Project for a New American Century. *Open Letter to President George W. Bush*. September 20, 2001. Available at https://web.archive.org/web/20131018052135/http://www.newamerican century.org/Bushletter.htm (last visited May 12, 2020).

RAND Corporation. "Military Doctrine." 2021. https://www.rand.org/topics/military-doctrine.html.

RAND Corporation. *Preliminary Design of a World-Circling Spaceship*. 1946. Available at https://www.rand.org/pubs/special_memoranda/SM11827.html (last visited May 25, 2020).

Reagan, Ronald. "Remarks in New York, New York, Before the United Nations General Assembly Special Session Devoted to Disarmament." *reaganlibrary.gov*. June 17, 1982. https://www.reaganlibrary.gov/research/speeches/61782a.

Reagan, Ronald. National Security Decision Directive 42, *National Space Policy*. July 4, 1982. Available at https://www.reaganlibrary.gov/sites/default/files/archives/reference/scanned-nsdds/nsdd42.pdf (last visited Apr. 6, 2020).

Reagan, Ronald. "Remarks at the Annual Convention of the National Association of Evangelicals in Orlando, Florida." March 8, 1983. Available at https://www.reaganfoundation.org/media/50919/remarks_annual_convention_national_association_evangelicals_030883.pdf (last visited Apr. 26, 2020).

Reagan, Ronald. "Address to the Nation on Defense and National Security." March 23, 1983. *Ronald Reagan Presidential Library and Museum*. https://www.reaganlibrary.gov/research/speeches/32383d (last visited Apr. 8, 2020).

Reagan, Ronald. NSDD-85. *Eliminating the Threat from Ballistic Missiles*. March 25, 1983. Available at https://aerospace.csis.org/wp-content/uploads/2019/02/NSDD-85-Eliminating-the-Threat-From-Ballisitc-Missiles.pdf (last accessed Apr. 29, 2020).

Reagan, Ronald. "Address to the 40th Session of the United Nations General Assembly in New York, New York." *reaganfoundation.org*. October 24, 1985. https://www.reaganfoundation.org/media/128611/assembly.pdf.

Roeder, Tom. "Space Force abolished? House bill would do just that." *The Gazette*. October 18, 2021. https://gazette.com/military/space-force-abolished-house-bill-would-do-just-that/article_7589e9f6-1bd5-11ec-9112-0f98af62e60b.html.

Ross-Nazzal, Jennifer. "Détente on Earth and in Space: The Apollo-Soyuz Test Project." *OAH Magazine of History* (July 2010).

Sambaluk, Nicholas Michael. *The Other Space Race: Eisenhower and the Quest for Aerospace Security*. Annapolis, MD: Naval Institute Press, 2015.

Schriever, Bernard A. "ICBM: A Step Toward Space Conquest." Speech to the Astronautics Symposium. February 19, 1957. Available at Schriever, Bernard A. "ICBM: A Step

Toward Space Conquest." *Air Force Magazine*. https://www.airforcemag.com/PDF/MagazineArchive/Documents/2007/February%202007/0207keeperfull.pdf (last visited June 10, 2020).

Schriever Space Force Base. "Fact Sheet: Peterson-Schriever Garrison." *Schriever Space Force Base*. July 24, 2020. https://www.schriever.spaceforce.mil/About-Us/Fact-Sheets/Display/Article/2287613/peterson-schriever-garrison/.

Secretary of the Air Force Public Affairs. "U.S. Space Force unveils name of space professionals." *United States Space Force: Space Force News*. December 18, 2020. https://www.spaceforce.mil/News/Article/2452593/us-space-force-unveils-name-of-space-professionals/.

Secretary of the Air Force Public Affairs. "Space Force Acquisition Council looks to safeguard space industrial base from COVID-19 impacts." *United States Space Force: Space Force News*. April 29, 2020. https://www.spaceforce.mil/News/Article/2168917/space-force-acquisition-council-looks-to-safeguard-space-industrial-base-from-c/.

Siddiqi, Asif A. "Soviet Space Power During the Cold War." *Harnessing the Heavens: National Defense through Space*. Paul G. Gillespie and Grant T. Weller, eds. Chicago: Imprint Publications, 2008.

Singer, Jeremy. "Armor Urges Creation of Space Corps Within the US Air Force." *Space News*. November 16, 2007. https://spacenews.com/armor-urges-creation-space-corps-within-us-air-force/.

Slaughter, Anne-Marie. "Liberal International Relations Theory and International Economic Law." 10 *American University Journal of International Law and Policy* 2, 724 (1995).

Smith, Marcia S. Congressional Research Service. *China's Space Program: An Overview*. 2003.

Space Launch Delta 45. "Space Launch Delta 45 History." *patrick.spaceforce.mil*. https://www.patrick.spaceforce.mil/history/.

Space Operations Command. "About Space Operations Command." *spoc.spaceforce.mil*. https://www.spoc.spaceforce.mil/About-Us/About-Space-Operations-Command.

Space Operations Command. "Fact Sheets—Space Delta 9." *spoc.spaceforce.mil*. September 2020. https://www.spoc.spaceforce.mil/About-Us/Fact-Sheets/Display/Article/2550598/space-delta-9.

Space Operations Command. "Fact Sheets—Space Delta 2." *spoc.spaceforce.mil*. July 24, 2020. https://www.spoc.spaceforce.mil/About-Us/Fact-Sheets/Display/Article/2334029/space-delta-2.

Space Operations Command. "Fact Sheets—Space Delta 4." *spoc.spaceforce.mil*. July 2020. https://www.spoc.spaceforce.mil/About-Us/Fact-Sheets/Display/Article/2334034/space-delta-4.

Space Operations Command. "Fact Sheets—Space Delta 6." *spoc.spaceforce.mil.* July 2020. https://www.spoc.spaceforce.mil/About-Us/Fact-Sheets/Display/Article/2334044/space-delta-6.

Space Operations Command. "Fact Sheets—Space Delta 7." *spoc.spaceforce.mil.* July 2020. https://www.spoc.spaceforce.mil/About-Us/Fact-Sheets/Display/Article/2334032/space-delta-7.

Space Operations Command. "Fact Sheets—Space Delta 8." *spoc.spaceforce.mil.* July 2020. https://www.spoc.spaceforce.mil/About-Us/Fact-Sheets/Display/Article/2334040/space-delta-8.

Space Operations Command. "Fact Sheets—Space Operations Command." *spoc.spaceforce.mil.* March 25, 2021. https://www.spoc.spaceforce.mil/About-Us/Fact-Sheets/Display/Article/2550627/space-operations-command.

Space Systems Command. "About Space Systems Command." *ssc.spaceforce.mil.* https://www.ssc.spaceforce.mil/About-Us/About-Space-Systems-Command.

Space Training and Readiness Command. "What We Do." *starcom.spaceforce.mil.* https://www.starcom.spaceforce.mil/About-Us/What-We-Do/.

Space Training and Readiness Command. "Space Delta 1—Training." *starcom.spaceforce.mil.* August 2021. https://www.starcom.spaceforce.mil/About-Us/How-We-Do-It/Space-Delta-1-Training/.

Space Training and Readiness Command. "Space Delta 10—Doctrine and Wargaming." *starcom.spaceforce.mil.* August 2021. https://www.starcom.spaceforce.mil/About-Us/How-We-Do-It/Space-Delta-10-Doctrine-Wargaming/.

Space Training and Readiness Command. "Space Delta 11—Range and Aggressors." *starcom.spaceforce.mil.* August 2021. https://www.starcom.spaceforce.mil/About-Us/How-We-Do-It/Space-Delta-11-Range-Aggressors/.

Space Training and Readiness Command. "Space Delta 12—Test and Evaluation." *starcom.spaceforce.mil.* August 2021. https://www.starcom.spaceforce.mil/About-Us/How-We-Do-It/Space-Delta-12-Test-and-Evaluation/.

Space Training and Readiness Command. "Space Delta 13—Education." *starcom.spaceforce.mil.* August 2021. https://www.starcom.spaceforce.mil/About-Us/How-We-Do-It/Space-Delta-13-Education/.

Spectar, J.M. *Elephants, Donkeys, or Other Creatures? Presidential Election Cycles & International Law of the Global Commons.* 15 AM. U. INT'L L. REV. 5, 975 (2000).

Spinetta, Lawrence J. *White vs. LeMay: The Battle Over Ballistic Missiles.* AIR FORCE MAGAZINE 96 No. 1, 56. (January 2013).

Stares, Paul B. *The Militarization of Space: U.S. Policy, 1945–1984.* Ithaca, NY: Cornell University Press, 1985.

Stassinopoulos, E.G. "The STARFISH Exo-atmospheric, High-altitude Nuclear Weapons Test." Hardened Electronics and Radiation Technology (HEART) 2015 Conference. Chantilly, VA. April 22, 2015. Available at https://nepp.nasa.gov/files/26652/2015-561-Stassinopoulos-Final-Paper-Web-HEART2015-STARFISH-supplemental-TN26292.pdf.

Statute of the International Atomic Energy Agency, July 29, 1957, 8 U.S.T. 1093, 276 U.N.T.S. 3 (amended Oct. 4, 1961, 14 U.S.T. 135, 471 U.N.T.S. 333).

Stokes, Mark A. & Dean Cheng. *China's Evolving Space Capabilities: Implications for U.S. Interests*. Report Prepared for the U.S.-China Economic & Security Review Commission. April 26, 2012. Available at https://www.hsdl.org/?view&did=708400 (last accessed May 5, 2020).

Strassler, Robert B. ed., *The Landmark Thucydides*. New York: Free Press/Simon & Schuster, 1996.

Strout, Nathan. "Space Systems Command is more than a name change, says new commander." *C4ISRNet.com*. August 25, 2021 https://www.c4isrnet.com/smr/space-competition/2021/08/25/space-systems-command-is-more-than-a-name-change-says-new-commander/.

Sukhankin, Sergey. "COVID-19 as a Tool of Information Confrontation: Russia's Approach." *University of Calgary SPP Communiqué*, 13:3, 1. April 2020, available at https://www.policyschool.ca/wp-content/uploads/2020/03/COVID-19-Tool-of-Information-Sukhankin.pdf (last visited May 14, 2020).

Tang, Shiping. "The Security Dilemma: A Conceptual Analysis." 18 *Security Studies* 3, 587 (2009).

Terrill, Jr., Delbert R. *The Air Force Role in Developing International Outer Space Law*. 1999. Available at https://media.defense.gov/2010/Sep/22/2001330058/-1/-1/0/AFD-100922-019.pdf (last visited Apr. 24, 2020).

Todd, David. "ISS alarm caused by threatening debris cloud which Russia created via an Anti-Satellite (ASAT) missile strike on dead Cosmos 1408 satellite (Updated)." *Seradata Space Intelligence*. November 15, 2021. https://www.seradata.com/iss-alarm-caused-by-threatening-debris-cloud-which-russia-may-have-created-via-an-anti-satellite-asat-missile-strike-on-dead-cosmos-1408-satellite/.

Treaty Banning Nuclear Weapon Tests in the Atmosphere, in Outer Space and Under Water. August 5, 1963. 14 U.S.T. 1313, 480 U.N.T.S. 43.

Treaty on the Limitation of Anti-Ballistic Missile Systems, May 26, 1972, U.S.-U.S.S.R., 23 U.S.T. 3435, T.I.A.S. No. 7503.

Treaty on Principles Governing the Activities of States in the Exploration and Use of Outer Space, Including the Moon and Other Celestial Bodies. January 27, 1967. 18 U.S.T. 2410, 610 U.N.T.S. 205.

Trump, Donald J. "Executive Orders: Presidential Executive Order on Reviving the National Space Council." *WhiteHouse.gov*. June 30, 2017. https://trumpwhitehouse.archives.gov/presidential-actions/presidential-executive-order-reviving-national-space-council/.

Trump, Donald J. "Space Policy Directive 1—Presidential Memorandum on Reinvigorating America's Human Space Exploration Program." *WhiteHouse.gov*. December 11, 2017. https://trumpwhitehouse.archives.gov/presidential-actions/presidential-memorandum-reinvigorating-americas-human-space-exploration-program/.

Trump, Donald J. "Space Policy Directive-2, Streamlining Regulations on Commercial Use of Space." *Trump White House Archives*. May 24, 2018. https://trumpwhitehouse.archives.gov/presidential-actions/space-policy-directive-2-streamlining-regulations-commercial-use-space/.

Trump, Donald J. "Space Policy Directive-3, National Space Traffic Management Policy." *Trump White House Archives*. June 18, 2018. https://trumpwhitehouse.archives.gov/presidential-actions/space-policy- directive-3-national-space-traffic-management-policy/.

Trump, Donald J. "Text of a Memorandum from the President to the Secretary of Defense Regarding the Establishment of the United States Space Command." *WhiteHouse.gov*. December 18, 2018. https://trumpwhitehouse.archives.gov/briefings-statements/text-memorandum-president-secretary-defense-regarding-establishment-united-states-space-command/.

Trump, Donald J. "Text of Space Policy Directive-4: Establishment of the United States Space Force." *Trump White House Archives*. February 19, 2019. https://trumpwhitehouse.archives.gov/presidential-actions/text-space-policy-directive-4-establishment-united-states-space-force/.

Trump, Donald J. "Memorandum on Space Policy Directive-5—Cybersecurity Principles for Space Systems." *Trump White House Archives*. September 4, 2020. https://trumpwhitehouse.archives.gov/presidential- actions/memorandum-space-policy-directive-5-cybersecurity-principles-space-systems/.

Trump, Donald J. National Space Policy of the United States of America. *Trump White House Archive*. December 9, 2020. Available at https://trumpwhitehouse.archives.gov/wp-content/uploads/2020/12/National-Space-Policy.pdf.

Trump, Donald J. "Memorandum on the National Strategy for Space Nuclear Power and Propulsion (Space Policy Directive-6)." *Trump White House Archives*. December 16, 2020. https://trumpwhitehouse.archives.gov/presidential-actions/memorandum-national-strategy-space-nuclear-power- propulsion-space-policy-directive-6/.

Trump, Donald J. "Memorandum on Space Policy Directive 7." *Trump White House Archives*. January 15, 2021. https://trumpwhitehouse.archives.gov/presidential-actions/memorandum-space-policy-directive-7/.

United Nations Committee on the Peaceful Uses of Outer Space, Legal Subcommittee. *Summary Record of the Sixty-Fifth Meeting—Held at the Palais des Nations, Geneva, on Monday, 25 July 1966, at 10:30 a.m.* 5th Session. UN Doc. A/AC.105/C.2/SR.66. October 21, 1966.

United Nations Committee on the Peaceful Uses of Outer Space, Legal Subcommittee. *Summary Record of the Sixty-Fifth Meeting—Held at the Palais des Nations, Geneva, on Friday, 22 July 1966, at 10:30 a.m.* 5th Session. UN Doc. A/AC.105/C.2/SR.65. October 24, 1966.

United Nations Committee on the Peaceful Uses of Outer Space, Legal Subcommittee. *Activities being carried out or to be carried out on the Moon and other celestial bodies, international and national rules governing those activities and information received from States parties to the Agreement Governing the Activities of States on the Moon and Other Celestial Bodies about the benefits of adherence to that Agreement*. 47th Session. U.N. Doc. A/AC.105/C.2/L.271. January 25, 2008.

United Nations Committee on the Peaceful Uses of Outer Space, Legal Subcommittee. *Status of International Agreements relating to activities in outer space as at 1 January 2019*. 58th Session. U.N. Doc. A/AC.105/C.2/2019/CRP.3. April 1, 2019.

United Nations First Committee. *Verbatim Record of the Twelve Hundred and Eighty-Ninth Meeting. 17th Session*. U.N. Doc. A/C.1/PV.1289. December 3, 1962.

United Nations General Assembly. Resolution 1348(XIII). December 13, 1958.

United Nations General Assembly. Resolution 1472(XIV). December 12, 1959.

United Nations General Assembly. Resolution 1962 (XVIII). *Declaration of Legal Principles Governing the Activities of States in the Exploration and Use of Outer Space. 18th Session*. U.N. Doc A/RES/1962(XVIII). December 13, 1963.

United Nations General Assembly. Resolution 2222 (XXI). *Treaty on Principles Governing the Activities of States in the Exploration and Use of Outer Space, including the Moon and Other Celestial Bodies*. 21st Session. December 19, 1966.

United Nations General Assembly. Resolution 2777(XXVI). November 29, 1971.

United Nations General Assembly. "Agenda item 98 (d) Prevention of an arms race in outer space: reducing space threats through norms, rules and principles of responsible behaviours." 76th Session. U.N. Doc. A/C.1/76/L.52. October 14, 2021.

United Nations Office for Outer Space Affairs. *Convention on International Liability for Damage Caused by Space Objects—Travaux Préparatoires*. UNOOSA.org. https://www.unoosa.org/oosa/en/ourwork/spacelaw/treaties/travaux-preparatoires/liability-convention.html (last visited Mar. 31, 2020).

United Nations Treaty Collection. *Convention on the international liability for damage caused by space objects*. TREATIES.UN.ORG. March 31, 2020. https://treaties.un.org/pages/showDetails.aspx?objid=0800000280109 8c7.

United Nations Treaty Collection. "Depositary—Convention on registration of objects launched into outer space." *treaties.un.org*. March 31, 2020. https://treaties.un.org/Pages/ViewDetailsIII.aspx?src=TREATY&mtdsg_no=XXIV-1&chapter=24&Temp=mtdsg3&clang=_en.

United States Air Force Historical Foundation. *The US Air Force in Space: 1945 to the Twenty-First Century*. (Proceedings of the Air Force Historical Foundation Symposium. September 21–22, 1995). 1998.

United States Air Force Space Command. "Air Force Space Command History." *afspc.af.mil*. https://www.afspc.af.mil/About-Us/AFSPC-History/ (last visited Apr. 8, 2020).

United States Army. "Redstone Rocket." US Army Aviation and Missile Life Cycle Management Command. https://history.redstone.army.mil/space-redstone.html.

United States Defense Intelligence Agency. *Challenges to Security in Space*. January 2019.

United States Department of the Air Force. Air Force Manual 1-6, *Military Space Doctrine*. Aerospace Basic Doctrine. October 15, 1982.

United States Department of the Air Force.. Air Force Doctrine Document 2-2, *Space Operations*. August 23, 1998.

United States Department of the Air Force. Air Force Doctrine Document 2-2.1, *Counterspace Operations*. August 2, 2004.

United States Department of the Air Force. Air Force Doctrine Document 2-2, *Space Operations*. November 27, 2006.

United States Department of the Air Force. Curtis E. LeMay Center for Doctrine Development and Education. Annex 3–14, *Space Operations*. June 19, 2012. Available at https://fas.org/irp/doddir/usaf/3-14-annex.pdf.

United States Department of the Air Force. Curtis E. LeMay Center for Doctrine Development and Education, Annex 3–14, *Counterspace Operations*. August 27, 2018. https://www.doctrine.af.mil/Portals/61/documents/Annex_3-14/Annex-3-14-Counterspace-Ops.pdf.

United States Department of the Air Force. *Comprehensive Plan for the Organizational Structure of the U.S. Space Force*. Report to Congressional Committees. February 2020. Available at https://www.airforcemag.com/app/uploads/2020/02/Comprehensive-Plan-for-the-Organizational-Struccture-of-the-USSF_Feb-2020.pdf.

United States Department of Defense. *United States Space Force*. Strategic Overview. February 2019. Available at https://media.defense.gov/2019/Mar/01/2002095012/-1/-1/1/UNITED-STATES-SPACE-FORCE-STRATEGIC-OVERVIEW.PDF.

United States Department of Defense. Joint Publication 3–14. *Joint Doctrine for Space Operations*. August 9, 2002.

United States Department of Defense. Joint Publication 3–14, *Joint Doctrine for Space Operations*. January 6, 2009.

United States Department of Defense. Joint Publication 3–14, *Joint Doctrine for Space Operations*. May 29, 2013.

United States Department of Defense. *Summary of the 2018 National Defense Strategy of the United States of America: Sharpening the American Military's Competitive Edge*. January 2018.

United States Department of Defense. Joint Publication 3–14. *Space Operations*. April 10, 2018.

United States Department of Defense. *Final Report on Organizational and Management Structure for the National Security Space Components of the Department of Defense*. Report to Congressional Defense Committees. August 9, 2018. Available at https://secureservercdn.net/198.71.233.197/b13.8cb.myftpupload.com/wp-content/uploads/2018/08/Space-Force-report-Aug-9-2018.pdf.

United States Department of State. *The Department of State Bulletin, Vol XXXVI*. No. 920. February 11, 1957.

United States Department of State. *U.S. Participation in the UN—Report by the President to the Congress for the Year 1957*. Department of State Publication 6654. June 1958.

United States Department of State. *The Department of State Bulletin Vol. XXXIX*. No. 1003. September 15, 1958.

United States Department of State. *U.S. Department of State, Foreign Relations of the United States, 1955–1957, Vol. XI*. 1988. Available at https://history.state.gov/historicaldocuments/frus1955-57v11/d348.

United States Department of Defense & Office of the Director of National Intelligence. *National Security Space Strategy—Unclassified Summary*. January 2011.

United States. *U.S. National Space Policy*. NSPD-49. August 31, 2006. Available at https://fas.org/irp/offdocs/nspd/space.pdf (hereinafter *2006 NSP*).

United States. *National Space Policy of the United States of America*. PPD-4. June 28, 2010.

United States House of Representatives. "Report of the Committee on Appropriations Together With Minority Views." Department of Defense Appropriations Bill, 2022. Report 117–88. 117th Congress. July 15, 2021. Available at https://www.congress.gov/congressional-report/117th-congress/house-report/88.

United States House of Representatives. *S.1790—National Defense Authorization Act for Fiscal Year 2020*. "Text: S.1790—116th Congress (2019–2020): Engrossed Amendment House (09/17/2019)." Available at https://www.congress.gov/bill/116th-congress/senate-bill/1790/text/eah.

United States House of Representatives. H.R. 2810. 115th Congress. 1st Session. July 6, 2017. Available at https://www.congress.gov/115/bills/hr2810/BILLS-115hr2810rh.pdf.

United States House of Representatives. *Toward the Endless Frontier: History of the Committee on Science and Technology, 1959–79*. 1980.

United States Office of Space Commerce. *National Space Council Directives*. 2019. https://www.space.commerce.gov/policy/national-space-council-directives/.

United States Senate. "Roll Call Vote 116th Congress—1st Session: On Passage of the Bill (S. 1790, As Amended." June 27, 2019. Available at https://www.senate.gov/legislative/LIS/roll_call_votes/vote1161/vote_116_1_00188.htm.

United States Senate. *Document No. 18, Documents on International Aspects of the Exploration and Use of Outer Space, 1954–1962*. Staff Report Prepared for the Committee on Aeronautical and Space Sciences. May 9, 1963.

United States Senate Armed Services Committee. *Preparedness Subcommittee Recommendations for America's Defenses*. 85th Congress. 2nd Session. 104 Congressional Record, Part 15 (1958).

United States Senate Committee on Foreign Relations. *Treaty on Outer Space. Hearings before the Committee on Foreign Relations*. 90th Congress, 1st Session. March 7, 13, and April 12, 1967.

United States Space Force. "What's the Space Force?" *spaceforce.mil*. https://www.spaceforce.mil/About-Us/FAQs/Whats-the-Space-Force.

United States Space Force. *Spacepower: Doctrine for Space Forces*. Space Capstone Document. June 2020. Available at https://www.spaceforce.mil/Portals/1/Space%20Capstone%20Publication_10%20 Aug%202020.pdf.

Vandenberg Space Force Base. "History." *Vandenberg.spaceforce.mil*. https://www.vandenberg.spaceforce.mil/About-Us/History/.

Vecchiatto, Jean-Claude. "The latest developments of the French Space Military Command." *Bird & Bird*. January 2021. https://www.twobirds.com/en/news/articles/2021/france/the-latest-developments-of-the-french-space-military-command.

Verspieren, Quentin. "The United States Department of Defense space situational awareness sharing program: Origins, development and drive towards transparency." *Journal of Space Safety Engineering*, 8:1, (March 2021).

Viswanathan, Vivek. "Fallout From Reykjavik: Reagan's Stand and the Fate of Arms Control." *New York History*, 87:1, 135–43 (Winter 2006).

von Kries, Wulf. "The demise of the ABM Treaty and the militarization of outer space." *Space Policy*. 2002.

"Vought ASM-135A Anti-Satellite Missile." Fact Sheet. National Museum of the United States Air Force. Available at https://www.nationalmuseum.af.mil/Visit/Museum-Exhibits/Fact-Sheets/Display/Article/198034/vought-asm-135a-anti-satellite-missile/.

Waltz, Kenneth N. *Man, the State and War: A Theoretical Analysis*. New York: Columbia University Press, 1959.

Weinberger, Sharon. *The Imagineers of War: The Untold History of DARPA, the Pentagon Agency that Changed the World*. New York: Knopf, 2017.

Weiss, Thomas G. and Rorden Wilkinson, eds. *International Organization and Global Governance*. 2nd Edition. London: Routledge, 2018.

Westwick, Peter J. "'Space-Strike Weapons' and the Soviet Response to SDI." *Diplomatic History*, 32:5, 958 (November 2008).

White House. "President Donald J. Trump is Unveiling an America First National Space Strategy." *WhiteHouse.gov*. March 23, 2018. https://www.whitehouse.gov/briefings-statements/president-donald-j-trump-unveiling-america-first-national-space-strategy/.

White House. "Remarks by President Trump at a Meeting with the National Space Council and Signing of Space Policy Directive-3." *Trump White House Archives*. June 18, 2018. https://trumpwhitehouse.archives.gov/briefings-statements/remarks-president-trump-meeting-national-space-council-signing-space-policy-directive-3/.

Whittington, Michael C. *A Separate Space Force: An 80-Year-Old Argument*. Air War College, Maxwell Paper No. 20. 2000. Available at https://apps.dtic.mil/dtic/tr/fulltext/u2/a378853.pdf (last visited May 25, 2020).

Wikipedia. "Jimmy Carter." *Wikipedia.org*. March 30, 2020. https://en.wikipedia.org/wiki/Jimmy_Carter#Presidency_(1977–1981) (lasted visited Apr. 1, 2020).

Ziarnick, Brent D. T*ough Tommy's Space Force: General Thomas S. Power and the Air Force Space Program*. Air University Press, Drew Paper No. 34. 2019.

Ziarnick, Brent D. "The commander the Space Force needs." *The Hill*. August 6, 2019. https://thehill.com/opinion/national-security/456400-the-commander-the-space-force-needs.

Index

www.ingramcontent.com/pod-product-compliance
Ingram Content Group UK Ltd.
Pitfield, Milton Keynes, MK11 3LW, UK
UKHW022209051026
15624UKWH00001B/72

9 789004 523128